CHART YOUR SUCCESS

ON THE

COMPASS

TEST

COMputer-adaptive Placement Assessment and Support System

THIRD EDITION

Nannette Commander
GEORGIA STATE UNIVERSITY

Walter Cotter
FLOYD COLLEGE

Carol Callahan
formerly FLOYD COLLEGE

CPC **CONTEMPORARY PUBLISHING COMPANY OF RALEIGH, INC.**

6001-101 Chapel Hill Road, Raleigh, NC 27607 • (919) 851-8221

Publisher: Charles E. Grantham
Editorial Assistant: Sherri Powell
Marketing Director: J. Wesley Carnes
Production Manager: Erika Kessler
Cover Design: Contemporary Publishing Company of Raleigh, Inc.
Printer: Edwards Brothers, Inc.

ISBN: 0-89892-302-6

Printed in the United States of America

Printing 10 9 8 7 6 5 4 3 2

This book is in memory of Carol Callahan (1945-2000), our esteemed colleague. Her dedication to quality, generosity to others, and sense of humor will be sorely missed. Our friendship with Carol enriched our lives in countless ways, both professionally and personally.

This project would not have been possible without her efforts.

TABLE OF CONTENTS

PREFACE

Computerized Adaptive Testing (CAT) is changing the way institutions test entering students. Computer testing provides shorter testing time with more accurate results. While there are attractive features to computerized testing, there are some differences that require a shift in the students' approach to testing. For example, because of the smaller number of items needed to place students, each item is critically important—a mini-test in itself. This book is designed to help students understand the COMPASS test, review the skills necessary to perform well on COMPASS, and take practice tests similar to the COMPASS test.

The book is divided into four parts—Introduction, Mathematics, Composition, and Reading. The first section relates information about adaptive testing, COMPASS features, and general test-taking hints. This section helps students become comfortable with adaptive testing and computer keyboard functions. Sections II, III, and IV provide content information based on the design of the COMPASS test. They are developed for a concise review of necessary skills. Practice tests designed to mimic items and responses in the COMPASS style complete each of these sections.

INTRODUCTION TO COMPASS

WHAT IS COMPASS?

COMPASS (the computer-adaptive placement assessment and support system) is a test designed by the American College Testing Program. It tests reading, mathematics, and writing skills and is designed to help accurately place you in college courses. It may also, in some cases, be used as an exit test. **COMPASS** differs from many tests in that it is a computerized test. It is also adaptive. Adaptive means that the test administers questions based on your answers. If you answer easy questions correctly, the test will give you more difficult questions. The number of questions on your test will be determined by the answers you give. There is no time limit, so test takers will complete the test at their own rate. Your test will be different from everyone else's.

C
O
MPUTER-ADAPTIVE
PLACEMENT
ASSESSMENT AND
SUPPORT
SYSTEM

This book is designed to help you prepare for the **COMPASS** test. Although it was originally written to accompany the DOS version, information pertaining to the newer Windows version has been added to the Introduction. *Chart Your Success on the COMPASS Test* will provide plenty of practice for students taking either version of the test.

The first chapter will help you to (a) prepare for tests in general, (b) understand features specific to the **COMPASS** test, (c) learn how the **COMPASS** test can work for you, and (d) know what your results mean. The subsequent chapters will give you basic instruction and sample items in the areas tested by **COMPASS**: mathematics, composition, and reading. Chapters 7, 10, and 13 provide practice tests in these subject areas that contain items similar to those on the test.

TEST–WISENESS

Many college students express worry and anxiety over tests and will often complain about the need for taking them. There is bad news and good news regarding tests. First, THE BAD NEWS—tests are a serious part of the business of being a successful student. You will at times feel like tests are coming at you from all directions. You may, because of negative test experiences in the past, view yourself as a poor "test-taker" and feel a great deal of apprehension regarding tests. Now, THE GOOD NEWS—through knowledge and application of a few simple techniques, you can significantly improve your ability to take tests. "Test-wiseness" is the ability to take a test as effectively and efficiently as possible. For the most part, your performance on a test reflects your mastery of a skill or your understanding of a body of knowledge. However, using "test-wiseness" techniques before, during, and after a test can improve your score. We recommend the following strategies for you to achieve your highest potential in any test situation.

Before the Test

1. **Eat right.**

    In the days and hours before a test, eat a diet high in protein and complex carbohydrates—meat (or protein substitute), vegetables, and fruits. Drink plenty of water and avoid overuse of caffeine. Avoid simple sugars, especially the day of the test. Sugar raises your blood sugar quickly, but the stress of the test can cause it to drop dramatically, leaving you weak and shaky.

2. **Get plenty of sleep.**

    It is often difficult to sleep well the night or two before an important test. You may need to "bank" your sleep by ensuring that you sleep well the week before the test. Then, if you cannot sleep well the night before the test, you still will have rested enough to stay alert throughout the test.

3. **Stick to your exercise schedule.**

    You should follow some regular exercise program several times a week. Don't skip this routine before a test. Exercise has an important effect on the body. It increases circulation, allowing more oxygen to feed your memory cells. Exercise also reduces stress, and it causes the body to release hormones that make you feel good.

4. **Plan to arrive at the test site early.**

    Allow plenty of time to arrive at the testing area. If you're unfamiliar with the location, plan a practice run ahead of time. Plan to arrive early and, if you are too early, take a walk around the area and relax as much as possible.

During the Test

1. **Concentrate on the test.**

    Focus on the test questions and tune out any external and internal distractions. If there is noise or movement in the room that is bothering you, discuss it with the test administrator. If you find that your mind is starting to wander, take a few deep breaths to relax. Tell yourself you will "think about that later," and reread the test question.

2. Follow directions.

Take your time reading the directions on any test. If there is any confusing information, ask the test administrator for clarification. Be sure you understand how the test is set up before you begin. A few minutes previewing the test and doing some practice items can pay off in accuracy.

3. Think.

In many test situations it is one's ability to persist on an item that results in the right answer. While you don't want to spend too long on any one item, don't give up too easily either. Use logic, knowledge, and common sense, and have confidence in your ability to reason through the question.

4. Don't pay attention to other test-takers.

Others may finish the test before you do for a variety of reasons. Don't allow students' leaving the test to intimidate you and cause you to feel anxiety about your performance. They may have finished more quickly at the expense of accuracy.

5. Have a plan to deal with stress.

Stress is not all bad. Without some stress we would not be motivated to do our best on tests. Harmful stress, however, is something that we need to learn to deal with since it can hinder our performance on tests. Learn to monitor your stress level at various times by asking yourself, "What things trigger my anxiety?" Consider what coping strategies would be helpful to you. For example, being late can cause stress. Some people learn to schedule their time better so they are not continually late, while others resist change and remain stressed unnecessarily. You also should have some plan in case of panic while taking a test. Positive statements such as "I know I will do well on this test" and "I've got the skills I need to achieve" can make a difference. Breathing exercises are proven to help deal with symptoms of stress. Try this: (a) breathe in deeply for a slow count of 3, (b) hold your breath for a slow count of 12, and (c) force the air out of your body for a slow count of 6 . . . Repeat this exercise seven times. Practice breathing exercises before the test situation.

After the Test

1. Review your results.

Analyze whether the results of your test reflect your knowledge and preparation. Discuss your performance with an academic advisor or a professor.

2. Modify your preparation.

As a student you will constantly be taking tests and analyzing your results. If you never make changes in the way you prepare for tests, your chances of improving are slim. Even if your score was extremely high on a test, improved test-taking skills may allow you to achieve the same high results with less preparation. On the other hand, you may need to spend more time preparing for the test. If you are unsure, discuss the way you prepared and your results with a learning specialist on your campus.

3. Pat yourself on the back.

Don't forget to reward yourself for your efforts. Academic achievement takes talent, hard work, and persistence. Positive reinforcement will keep you motivated.

DOS VERSION

FEATURES SPECIFIC TO COMPASS (DOS)

You have probably learned from experience that all tests differ. They all have features specific to them. There are features within **COMPASS** that are specific to each subtest: mathematics, writing, and reading. For example, there are some computer keys that have special functions. There are also different types of questions and rules for each area. Here is a list of rules, features, and important keys that apply to the DOS version of the COMPASS Test.

Mathematics

▶ You are not allowed to use a calculator on the mathematics portion of the test. (This applies to the DOS version only.)

▶ All of the mathematics items are multiple choice.

▶ Once you choose an answer you cannot go back and change it.

▶ You may not skip any problems and come back to them.

▶ Paper and pencil will be provided for the mathematics subtest.

Writing

▶ The writing test requires you to edit an essay.

▶ You may have to move a pointer to a place in the text and then choose an answer from a list of items.

▶ You may have to highlight a portion of text and then edit it.

▶ You will be asked to press F when you finish editing the essay. After doing so, you will not be allowed to make any changes.

▶ You may not use paper and pencil on the writing subtest.

Reading

▶ On the reading test you have to toggle (go back and forth) between the passage and the questions. You cannot see the passage and the questions on the same screen.

▶ When you have responded to all of the questions for a particular passage, you may go back and revise your answers before continuing.

▶ You may not use paper and pencil for the reading subtest.

DOS VERSION

COMPUTER KEYBOARD FUNCTIONS

Following is a list of keys on the computer keyboard that you need to be familiar with for the DOS version of the COMPASS Test.

Arrow Keys   These keys have several uses on the test. For one, they are used to move to the letter (A, B, C, D, or E) that you think is the correct answer to the question on the screen. They are also used to indicate where you would insert a mark of punctuation or to indicate what part of the text you wish to highlight. Finally, the arrow keys are used to scroll up or down in the text.

Y for Yes & N for No   You will be prompted to verify your name and social security number, to begin or end a test, and to confirm an answer before moving on to the next question. At all of these points, you will type Y for "yes" and N for "no."

Letters A through E   You can choose the letter of the best answer for a multiple-choice question by pressing that key and *enter* (or *return* on some keyboards) or by using the arrow keys.

S for Toggling   The S key is used for toggling back and forth between screens. This feature is used in the reading section of the test where a passage and the related set of questions are on separate screens.

H for Help   Throughout the entire test you may press the H key to reach a help screen.

Home & End   The Home key places the cursor at the beginning of a line. The End key places it at the end of a line.

Enter   The COMPASS test prompts you to use this key to verify your answer choice.

Space Bar   This key is used to move the highlighter to positions in the text.

Esc   This key is used when you want to change an answer you have just entered.

The most important thing to remember is always READ the screen, since COMPASS will tell you which keys are presently active.

WINDOWS VERSION

FEATURES SPECIFIC TO COMPASS (Windows)

The COMPASS Test is now available for Windows. The format of this version is different from the DOS version. For example, the DOS screens are dark with light text, whereas the Windows screens are white with black text. The Windows version has squares beside each answer choice instead of circles. Certain rules have been changed as well, such as the use of calculators. Find out if your institution has adopted the Windows version, so you will know what to expect on the day of the test. The more familiar you are with the content, rules, and format, the more confident you will be.

Mathematics

You ARE allowed to use calculators on the Windows version of COMPASS. You may use the on-screen pop-up calculator or bring your own. If you choose to bring your own, make sure it is an approved model. Calculators with a QWERTY keypad (like a keyboard) are not allowed. Graphing and scientific models are allowed, provided they meet all guidelines. For a list of calculator guidelines, visit the following website: *www.act.org/compass/sample/calc.html* . Or, you can call ACT (the test publisher) at 1-800-498-6481 to get a recorded message about approved models.

Before you plan on bringing a calculator, make certain that your institution is using the Windows version of COMPASS. Also, make sure yours is an approved model. Nothing will shake your confidence more than showing up on test day and being told you cannot use a calculator when you were planning on it.

Writing

Note: This is the only section of the test that *requires* the use of a mouse. If you are not accustomed to using a mouse, ask the testing center at your institution for some practice.

On the Writing Skills Test, you will be able to see the essay and test item on the same screen. Your task is to edit the essay that appears in a box on the left. Any time you use the mouse and click on a part of the passage, a portion of that text will become highlighted. A box on the right will then display five options. Choice **A** is always the same as the highlighted text. The next four choices will rewrite that portion of the essay.

When you think you have corrected all the errors in the passage, click on the button labelled "Finished editing the passage." Next, you will be asked several questions concerning strategy, organization, and style. This section of the Writing Skills Test will look similar to the Reading Test screen.

Reading

In this section of the Test, a passage will appear on the left and a question on the right. Only one question will be displayed at a time. To move to a different question, click on the square with the question number you wish to move to. Or, simply press the that number on the keyboard. You will not be allowed to go on to the next passage until you have answered all the questions for that current passage.

WINDOWS VERSION

SAMPLE SCREEN

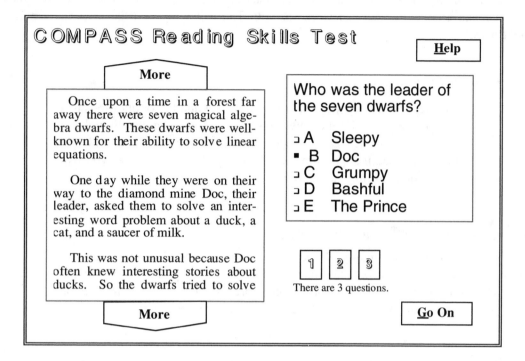

COMPUTER KEYBOARD FUNCTIONS

KEY	FUNCTION	SECTION
A, B, C, D, or E	selects answer A, B, C, D, or E	M, W, R
F	indicates you have finished editing the essay	W
G	confirms the selected answer and moves you to the next question	M, W, R
H	activates the Help screen	M, W, R
L	activates the pop-up calculator	M
1, 2, 3...	moves you to a different numbered question	W, R
Up and Down arrow keys	scrolls through the essay/passage	W, R
Left and Right arrow keys	moves you to a different numbered questions	W, R

M = Math   W = Writing   R = Reading

The mouse can be used to perform all of these functions. It is up to you which way you wish to enter your answers. Once you press G or click the "Go On" button, your answer to the Math question on the screen or to all the questions relating to a single essay/passage are confirmed. COMPASS will then move you to the next Math question, Writing essay, or Reading passage. Remember, there is no going back once you "Go On."

HOW THE COMPASS TEST CAN WORK FOR YOU

Because **COMPASS** is a computerized test, it will be a different experience for every student. It may be a challenge. If you are aware of what material is covered and the best approach to the test, you can make a computerized test work for you. The following is a list of the advantages of **COMPASS**.

1. **COMPASS is an untimed test**.

   The stress produced by having to answer a set number of questions in a certain time period is eliminated. Take your time, and move through the test at your own pace. Do not choose an answer until you are completely sure of it. Read the questions slowly and go back as often as you like before you confirm your answer.

2. **COMPASS offers practice exercises**.

   Before the beginning of each test, there are several practice items to allow you to become familiar with the mechanical part of answering the questions. Be sure that you feel comfortable with the keyboard and the process of answering questions before you proceed.

3. **COMPASS gives you immediate score results**.

   Your results are available right after you take the test, and they are easy to interpret. You may receive them at the testing center or shortly after from a professional who can interpret the results with you. Be sure you understand the decisions that will be made based on your results. What course placement is recommended? Are there areas of weakness you can improve or strengths that you can build on?

4. **COMPASS is a personalized test**.

   The test you take is unlike anyone else's. You will not be answering the same questions as the person next to you. If you take the test more than once, you will not be answering the same set of questions each time. You will receive an individualized report of your skill level. Ask the person who gives you the results to explain every part of your score report. Because **COMPASS** is a personalized test, it is a more accurate estimate of your ability than a paper-and-pencil test.

5. **COMPASS operates at your comfort level**.

   The **COMPASS** test adjusts to your responses and comfort level instead of your frustration level. It is unlikely you will feel bored or impatient during the test. By tailoring the items to your skill level, the test will challenge but not discourage you.

6. **COMPASS requires different tasks**.

   This test does not rely only on multiple-choice questions, so you have different opportunities for communicating your knowledge. For instance, in the reading test there are text-highlighting items that ask a question and then require you to locate within a passage a specific segment of text that answers the question. You may also be asked questions that are not about the content of the passage but about your prior knowledge regarding the subject.

7. **COMPASS can be taken when you want to take it**.

   In place of the traditional paper-and-pencil test given only during certain times on certain dates to a large group, computerized adaptive testing allows you to take the test when you want, in a relatively small group, in a comfortable setting.

8. **COMPASS is a short test**.

   You will have to answer fewer items than on a traditional paper-and-pencil test. This is good because sometimes on a long test students may become tired and lose their concentration.

9. **COMPASS prompts you to remember the things you should do on a test**.

   You are told to go back and reread the essay you have edited. It prompts you to check each answer before going on.

10. **COMPASS does not penalize you for guessing**.

    If you are not sure of an answer, make your best guess. You can only benefit from guessing.

WHAT YOUR RESULTS MEAN

Again, there is good news and bad news. The good news is that as soon as you finish the test your results are ready. The results will be immediate, accurate, and fair. The bad news is that we cannot guarantee you will pass the test. However, the fact that you are taking the time to read this book and prepare means you are doing your best to do well on the test. This preparation will give you an advantage on test day.

How your results are reported to you depends entirely on where you take the test. Some testing sites will give you your results before you leave the room. Other sites will have you meet with a counselor to review your results. Another site might mail you the results at a later date. It all depends on how your testing site is set up.

The most common way to get your scores is from the **COMPASS** Standard Individual Report. This report is usually printed out before you leave the testing center.

▶ The first section will have your name, ID#, location of the test, test date and test session.

▶ The next section may show your answers to the demographic questions that you answered before the actual test began. (Often, this demographic section is not included.)

▶ The next section of the report will describe the Administration Mode and the Placement Group used to give you your test. These facts are rarely of any importance to you.

▶ The next section(s) contains your test scores, times, and recommendations. If your test was taken for placement your score will be given as a range. For example, a range of 69-100 would mean you scored somewhere between 69 and 100. If your test was taken for a score then you will get a number (for example, 73). The test will also report how long it took you to take the test (for example, 19 mins, 17 sec). This time has no effect on your grade or placement. Recommendations are the last portion of this section. Recommendations are messages to you about your test score. These messages will help you and an advisor determine what courses you should take. If you are taking the test as an exit exam, then whether or not you passed or failed will be written here.

▶ The last section of the report is a release that allows the testing center to share your results with other educational institutions.

Whoever is proctoring your test will be able to explain your results or direct you to an academic advisor who will be able to tell you more about your test scores and how they affect your plans.

RESOURCES ON THE WEB

American College Testing (ACT), the publisher of the COMPASS Test, maintains a website that you can visit for additional information on COMPASS. The site address is: *www.act.org/compass/index.html* . For additional support in preparing for the mathematics test on COMPASS, please visit the website: *www.fc.peachnet.edu/wcotter/compass.htm* .

ADAPTIVE TESTING

The following graphs explain how questions adapted to your skill level are used to arrive at your score.

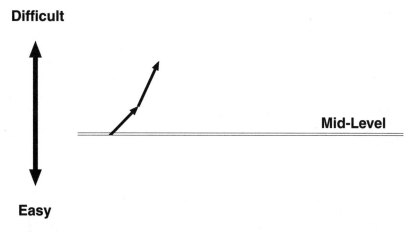

An adaptive test starts with a mid-level question. If you get the question right, you will be asked a harder question.

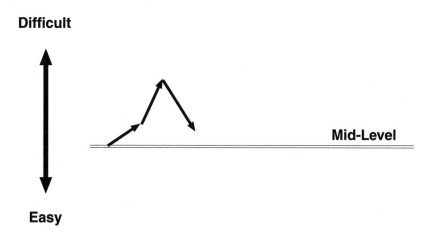

If you answer incorrectly, the test will give you an easier question.

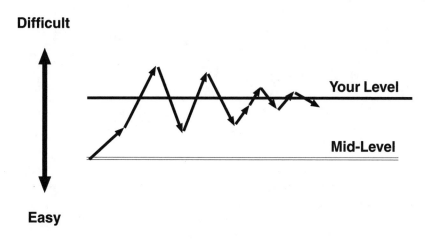

This process continues until the computer is confident that it has found your level of performance. This is your score.

INTRODUCTION TO MATHEMATICS

COMPASS Mathematics Sections:

Pre–algebra/Numerical Skills
Algebra
College Algebra
Geometry
Trigonometry

INTRODUCTION

The mathematics portion of the **COMPASS** test has five sections: pre-algebra/numerical skills, algebra, college algebra, geometry, and trigonometry. Each section has a pool of about 200 test items. **COMPASS** will select problems from this pool for you according to how well you do. If you answer questions correctly, **COMPASS** will give you harder questions. If you answer incorrectly, **COMPASS** will give you easier questions. Because the selection process is based on how well you do, the test you take will be different from those taken by other test-takers, even on the same day. Most people will answer fewer than 17 questions in a particular section.

If you do very well in one section, **COMPASS** will move you to the next section. If you do poorly in a section, **COMPASS** will move you back a section. This process continues until **COMPASS** finds the hardest section of the test that you can do well. **COMPASS** will not tell you when you move from one section to the next. Some people will only see one section, others two. Very few people will see more than two, but it is possible.

KNOW WHAT TO STUDY

Some schools will not use certain sections of the test. For example, some schools use the geometry section of the test, some do not, and others let the **COMPASS** program decide. Make sure that you know what sections of the test you might be tested on. There is no point in spending test preparation time on something you will not be tested over. If you have very limited time to study, start with the Algebra chapter, chapter number three.

KNOW HOW TO ANSWER

Before you take the test you will be given a chance to practice inputting answers on some example items that do not count towards your test score. Each item has five options just like the real test. You can select your answer in one of three ways:

1) Use the space bar until your choice is highlighted, then press enter.

2) Press the key (A, B, C, D, or E), then press enter.

3) Use the pointer/arrow to select your answer by moving the mouse, then press enter.

After you select your answer **COMPASS** will ask you to confirm your answer by pressing enter again. Once you confirm your answer, you cannot go back and change it later.

FORMAL LANGUAGE

Mathematics is its own language. Every language has different styles. People from England speak a very different English than the people from the Southeastern United States. The mathematical language on this test is a little different from the everyday mathematical language spoken in most classrooms. The language on the test is much more formal and "correct." Do not let this formal style distract or intimidate you. For the most part this language can be ignored, and you can focus on the real questions.

Here are a few examples of phrases which you may or may not be familiar with.

▶ For all x such that ...   (meaning: x can be anything)

▶ For $x \neq 4$...   (meaning: x can be anything BUT 4, because 4 is not in the domain, probably because it would cause a zero to be in the denominator)

▶ If $i^2 = -1$, then...   (meaning: this problem deals with complex numbers)

Usually you can ignore most prepositional phrases. These phrases provide a context for the problem. Once you recognize the context, concentrate on the rest of the information provided.

CALCULATORS

Calculators are not permitted on the DOS version of the COMPASS Test. However, they are allowed on the Windows version. If your school is using the Windows version of COMPASS, make sure that you have an approved calculator. The following web page lists which are approved and which are not: *www.act.org/compass/sample/calc.html* . The site is updated as new models become available. Or, call ACT (the Test publisher) at 1-800-498-6481 for current information.

TEST HINTS

► **TIME** is the number one thing. This test is not timed. The longer you take on the test the better for you. Relax and do your best on each question.

► On the test day make sure you have several hours to take the test. Do not plan anything after your test that could make you rush. Some people will take the test in 20 minutes; others may take over three hours. Give yourself the time to do your best.

► Each question is its own test. Concentrate only on the question that is on the screen. Forget about questions you have already answered. Don't worry about the next question. Once you have answered and confirmed your answer, it is gone. Forget about it, and move on to the new question that is now on the screen.

► Even if you feel very confident about an answer, make sure you check and recheck your answer. Time is not important.

► When you get a question right, a harder question is your reward. Eventually you will get one that is too hard. Do not let this worry you. Some questions will be too hard for you. That is the way that the test is designed.

► Touch the screen. Use your finger, the eraser of your pencil, or the mouse to help you read and concentrate on parts of the problem. This is especially important on graphs, where you may need to count the location of different points.

► Most people who take **COMPASS** start in the algebra section. Do most of your studying here, as colleges use this information to help them decide what math course to place you in.

► Make sure you are answering the question asked. Sometimes the question will ask for the value of x^2, not of x.

► The number one mistake is a sign (+/−) error. The test will have the right answer, and it will also have the right answer with the wrong sign.

► Memorize the first 16 perfect squares. They show up often, especially in factoring.

N	1	2	3	4	5	6	7	8	9	10	11	12	13	14	15	16
N^2	1	4	9	16	25	36	49	64	81	100	121	144	169	196	225	256

► Become familiar with the perfect cubes:

N	1	2	3	4	5	6	7	8
N^3	1	8	27	64	125	216	343	512

► Do **not** bring a watch. Time is **not** important.

HELP ON THE WEB

For more information on preparing for the mathematics test on COMPASS, visit the following website: *www.fc.peachnet.edu/wcotter/compass.htm* .

CHAPTER TWO

PRE-ALGEBRA/NUMERICAL SKILLS

The pre-algebra section covers these topics:

> P1 **Basic Operations with Integers**
> P2 **Basic Operations with Fractions**
> P3 **Basic Operations with Decimals**
> P4 **Exponents**
> P5 **Order of Operations**
> P6 **Ratios and Proportions**
> P7 **Percentages**
> P8 **Averages (Means)**
> •
> P9 **Multiples and Factors of Integers**
> P10 **Absolute Values of Numbers**
> P11 **Greater Than / Less Than**
> P12 **Conversions Between Fractions and Decimals**

Over 85% of the pre-algebra section will come from the first 8 topics. Concentrate your studies on these.

P1 BASIC OPERATIONS WITH INTEGERS

Basic operations with integers include addition, subtraction, multiplication and division. These problems are the most basic on the test, but do not rush through these items. Make sure you spend enough time to get the problem correct. The number one mistake a person will make on a problem in this section is to get a + or − sign wrong.

ADDITION

$$7 + (-9) = -2 \qquad -5 + (-8) = -13 \qquad 18 + (-12) = 6$$

In an addition problem like $7 + (-9) = -2$, 7 and −9 are called **addends.** The answer −2 is called the **sum.**

SUBTRACTION

$$16 - (-5) = 21 \qquad -8 - (-12) = 4 \qquad 13 - 22 = -9$$

In a subtraction problem $16 - (-5) = 21$; 16 is called the **minuend** and −5 is called the **subtrahend**. The answer 21 is called the **difference**. If you are not good at subtracting signed numbers, try changing the sign of the subtrahend and adding.

$$16 - (-5) = 16 + (5) = 21 \qquad -8 - (-12) = -8 + (12) = 4 \qquad 13 - 22 = 13 + (-22) = -9$$

MULTIPLICATION

When multiplying $8 \times 7 = 56$, 8 and 7 are called **factors**. The answer 56 is called the **product**. Multiplication can be written many different ways. In the following examples, notice what happens to the sign of the product when we change the signs of the factors.

With an x

$8 \times 7 = 56$ $8 \times -7 = -56$ $-8 \times 7 = -56$ $-8 \times -7 = 56$

With a •

$8 \bullet 7 = 56$ $8 \bullet -7 = -56$ $-8 \bullet 7 = -56$ $-8 \bullet -7 = 56$

With juxtaposition (placing two factors next to each other)

$(8)(7) = 56$ $(8)(-7) = -56$ $(-8)(7) = -56$ $(-8)(-7) = 56$

DIVISION

When dividing $20 \div 4 = 5$, 20 is called the **dividend** and 4 is called the **divisor**. The answer 5 is called the **quotient**.

$20 \div 4 = 5$ $(-35) \div 7 = -5$ $\dfrac{42}{-7} = -6$

SIGNS OF TERMS

For multiplication and division only, if there is just one term in an expression (no addition or subtraction), then count the number of negative signs. If there is an odd number of negative signs, then your answer is negative. If there is an even number of negative signs, then the result will be positive.

P1   Practice simplifying.

a. $33 + (-13) + 22 + (-9) + 15$

b. $23 + (-15) + 22 + (-17) + 16$

c. $43 - (-23) + 25 - (9) + 33$

d. $38 - (-22) + 30 - (-17) + 24$

(*Answers* to all practices in Chapter Two are found on p. 28.)

P2 BASIC OPERATIONS WITH FRACTIONS

Basic operations with fractions include addition, subtraction, multiplication and division. These are the same operations that were discussed in P1.

COMMON DENOMINATOR

In a fraction, the top is called the **numerator,** and the bottom is called the **denominator**. When adding or subtracting fractions with different denominators, the fractions must first be converted to make their denominators the same. Suppose we wanted to add $5/6$ and $3/8$. Since 6 and 8 are unlike denominators, we must first convert these fractions into two fractions with a common denominator. The smallest number that both 6 and 8 will divide into is 24. Multiply $5/6$ by $4/4$ and $3/8$ by $3/3$. When we multiply by $4/4$ and $3/3$, we are actually multiplying by the number 1 so the value of $5/6$ and $3/8$ is not changed, just the way that they look.

$$\frac{\textbf{numerator}}{\textbf{denominator}} = \frac{5}{6} = \left(\frac{5}{6}\right)\left(\frac{4}{4}\right) = \frac{20}{24} \qquad \frac{\textbf{numerator}}{\textbf{denominator}} = \frac{3}{8} = \left(\frac{3}{8}\right)\left(\frac{3}{3}\right) = \frac{9}{24}$$

With a common denominator, we can now combine the fractions and then add the numerators:

$$\frac{20}{24} + \frac{9}{24} = \frac{20+9}{24} = \frac{29}{24}$$

If you are able to reduce the resulting fraction, the denominator will change again. Section **P9** has more information about finding common denominators.

Caution. When you are adding and subtracting fractions you must find a common denominator, but do not forget about signs. If you forget about signs, you will get the problem just as wrong as the person who could not find the common denominator.

ADDITION

Example 1

$$\frac{7}{10} + \frac{3}{8} = \frac{28}{40} + \frac{15}{40} = \frac{28+15}{40} = \frac{43}{40}$$

Example 2

$$\frac{2}{5} + \frac{6}{11} = \frac{22}{55} + \frac{30}{55} = \frac{22+30}{55} = \frac{52}{55}$$

SUBTRACTION

Subtraction has the same rules about common denominator that addition has. Just subtract after you find the common denominator.

Example 3

$$\frac{7}{12} - \frac{3}{10} = \frac{35}{60} - \frac{18}{60} = \frac{35-18}{60} = \frac{17}{60}$$

MULTIPLICATION

Multiplication and division are much easier than addition and subtraction since a common denominator is not required. Just multiply numerator by numerator and denominator by denominator.

Example 4

$$\frac{2}{5} \times \frac{3}{14} = \frac{6}{70} = \frac{3}{35}$$

You may find it easier to cancel before multiplying in order to get the answer in lowest terms:

$$\frac{2}{5} \times \frac{3}{14} = \frac{1}{5} \times \frac{3}{7} = \frac{3}{35}$$

The answer to a multiplication problem is called a **product.** Consider what is necessary for the product of a pair of fractions to equal 1. For example, $\frac{2}{3} \times \frac{3}{2} = \frac{6}{6} = 1$. $\frac{3}{2}$ is the **reciprocal** of $\frac{2}{3}$. Every number except 0 has a reciprocal. A number multiplied by its reciprocal will always equal 1. To find the reciprocal of a number, simply flip the number over:
The reciprocal of $\frac{5}{2}$ is $\frac{2}{5}$; the reciprocal of $\frac{15}{14}$ is $\frac{14}{15}$; the reciprocal of 8 is $\frac{1}{8}$.

DIVISION

To perform division take the reciprocal of the divisor and then multiply. (Don't ask why . . . just flip and multiply.)

Example 5

$$\frac{4}{7} \div \frac{9}{5} = \frac{4}{7} \times \frac{5}{9} = \frac{20}{63}$$

COMBINATIONS

Do multiplications and divisions in order from left to right **before** performing addition and subtraction in order from left to right.

Example 6

$$\frac{2}{5} + \left(\frac{7}{10} \cdot \frac{-3}{2} \right) - \frac{4}{15}$$

$$= \frac{2}{5} + \frac{-21}{20} - \frac{4}{15}$$

$$= \frac{24}{60} + \frac{(-63)}{60} - \frac{16}{60}$$

$$= \frac{24 + (-63) - 16}{60}$$

$$= \frac{-55}{60} = \frac{-11}{12}$$

Example 7

$$\frac{3}{4} \div \left(\frac{1}{15} + \frac{2}{3} \right) \div \left(\frac{-2}{7} \right)$$

$$= \left(\frac{3}{4} \cdot \frac{15}{1} \right) + \left(\frac{2}{3} \cdot \frac{-7}{2} \right)$$

$$= \frac{45}{4} + \frac{-7}{3}$$

$$= \frac{135}{12} + \frac{-28}{12}$$

$$= \frac{135 + -55}{12} = \frac{107}{12}$$

P2 Practice. Simplify.

a. $\left(\frac{-18}{14} \right) \left(\frac{49}{-6} \right)$

b. $\frac{2}{5} + \frac{3}{7}$

c. $\frac{3}{4} + \frac{4}{9} \cdot \frac{-5}{2} - \frac{3}{4}$

P3 BASIC OPERATIONS WITH DECIMALS

ADDITION AND SUBTRACTION

When adding and subtracting decimal numbers, don't forget to line up the decimals.

$3.85 + 1.2 + (-0.15) = 4.9$

$$
\begin{array}{r}
3.85 \\
1.2 \\
+ \quad (-0.15) \\
\hline
4.9
\end{array}
$$

MULTIPLICATION

When multiplying decimals, count the number of digits behind the decimal in the factors. This is where you will place the decimal point in the answer.

$3.6 \times 4 = 14.4$ $\qquad\qquad$ $2.1 \times 0.63 = 1.323$

When multiplying, the numbers that are multiplied together (3.6 and 4) are called **factors.** The answer (14.4) is called a **product.** A product is the result of multiplying two factors.

DIVISION

In the following division problem, 20.5 is called the **dividend,** 0.5 is the **divisor,** and 41 is the **quotient.**

$20.5 \div 0.5 = 41$

When dividing, if the divisor has a decimal, move it to the end of the number. 0.5 would become 5. For this to be legal, you must make a corresponding move in the dividend; therefore, 20.5 becomes 205. Now just divide as usual.

$0.5\overline{)20.5}$ $\qquad \rightarrow \qquad$ $5\overline{)205}$ $\qquad = \qquad 41$

Another way of writing this problem would be as a fraction. The dividend becomes the numerator, and the divisor becomes the denominator. We move the decimal point by multiplying the top and the bottom by the same number.

$$\frac{20.5}{0.5} = \left(\frac{20.5}{0.5}\right)\left(\frac{10}{10}\right) = \frac{205}{5} = 41$$

P3 Practice. Simplify.

a. $12.5 + 3.7 - 13.002$ $\qquad$ b. $1.2 \bullet 3.0$ $\qquad$ c. $36 \div 0.4$ $\qquad$ d. $\dfrac{6.5}{0.13}$

P4 EXPONENTS

2^3 2 is called the **base**. 3 is called the **exponent**. 2^3 is read as "2 raised to the third power" or "2 to the third." The meaning of 2^3 is "use 2 three times as a factor."

Here is a mathematical way of writing that definition.

$2^3 = 2 \cdot 2 \cdot 2 = 8$

What is the exponential notation for $5 \cdot 5 \cdot 5 \cdot 5$?   Answer: 5^4

Notice what happens to the sign of our product when the exponent is odd or even.

$(-3)^2 = (-3)(-3) = 9$

$(-3)^3 = (-3)(-3)(-3) = -27$

$(-3)^4 = (-3)(-3)(-3)(-3) = 81$

$(-3)^5 = (-3)(-3)(-3)(-3)(-3) = -243$

$(-3)^6 = (-3)(-3)(-3)(-3)(-3)(-3) = 729$

Whenever the exponent is an even number, the answer is positive. If the exponent is an odd number, the sign will be the same one that you started with.

Here are two expressions that look alike, but are very different.

$(3x^2)$ $(3x)^2$

The difference between these two expressions is what the exponent affects. The square on the left affects only the x. The square on the right applies to the 3 *and* the x because of the parentheses.

$(3x^2) = 3x^2$ $(3x)^2 = 9x^2$

P4   Practice.

Write the exponential notation.

a. $x \cdot x \cdot x \cdot x \cdot x$ b. $7 \cdot 7 \cdot 7 \cdot 7 \cdot 7$ c. $5 \cdot 5 \cdot 5 \cdot A \cdot A \cdot A \cdot B \cdot B$

Simplify.

d. 4^3 e. $(-1)^{83}$ f. $(4a)^2$ g. 1^8

P5 ORDER OF OPERATIONS

When evaluating mathematical expressions, it is important that you perform operations in the correct order. Consider $3 + 4 \times 5 - 8$. What should be done first?

Correct

$3 + 4 \times 5 - 8$	Multiply first
$= 3 + 20 - 8$	Add
$= 23 - 8$	Subtract
$= 15$	

Incorrect

$3 + 4 \times 5 - 8$	(addition done before
$= 7 \times (-3)$	multiplication)
$= -21$	

Because the incorrect way looks correct, we must guard against doing the problem that way. The **order of operations** is the method you use to make sure that you are doing everything in the correct order.

THE ORDER OF OPERATIONS

1. **P** Do everything inside **Parentheses** ( ) or any other grouping symbol, such as brackets [ ], first.
2. **E** Do all **Exponents**.
3. **MD** Do all **Multiplications** and **Divisions** in order from left to right.
4. **AS** Do all **Additions** and **Subtractions** in order from left to right.

Here is a silly way to remember the Order of Operations:

1. **P** Please **Parentheses**
2. **E** Excuse **Exponent**
3. **MD** My Dear **Multiplication** and **Division**
4. **AS** Aunt Sally **Addition** and **Subtraction**

Example 1

$8 - 10 \div 2 + 4 \bullet 3$	Divide
$= 8 - 5 + 4 \bullet 3$	Multiply
$= 8 - 5 + 12$	Subtract
$= 3 + 12$	Add
$= 15$	

Example 2

$3^2 + 5 \bullet 2 - (8 + 9)$	Parentheses
$= 3^2 + 5 \bullet 2 - 17$	Exponent
$= 9 + 5 \bullet 2 - 17$	Multiply
$= 9 + 10 - 17$	Add
$= 19 - 17$	Subtract
$= 2$	

P5 Practice. Simplify.

a. 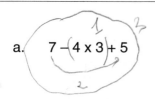 $7 - 4 \times 3 + 5$

b. $2^2 + 9 \times 3^3 + 4 - 6$

c. $\dfrac{12 - 7}{3^2 + 4^2}$

d. $\dfrac{4(6 - 2) + 5(2 + 6)}{33 - (-2)}$

23

P6 RATIOS AND PROPORTIONS

A **ratio** is an expression of the relationship between two or more things. Fractions are ratios. Here are some examples of how ratios are written.

$$\frac{a}{b} \qquad\qquad a \text{ to } b \qquad\qquad a{:}b$$

A **proportion** is a statement of equality about two ratios.

$$\frac{3}{4} = \frac{9}{12} \qquad\qquad \frac{A}{B} = \frac{C}{D} \qquad\qquad \frac{20}{4} = \frac{5}{1}$$

If a proportion is true then you can cross multiply and get a true answer. **Cross multiplication** means multiplying the denominator of one fraction by the numerator of the other. This method can be used to determine if two fractions are equal.

$$\frac{3}{4} = \frac{9}{12} \qquad \rightarrow \qquad 3 \cdot 12 = 9 \cdot 4 \qquad \rightarrow \qquad 36 = 36$$

When we have a proportion with one part missing or unknown we can use cross multiplication to find the missing part.

$$\frac{x}{3} = -\frac{8}{12}$$

$$x \cdot 12 = -8 \cdot 3$$

$$12x = -24$$

$$\frac{12x}{12} = -\frac{24}{12}$$

$$x = -2$$

P6 Practice.
Solve these proportions.

a. $\dfrac{w}{5} = \dfrac{7}{10}$

b. $\dfrac{8}{13} = \dfrac{X}{39}$

c. $\dfrac{36}{8} = \dfrac{9}{Y}$

d. $\dfrac{-1.2}{Z} = \dfrac{4}{5}$

P7 PERCENTAGES

Per means part and **cent** means 100, therefore percentage means "part of 100." In other words, what would the numerator be if the denominator were 100?

Example 1 What percent of 25 is 8?

$$\frac{8}{25} = \frac{8}{25} \cdot \left(\frac{4}{4}\right) = \frac{32}{100} = 32\%$$

Example 2 What percent of 225 is 27?

"Of" means multiply and "is" means =, therefore

$W\%$ *of* 225 *is* 27

$$\frac{W}{100} \cdot 225 = 27$$

$$\frac{W}{100} = \frac{27}{225}$$

$$W = \frac{27 \cdot 100}{225} = \frac{27 \cdot 4}{9} = 3 \cdot 4 = 12$$

$$W = 12\%$$

Example 3 What is 30% of 45?

"Of" means multiply and "is" means =, therefore

30% *of* 45 *is* W

$$\frac{30}{100} \cdot 45 = W$$

$$\frac{3}{10} \cdot 45 = W$$

$$\frac{3}{2} \cdot 9 = \frac{27}{2} = 13.5 = W$$

Example 4 80% of what number is 36?

Just divide 0.8 into 36.

$$\frac{36}{0.8} = \frac{360}{8} = 45$$

P7 Practice.

a. 8 is what percent of 32?

b. What number is 85% of 360?

c. 22 is 20% of what number?

P8   AVERAGES (MEANS)

Finding the **mean** of a group of numbers is exactly like finding the average grade for a group of tests. First add all of the test grades. Then divide by the number of tests.

Example 1
Find the mean of these tests grades: 78, 83, 85, and 75.

$$\frac{78 + 83 + 85 + 75}{4} = \frac{321}{4} = 80.25$$

P8   Practice.

a. Find the mean of 17, 22, 19, and 30.

b. Find the mean of 7, 12, 39, 4, and 3.

c. Find the mean of 16, 0, and 11.

P9   MULTIPLES AND FACTORS OF INTEGERS

MULTIPLES

Consider all the numbers that 4 will divide evenly. For example, 16 is divisible by 4, as is 484 and 4,444,444. Because these numbers are divisible by 4, they are considered **multiples** of 4. To list all the multiples of 4, you would begin with 4, 8, 12, 16, 20, . . . To list all of the multiples of 6, you would begin 6, 12, 18, 24, 30, 36, 42, . . . Comparing the two lists of multiples we find some numbers in common.

Multiples of 4: 4, 8, **12,** 16, 20, **24,** 28, 32, **36,** 40
Multiples of 6: 6, **12,** 18, **24,** 30, **36,** 42, . . .

The numbers which occur in both lists—12, 24, and 36—are common multiples. Since 12 is the smallest common multiple in this group it is called the **least common multiple (LCM).** The least common denominator (LCD) is sometimes referred to as the LCM. Thus, the LCM is very important for adding fractions. In the following addition of fractions problem, the LCM of 4 and 6 is used to solve the problem.

$$\frac{1}{4} + \frac{1}{6} = \frac{3}{12} + \frac{2}{12} = \frac{3 + 2}{12} = \frac{5}{12}$$

FACTORS

A factor is both a noun (thing) and a verb (action). Factor (noun) means the numbers that are multiplied together to get a product. When we factor (verb), we start with the product and find numbers that will divide into the product. For example, in the equation $36 = 9 \cdot 4$, 36 is the product of the factors 9 and 4. Also, $9 \cdot 4$ is a **factorization** of 36. Since neither 4 or 9 is a prime number, $9 \cdot 4$ is not a **prime factorization** of 36. A prime factorization is a list of prime factors of a number such that when you multiply them all together you get the product you are interested in. For 36 the prime factorization is $2 \cdot 2 \cdot 3 \cdot 3$. More often it is written $36 = 2^2 \cdot 3^2$. Every number has its own unique prime factorization.

FACTORS AND LCMS

Prime factorization is a powerful tool we can use to find the LCM of a group of numbers. For example, let's find the LCM of 12, 18 and 24.

$$12 = 2 \cdot 2 \cdot 3 \qquad\qquad 18 = 2 \cdot 3 \cdot 3 \qquad\qquad 24 = 2 \cdot 2 \cdot 2 \cdot 3$$

Now use each factor the <u>most</u> times it was used in any of the three factorizations.

$$LCM = 2 \cdot 2 \cdot 2 \cdot 3 \cdot 3 = 72$$

Therefore, 72 is the smallest number that 12, 18, and 24 will all divide into evenly.

P9   Practice.

a. Find the LCM of 8 and 12.

b. Find the LCM of 9, 12, and 4.

c. Find the prime factorization of 96.

d. Find the prime factorization of 360.

P10   ABSOLUTE VALUES OF NUMBERS

The **absolute value** of a number is the distance that number is away from zero.

$$|-8| = 8$$

Read this as "the absolute value of negative 8 is 8."

$$|-8| = 8 \qquad\qquad |5| = 5 \qquad |-3.8| = 3.8 \qquad |0| = 0$$

One of the few guarantees in life is that a negative value will never come out of an absolute value sign.

P11   GREATER THAN / LESS THAN

Sometimes we want to compare numbers that we know are not equal to each other. To do this we use an inequality sign. The small end of the **greater than / less than sign** always points towards the smaller value. The larger end always opens towards the largest value.

$$3 < 5 \qquad\qquad 5 > 3 \qquad\qquad -1.02 < -1.01 \qquad\qquad -7 < 5$$

P12 CONVERSIONS BETWEEN FRACTIONS AND DECIMALS

To change a fraction to a decimal, divide the numerator by the denominator.

$$\frac{7}{8} = 0.875$$

To change a decimal to a percent, move the decimal point two places to the right.

$$0.875 = 87.5\%$$

To change a percent to a decimal, move the decimal point two places to the left.

$$112\% = 1.12$$

To change a decimal to a fraction, place the number over 1.0 and then multiply the top and the bottom by whatever it takes (10, 100, 1000) to move the decimal point to the last significant digit of the numerator. In this example we want to move the decimal point two spots, so we will use 100 over 100 as the multiplier.

$$1.15 = \frac{1.15}{1.0} \cdot \left(\frac{100}{100}\right) = \frac{115}{100} = \frac{23}{20}$$

P12 Practice. Complete this table.

Fraction	Decimal	Percent
³⁄₈		
	0.35	
		8%

ANSWERS TO PRACTICES

P1 Answers
a. 48
b. 29
c. 115
d. 131

P2 Answers
a. $^{21}/_2$
b. $^{29}/_{35}$
c. $-^{10}/_9$

P3 Answers
a. 3.198
b. 3.6
c. 90
d. 50

P4 Answers
a. x^5
b. 7^5
c. $5^3A^3B^2$
d. 64
e. -1
f. $16a^2$
g. 1

P5 Answers
a. 0
b. 245
c. $^1/_5$
d. $^8/_5$

P6 Answers
a. $w = 3.5$
b. $X = 24$
c. $Y = 2$
d. $Z = -1.5$

P7 Answers
a. 25%
b. 306
c. 110

P8 Answers
a. 22
b. 13
c. 9

P9 Answers
a. 24
b. 36
c. $96 = 2^5 \cdot 3$
d. $2^3 \cdot 3^2 \cdot 5$

P12 Answers
$^3/_8 = .375 = 37.5\%$
$^7/_{20} = .35 = 35\%$
$^2/_{25} = .08 = 8\%$

CHAPTER THREE

ALGEBRA

The content of the Algebra section falls into three major categories: Elementary Algebra, Intermediate Algebra, and Coordinate Geometry.

Elementary Algebra   (about 60%)

A1   Substituting values into algebraic expressions

A2   Setting up equations for given situations

A3   Basic operations with polynomials

A4   Factorization of polynomials

A5   Solving polynomial equations by factoring

A6   Formula manipulation and field axioms

A7   Linear equations in one variable

A8   Exponents

A9   Linear inequalities in one variable

Intermediate Algebra   (about 20%)

A10   Rational Expressions

A11   Exponents

A12   Systems of linear equations in two variables

A13   Quadratic formulas

A14   Absolute value equations and inequalities

Coordinate Geometry   (about 20%)

A15   Linear equations in two variables

A16   Distance formula in the plane

A17   Graphing conics (parabolas, circles)

A18   Graphing systems of equations and rational functions

A19   Midpoint formula

A1 SUBSTITUTING VALUES INTO ALGEBRAIC EXPRESSIONS

This is also known as "plug and chug." You are going to plug values into equations, and then chug along until the expression is simplified. You must be careful to keep track of signs and to follow the order of operations. (The order of operations was discussed in P5.)

Evaluate $x^3 + 2(x + 1)^2 + x - 5$ when $x = 3$. Whenever you substitute into an equation, use parentheses for each substitution. This will help you keep track of signs.

$$
\begin{aligned}
&= (3)^3 + 2((3)+1)^2 + (3) - 5 &&\text{substitute} \\
&= (3)^3 + 2(4)^2 + (3) - 5 &&\text{add inside the parentheses} \\
&= 27 + 2(16) + 3 - 5 &&\text{calculate the exponents} \\
&= 27 + 32 + 3 - 5 &&\text{multiply} \\
&= 57 &&\text{add and subtract}
\end{aligned}
$$

When substituting values into algebraic expressions, it is extremely important to keep track of signs. You can do all of the multiplication, division, addition, and subtraction exactly right, but if you miss just one sign you will get the problem just as wrong as the person who could not do the simplest addition. Perhaps the most dangerous substitution is plugging a negative value into an expression that has subtraction:

Find the value of the expression $2x^2 - 4x + 5$ when $x = -6$.

$$
\begin{aligned}
&= 2(-6)^2 - 4(-6) + 5 \\
&= 2(36) - 4(-6) + 5 \\
&= 72 - 24 + 5 \\
&= -43 \quad \text{INCORRECT}
\end{aligned}
\qquad
\begin{aligned}
&= 2(-6)^2 - 4(-6) + 5 \\
&= 2(36) - 4(-6) + 5 \\
&= 72 + 24 + 5 \\
&= 96 + 5 = 101 \quad \text{CORRECT}
\end{aligned}
$$

Also, pay careful attention to signs when calculating exponents:

What is the difference between -2^2 and $(-2)^2$?

$$
-2^2 = -(2)(2) = -4 \qquad\qquad (-2)^2 = (-2)(-2) = 4
$$

A1 Practice.

1. Evaluate $2X^2 + 9X - 5$ for $X = -2$.

2. Evaluate $y^2 - 10y + 25$ for $y = 5$.

3. Evaluate $z^2 + 5z - 8$ for $z = -3$.

4. Evaluate $a^2 - 3a + 2ab - 6b$, for $a = -3$ and $b = 2$.

(*Answers* to all practices in Chapter Three are found on pp. 65-66.)

A2 SETTING UP EQUATIONS FOR GIVEN SITUATIONS

Some questions will be word problems. But, rather than coming up with the "answer," you will have to determine an equation to solve the problem. In translating a word problem into algebra, it is useful to know that some words are associated with particular operations.

+ **Addition**	− **Subtraction**	• x ( ) **Multiplication**	÷ / **Division**	= **Equal**
sum more than together and	difference less than fewer than	product of times twice	divided quotient	is was will be (any form of be)

Usually you will have to use more than one operation in combination. When doing this you must pay attention to the difference between the algebraic order of operation (**PEMDAS**) and the order of operations called for in the word problem. For example, the ***sum of the products*** means something different than the ***product of the sums***.

The sum of the products of a times b and d times c $\qquad$ ab + dc
The product of the sums of a and b times d and c $\qquad$ (a + b)(d + c)

If we substitute values of a = 2, b = 3, c = 4, and d = 5, we see how different these two similar things actually are.

ab + dc = (2)(3) + (4)(5) = 6 + 20 = 26
(a + b)(d + c) = (2 + 3)(4 + 5) = (5)(9) = 45

Once you come up with what you think is the correct equation, try plugging in some values to see if your equation gives you what you think it should.

A2 Practice. Select the best answer.

1. Find the sum of the product of 2 times x and 3 times y.

    a) (2 + x)
    b) 6(x + y)
    c) 6xy
    d) 2x + 3y
    e) 6x + 6y

2. What is the sum of three consecutive integers?

    a) x + y + z
    b) x + (x + 1) + (x + 2)
    c) x + 1 + 2
    d) x + (x + 2) + (x + 4)
    e) x + 2x + 3x

3. Susan gets paid a salary of D dollars a week, plus a commission of 6%, based on her sales total (S). Which expression below best describes Susan's pay?

    a) D + S
    b) 6D + S
    c) D + 6S
    d) D + .06S
    e) .06(D + S)

4. A piece of rope 135 feet long is cut into three pieces. The second piece is twice as long as the first piece. The third piece is 3 times as long as the second.

    a) x + (x + 2) + (x + 3) =135
    b) x + 2(x + 3) =135
    c) x + 2x + 6x = 135
    d) 3x + 2x + x = 135
    e) 6x = 135

A3   BASIC OPERATIONS WITH POLYNOMIALS

POLYNOMIALS

Poly means many and **nominal** means terms. Therefore, polynomial means many terms. Even though the name literally means many terms, polynomials can have just one term. If it is just a one-term polynomial, it has a special name, **monomial**. Terms are always separated from each other by addition or subtraction signs.

1 term Monomials	2 terms Binomials	3 terms Trinomials	4 or more (no special name)
a	a + b	a + b + c	a + b + c + d
$-2x$	c − 5	$x^2 - 8x + 15$	$x^3 - x^2 + 2x + 9$
$4y^2$	$x^2 - y^2$	$x^4 - x + y$	$5a - 4b + 3c - 2d - 5e + 8f - 9$

ADDITION

When adding polynomials, drop parentheses and combine like terms.

$$(x^2 - 8x + 15) + (x^3 - x^2 + 2x + 9) = x^2 - 8x + 15 + x^3 - x^2 + 2x + 9 = x^3 - 6x + 24$$

SUBTRACTION

When subtracting, make sure to change all of the signs in the subtrahend, then add.

$$(a + b + c) - (a - b) = a + b + c - a + b = 2b + c$$

$$(x^2 - 8x + 15) - (x^3 - x^2 + 2x + 9) = x^2 - 8x + 15 - x^3 + x^2 - 2x - 9 = -x^3 + 2x^2 - 10x + 6$$

MULTIPLICATION

Distribution is the basis for multiplication of polynomials.

$$a(b + c) = ab + ac$$

$$2(x + 5) = 2x + 10$$

When multiplying polynomials be aware of how many terms you are multiplying together. In the example above, $a(b + c) = ab + ac$, we multiplied a binomial by a monomial, so 1 x 2 = 2 multiplications had to be performed. If you are multiplying a binomial times a binomial, you will have 2 x 2 = 4 multiplications to perform. If you are multiplying a trinomial by a binomial, you will have 3 x 2 = 6 multiplications to perform.

FOIL

When multiplying a binomial by a binomial remember the acronym **FOIL** (First Outside Inside Last).

$$(x + 4)(x - 3) \quad = \quad (x + 4)\,(x - 3)$$

F	First	Multiply the **First** terms of both binomials	$x \cdot x = x^2$
O	Outside	Multiply the **Outside** terms of both binomials	$x \cdot (-3) = -3x$
I	Inside	Multiply the **Inside** terms of both binomials	$4 \cdot x = 4x$
L	Last	Multiply the **Last** terms of both binomials	$4 \cdot (-3) = -12$

$$(x + 4)(x - 3) = x^2 - 3x + 4x - 12 = x^2 + x - 12$$
$$\text{F} \quad \text{O} \quad \text{I} \quad \text{L}$$

When squaring a binomial just write the binomial down twice and **FOIL**.

$$(a + 3)^2 = (a + 3)(a + 3) = a^2 + 3a + 3a + 9 = a^2 + 6a + 9$$

When multiplying a trinomial by a binomial, think of it as two monomials being **distributed** through a trinomial, then combine like terms.

$$(b + 3)(b^2 - 2b - 15) = (b^3 - 2b^2 - 15b) + (3b^2 - 6b - 45) = b^3 + b^2 - 21b - 45$$

DIVISION

When dividing a polynomial by a monomial, just divide each term by the monomial.

$$\frac{4x^3 + 16x^2 - 10x}{2x} = \frac{4x^3}{2x} + \frac{16x^2}{2x} - \frac{10x}{2x} = 2x^2 + 8x - 5$$

Division of polynomials by binomials will require factorization, which is the next topic (**A4**).

A3   Practice.

1. Add $(3x^5 + 5x^3 - 5x^2 + 6x - 7) + (3x^4 + 2x^2 - 9x + 5)$

2. Subtract $(7x^5 + 3x^3 - 5x^2 + 5x - 7) - (2x^4 - 2x^3 + 7x^2 - 7x + 6)$

3. Multiply $(A + 7)(A + 2)$

4. Multiply $(B - 4)(B + 2)$

5. Multiply $(2C + 3)(C - 4)$

6. Multiply $(4D^3 + 3D^2 - 4D + 5)(2D - 5)$

33

A4 FACTORIZATION OF POLYNOMIALS

In the previous section, A3, we reviewed multiplication of polynomials. In this section, we will reverse the process and factor polynomials. When a polynomial is factored, it changes from being addition and subtraction to multiplication. Thus, it changes from being a polynomial to being a monomial. This process is essential for solving many types of equations.

GREATEST COMMON FACTOR (GCF)

The first tool to use when attempting to factor a polynomial is to find the **Greatest Common Factor** (GCF). The GCF is the largest factor that will divide evenly into all of the terms of the polynomial. Consider $4x + 10$. The largest factor that will divide evenly into both 4 and 10 is 2. Therefore, 2 is the GCF.

$$4x + 10 = 2(2x + 5)$$

Whenever you want to check a factorization, just multiply. You should get what you started with.

$$2(2x + 5) = 4x + 10$$

Here is another expression that can be factored.

$$42x^2 + 30x$$

Notice that the binomial could be factored several different ways:

$$42x^2 + 30x = 2(21x^2 + 15x)$$
$$42x^2 + 30x = 3(14x^2 + 10x)$$
$$42x^2 + 30x = 2x(21x + 15)$$
$$42x^2 + 30x = 3x(14x + 10)$$
$$42x^2 + 30x = 6x(7x + 5)$$

While none of these factorizations are incorrect, the best factorization is the last one. It is the one that pulls out the GCF.

FACTORING BINOMIALS

If you are factoring a binomial, check to see if it is the **difference of squares**.

Example 1 $X^2 - 25 = (X + 5)(X - 5)$

Example 2 $a^2 - 16 = (a + 4)(a - 4)$

Example 3 $m^2 - 144 = (m + 12)(m - 12)$

This will only work when there is subtraction. $A^2 + B^2$, the sum of squares, will not factor in the real number system.

Sometimes there can be a problem within a problem. After the first factorization in the problem below there is a factor, $(B^2 - 4)$, which can be factored further.

Example 4 $(B^4 - 16) = (B^2 + 4)(B^2 - 4) = (B^2 + 4)(B + 2)(B - 2)$

If the binomial is a **sum of cubes** or a **difference of cubes** it can be factored according to these formulas.

Sum of Cubes Formula: $\boxed{a^3 + b^3 = (a + b)(a^2 - ab + b^2)}$

Example 3 $\qquad x^3 + 8 = (x + 2)(x^2 - 2x + 4)$

Example 4 $\qquad 27y^3 + 64 = (3y + 4)(9y^2 - 12y + 16)$

Difference of Cubes Formula: $\boxed{a^3 - b^3 = (a - b)(a^2 + ab + b^2)}$

Example 5 $\qquad x^3 - 8 = (x - 2)(x^2 + 2x + 4)$

Example 6 $\qquad 8y^3 + 125 = (2y + 5)(4y^2 - 10y + 25)$

Notice how similar the formulas are; the only difference is the signs.

FACTORING TRINOMIALS

When you are faced with factoring a trinomial, check first to see if it is a **perfect square trinomial** by answering these three questions:

$$x^2 + 10x + 25$$

Is the first term a perfect square?	Yes	$\sqrt{x^2} = x$
Is the last term a perfect square?	Yes	$\sqrt{25} = 5$
Is the middle term equal to twice the product of the roots of the first and last terms?	Yes	$10x = 2 \bullet x \bullet 5$

Since we answered yes to all three questions, we know that we have a perfect square trinomial. The factorization of any perfect square trinomial will be a binomial squared.

$$x^2 + 10x + 25 = (x + 5)(x + 5) = (x + 5)^2$$

Here are some more examples. Notice that the sign of the last term must always be positive, and the sign used in the factor is always the same as the middle term.

Example 7 $\qquad x^2 - 8x + 16 = (x - 4)(x - 4) = (x - 4)^2$

Example 8 $\qquad x^2 + 12x + 36 = (x + 6)(x + 6) = (x + 6)^2$

Example 9 $\qquad 4x^2 + 12x + 9 = (2x + 3)(2x + 3) = (2x + 3)^2$

Example 10 $\qquad 9x^2 - 30x + 25 = (3x - 5)(3x - 5) = (3x - 5)^2$

To verify any of these results, **FOIL** out the binomial.

If a trinomial is not a perfect square trinomial, then a different approach to factoring is required. We shall consider two: **inspection** and **grouping**.

INSPECTION

The inspection method of factoring trinomials requires you to consider two things. First, what are all the factors of the last term? Second, which of these factors add up to equal the number, or **coefficient,** of the middle term? The inspection method is easiest when the coefficient of the first term is 1. In Examples 11 and 12, since no number is written in front of the x^2 we know that the coefficient is 1.

Example 11 Factor $x^2 + 7x + 12$ by inspection.

To solve by inspection, we need the factors of 12 that add together to equal 7.

What are the factors of 12?	What is the sum of each set of factors?
$12 = 1 \cdot 12$	$1 + 12 = 13$
$12 = 2 \cdot 6$	$2 + 6 = 8$
$12 = 3 \cdot 4$	**$3 + 4 = 7$**

Since $3 + 4 = 7$, the middle term of the trinomial, we use the factors 3 and 4 to write the factorization of $x^2 + 7x + 12$: $x^2 + 7x + 12 = (x + 3)(x + 4)$. As with all factorizations, check by multiplying. These problems can become quite complex, especially when we mix signs.

Example 12 Factor $x^2 + 2x - 48$ by inspection.

What are the factors of –48?	What is the sum of each set of factors?
$48 = -1 \cdot 48$	$-1 + 48 = 47$
$48 = -2 \cdot 24$	$-2 + 24 = 22$
$48 = -3 \cdot 16$	$-3 + 16 = 13$
$48 = -4 \cdot 12$	$-4 + 12 = 8$
$48 = -6 \cdot 8$	$-6 + 8 = 2$

Since $-6 + 8 = 2$, the middle term of the trinomial, we use those factors to write the factorization of $x^2 + 2x - 48$: $x^2 + 2x - 48 = (x - 6)(x + 8)$.

Factoring by inspection is another way of saying *guess the factorization* until you come up with the correct factors. Factoring by inspection is a skill that requires some practice. The more you factor, the better you will get at it. It is essential that you check your factorization by FOIL.

GROUPING

Factoring by grouping requires less skill than inspection, but it usually takes more time. In grouping, we are going to split the middle term into two terms and pull out the GCF three times. First let's consider the general form of a trinomial written in descending order: $ax^2 + bx + c$

STEPS FOR FACTORING BY GROUPING

Step 1. Multiply $(a \cdot c)$. Pay attention to the sign.

Step 2. List all the factors of $a \cdot c$.

Step 3. If the sign of $(a \cdot c)$ is *positive,* ADD all the pairs of factors of $(a \cdot c)$ until you find a pair that will sum to b.

If the sign of $(a \cdot c)$ is *negative,* find the DIFFERENCE of all the pairs of factors $(a \cdot c)$ until you find a pair that has a difference of b.

Step 4. Rewrite the trinomial into a four term polynomial using the factor pair found in step 3 to replace the bx term.

Step 5. Factor out the GCF of the first two terms. Factor out the GCF of the last two terms. The result is two terms. Each term is a monomial times a binomial.

Step 6. Factor out the GCF of the two terms, and you are finished.

Example 13 $3x^2 - 13x - 10$

Step 1.   Multiply (a • c): $3(-10) = -30$

Steps 2 and 3.   Since (a • c) is a negative, we will look for a difference:

Factors of –30		Difference
1	30	29
████	████	████
3	10	7
5	6	1

Step 4.   Since the difference of 2 and 15 is 13, this is the pair of factors we use to rewrite the trinomial. Since we want to replace a –13, we let the 15 be negative and the 2 be positive.

$$3x^2 - 13x - 10 = 3x^2 - 15x + 2x - 10$$

Step 5.   Now we pull the GCF (3x) of the first group ($3x^2 - 15x$) and then the GCF (2) of the second group ($2x - 10$). This is where the name of this method, **factor by grouping**, comes from.

$$3x^2 - 15x + 2x - 10 = (3x^2 - 15x) + (2x - 10)$$
$$= 3x(x - 5) + 2(x - 5)$$

Step 6.   Now we have a binomial with two terms. The first term is $3x(x - 5)$ and the second term is $2(x - 5)$. The GCF is $(x - 5)$. Factor out the GCF.
$$= 3x(x - 5) + 2(x - 5)$$
$$= (x - 5)(3x + 2)$$

Factoring is complete. Check by multiplying, using the FOIL method.

Example 14   Factor $6x^2 - x - 40$ by grouping.

Find the factors of $6 • (40) = -240$ that have a difference of –1.

Factors of 6 • (40) = –240		Difference
1	240	239
2	120	118
3	80	77
4	60	56
5	48	43
6	40	34
8	30	22
10	24	14
12	20	8
████	████	████

Since 15 and 16 differ by 1, we can rewrite the trinomial into a four term polynomial ready for factoring. Since we want a negative 1, 16 will be negative and 15 will be positive ($-16 + 15 = -1$). The order you write –16 and 15 in does not matter.

$$6x^2 - x - 40 = 6x^2 - 16x + 15x - 40 = (6x^2 - 16x) + (15x - 40)$$
$$= 2x(3x - 8) + 5(3x - 8) = (2x + 5)(3x - 8)$$

Check by multiplication, using FOIL.

FACTORING OTHER POLYNOMIALS

If you have more than three terms, try factoring by grouping.

Example 15

$ac + ad + bc + bd$
$= (ac + ad) + (bc + bd)$
$= a(c + d) + b(c + d)$
$= (a + b)(c + d)$

Example 16

$2cd + 16c - 3d - 24$
$= (2cd + 16c) + (-3d - 24)$
$= 2c(d + 8) + -3(d + 8)$
$= (2c - 3)(d + 8)$

Example 17

$x^3 - 2x^2 + 3x - 6$
$= (x^3 - 2x^{2)} + (3x - 6)$
$= x^2(x - 2) + 3(x - 2)$
$= (x^2 + 3)(x - 2)$

Some problems call for a combination of methods:

Example 18

$x^3 + 7x^2 - 4x - 28$
$= (x^3 + 7x^2) + (-4x - 28)$ Begin with grouping.
$= x^2(x + 7) + -4(x + 7)$
$= (x^2 - 4)(x + 7)$ Notice the difference of squares.
$= (x + 2)(x - 2)(x + 7)$

PRIME POLYNOMIALS

Consider the polynomial $x^2 + 8x + 10$. If we were to try to factor this polynomial by inspection, we would need to find factors of 10 that would also add up to 8. The factors of 10 are (1, 10) and (2, 5). Since neither of these factor pairs will produce the required sum of 8, we know that $x^2 + 8x + 10$ cannot be factored. If a polynomial cannot be factored, it is called a **prime polynomial.**

FACTORING SURVIVAL

Factoring is a skill that you can get better at with practice. Whenever you must factor a polynomial and cannot decide where to start, try these steps.

A) **GCF**: Always try to factor out a **GCF**. If this is possible, the rest of the problem will be easier.

B) Count the number of terms. This will tell you what to do next.

- *One Term* – no need to factor

- *Two Terms* – check for the **difference of squares, sum of cubes, or difference of cubes**, and follow these formulas. Remember, the sum of squares will not factor in the real number system.

prime polynomial (will not factor)	$a^2 + b^2$
difference of squares	$a^2 - b^2 = (a + b)(a - b)$
sum of cubes	$a^3 + b^3 = (a + b)(a^2 - ab + b^2)$
difference of cubes	$a^3 - b^3 = (a - b)(a^2 + ab + b^2)$

- *Three terms* – Check for a **perfect square trinomial**.

$$a^2 + 2ab + b^2 = (a + b)(a + b) = (a + b)^2$$
$$a^2 - 2ab + b^2 = (a - b)(a - b) = (a - b)^2$$

If that does not work, try **inspection** or **grouping**.

- *Four terms* – Grouping

FACTORING SURVIVAL, continued

C) Factor completely. Watch out for combinations of two or more methods.

D) Check by multiplying. With this type of test, you have time to work backwards from the answers that are given on the test.

An important thing to remember about a test like the COMPASS is that you can often work backwards from the answers to determine the correct response. For example, suppose you were given an item like this:

For all x, $x^2 + 3x - 40$

   a) $(x + 5)(x + 8)$
   b) $(x + 5)(x - 8)$
   c) $(x - 5)(x + 8)$
   d) $(x - 5)(x - 8)$
   e) $(x - 4)(x + 10)$

If you did not have any idea about how to factor this polynomial, you could multiply each of the answers out until you found the one that matched the question.

For all x, $x^2 + 3x - 40$

   a) $(x + 5)(x + 8) = x^2 + 8x + 5x + 40 = x^2 + 13x + 40$
   b) $(x + 5)(x - 8) = x^2 - 8x + 5x - 40 = x^2 - 3x - 40$
   c) $(x - 5)(x + 8) = x^2 + 8x - 5x - 40 = \mathbf{x^2 + 3x - 40}$
   d) $(x - 5)(x - 8) = x^2 - 8x - 5x + 40 = x^2 - 13x + 40$
   e) $(x - 4)(x + 10) = x^2 + 10x - 4x - 40 = x^2 + 6x - 40$

So, choice "c" is the correct answer. Because COMPASS is not a timed test, you are free to work problems like this the long way.

A4 Practice.
Factor completely. If a polynomial is prime, state so.

1. $2X^2 + 9X - 35$ 2. $X^2 - 10X + 25$

3. $X^4 - 81$ 4. $X^2 + 5X - 8$

5. $a^2 - 3a + 2ab - 6b$ 6. $A^2 - 13A + 42$

7. $2B^2 - 3B - 20$ 8. $12C^2 + 46C + 40$

9. $12D^3 + 22D^2 - 70D$ 10. $X^2 - 16X + 64$

11. $3y^3 + 27y + 18y^2$ 12. $A^8 - 256$

13. $4b^2 - 16c^2$ 14. $36c^2 - 12c + 1$

A5 SOLVING POLYNOMIAL EQUATIONS BY FACTORING

In this section we will see how factoring is used to solve equations.

THE PRINCIPLE OF ZERO PRODUCTS

What types of multiplication problems have zero as an answer? Only those that use zero as a factor. For example: $0 \cdot 0 = 0$; $0 \cdot -7 \cdot 4.238 = 0$; $110 \cdot 0 \cdot 82 \cdot 2 \cdot 5 = 0$. So, if we see a multiplication problem like this: $25 \cdot x \cdot 53 \cdot 7 \cdot 205 = 0$, we know that x has to be equal to 0. The reasoning that supports this claim is known as the **Principle of Zero Products:**

If a • b = 0, then either a = 0 or b = 0.

The Principle of Zero Products allows us to look at a multiplication problem like $(x = 8)(x - 5) = 0$ and reason that either $(x + 8) = 0$ or $(x - 5) = 0$. Thus, $x = -8$ or $x = 5$. These are the only values that will produce a zero factor, hence a zero product.

If you are given a polynomial such as $2x^2 = 16x - 30$ to solve, you can use the Principle of Zero Products to find the solutions:

$2x^2 = 16x - 30$	First, set the polynomial equal to 0.
$2x^2 - 16x = 30 = 0$	Now factor out the GCF, which is 2.
$2(x^2 - 8x = 15) = 0$	Try to factor the remaining polynomial.
$2(x - 3)(x - 5) = 0$	Set each of the three factors equal to 0.
$2 = 0$	Since $2 = 0$ will never be true, this factor will not make a contribution to the solution set.
$x - 3 = 0$	
$x = 3$	So 3 is a member of the solution set.
$x + 5 = 0$	
$x = -5$	So -5 is a member of the solution set.
$x = \{-5, 3\}$	The solution set is $\{-5, 3\}$.

Example 1   Solve $x^2 + 5x + 6 = 0$.

This equation is a trinomial. We will factor, which will change it into a multiplication problem. Then use the Principle of Zero Produts to find solutions.

$$x^2 + 5x + 6 = 0$$
$$(x + 3)(x + 2) = 0 \qquad \text{Set each factor} = 0$$
$$(x + 3) = 0 \qquad (x + 2) = 0$$
$$x = -3 \qquad\quad x = -2 \qquad \text{The solution set is } x = \{-3, -2\}$$

Example 2   Solve $2X^2 + 9X = 35$.

Sometimes problems are not set equal to zero. Therefore, you must set the equation equal to zero before you factor. That is always the first step.

$$2X^2 + 9X = 35$$
$$2X^2 + 9X - 35 = 0$$
$$(2X - 5)(X + 7) = 0 \qquad \text{Set each factor} = 0$$
$$(2X - 5) = 0 \qquad (X + 7) = 0$$
$$2X = 5 \qquad\qquad X = -7$$
$$X = \frac{5}{2} \qquad\qquad\qquad \text{The solution set is } X = \left\{\frac{5}{2}, -7\right\}$$

40

Example 3   Solve $12x^3 + 22x^2 = 70x$.

In this problem, first set the equation equal to zero. Then, factor out the GCF, which is $2x$. Next, factor the trinomial, which gives us three factors. Finally, set each factor equal to zero to find the solution set.

$$12x^3 + 22x^2 = 70x$$
$$12x^3 + 22x^2 - 70x = 0$$
$$2x(6x^2 + 11x - 35) = 0$$
$$2x(2x + 7)(3x - 5) = 0$$

$2x = 0$	$2x + 7 = 0$	$3x - 5 = 0$
$2x = 0$	$2x = -7$	$3x = 5$
$x = \dfrac{0}{2}$	$x = -\dfrac{7}{2}$	$x = \dfrac{5}{3}$

$$x = \left\{ 0, -\frac{7}{2}, \frac{5}{3} \right\}$$

Example 4   Solve $X^2 + 8X = -16$.

Sometimes quadratic equations have only one solution. For example, $X^2 + 8X = -16$ is a perfect square trinomial. Whenever the equation is a perfect square trinomial, you will only have one solution.

$$X^2 + 8X = -16$$
$$X^2 + 8X + 16 = 0$$
$$(X + 4)(X + 4) = 0$$
$$(X + 4)^2 = 0 \qquad\qquad \text{Set each factor} = 0$$
$$X + 4 = 0 \qquad X + 4 = 0$$
$$X = \{-4\}$$

Example 5   Solve $3x^2 + 6x = 0$.

If you have a quadratic but no "c" term, then factor out the common factor of x.

$$3x^2 + 6x = 0$$
$$3x(x + 2) = 0 \qquad\qquad \text{Set each factor} = 0$$

$3x = 0$	$x + 2 = 0$
$x = 0$	$x = -2$

$$x = \{0, -2\}$$

Whenever you have a monomial factor that contains the variable, then you will have a zero in the solution set. See Example 3: $2x$ and Example 5: $3x$.

Example 6   Solve $X^2 = 5X + 8$.

Sometimes equations will have no rational solution. This is one such equation.

$$X^2 = 5X + 8 \qquad\qquad X^2 - 5X - 8 = 0$$

The factors of 8 are $(1, 8)$ and $(2, 4)$. There is no way to combine these factors and come up with a -5; therefore, this quadratic is not factorable. This means it has no rational solutions. Later we will see how to find irrational solutions to this type of equation.

A5   Practice. Solve.

1.	$X^2 = 36$		2.	$X^2 = 5X$
3.	$(X + 2)(X - 3) = 0$		4.	$X^2 = 7X - 12$
5.	$X^2 - X = 6$		6.	$A^2 - 13A = -42$
7.	$B^2 + 3B + 20 = 0$		8.	$X^3 + 2X^2 - 9X - 18 = 0$

41

A6 FORMULA MANIPULATION AND FIELD AXIOMS

Formula manipulation means solving for a particular variable. When solving for a variable, let's call that variable the **target.** What you want to do is get everything away from the target and have the target alone on either side of the equal sign.

When dealing with a target that has no exponents, try this procedure:

Step 1. Remove all grouping symbols.

Step 2. Move all terms containing the target on one side of the equation.

Step 3. Move all other terms to the other side of the equation.

Step 4. If you have two or more unlike terms with the target in them, factor out the target.

Step 5. Multiply by the reciprocal of the coefficient of the target.

Example 1   Solve for x. $C + 2x = a(x + 3) + x$

$C + 2x = a(x + 3) + x$ 1. Remove all grouping symbols.
$C + 2x = ax + 3a + x$ 2. Collect the target variable terms on one side.
$C = ax + 3a - x$ 3. Move everything else to the other side.
$C - 3a = ax - x$ 4. Factor.
$C - 3a = x(a - 1)$ 5. Divide by the coefficient.
$\dfrac{C - 3a}{a - 1} = x$

Example 2   Solve for b_2. $A = \dfrac{1}{2}(b_1 + b_2)H$

$A = \dfrac{1}{2}(b_1 + b_2)H$ 1. Remove all grouping symbols.
                                              Distribute $\frac{1}{2}$.
$A = (\dfrac{1}{2}b_1 + \dfrac{1}{2}b_2)H$ Distribute the H.
                                          2. Collect the target variables on one side.
$A = \dfrac{1}{2}b_1 H + \dfrac{1}{2}b_2 H$ (Not needed)
                                          3. Move everything else to the other side.
$A - \dfrac{1}{2}b_1 H = \dfrac{1}{2}b_2 H$ 4. Factor. (Not needed)
                                          5. Multiply by the reciprocal of the coefficient.
$\dfrac{2}{H} \cdot \left(A - \dfrac{1}{2}b_1 H\right) = \left(\dfrac{1}{2}b_2 H \cdot \dfrac{2}{H}\right)$

$\dfrac{2A}{H} - b_1 = b_2$

Sometimes it is easier to follow a different procedure to get the same result.

$A = \dfrac{1}{2}(b_1 + b_2)H$ 1. Multiply both sides by 2.

$2A = (b_1 + b_2)H$ 2. Divide by H.

$\dfrac{2A}{H} = (b_1 + b_2)$ 3. Subtract b_1.

$\dfrac{2A}{H} - b_1 = b_2$

FIELD AXIOMS

In field axioms, you will be given a made-up rule and then be asked to apply it.

> *Example 3*   Choose the best answer.
>
> The operation a ∘ b means "take 3a and add it to 2b." Find (6x) ∘ (7y) when x = 4 and y = 5.
>
> A. 72   B. 70   C. 2   D. 5040   E. 142

Plug in 6x for a and 7y for b: $3(6x) + 2(7y) = 3(6(4)) + 2(7(5)) = 3(24) + 2(35) = 72 + 70 = 142$. Therefore, the correct answer is E. 142. Notice that the incorrect answers all have something to do with the correct solution. This is very common on multiple choice tests. Often the incorrect answers you are given are only wrong by a sign or some other simple error.

This type of problem is not very common. If you work carefully and check your answer against those provided with the problem it should not be too difficult.

K PROBLEMS

Another type of problem will involve "k". "K" will be the missing part of some situation. You will need to figure out the value of "k" before you can do anything else with the problem.

> *Example 4*   Choose the best answer.
>
> If x = 4 and y = kx + x, then y = 5. What is *the value of y when x = 8?*
>
> A. 8   B. 10   C. 16   D. 20   E. 24

To find the solution, we must first find the value of k. Then we will use that k value and x = 8 to find *the value of y when x = 8.*

$$y = kx + x \qquad\qquad \text{Solve for k.}$$
$$(5) = k(4) + (4)$$
$$5 - 4 = 4k$$
$$1 = 4k$$
$$\frac{1}{4} = k \qquad\qquad \text{Now, substitute 8 for x and } \frac{1}{4} \text{ for k.}$$
$$y = \left(\frac{1}{4}\right)(8) + (8) = 2 = 8 = 10 \qquad \text{Therefore, the answer is B.}$$

A6   Practice.

1. Solve $A = \pi rs + \pi r^2$ for s.

2. Solve $P = 2l + 2w$ for l.

3. Solve $\dfrac{1}{x} + \dfrac{1}{y} = \dfrac{1}{z}$ for x.

4. If x = 4 and y = kx + 2x, then y = 9. What is the value of y when x = 2?

5. If x = 6 and y = kx + x, then y = 18. What is the value of y when x = 8?

6. If x = 9 and y = kx + x, then y = 12. What is the value of y when x = 6?

43

A7 LINEAR EQUATIONS IN ONE VARIABLE

This section is very similar to the first half of the previous section, A6. We have added step 6 (Check your answer). Often there will be other, more efficient ways to solve particular problems, but this way will always work.

Step 1.   Remove all grouping symbols.

Step 2.   Collect all terms containing the target on one side of the equation.

Step 3.   Move all other terms to the other side of the equation.

Step 4.   If you have two or more unlike terms with the target in them, factor out the target.

Step 5.   Multiply by the reciprocal of the coefficient of the target.

Step 6.   Check by plugging your answer into the original equation.

Example 1

$$3(x + 5) = 21 + x$$
$$3x + 15 = 21 + x$$
$$3x - x + 15 = 21$$
$$3x - x = 21 - 15$$
$$2x = 6$$
$$x = 3$$

1. Remove all grouping symbols.
2. Collect the target variable terms on one side.
3. Move everything else to the other side.
4. It is not necessary to Factor this example.
5. Divide by the coefficient.

$$3((3) + 5) = 21 + (3)$$
$$3(8) = 21 + 3$$
$$24 = 24 \quad \text{Correct.}$$

6. Check.

Whenever you encounter a fraction in an equation, you can get rid of it by multiplying by the LCD of all the denominators.

Example 2

$$\frac{2x}{3} + \frac{x}{2} = x + 3$$

$$(6) \cdot \left(\frac{2x}{3} + \frac{x}{2}\right) = (x + 3) \cdot (6)$$

$$\frac{12x}{3} + \frac{6x}{2} = 6x + 18$$

$$4x + 3x = 6x + 18$$
$$7x = 6x + 18$$
$$x = 18$$

The numbers 3 and 2 are the denominators so 6 is the LCD.

Check:

$$\frac{2(18)}{3} + \frac{18}{2} = 18 + 3$$
$$12 + 9 = 21$$
$$21 = 21$$
Correct!

A7   Practice.   Solve.

a. $X + 6 = -19$

b. $66 = 6Y$

c. $6A - 4 = 41$

d. $-67 = 7B - 4$

e. $9C - 5 = 4C + 20$

f. $D + \dfrac{D}{4} = 20$

44

A8 EXPONENTS

PRODUCT RULE OF EXPONENTS

$a^4 \cdot a^3 = a^{4+3} = a^7$

When **multiplying** like bases, **add** the exponents. (Multiplication becomes addition)

Examples:

$(X^5 Y^2)(X^4 Y^3) = X^9 Y^5$ $\qquad$ $(s^2t)(s^3 t^4) = s^5t^5$ $\qquad$ $(5z^2)(3z^3) = 15z^5$

QUOTIENT RULE OF EXPONENTS

$\dfrac{a^9}{a^3} = a^{9-3} = a^4$

When **dividing** like bases, **subtract** exponents. (Division becomes subtraction)

Examples

$\dfrac{X^6Y^4}{X^4Y^3} = X^2Y$ $\qquad$ $\dfrac{s^4t}{s^3} = st$ $\qquad$ $\dfrac{5z^{10}}{3z^3} = \dfrac{5z^7}{3}$

ZERO EXPONENT RULE

$C^0 = 1$

Anything (except zero) raised to the zero power is 1.

Examples

$5^0 = 1$ $\qquad$ $X^0 = 1$ (assume $X \neq 0$) $\quad$ $0^0 =$ undefined

THE POWER RULE OF EXPONENTS

$(D^4)^3 = D^{4 \cdot 3} = D^{12}$

When taking a power to a power, multiply the exponents.

$(X^5 Y^2)^3 = X^{15} Y^6$ $\qquad$ $(s^2t)^4 = s^8t^4$ $\qquad$ $(3z^3)^2 = 9z^6$

Raising a product or a quotient to a power: $\quad \left(\dfrac{C}{D}\right)^3 = \dfrac{C^3}{D^3}$ $\qquad$ $(AB)^3 = A^3B^3$

What is the difference between the product rule and the power rule?

Product Rule
$a^4 \cdot a^3 = a^7$

ADD

Notice there are two "a" bases and two exponents.

$aaaa \cdot aaa = aaaaaaa = a^7$

Power Rule
$(D^4)^3 = D^{12}$

MULTIPLY

Notice there is only one "D" base and two exponents.

$(D^4)(D^4)(D^4) = (DDDD)(DDDD)(DDDD)$
$= DDDDDDDDDDDD = D^{12}$

What about regular addition?

$a^4 + a^3 = a^4 + a^3$

Addition will not change exponents.
We cannot combine unlike terms.

What about signs? Does $-3^2 = (-3)^2$?

No! $-3^2 = -(3)(3) = -9$ $\qquad$ $(-3)^2 = (-3)(-3) = 9$

1. $K^5 \cdot K^3$ 2. $\dfrac{X^7Y^8}{X^2Y^3}$ 3. $(M^3N^4)^5$ 4. 13^0

A9   LINEAR INEQUALITIES IN ONE VARIABLE

The basic difference between a linear equality and a linear inequality is that an equality has one answer and an inequality has an infinite number of answers.

Equality

$x + 2 = 7$

$x = 7 - 2$ Subtract 2 from both sides

$x = 5$

Inequality

$x + 2 \geq 7$

$x \geq 7 - 2$

$x \geq 5$

Graph.

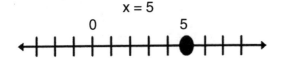

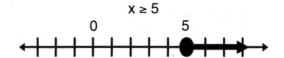

To solve a linear inequality, do everything exactly as you would with a linear equality; however, if you ever have to multiply or divide by a negative number, you must reverse the sign of the inequality.

Example 1

$-7Y + 5 \leq 33$ The act of dividing by –7 reverses the direction of the inequality.

$-7Y \leq 33 - 5$

$-7Y \leq 28$

$\dfrac{-7Y}{-7} \geq \dfrac{28}{-7}$

$Y \geq -4$

Check this problem by inserting any number greater than –4 into the original equation and see if it true. For example, let y = 3.

$-7(3) + 5 \leq 33$

$-21 + 5 \leq 33$

$-16 \leq 33$ True.

1. $3x + 8 \leq 35$

2. $12 - 4y > 2y + 18$

3. $9(z + 3) - 18 \geq -9$

4. $14C - 5 \leq 4C + 20$

A10 RATIONAL EXPRESSIONS

Rational expressions have variables in the denominator. All of the rules about fractions apply to rational expressions. One of the most important rules in algebra is that denominators can never equal zero. Consider the following expression:

$$\frac{20}{x-3}$$

If x were 8, we could plug it in and get a value of 4 for the expression. However, if we tried to plug in a 3 for x, we would get a zero in the denominator. And a zero in the denominator is the worst thing that can ever happen in your life! To find the value(s) for which a rational expression is undefined, set the denominator equal to zero and solve for x:

$$x - 3 = 0$$
$$x = 3$$

In other words, x = 8 is a meaningful replacement, but the expression is undefined for x = 3.

ADDITION AND SUBTRACTION

Adding or subtracting rational expressions requires a common denominator. Then the operation can be performed on the numerators.

$$\frac{4}{x^2 + x - 6} - \frac{2}{x^2 + 3x - 10}$$

$$= \frac{4}{(x + 3)(x - 2)} - \frac{2}{(x + 5)(x - 2)}$$

$$= \frac{4(x + 5)}{(x + 3)(x - 2)(x + 5)} - \frac{2(x + 3)}{(x + 3)(x - 2)(x + 5)}$$

$$= \frac{4(x + 5) - 2(x + 3)}{(x + 3)(x - 2)(x + 5)}$$

$$= \frac{4x + 20 - 2x - 6}{(x + 3)(x - 2)(x + 5)}$$

$$= \frac{2x + 14}{(x + 3)(x - 2)(x + 5)}$$

Sometimes finding the LCD requires factoring. In this example, after the denominators are factored, we only have three factors: $(x + 3)$, $(x - 2)$, and $(x + 5)$. The LCD is the smallest number that contains these factors. Thus, the LCD is $(x + 3)(x - 2)(x + 5)$. Once found, the LCD will not change for the rest of the problem.

Notice that the negative 2 is distributed all the way through the $(x + 3)$ numerator to become $-2x - 6$ in the next to last step.

MULTIPLICATION

When multiplying rational expressions, just multiply numerator by numerator and denominator by denominator.

When you are instructed to simplify the multiplication of rational expressions, you need to factor and then cancel. Do not multiply.

$$\frac{x^2 + x - 6}{x^2 - x - 12} \cdot \frac{x^2 - 16}{x^2 + 3x - 10}$$

$$= \frac{(x + 3)(x - 2)}{(x + 3)(x - 4)} \cdot \frac{(x + 4)(x - 4)}{(x + 5)(x - 2)}$$

$$= \frac{(x + 4)}{(x + 5)}$$

DIVISION

When dividing, multiply by the reciprocal of the divisor. (When dividing, *don't ask why just flip and multiply.*)

$$\frac{a}{b} \div \frac{c}{d} = \frac{a}{b} \cdot \frac{d}{c} = \frac{ad}{bc}$$

A10 Practice.

1. For what values of x is the expression undefined? $\dfrac{3}{2x + 8}$

2. For what values of y is the expression undefined? $\dfrac{-5}{2y}$

3. Add

$$\frac{x}{2} + \frac{3}{x}$$

$$\frac{x^2 + 6}{2x}$$

4. Subtract

$$\frac{3}{x^2 + 5x + 6} - \frac{2}{x^2 - 4}$$

5. Multiply

$$\frac{x^2 + 10x + 25}{x^2 - x - 2} \cdot \frac{x^2 + x - 6}{x^2 - 25}$$

6. Divide

$$\frac{x^2 + x + 2}{x^2 + 4x + 3} \div \frac{x + 2}{x + 3}$$

A11　EXPONENTS

Negative exponents have nothing to do with whether a number is positive or negative. Negative exponents tell us to switch the position of the base from the numerator to the denominator or from the denominator to the numerator. In other words, if a base in the numerator has a negative exponent, move it to the denominator, and the exponent is positive. For example: $x^{-2} = \dfrac{1}{x^2}$

Example 1　　　　Simplify.

$$\dfrac{a^{-2}b^3}{c^4d^{-5}} \qquad \dfrac{b^3d^5}{a^2c^4}$$

Example 2　　　The power rule is used to "distribute" an exponent across a term.

$$\left(\dfrac{3}{2}\right)^{-2} = \left(\dfrac{2}{3}\right)^{2} = \dfrac{2^2}{3^2} = \dfrac{4}{9}$$

Example 3

$$(2a^2b^{-3}c^4d^{-5})^{-2} = 2^{-2}a^{-4}b^6c^{-8}d^{10} = \dfrac{b^6d^{10}}{4a^4c^8}$$

Example 4

　　　　Notice the difference in what the exponent touches in A and B.

A)　$\dfrac{3}{(4x)^{-3}} = 4^3x^3 \cdot 3 = 64x^3 \cdot 3 = 192x^3$

B)　$\dfrac{3}{4x^{-3}} = \dfrac{3x^3}{4}$

SCIENTIFIC NOTATION

Negative exponents are very important in scientific notation. We use negative exponents to describe very small numbers.

$$0.00000123 = \dfrac{1.23}{1000000} = 1.23 \times 10^{-6}$$

On the other hand, positive exponents are used to indicate very large numbers.

$$123000000000 = 1.23 \times 100000000000 = 1.23 \times 10^{11}$$

A11　Practice. *Hafsa help*
Simplify.　Leave all exponents positive.

1.　$\dfrac{a^{-2}b^{-3}}{a^{-4}b^{-5}}$

2.　$\left(\dfrac{3a^2}{2a}\right)^{-2}$

3.　$(3x^3y^{-2}c^5d^{-3})^{-2}$

4.　$\dfrac{2a^{-2}}{(2a)^{-3}}$

5.　$\left(\dfrac{3a^{-1}}{5a^{-2}}\right)^{-2}$

6.　$\dfrac{s^{-2}t^{-8}}{s^3t^{-8}}$

A12 SYSTEMS OF LINEAR EQUATIONS IN TWO VARIABLES

A linear equation is a line. We will find out more about graphing lines in section A16. A system of linear equations in two variables consists of two lines. If you have two lines in a plane there are three possibilities for how they touch each other. First, they could be the same line. In such cases they are said to be **collinear** and they intersect at infinitely many points. Second, they could be **parallel**; these lines never intersect. Third, they could intersect at one point.

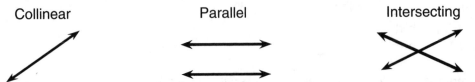

Collinear   Parallel   Intersecting

This section is about finding the one point of intersection if it exists. We will discuss two methods to find the point of intersection. One is called **substitution**, and the other is called **elimination**. Before using either method to find a solution, we need to discuss how to determine if your answer is correct.

CHECKING

First, what is an ordered pair? An **ordered pair** is two numbers arranged in order. Ordered pairs will always be in alphabetical order. So, if the system has a's and b's, the ordered pair (4, 9) means $a = 4$ and $b = 9$.

Example 1   Is the ordered pair (3, 2) a solution to this system?

$x + y = 5$
$x - y = 1$

Plug the ordered pair into each equation. If it is true for both, then it is a true solution for the system of equations. If it is false for either, it is false for the system.

$x + y = 5$	$x - y = 1$
$(3) + (2) = 5$	$(3) - (2) = 1$
$5 = 5$	$1 = 1$
True	True

Therefore, (3, 2) is a solution for the system.

Example 2   Is the ordered pair (8, 4) a solution to this system?

$2x - 3y = 4$
$x + y = 10$

Like before, we plug the ordered pair into each equation. It must be true for both to be a true solution for the system of equations.

$2(8) - 3(4) = 4$	$x + y = 10$
$16 - 12 = 4$	$(8) + (4) = 10$
$4 = 4$	$12 = 10$
True	False

Therefore, (8, 4) is not a solution for the system.

SUBSTITUTION

In substitution, we first solve for one variable in either equation. Then, we substitute that information back into the other equation. That will tell us what the value of one of the variables is. Finally, we plug that value into either of the equations, and that will reveal the value of the other variable.

Example 3

$2x + 3y = 5$

$x + 3y = 7$

⇨ $x = 7 - 3y$

Solving for x in the second equation is the easiest variable to solve for in this system.

$2(7 - 3y) + 3y = 5$
$14 - 6y + 3y = 5$
$14 - 3y = 5$
$-3y = 5 - 14$
$-3y = -9$
$\dfrac{-3y}{-3} = \dfrac{-9}{-3}$
$y = 3$

Plug the value obtained for x back into the other equation, and then solve for y.

⇨ $x = 7 - 3y$
$x = 7 - 3(3)$
$x = 7 - 9$
$x = -2$

Now that you have a y value, plug it back into either of the original equations to find x.

$2(-2) + 3(3) = 5$
$-4 + 9 = 5$
$5 = 5$

Plug back into an original equation to check. Since the check is true, we know $(-2, 3)$ is the solution to this system.

ELIMINATION

In substitution, one equation communicates with the other by the act of the substitution. In elimination, the communication takes place by adding the two equations together. The reason this method is called elimination is that we will alter the equations such that when we add them together one of the variables is eliminated.

Example 4 $2x - 3y = 5$ $x + 3y = 7$

$2x - 3y = 5$
+ $x + 3y = 7$
$3x \quad\;\; = 12$

Since $(-3y) + (3y) = 0$ we are already ready to eliminate y by adding the two equations.

$x = \dfrac{12}{3} = 4$

Solve for x and then substitute the value back into either equation to find the y value.

$x + 3y = 7$
$(4) + 3y = 7$
$3y = 7 - 4 = 3$

$\dfrac{3y}{3} = \dfrac{3}{3}$

$y = 1$

$2x - 3y = 5$
$2(4) - 3(1) = 5$
$8 - 3 = 5$
$5 = 5$

Check the ordered pair in the other equation.

Sometimes when you try substitution or elimination, you get what appears to be nonsense.

Example 5   Solve using elimination.

$-x + 3y = 5$
$2x - 6y = 4$

$(2) \cdot (-x + 3y) = (5) \cdot (2)$ Multiply both sides of the first equation by (2).
$-2x + 6y = 10$

$-2x + 6y = 10$ Add the two equations together.
$+\ 2x - 6y = 4$
_____
$\qquad 0 = 14$ False!

The procedure was executed correctly, but we got an obviously **false** result. This means that the system is inconsistent, parallel, and has no solution.

Example 6   Solve using substitution.

$2x - 8y = 16$
$x = 4y + 8$
$2(4y + 8) - 8y = 16$ Since the second equation is already solved for x just substitute (4y + 8) into the first equation for x.

$8y + 16 - 8y = 16$
$16 = 16$ True

True, but all of the variables are gone. This means that the system is collinear. It has an infinite number of answers. Any ordered pair that works for one equation will also work for the other.

If you are using one of these methods and all of the variables disappear, then the last statement will either be true or false, as in the last two examples. If the statement is false, then the system is inconsistent—parallel—no solution. If the statement is true, then the system is consistent–collinear—infinite solutions.

Collinear   **Parallel**   **Intersecting**
Consistent   Inconsistent   Consistent
Dependent   Dependent   Independent
∞ solutions   No solutions   One solution

Consistent or inconsistent means "do the lines touch?"
Dependent or independent means "do the lines go in the same direction?"

A12   Practice. Solve, using any method.

1. $x + y = 13$ 2. $2x - 4y = 3$ 3. $y = 2x - 3$
$\quad x - y = 1$ $3x + 5y = 10$ $4x - 5y = 9$

4. $x = 3y + 5$ 5. $y - 5 = x$ 6. $4x - 2y = -4$
$\quad 3x - 9y = 4$ $2x + 2y = 10$ $x + 3y = -15$

52

A13 QUADRATIC FORMULA

Memorize this formula. As soon as you begin the test, before you answer the first question, write the formula down on the provided scrap sheet of paper. Then, when you need to use it during the test, you won't have to worry about recalling it—you will already have it in front of you.

$$x = \frac{-b \pm \sqrt{b^2 - 4ac}}{2a}$$

Any equation of the form $ax^2 + bx + c = 0$ is called a quadratic equation. The quadratic formula will solve any quadratic equation. Any time you have a quadratic equation all you have to do is to identify a, b, and c and plug them into the formula.

Example 1   Solve $x^2 - 8x + 15 = 0$

$a = 1$ $b = -8$ $c = 15$ First identify a, b, and c. Pay attention to signs.

$x = \dfrac{-(-8) \pm \sqrt{(-8)^2 - 4(1)(15)}}{2(1)}$ Plug into the Quadratic Formula, then simplify.

$x = \dfrac{8 \pm \sqrt{64 - 60}}{2} = \dfrac{8 \pm \sqrt{4}}{2} = \dfrac{8 \pm 2}{2}$ The ± sign means work the problem twice.

$= \dfrac{8 + 2}{2} \qquad = \dfrac{8 - 2}{2}$

$= 5 \qquad\qquad = 3$ Thus, our equation $x^2 - 8x + 15 = 0$ has a solution set of $x = \{5, 3\}$.

When you get integer answers like these then you know that the equation would have factored. But, if you do not like to factor, you can always use the quadratic formula. It will always work, even with quadratics that will not factor—like the next one.

Example 2   Solve $x^2 + 5x + 3 = 0$

$a = 1$ $b = 5$ $c = 3$ Identify a, b, and c.

$x = \dfrac{-(5) \pm \sqrt{(5)^2 - 4(1)(3)}}{2(1)}$ Plug into the formula.

$= \dfrac{-5 \pm \sqrt{25 - 12}}{2} = \dfrac{-5 \pm \sqrt{13}}{2}$

$x = \left\{ \dfrac{-5 + \sqrt{13}}{2} \;,\; \dfrac{-5 - \sqrt{13}}{2} \right\}$ The square root of 13 will not simplify, so it shows up in your answer.

Sometimes the equation is not in standard form. Always write the equation in standard form before you identify a, b, and c.

Example 3   Solve $33 = 5x + 2x^2$

$33 = 5x + 2x^2$ First, set the equation equal to zero. Write
$0 = 2x^2 + 5x - 33$ the equation in descending order.
$a = 2$ $b = 5$ $c = -33$ Identify a, b, and c.
$x = \dfrac{-5 \pm \sqrt{5^2 - 4(2)(-33)}}{2(2)}$ Plug the values for a, b, and c into the Quadratic equation.

$x = \dfrac{-5 \pm \sqrt{25 + 264}}{4} = \dfrac{-5 \pm \sqrt{289}}{4} = \dfrac{-5 \pm 17}{4}$

$x = \dfrac{-5 - 17}{4} = \dfrac{-22}{4} = \dfrac{-11}{2} = -5.5$ or $x = \dfrac{-5 + 17}{4} = \dfrac{12}{4} = 3$

$x = \{-5.5, 3\}$

A13 Practice.

1. $x^2 + 6x + 8 = 0$

2. $y^2 + 5y = 24$

3. $7 - 11z = 3z^2 + 8z - 33$

4. $50 + 2x^2 = 20x$

5. $0 = x^2 + 4x - 7$

6. $0 = 2x^2 + x - 5$

A14 ABSOLUTE VALUE EQUATIONS AND INEQUALITIES

When variables are included within absolute value signs in an equation, you must work the equation twice, once for the positive case and once for the negative case.

Example 1 $|x| = 3$

$x = 3$ and $x = -3$ The solution set for x = $\{3, -3\}$.

Example 2 $|x + 5| = 7$

$x + 5 = 7$ $x + 5 = -7$

$x = 2$ and $x = -12$ The solution set for x = $\{2, -12\}$.

ABSOLUTE VALUES IN INEQUALITIES

Consider $|x| \leq 3$. What integer values would make this inequality false? Clearly, $\{4, 5, 6...\}$ would not satisfy the inequality. Neither would $\{...-6, -5, -4\}$. The integers in between these two sets will solve the inequality. So, $\{-3, -2, -1, 0, 1, 2, 3\}$ is part of the solution set.

These seven values are only the integer solutions. The complete answer to $|x| \leq 3$ would have to take into account all of the fractions and irrational numbers between 3 and -3. We would write the answer as (-3, 3). Note that this is the same notation used for ordered pairs. The only way to tell the two apart is by the context.

To solve this type of inequality algebraically, we must work the problem twice, just as we did with the absolute value equations in Examples 1 and 2 above. Recall that we work the equation once as it is written, but without the absolute value signs. The second time we work an equality, we introduce a negative sign. The procedure for working inequalities is similar. The only difference is that when a negative sign is introduced, the direction of the inequality sign must change.

Example 3 $3 \geq |x|$

$3 \geq x$ Work the problem once without the absolute value signs.

AND $-3 \leq x$ Work the problem a second time with a negative sign and a reversed inequality sign.

The final answer might be expressed in any of three ways:

Set notation $\{-3 \leq x \leq 3\}$

Interval notation $[-3, 3]$

Graphing

Note that the sign of the inequality was pointing towards the absolute value sign. Also note that the solution consists of one zone that runs from -3 to 3, inclusive. Suppose the sign pointed the other way?

Example 4 $5 \le |x|$

$5 \le x$ Work the problem once without the absolute value signs.

OR $-5 \ge x$ Work the problem a second time with a negative sign and a reversed inequality sign.

Again, the final answer might be expressed in three different ways:

Set notation $\{ x \le -5 \ \cup \ x \ge 5 \}$

Interval notation $(-\infty, -5) \ \cup \ (5, \infty)$

Graphing

The symbol $\cup$ stands for "union." This means that the answer is one of the two sets described on either side of the $\cup$ symbol.

Note that the sign of the inequality was pointing away from the absolute value sign. Also note that the solution consists of two zones that run from $-\infty$ to -5 or from 5 to ∞, where ∞ stands for "infinity."

A14   Practice. Solve.   All

a. $|w + 3| = 6$ b. $|2x - 2| = 10$ c. $7 < |y - 3|$ d. $|z| - 2 < 0$

A15   LINEAR EQUATIONS IN TWO VARIABLES

A linear equation with one variable usually has one answer.

x + 2 = 5   So, x = 3. There are no other solutions to this equation.

A linear equation with two variables has an infinite number of answers.

x + y = 5   (2, 3) is an ordered pair that means x = 2 and y = 3

How many answers can you think of?

. . .(–2, 7), (–1, 6), (0, 5), (1, 4), (2, 3), (3, 4), (4, 1), (5, 0), (6, –1), (7, –2) . . .

How about decimals?

. . . (1.5, 3.5), (1.6, 3.4), (1.7, 3.3) . . .

Rather than write all of these answers out, we can represent the solutions with a line. Any point in our list is included in the line, and any point on the line will fit into the equation.

Slope is the direction of a line. The line on the graph below goes down one unit for every unit it goes to the right. It is said to have a slope of negative one. Slope is defined by the formula:

$$m = \frac{y_2 - y_1}{x_2 - x_1} = \frac{\Delta y}{\Delta x} = \frac{\text{RISE}}{\text{RUN}}$$

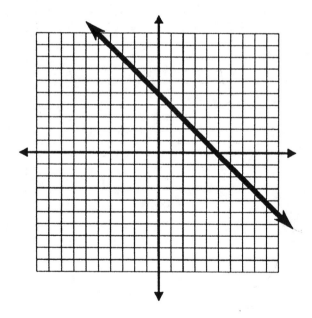

Memorize the formula above. Slope is m. The small numbers after the x's and y's are called subscripts. Subscripts are used to tell one ordered pair from another. x_2 and y_2 come from point two and x_1 and y_1 come from point one. Δy , pronounced "delta y," is the change in y. Δy is sometimes called "rise" because it describes how much a line changes in the up and down direction. Δx, "delta x," is the change in x. Δx is called "run" because it describes how much a line changes from left to right. The change, or Δ, is found by subtracting the x and y values of one point from another point. Slope is the change in y over the change in x, or rise over run.

Example 1   Find the slope of the line containing (7, 8) and (3, 5).

$$m = \frac{y_2 - y_1}{x_2 - x_1} = \frac{5 - 8}{3 - 7} = \frac{-3}{-4} = \frac{3}{4}$$

Remember that the *worst thing* that can ever happen in your life is to have zero in your denominator. If that situation occurs while you are computing the slope of a line, then what you have is an undefined slope. This happens with a vertical line.

Example 2   Find the slope of the line containing (2, 8) and (2, 5).

$$m = \frac{y_2 - y_1}{x_2 - x_1} = \frac{5 - 8}{2 - 2} = \frac{-3}{0}$$ Undefined

If a linear equation is solved for y, then the coefficient of x is the slope. So, to find the slope of any given equation, just solve for y.

Example 3   Find the slope of the line 2x + 3y = 6.

2x + 3y = 6	Move everything except the y term to the other side of the equation.
3y = -2x + 6	
$\frac{3y}{3} = \frac{-2x}{3} + \frac{6}{3}$	Divide by the coefficient of y.
$y = \frac{-2}{3}x + 2$	Now you have the form y = mx + b. The coefficient of the x term is –2/3. Therefore, –2/3 is the slope.

Example 4   Graph.

$$y = \frac{-2}{3}x + 2$$

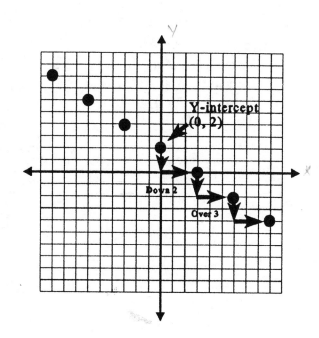

y = mx + b is called the **slope intercept** form of the line. It is the most useful form for graphing equations quickly.

The b term is where the line intersects the y–axis. Since 2 is the b term then the y-intercept is (0, 2).

The m coefficient gives the direction of the line. y = mx + b is all you need to graph a line. Just go to the intercept, then make the slope move down 2 and over 3. This will give you another point on the graph.

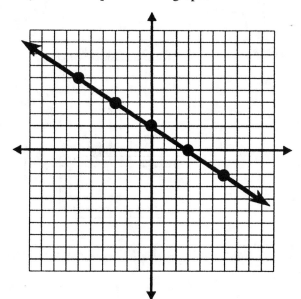

After you have found enough points, usually three, connect them, and you have a graph of the line.

57

Example 5 $4x - y = 8$

Another way of graphing a line is to just make a chart and find ordered pairs that fit into the equation until you have enough points to make a graph. Each row in the chart means that the problem was worked again.

$4x - y = 8$ Plug in values for x and solve for y.

x	y
0	−8
1	−4
2	0
3	4
4	8

When you have enough points, connect them for a graph.

Is the slope of this line positive or negative? What is the slope?
(answer below A15 Practice)

A15 Practice.

Find the slope of the line containing the given points.

1. 3, −5) and (−4, 7)   2. (3, −5) and (3, 7)   3. (3, −5) and (−4, −5)

Find the slope of the y-intercept of the line.
4. $5x - 3y = 9$ 5. $2x = 3y + 3$ 6. $-4x - 7y = -9$

Graph.
8. $y = 3x$ 9. $2x - 8y = 16$ 10. $x = 3y + 9$ 7. Find the slope and y-intercept of the line on the graph below.

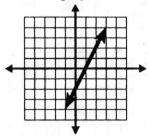

Answer to Example 5: positive $\dfrac{4}{1}$

58

A16   DISTANCE FORMULA IN THE PLANE

Pythagorean Theorem

$$a^2 + b^2 = c^2$$

Distance Formula

$$d = \sqrt{(x_2 - x_1)^2 + (y_2 - y_1)^2}$$

The distance formula in the plane is based on the Pythagorean Theorem. The distance formula is used to find the distance between two points in the plane.

Example 1   Find the distance between (4, -4) and (-2, 4)

$$d = \sqrt{(x_2 - x_1)^2 + (y_2 - y_1)^2}$$

$$d = \sqrt{(-2 - 4)^2 + (4 - (-4))^2}$$

$$d = \sqrt{(-6)^2 + (8)^2}$$

$$d = \sqrt{36 + 64}$$

$$d = \sqrt{100}$$

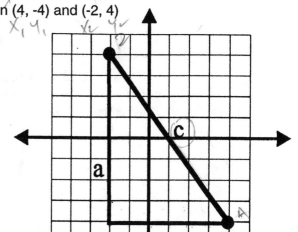

The Pythagorean Theorem can also be used to compute this distance.

$$a^2 + b^2 = c^2$$

$$8^2 + 6^2 = c^2$$

$$64 + 36 = c^2$$

$$100 = c^2$$

$$\sqrt{100} = \sqrt{c^2}$$

$$10 = c$$

a = the absolute value of the difference in the y values of the two points.

$$a = |4 - (-4)| = 8$$

b = the absolute value of the difference in the x values of the two points.

$$b = |(-2) - 4| = 6$$

A16   Practice.
Find the distance between the two points.

1. (0, 0), (5, 12)   2. (-1, 2), (3, 5)   3. (2, 7), (11, –5)

D =

A17 GRAPHING CONICS (PARABOLAS, CIRCLES)

PARABOLAS

$$y = ax^2 + bx + c$$

Here is a four-step method for graphing parabolas.

Step 1. When graphing equations of the form $y = ax^2 + bx + c$, the most important point is the **vertex**. This is where the parabola changes directions. The x value of the parabola can be found with this formula:

$$x = \frac{-b}{2a}$$

If this formula looks familiar, it should. It is the beginning of the quadratic formula. Once you find the x value, plug that into the original equation to find the corresponding y value.

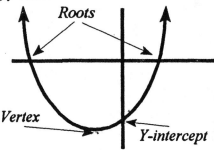

Step 2. Find the y-intercept. Just plug in a 0 for x. The y-intercept will be (0, c).

Step 3. Find the "roots" of the equation. The **roots** are another name for x-intercepts. Find the roots by factoring or the quadratic formula. This will give you either two, one, or no real answers.

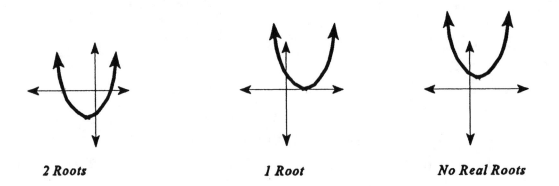

2 Roots   *1 Root*   *No Real Roots*

Step 4. Connect the points. If ax^2 is positive, then the parabola will point up (Smiley Face ☺). If ax^2 is negative, the parabola will point down (Frowny Face ☹). If you need more points plug values into the equation and make a xy chart.

Example 1

Graph $y = x^2 - 2x - 3$

This equation is in the form of $y = ax^2 + bx + c$. We know immediately that this is a parabola. Let's find the vertex, the y-intercept, and the roots so that we will have enough points to graph the equation.

$$x = \frac{-b}{2a} = \frac{-(-2)}{2(1)} = 1$$

1. Find the vertex.

$$y = (1)^2 - 2(1) - 3 = 1 - 2 - 3 = -4$$

$$vertex \ (1, -4)$$

$$y = (0)^2 - 2(0) - 3 = -3$$
$$y-intercept \ (0, -3)$$

2. Find the y-intercept.

$$0 = x^2 - 2x - 3$$
$$0 = (x - 3)(x + 1)$$
$$x = [3, -1]$$
$$roots \ (3, 0), \ (-1, 0)$$

3. Find the roots.

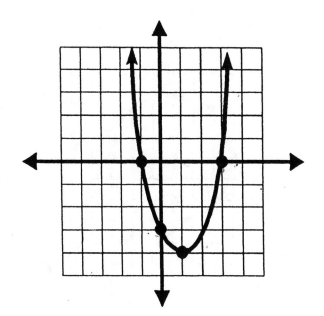

4. Now, plot the points and connect them to graph the parabola.

   $(1, -4)$

   $(0, -3)$

   $(3, 0)$

   $(-1, 0)$

CIRCLES

$$(x - h)^2 + (y - k)^2 = r^2$$

A circle is all of the points that are the same distance, r, the **radius**, from a particular point, called the **center**, in a plane. The circle formula is very similar to the distance formula. Circles are written in the form $(x - h)^2 + (y - k)^2 = r^2$, where (h, k) is the center of the circle and r is the radius.

Equation	Center	Radius
$(x - h)^2 + (y - k)^2 = r^2$	**(h, k)**	**r**
$(x - 3)^2 + (y + 5)^2 = 16$	(3, - 5)	4
$(x + 8)^2 + (y + 5)^2 = 25$	(-8, -5)	5

To graph a circle:

Step 1. Identify the center and the radius.

Step 2. Plot points North, South, East and West the specified distance away from the center. Add the radius to the y value of the center to get the North point. The x value for the North point will be the same as the centerpoint x value. Subtract to get the South point. Do the same with the x values to find the East point (add the radius to the centerpoint x value) and the West point (subtract). Use the centerpoint y value for the East and West points.

North (h, k+r)   South (h, k–r)
East   (h+r, k)   West (h–r, k)

Step 3. Connect the points in a smooth arc.

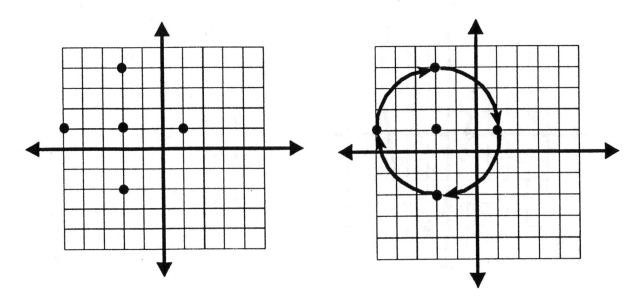

Example 1   Graph $(x + 2)^2 + (y - 1)^2 = 9$

1.   The center is at (-2, 1). Remember to change the signs. The radius is $\sqrt{9}$, which equals 3.

2.   By adding and subtracting 3 from the center (-2, 1), we find the values for the compass points: North (-2, 4), South (-2, -2), West (-5, 1), East (1, 1).

3.   Now, connect the points in an arc.

Find the vertex, y-intercept, and roots of the parabolas.

Find the center, radius, and North, South, East, and West points of the circles.

1. $y = x^2 - 6x + 8$

4. $(x + 3)^2 + (y - 2)^2 = 4$

2. $y = 4 - x^2$

5. $x^2 + y^2 = 36$

3. $y = 2x^2 - 4x - 6$

6. $(x - 4)^2 + (y + 3)^2 = 4$

A18   GRAPHING SYSTEMS OF EQUATIONS

To graph a system of equations, just graph one of the equations and ignore the other. When that one is done, graph the other. Make sure that you know where they intersect. Because finding the exact intersection by graphing is tricky, sometimes you should remember that you can always find this intersection algebraically by elimination or substitution.

Example 1   Solve by graphing.

$x + 2y = 5$
$x - 2y = 1$

$x + 2y = 5$

x	y
1	2
2	1.5
3	1

$x - 2y = 1$

x	y
1	0
2	0.5
3	1

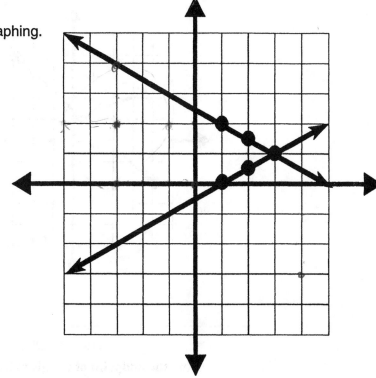

The solution for this system is (3, 1). (Just a reminder: substitution or elimination would have been a more efficient way of finding this intersection.)

A18   Practice.

Find the solution (the point of intersection) if such exists for each system.

1. $2x + 3y = 12$
     $4x - 2y = 8$

2. $y = 2x$
     $5x - 2y = 2$

3. $x + 3y = 2$
     $6y = 8 - 2x$

A19 MIDPOINT FORMULA

The **midpoint formula** will give the location of the center of a line segment. This point is the **midpoint**.

$$\left(\frac{x_2 + x_1}{2} \ , \ \frac{y_2 + y_1}{2}\right)$$

Another way to think about it is that the midpoint is the "average" point on the line.

Example 1

Find the midpoint of the line segment that has (3, 4) and (-4, -2) as endpoints.

$$\left(\frac{3 + -4}{2} \ , \ \frac{4 + -2}{2}\right) = \left(\frac{-1}{2}, \frac{2}{2}\right) = \left(\frac{-1}{2}, 1\right)$$

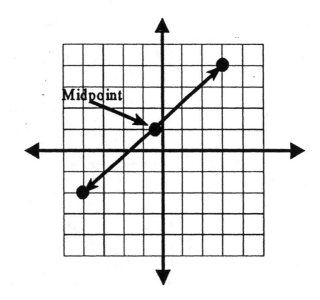

A19   Practice.

Find the midpoint of the given line segments.

1.   (3, 8) and (-9, 2)   2.   (-5, 7) and (-3, 2)

3.   (0, 0) and (−10, 20)   4.   (−8, 3) and (−9, 3)

ANSWERS TO PRACTICES

A1 Answers
1. −15
2. 0
3. −14
4. −6

A2 Answers
1. d
2. b
3. d
4. c

A3 Answers
1. $3x^5 + 3x^4 + 5x^3 − 3x^2 − 3x − 2$
2. $7x^5 − 2x^4 + 5x^3 − 12x^2 + 12x − 13$
3. $A^2 + 9A + 14$
4. $B^2 − 2B − 8$
5. $2C^2 − 5C − 12$
6. $8D^4 − 14D^3 − 23D^2 + 30D − 25$

A4 Answers
1. $(X + 7)(2X − 5)$
2. $(X − 5)^2$
3. $(X^2 + 9)(X + 3)(X − 3)$
4. Prime
5. $(a + 2b)(a − 3)$
6. $(A − 6)(A − 7)$
7. $(B − 4)(2B + 5)$
8. $2(2C + 5)(3C + 4)$
9. $2D(2D + 7)(3D − 5)$
10. $(X − 8)^2$
11. $3y(y + 3)^2$
12. $(A^4 + 16)(A^2 + 4)(A + 2)(A − 2)$
13. $4(b + 2c)(b − 2c)$
14. $(6c − 1)^2$

A5 Answers
1. $X = \{6, −6\}$
2. $X = \{0, 5\}$
3. $X = \{−2, 3\}$
4. $X = \{3, 4\}$
5. $X = \{−2, 3\}$
6. $A = \{6, 7\}$
7. No Solution
8. $X = \{−2, −3, 3\}$

A6 Answers
1. $s = \dfrac{A − \pi r^2}{\pi r}$
2. $l = \dfrac{p − 2w}{2}$
3. $x = \dfrac{yz}{y − z}$
4. $k = \dfrac{1}{4}$ $\quad y = \dfrac{9}{2}$
5. $k = 2$ $\quad y = 24$
6. $k = \frac{1}{3}$ $\quad y = 8$

A7 Answers
a. $X = −25$
b. $Y = 11$
c. $A = 7.5$
d. $B = −9$
e. $C = 5$
f. $D = 16$

A8 Answers
1. K^8
2. $X^5 Y^5$
3. $M^{15} N^{20}$
4. 1

A9 Answers
1. $x \leq 9$
2. $−1 > y$
3. $z \geq −2$
4. $c \leq 2.5$

A10 Answers
1. $x \neq −4$
2. $y \neq 0$
3. $\dfrac{x^2 + 6}{2x}$
4. $\dfrac{x − 12}{(x + 2)(x + 3)(x − 2)}$
5. $\dfrac{(x + 5)(x + 3)}{(x + 1)(x − 5)}$
6. 1

A11 Answers
1. $a^2 b^2$
2. $\dfrac{4}{9a^2}$
3. $\dfrac{y^4 d^6}{9x^6 c^{10}}$
4. $16a$
5. $\dfrac{25}{9a^2}$
6. $\dfrac{1}{s^5}$

A12 Answers
1. $(7, 6)$
2. $(2.5, .5)$
3. $(1, −1)$
4. Parallel, no solution

5. ?

6. ?

65

ANSWERS TO PRACTICES (CONTINUED)

A13 Answers
1. $x = \{-2, -4\}$
2. $y = \{3, -8\}$
3. $z = \{5/3, -8\}$
4. $x = \{5\}$
5. $-2 \pm \sqrt{11}$
6. $\dfrac{-1 \pm \sqrt{41}}{4}$

A14 Answers
a. $w = \{-9, 3\}$
b. $x = \{-4, 6\}$
c. $(-\infty, -4) \cup (10, \infty)$
d. $-2 < z < 2$

A15 Answers
1. $m = -12/7$
2. $m =$ undefined
3. $m = 0$
4. $m = 5/3$ $b = -3$
5. $m = 2/3$ $b = -1$
6. $m = -4/7$ $b = 9/7$
7. $m = 2$ $b = -2$

8.
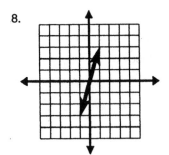

9.
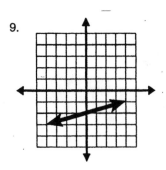

10.
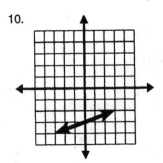

A16 Answers
1. 13
2. 5
3. 15

A17 Anwers
1. Vertex (3, −1), Y-int (0, 8)
   Roots (4,0), (2, 0)
2. Vertex (0, 4), Y-int (0, 4)
   Roots (−2,0), (2, 0)
3. Vertex (1, −8), Y-int (0, −6)
   Roots (3,0), (-1, 0)
4. Center (−3, 2) radius 2, North (−3, 4),
   South (−3, 0), East (−1, 2), West (−5, 2)
5. Center (0, 0) radius 6, North (0, 6),
   South (0, −6), East (6, 0), West (−6, 0)
6. Center (4, −3) radius 2, North (4, −1),
   South (4, −5), East (6, −3), West (2, −3)

A18 Answers
1. (3, 2)
2. (2, 4)
3. No solution

A19 Answers
1. (−3, 5)
2. (−4, 4.5)
3. (−5, 10)
4. (−8.5, 3)

CHAPTER FOUR

COLLEGE ALGEBRA

About 80% of the College Algebra portion of the **COMPASS** exam is concerned with functions, exponents, and complex numbers. The remaining 20% covers a wide variety of topics including: sequences and series, factorials, matrices, systems of equations, and roots of polynomials. Consequently, this chapter is divided into four sections corresponding to the weight **COMPASS** places on them.

C1   **Functions** (About 40%)

C2   **Exponents** (About 25%)

C3   **Complex numbers** (About 15%)

Other topics not included in this book (About 20%): arithmetic and geometric sequences and series, factorials, matrices (basic operations, equations and determinants), systems of linear equations in three or more variables, and logic and proof techniques.

C1 FUNCTIONS

Functions are extremely important during the freshman year of college mathematics. An understanding of functions is essential for calculus. But before we understand functions we must first understand what a correspondence is.

ORDERED PAIRS (DOMAIN, RANGE)

An ordered pair (x, y) is a partnership between two sets. The first is always the domain. The second is always the range. Notice how domain and range are in alphabetical order. Domain is usually x, and range is usually y.

CORRESPONDENCE

A correspondence is a rule that assigns one element from the domain to another element from the range. For example:

Two sets where D = the domain and R = the range: D = { a, b, c, d}   R = {1, 3, 5, 8}

Let F be a correspondence, a rule, that links D and R. F tells what happens when we input an element from the domain and which element we end up with from the range.

F = {(a, 1), (b, 5), (c, 3), (d, 8)}

(a, 1) is an ordered pair. It tells us that for an input "a" that "1" is the output. "a" and "1" are partners. The order they occur in tells us which is from the domain and which is from the range. Now if we have an input of d into the correspondence F we know that the output will be 8. This is the way we write an input of d and an output of 8:

F (d) = 8

Read this as, "F of d is 8." What is f (g) ? Look at the domain. There is no "g"; therefore, the mathematical way to answer this type of question is to say that "g" is not in the domain of F.

FUNCTION

A **function** is a special type of correspondence that assigns exactly one member of the range to a member of the domain.

Function
$G = \{(a,1), (b, 2), (c, 3), (d, 2)\}$

Not a Function
$H = \{(a,1), (b, 2), (a, 3), (d, 2)\}$

• 2 can occur twice as output
• Ranges can repeat with new partners

• a is listed with two domain elements
• Domains cannot repeat with new partners

A **function** is a relation in which no two ordered pairs have the same first coordinate with different second coordinates.

VERTICAL LINE TEST

If the graph of a relation is intersected more than once by any vertical line, that relation is not a function.

Function

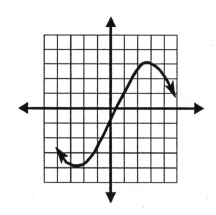

Not a Function, fails the vertical line test

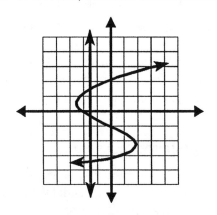

FUNCTIONAL NOTATION

In functional notation $y = 2x + 3$ could be written as $F(x) = 2x + 3$. $F(x)$ does **not** mean multiply $F \cdot x$. $F(x)$ does mean plug in an x value and find the y value. $F(x)$ is the same as y.

Functional notation is shorthand for writing down instructions about algebra.

For example,
Can be written:

Find the value of y when $y = 2x + 3$ and $x = 3$.
$F(3) = 2x + 3$

When working with functions it is often useful to make an x-y chart. The headings of these charts can be different, but they all mean the same thing.

Input	Output
Independent	Dependent
x	F(x)
x	y
0	3
2	7
8	19

$F(x) = 2x + 3$

Different Possible Headings that mean exactly the same thing.

For each row, pick an x value and then calculate the F(x).

DIFFERENT TYPES OF FUNCTIONS

POLYNOMIAL FUNCTIONS

There are actually an infinite number of different types of polynomial functions. We will consider the first four types: constant, linear, quadratic, and cubic.

CONSTANT FUNCTIONS $\boxed{F(x) = c}$

A constant function always stays the same no matter what the input is. For example:

$$F(x) = 3$$

Input	Output
x	y
x	F (x)
3	3
2	3
1	3
0	3
−1	3
−2	3

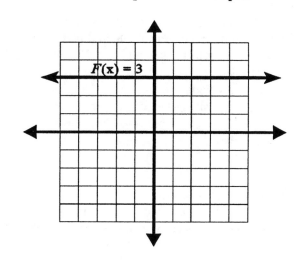

LINEAR FUNCTIONS $\boxed{F(x) = mx + b}$

(See also A7 and A16)

The simplest type of linear function is the constant function we just talked about. The slope of a constant function is 0. Usually when we think of linear functions we think of lines with slopes other than zero. $3x + 2y = 12$ is a linear equation in standard form. If we solve for y we get the equation into the slope intercept form of the line, $y = mx + b$. Recall that the coefficient of the x variable, m, is called the slope. Slope tells exactly the direction a line will take. Now, if we just replace y with functional notation, we will have a linear function.

Example 1   Write $3x + 2y = 12$ as a function.

$3x + 2y = 12$
$2y = -3x + 12$
$\dfrac{2y}{2} = \dfrac{-3x}{2} + \dfrac{12}{2}$
$y = \dfrac{-3x}{2} + 6$
$G(x) = \dfrac{-3x}{2} + 6$

Linear functions are always straight lines when graphed. Calculate at least three points to graph.

x	G(x)
0	6
2	3
4	0

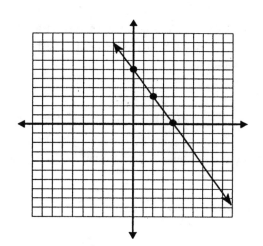

QUADRATIC FUNCTIONS

(See also A14 and A18)

Quadratic functions are second degree polynomials. The most important point of a quadratic function is the vertex. The vertex is the point where the parabola will change direction. This is also where the maximum or minimum value of the parabola will occur.

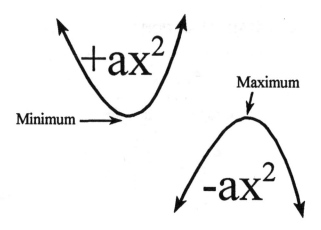

$$F(x) = ax^2 + bx + c$$

Direction

Parabolas always change direction. Part of the time they will go up and part of the time they will go down. The "a" of the ax^2 term decides the direction of the function and how wide or narrow it is. If ax^2 is positive, the parabola will turn up on the ends, like a smiley face [+, ☺]. If ax^2 is negative, the parabola will turn down on the ends, like a frowny face [–, ☹].

Maximum and Minimum

The maximum or minimum of any quadratic always occurs at the vertex. In section A17 of the previous chapter, we saw that to find the x value of a vertex we can use the formula:

$$x = \frac{-b}{2a}$$

This formula only gives you half of the vertex. To find the y value of the vertex, evaluate the quadratic at the x value given by the above formula. With this information you will be able to answer questions like the following:

Example 1

On which interval does the maximum value of $f(x) = -2x^2 + 16x - 14$ occur?

a) $(-\infty, -7)$
b) $(-7, -1)$
c) $(-1, 1)$
d) $(1, 7)$
e) $(7, \infty)$

First identify a and b. Remember the equation for a quadratic function: $f(x) = ax^2 + bx + c$. In this example, $a = -2$ and $b = 16$. Now use the vertex formula to identify the x value of the maximum point of the parabola.

$$x = \frac{-b}{2a} = \frac{-16}{2(-2)} = \frac{16}{4} = 4$$

The value x = 4 falls in the interval (1, 7), so the answer is *d*.

70

Width

The smaller the value of *a,* the wider the parabola. As the absolute value of *a* increases, the parabola becomes more narrow.

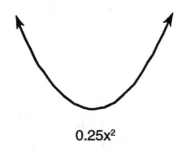
$0.25x^2$

$1x^2$

$4x^2$

Y–Intercept

The y–intercept occurs when x $= 0$. In other words, the y–intercept is located at $(0, c)$.

Roots or Zeros

The x–intercepts, or roots, occur when the value of the polynomial is zero. A second degree polynomial can have none, one, or at most two real roots. If $F(3) = 0$, then 3 is a root of the polynomial.

We already have two methods of finding the zeros of a quadratic equation.

- Factoring (section A4)
- The quadratic formula (section A14)

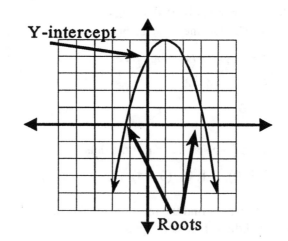

CUBIC FUNCTIONS

$$F(x) = ax^3 + bx^2 + cx + d$$

A cubic equation is a third degree polynomial. If *a* is positive, the graph will start low and end high (from left to right). If *a* is negative, then the graph will start high and end low.

$+ax^3$

$-ax^3$

The y–intercept is located at $(0, d)$. To find the zeros try to factor the equation.

CUBIC FUNCTIONS, continued

Example 1

Graph $H(x) = x^3 + x^2 - 4x - 4$

First, find the zeros. Next, set the polynomial equal to zero. Finally, try to factor.

$0 = x^3 + x^2 - 4x - 4$

$0 = (x^3 + x^2) + (-4x - 4)$

$0 = x^2(x + 1) + (-4)(x + 1)$

$0 = (x + 1)(x^2 - 4)$

$0 = (x + 1)(x + 2)(x - 2)$

$x = \{-1, -2, 2\}$

Therefore, the roots are:

(-1, 0), (-2, 0) and (2, 0)

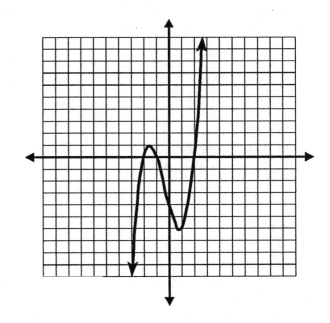

The y–intercept is (0, d) or (0, –4).
Now calculate the value of F(1):

$F(1) = (1)^3 + (1)^2 - 4(1) - 4$

$= 1 + 1 - 4 - 4$

$= -6$

Plot the points and connect the dots.

(–2, 0), (–1, 0), (0, –4), (1, –6), (2, 0)

If you cannot find the roots, just make an x–y chart, plug in several values, plot the points on a graph, and then connect the points.

DOMAIN

Domain, as we saw earlier, is the input, or the source, for the function. In polynomial functions the input can be any real number. There is never any danger with what you input into polynomial functions. In other words, x can be anything. Mathematically, this type of domain can be written:

$$\{x | x \in \mathbb{R}\}$$

Read this as "x such that x is an element of the real numbers." This is another way of saying x can be anything.

Often questions on the test will begin with a phrase, "For all x ≠..." This phrase indicates you are working with a problem that has a restriction on the domain. The problem probably contains a rational expression. For the most part, you can ignore the phrase and just concentrate on the subject and verb of the question.

RATIONAL FUNCTIONS

The word "rational" is usually associated with fractions in mathematics. The name "rational function" implies a function that involves fractions. **Rational functions** can be defined as the quotient of two polynomial functions. In other words, one polynomial divided by another. This means that a variable will be located in the denominator. Before we allow variables into a denominator we must be aware of a very important fact: having a zero in the denominator is the *worst* thing that can happen in your entire life!

The point is that by allowing variables into the denominator we might sometimes, just by accident, allow a zero to slip into the denominator. That would be so bad that we must constantly guard against this occurrence. When someone, or some situation, tries to place a zero in your denominator, you must not hesitate, identify the offending element, the one that would force a zero in the denominator, and declare, "This element is not in the domain of this function!" For example, consider the function K(x):

$$K(x) = \frac{2x + 5}{x + 3}$$

If x = −3 the numerator would evaluate to be −1. But the denominator would be 0. This must *never* be allowed to happen. So we say x ≠ −3. Or, more formally, we can say:

$$\{x | x \in \mathbb{R}, x \neq -3\}$$

Read this as "x such that x is a member of the real numbers, x cannot equal negative three." The value of K(−3) is undefined.

OPERATIONS ON POLYNOMIALS +, −, x, ÷

We can add, subtract, multiply, and divide polynomials in a straightforward manner.

Example 1   Let F(x) = 2x + 5 and G(x) = 3x − 6.
Find F(x) + G(x). Find F(x) − G(x). Find F(x)G(x). Find F(x)/G(x).

F(x) + G(x) = (2x + 5) + (3x − 6) = 2x + 5 + 3x − 6 = 5x − 1

F(x) − G(x) = (2x + 5) − (3x − 6) = 2x + 5 − 3x + 6 = −x + 11

F(x)G(x) = (2x + 5)(3x − 6) = $6x^2$ − 12x + 15x − 30 = $6x^2$ + 3x − 30

$$F(x) \div G(x) = \frac{(2x + 5)}{(3x - 6)}$$

Also note that we can write the sum, difference, product and quotient of functions in two different ways:

F(x) + G(x) = (F + G)(x)
F(x) − G(x) = (F − G)(x)
F(x)G(x) = FG(x)
F(x)/G(x) = (F/G)(x)

When we found F(x)/G(x) we placed a variable in the denominator so we must place a restriction on the domain. To find the restriction set G(x) equal to 0.

G(x) = 3x − 6 = 0
3x = 6
x = 2

So the domain of F(x)/G(x) is {x | x ∈ ℝ, x ≠ 2}.

COMPOSITE FUNCTIONS

Another way of combining functions is to put one inside the other. In other words, one function becomes the variable for the other function.

Let $f(x) = 4x - 5$ and $g(x) = x^2 + 2$.

Now let's put $g(x)$ inside of $f(x)$:

$$f(g(x)) = 4(g(x)) - 5 = 4(x^2 + 2) - 5 = 4x^2 + 8 - 5 = 4x^2 + 3$$

The composition of functions can be written two different ways.

$$f(g(x)) = f \circ g (x)$$
$$g(f(x)) = g \circ f (x)$$

Note: $f \circ g (x) \neq g \circ f (x)$

$$f \circ g (x) = 4(g(x)) - 5 = 4(x^2 + 2) - 5 = 4x^2 + 8 - 5 = 4x^2 + 3$$
$$g \circ f (x) = (4x - 5)^2 + 2 = (16x^2 - 40x + 25) + 2 = 16x^2 - 40x + 27$$

Application

Given a Fahrenheit temperature, this function will produce an equivalent Celsius:

$$C(F) = \frac{5}{9}(F - 32)$$

Given a Celsius temperature, this function will produce an equivalent Kelvin:

$$K(C) = C + 273$$

Find a function H(F) that will produce a Kelvin reading given a Fahrenheit temperature.

Example 1 $\quad H(F) = K \circ C(F) = K\left(\frac{5}{9}(F - 32)\right) = \frac{5}{9}(f - 32) + 273$

INVERSE OF A FUNCTION

An **inverse** of a function swaps inputs and outputs. For example, if the function G is defined to be G = {(a, 1), (b, 2), (c, 3)}, then the inverse must be G^{-1}= {(1, a), (2. b), (3, c)}. Notice the notation for the inverse, $G^{-1}(x)$ looks like G raised to the negative one power. It actually reads as "the inverse of G of x."

To find the inverse function of a function (if it exists) follow this four-step procedure.

Step 1.   Replace f(x) with y.

Step 2.   Swap x and y.

Step 3.   Solve for y.

Step 4.   Replace y with $f^{-1}(x)$.

Example1   Find the inverse of f(x) = 2x + 3.

$f(x) = 2x + 3$ 1. Replace f(x) with y.
$y = 2x + 3$

$x = 2y + 3$ 2. Swap x and y.

$x - 3 = 2y$

$\dfrac{x - 3}{2} = \dfrac{2y}{2}$ 3. Solve for y.

$\dfrac{x - 3}{2} = y$

$f^{-1} = \dfrac{x - 3}{2}$ 4. Replace y with f⁻¹(x).

These two charts show a few values for the function and its inverse. From the chart, notice that when x = 0, then f(x) = 3. Also notice that if x = 3, then f⁻¹(x) = 0. The inverse of a function will return the original input.

x	f(x)
0	3
1	5
2	7

x	f⁻¹(x)
3	0
5	1
7	2

Graphs of inverses are reflections across the line y = x. If a function intersects its inverse the intersection must be on the line y = x.

The inverses of some functions are not functions themselves. These relations that are not functions will fail the vertical line test. For the inverse of a function to produce another function it must be what is called a one–to–one function. A function is one–to–one if for every input there is a different output. The easiest way to tell if a function is one–to–one is with the horizontal line test.

To the right is a graph of the equation g(x) = x² + 6x + 5 and its inverse correspondence; notice that g(x) fails the horizontal line test, therefore, the inverse of g(x) does not pass the vertical line test. This inverse correspondence is not a function.

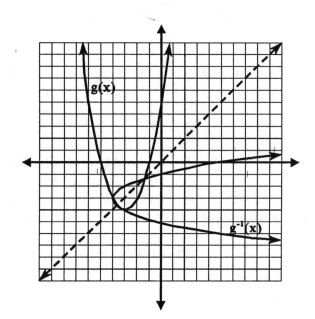

75

RADICAL FUNCTIONS

Radical functions are functions that have variables inside radicals. For example:

$$F(x) = \sqrt{x}$$

x	F(x)
0	0
1	1
4	2
9	3

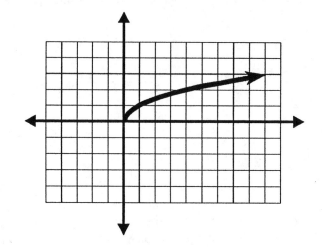

Notice that there is only one arrow on the drawing of the function. This is because the graph only extends in one direction.

DOMAIN OF A RADICAL FUNCTION

What is the square root of –25? It cannot be 5 because 5 • 5 = 25. It cannot be –5 because (–5) • (–5) = 25. It has to be a number that, when you square it, you get –25. There is no such number in the real number system, because when a positive is squared $(+)^2 = (+)(+) = (+)$. And when a negative is squared $(-)^2 = (-)(-) = (+)$. Since there is no solution to negatives inside radicals in the real number system, we say that negatives are not allowed in the domain of radicals.

If the very *worst* thing that can happen in your life is have a zero in the denominator, then a very distant second is to have a negative radicand. So anytime there is a radical with an even number index we must guard against the radicand becoming negative, just as we would guard against zeros in the denominator. To determine the domain of a radical function, set the radicand greater than or equal to zero, and then solve.

$$H(x) = \sqrt{x + 3} - 5$$

Example 1   Determine the domain of H(x).

$$x + 3 \geq 0$$
$$x \geq -3$$

Therefore the domain of H(x) is $\{x | x \geq -3\}$.

If the index is odd you do not have to worry about negatives, since the domain is all real numbers. The cube root of (–27) is –3 because (–3)(–3)(–3) = –27.

(In C3, we discuss a way around the problem of negative radicands.)

76

Example 2   Graph $g(x) = \sqrt{x + 4} - 3$.

The domain is $\{x | x \geq -4\}$, so start computing values at $x = -4$.

x	g(x)
-4	-3
-3	-2
0	-1
5	0
12	1

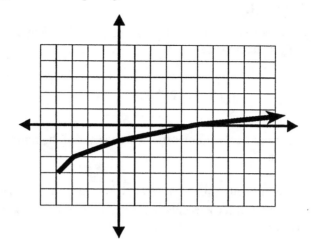

C1   Practice.

1.   On which interval does the maximum value of $h(x) = -x^2 + 8x + 15$ occur?   a. (-5, -3)   b. (-3, -1)   c. (3, 5)   d. (5, 7)   e. (1, 3)

2.   Let $f(x) = x^2 + 4x + 4$ and $g(x) = 2x - 7$. Find the following:

   a) $(f + g)(x)$

   b) $(f - g)(x)$

   c) $(f)(g)(x)$

   d) $(f/g)(x)$

   e) $f \circ g(x)$

   f) $g \circ f(x)$

3.   If $y = 10x - 20$ and $z = 3y - 8$, find an expression for z in terms of x.

4.   If H(x) contains the point (3, 7) then $H^{-1}(x)$ must contain the point _____.

5.   What is the domain of each of these functions?

   a) $f(x) = \dfrac{7}{2x + 6}$

   b) $g(x) = \sqrt{x + 8} - 7$

(*Answers* to all practices in Chapter Four are found on p. 86.)

C2 EXPONENTS *(see also A8)*

RATIONAL EXPONENTS

A rational exponent is a fraction used as an exponent. Rational exponents give us a different notation for writing radical expressions.

$$\sqrt{a} = a^{\frac{1}{2}} \qquad \sqrt[3]{b^2} = b^{\frac{2}{3}} \qquad \sqrt[y]{c^x} = c^{\frac{x}{y}}$$

The index of the radical becomes the denominator of the rational exponent. The regular exponent is the numerator.

The basics of exponents have been discussed in A8 and A12. The same rules apply for rational exponents. Below you will see a review of the rules with integer exponents followed by an example with rational exponents.

PRODUCT RULE OF EXPONENTS

Example 1

$$a^4 \cdot a^3 = a^{4+3} = a^7$$

When **multiplying** like bases, **add** the exponents.
(Multiplication becomes addition)

Example 2

$$a^{\frac{2}{3}} \cdot a^{\frac{1}{2}} = a^{\left(\frac{2}{3} + \frac{1}{2}\right)} = a^{\left(\frac{4}{6} + \frac{3}{6}\right)} = a^{\frac{7}{6}}$$

Recall that when adding fractions you must find a common denominator.

QUOTIENT RULE OF EXPONENTS

Example 1

When **dividing** like bases, **subtract** exponents. (Division becomes subtraction)

$$\frac{b^8}{b^5} = b^{8-5} = b^3$$

Example 2

Requires a common denominator.

$$\frac{b^{\frac{3}{4}}}{b^{\frac{1}{5}}} = b^{\left(\frac{3}{4} - \frac{1}{5}\right)} = b^{\left(\frac{15}{20} - \frac{4}{20}\right)} = b^{\frac{11}{20}}$$

ZERO EXPONENT RULE

$$C^0 = 1 \qquad \text{Anything (except zero) raised to the zero power is 1.}$$

Example 1

$$\frac{c^{\frac{2}{5}}}{c^{\frac{2}{5}}} = c^{\left(\frac{2}{5} - \frac{2}{5}\right)} = c^{\left(\frac{0}{5}\right)} = c^0 = 1$$

THE POWER RULE OF EXPONENTS

Example 1 $\qquad (D^4)^3 = D^{4 \cdot 3} = D^{12}$

When taking a power to a power, multiply the exponents.
(Power to a Power—exponents become multiplication)

$$\left(d^{\frac{2}{3}}\right)^{\frac{1}{2}} = d^{\left(\frac{2}{3} \cdot \frac{1}{2}\right)} = d^{\left(\frac{1}{3}\right)} \qquad \text{No need for a common denominator.}$$

Example 2

Translating radical expressions into rational exponential expressions gives us a familiar set of rules (adding fractions) to apply when multiplying unlike radicals.

$$\sqrt{a} \bullet \sqrt[3]{a} = a^{\frac{1}{2}} \bullet a^{\frac{1}{3}} = a^{\left(\frac{1}{2} + \frac{1}{3}\right)} = a^{\left(\frac{3}{6} + \frac{2}{6}\right)} = a^{\frac{5}{6}} = \sqrt[6]{a^5}$$

Example 3

Once you find a common denominator you can go back to radical notation.

$$\sqrt[3]{a} \bullet \sqrt[4]{b} = a^{\frac{1}{3}} \bullet b^{\frac{1}{4}} = a^{\frac{4}{12}} \bullet b^{\frac{3}{12}} = \sqrt[12]{a^4 b^3}$$

EXPONENTIAL FUNCTIONS

Exponential functions are functions that have a variable in the exponent.

Consider $F(x) = 2^x$. When graphing exponential functions, try using 3, 2, 1, 0, –1, –2, –3 as the domain to get you started.

x	F(x)
3	8
2	4
1	2
0	1
–1	$^1/_2$
–2	$^1/_4$
–3	$^1/_8$

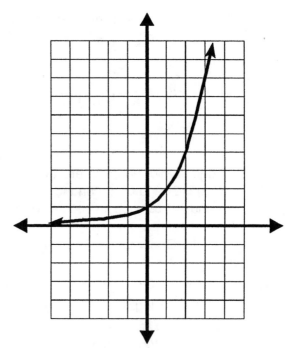

Notice that F(–1) is the reciprocal of F(1), and F(2) is the reciprocal of F(–2), and so forth. When graphing exponential functions by just inputting values into the function, it is important to use enough points to see the true character of the line.

LOGARITHMIC FUNCTIONS

$$\log_5 25 = 2$$

Read this as, "log base 5 of 25 is 2." One way to think about it is, "What exponent do I use on 5 to get 25? 2." The logarithm on the left side is equal to the exponent on the right. That makes a logarithm an exponent.

THREE COOL FACTS ABOUT LOGARITHMIC FUNCTIONS

Logarithmic functions can be intimidating, but just remember these three facts:

Fact #1 $a^b = c$ is the same as $\log_a c = b$

Fact #2   logarithmic functions are the inverses of exponential functions.

Fact #3   A logarithm is an exponent and follows the same rules.

Fact #1

The fact that $a^b = c$ is the same as $\log_a c = b$ is just a definition. You *must* commit it to memory; then you can apply it to different situations. This will allow you to rewrite exponential form to logarithmic form and vice versa.

Example 1   Rewrite using logarithmic notation.

    a) $6^2 = 36$ $\log_6 36 = 2$

    b) $x^3 = 64$ $\log_x 64 = 3$

    c) $1.5^4 = 5.0625$ $\log_{1.5} 5.0625 = 4$

Notice that each time you convert to logarithms, the base becomes the small number beside the word "log." The exponent goes off by itself to the other side of the equation. The answer to the exponential becomes the argument of the logarithmic.

Example 2   Rewrite using exponential notation.

    a) $\log_3 81 = 4$ $3^4 = 81$

    b) $\log_7 49 = 2$ $7^2 = 49$

    c) $\log_2 \left(\dfrac{1}{8} \right) = -3$ $2^{-3} = \dfrac{1}{8}$

Fact #2

Logarithmic functions are the inverse of exponential functions. Consider $G(x) = 2^x$ and $G^{-1}(x)$ on the same graph. First, let's find the inverse of $G(x)$ using the four step procedure described at the end of C1 for finding an inverse.

$G(x) = 2^x$		
$y = 2^x$	**Step 1.**	Replace $G(x)$ with y.
$x = 2^y$	**Step 2.**	Swap x and y.
$y = \log_2 x$	**Step 3.**	Solve for y by converting to a logarithm.
$G^{-1}(x) = \log_2 x$	**Step 4.**	Replace y with $G^{-1}(x)$.

x	G(x)
3	8
2	4
1	2
0	1
−1	$1/2$
−2	$1/4$
−3	$1/8$

x	$G^{-1}(x)$
8	3
4	2
2	1
1	0
$1/2$	−1
$1/4$	−2
$1/8$	−3

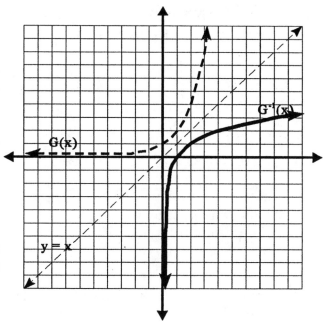

Notice that the inputs and the outputs have swapped, and that the graph of $G^{-1}(x)$ is a reflection of G(x) in the line y = x.

Fact #3

A logarithm is an exponent and therefore follows the same rules as exponents. This leads to the properties of logarithms that are associated with the rules about exponents.

PROPERTY 1: **The Product Rule** $\boxed{\log_a (M \cdot N) = \log_a M + \log_a N}$

Example 3 $\log_2 (4 \cdot 8) = \log_2 4 + \log_2 8 = 2 + 3 = 5$
$\log_2 (4 \cdot 8) = \log_2 32 = 5$

PROPERTY 2: **The Power Rule** $\boxed{\log_a M^p = p \cdot \log_a M}$

Example 4 $\log_2 4^3 = 3 \cdot \log_2 4 = 3 \cdot 2 = 6$
$\log_2 4^3 = \log_2 64 = 6$

PROPERTY 3: **The Quotient Rule** $\boxed{\log_a \left(\dfrac{M}{N}\right) = \log_a M - \log_a N}$

Example 5 $\log_2 \left(\dfrac{32}{8}\right) = \log_2 32 - \log_2 8 = 5 - 3 = 2$

$\log_2 \left(\dfrac{32}{8}\right) = \log_2 4 = 2$

PROPERTY 4: $\boxed{\log_a a^x = x}$

Example 6 $\log_2 2^x = ?$

Apply the Power Rule:

$\log_2 2^x = x \cdot \log_2 2$

Again, using the Power Rule ($\log_a M^p = p \cdot \log_a M$), we know that $\log_2 2 = 1$. If we plug that into $x \cdot \log_2 2$, we get:

$x \cdot (1) = x$ So, $\log_2 2^x = x$.

81

Using these properties, logarithmic expressions can be written in a variety of ways.

Example 7   Express as a single logarithm.

$$\frac{2}{3} \log_a X + 4 \log_a Y - 3 \log_a Z =$$

1. The Power Rule.
$$\log_a X^{\frac{2}{3}} + \log_a Y^4 - \log_a Z^3 =$$

2. The Product and the Quotient Rule.
$$\log_a \frac{X^{\frac{2}{3}} Y^4}{Z^3} =$$

3. Rewrite the rational exponent as a radical.
$$\log_a \frac{Y^4 \sqrt[3]{X^2}}{Z^3}$$

Example 8   Express in terms of logarithms.

1. Rewrite radicals as rational exponents and simplify.
$$\log_a \sqrt[4]{\frac{x^8}{y^4 z^3}} = \log_a \frac{x^{\frac{8}{4}}}{y^{\frac{4}{4}} z^{\frac{3}{4}}} = \log_a \frac{x^2}{y z^{\frac{3}{4}}} =$$

2. Quotient Rule.
$$\log_a x^2 - \log_a y - \log_a z^{\frac{3}{4}} =$$

3. Power Rule.
$$2\log_a x - \log_a y - \frac{3}{4} \log_a z$$

C2 Practice.

1. Simplify.
$$a^{\frac{2}{5}} \cdot a^{\frac{1}{6}}$$

2. Simplify.
$$\frac{b^{\frac{3}{5}}}{b^{\frac{2}{3}}}$$

3. Simplify.
$$\left(c^{\frac{2}{5}}\right)^{\frac{3}{4}}$$

4. Simplify.
$$\sqrt[4]{a^3} \cdot \sqrt[3]{a}$$

5. Simplify.
$$\sqrt[3]{b^2} \cdot \sqrt[5]{2}$$

6. Express as a single logarithm.
$$\frac{1}{4} \log_a x - \frac{3}{4} \log_a y$$

7. Express in terms of logarithms.
$$\log_a \sqrt[3]{\frac{x^{12} y^6}{z}}$$

C3 COMPLEX NUMBERS

IMAGINARY NUMBERS

$$\sqrt{-1} = i$$

$$(\sqrt{-1})^2 = -1$$

$$i^2 = -1$$

Before we can have **complex numbers** we need **imaginary numbers**. The number i is defined to be the square root of negative 1.

The square root of -1 squared is -1.

Therefore, i squared is -1.

AUTOMATICS INVOLVING i

• Whenever you have a negative inside a radical, the next turn you will have an i outside the radical and no more negative inside.

• Whenever you have an i^2, the next turn you will have a -1 and no i.

POWERS OF i

Memorize the first four: 1, i, -1, - i

Powers of i
$i^0 = 1$
$i^1 = i$
$i^2 = -1$
$i^3 = (i)^2(i) = -i$

more powers of i

$i^4 = (i)^2(i)^2 = (-1)(-1) = 1$

$i^5 = i^4 i = i$

$i^6 = i^4\ i^2 = i^2 = -1$

$i^7 = i^4 \cdot i^3 = -i$

Because the powers of i repeat every fourth time, finding values like i^{66} (i to the 66th power) is easy. To find the value of i raised to some power, divide the power by 4. The remainder is the new exponent. So if the exponent were 66, you would divide by 4, the remainder would be 2 and the new exponent would be 2. Then refer to the powers of i chart. i^2 is -1. Therefore $i^{66} = i^2 = -1$.

Example 1   What is i^{27} ?

Divide 27 by 4 and you get 6 with a remainder of 3.
So, the answer should be i^3, which equals - i.
$(i^4)^6(i^3) = (1)^6(-i) = -i$

COMPLEX NUMBERS

A complex number is any number that can be written in "a + bi" form. The first part "a" is the real part. The second part "bi" is called the imaginary part.

ADDITION AND SUBTRACTION

When adding or subtracting complex numbers, just drop the parentheses and combine like terms. Write your final answer in "a + bi" form.

Example 2   Add.

$(3 + 2i) + (4 - 8i) = 3 + 2i + 4 - 8i = 7 - 6i$

Example 3   Subtract.

$(5 + 6i) - (7 - 8i) = 5 + 6i - 7 + 8i = -2 + 14i$

Be careful to distribute the negative sign.

MULTIPLICATION

Multiplication is straightforward except you must substitute a (-1) for any i^2. Write your final answer in "a + bi" form.

Example 4   Multiply.

a) $4i \cdot 5 = 20i = 0 + 20i$

b) $3i \cdot 8i = 24i^2 = -24 = -24 + 0i$

c) $3i(5 + 6i) = 15i + 18i^2 = 15i - 18 = -18 + 15i$

d) $(3 + 2i)(4 - 5i) = 12 - 15i + 8i - 10i^2 = 12 - 7i + 10 = 22 - 7i$

DIVISION

Division of complex numbers is accomplished with a particular type of multiplication by the number one. Look at the denominator. If it is a monomial with an i, multiply the top and bottom by i. If the denominator is in "a + bi" form, multiply the top and the bottom by "a − bi". What should happen in both cases is that there will be no "i" value in the denominator when you are done.

Example 5   Divide.

a) $\dfrac{3}{2i} = \dfrac{3}{2i} \cdot \dfrac{i}{i} = \dfrac{3i}{2i^2} = \dfrac{3i}{-2} = 0 - \dfrac{3}{2}i$

b) $\dfrac{5}{4 - 3i} = \dfrac{5}{4 - 3i} \cdot \dfrac{4 + 3i}{4 + 3i} = \dfrac{5(4 + 3i)}{16 + 12i - 12i - 9i^2}$

$= \dfrac{5(4 + 3i)}{16 + 9} = \dfrac{5(4 + 3i)}{25} = \dfrac{4 + 3i}{5} = \dfrac{4}{5} + \dfrac{3}{5}i$

i AND THE QUADRATIC FORMULA

Because *i* allows us to have negatives inside the radical, we can now solve any quadratic equation.

Example 6   Solve $x^2 + 2x + 5 = 0$

$$a = 1 \quad b = 2 \quad c = 5$$

$$x = \frac{-b \pm \sqrt{b^2 - 4ac}}{2a}$$

$$x = \frac{-(2) \pm \sqrt{(2)^2 - 4(1)(5)}}{2(1)}$$

$$x = \frac{-(2) \pm \sqrt{4 - 20}}{2}$$

$$x = \frac{-(2) \pm \sqrt{-16}}{2}$$

$$x = \frac{-(2) \pm 4i}{2}$$

$$x = -\frac{2}{2} \pm \frac{4i}{2}$$

$$x = 1 \pm 2i$$

C3 Practice.
Leave all of your answers in a + bi form.

1. Add
   $(7 + 2i) + (8 - 5i)$

2. Subtract
   $(4 - 3i) - (8 - 5i)$

3. Multiply
   $(2 + 3i)(7 + 2i)$

4. Divide
   $$\frac{2 + 3i}{2 - 3i}$$

5. Solve
   $2x^2 + 2x = -5$

6. Solve
   $x^2 + 8 = 3x$

ANSWERS TO PRACTICES

C1 Answers

1. The maximum value occurs at the vertex 4. Therefore C is the answer because 4 is between 3 and 5

2.
   a) $x^2 + 6x - 3$
   b) $x^2 + 2x + 11$
   c) $2x^3 + x^2 - 20x - 28$
   d) $\dfrac{(x^2 + 4x + 4)}{(2x - 7)}$
   e) $4x^2 - 20x + 25$
   f) $2x^2 + 8x + 1$

3. $z = 3(10x - 20) - 8 = 30x - 60 - 8 = 30x - 68$

4. $(7, 3)$

5.
   a) $\{x \mid x \in \mathbb{R}, x \neq -3\}$
   b) $\{x \mid x \in \mathbb{R}, x \geq -8\}$

C2 Answers

1. $a^{\frac{17}{30}}$ 　 2. $\dfrac{1}{b^{\frac{1}{15}}}$ 　 3. $c^{\frac{3}{10}}$ 　 4. $a^{\frac{13}{12}}$ 　 5. $\sqrt[15]{8b^{10}}$

6. $\log_a \sqrt[4]{\dfrac{x}{y^3}}$ 　 7. $4\log_a x + 2\log_a y - \dfrac{1}{3}\log_a z$

C3 Answers

1. $15 - 3i$
2. $-4 + 2i$
3. $8 + 25i$
4. $-\dfrac{5}{13} + \dfrac{12}{13}i$
5. $-\dfrac{1}{2} \pm \dfrac{3}{2}i$
6. $\dfrac{3}{2} \pm \dfrac{\sqrt{23}}{2}i$

CHAPTER FIVE

GEOMETRY

About 85% of the Geometry portion of the **COMPASS** exam is concerned with triangles, circles, and angles. The remaining 15% covers a wide variety of topics including: rectangles, trapezoids, parallelograms, and composite shapes. Consequently, this chapter is divided into four sections corresponding to the weight **COMPASS** places on them.

G1	**Angles**	**Supplementary, complementary, adjacent, vertical**
G2	**Triangles**	**Perimeter, area, Pythagorean Theorem, Triangle Angle Sum, exterior angle, similar triangles**
G3	**Circles**	**Perimeter, area, arcs**
G4	**Other**	**Rectangles, parallelograms, trapezoids, composites**

G1 ANGLES

Much of geometry relies on definition, so to get us started, here are some definitions.

▶ **Point** - A thing so small, it has no shape or size, only location. Points are labeled with capital letters.

▶ **Line** - A collection of points in a straight path that has no end and no beginning. Since it is made out of points it has no height, no width, only infinite length. Lines are named by using any two points on the line. The order of the points is not important. Lines can also be named with just one lowercase letter.

▶ **Ray** - A half line. A ray has a beginning point called an endpoint. A ray extends forever away from the endpoint. Rays are named by the endpoint and any other point on the ray. The order of the points is important, Ray AB is different than Ray BA.

▶ **Line segment** - A part of a line, it is a collection of points between two endpoints. A line segment is named by using the two endpoints. The order of the points is not important.

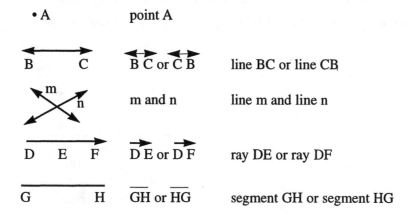

•A		point A
B C	$\overleftrightarrow{BC}$ or $\overleftrightarrow{CB}$	line BC or line CB
m, n	m and n	line m and line n
D E F	$\overrightarrow{DE}$ or $\overrightarrow{DF}$	ray DE or ray DF
G H	$\overline{GH}$ or $\overline{HG}$	segment GH or segment HG

► **Angle** - An angle is formed when two rays share the same endpoint. The shared endpoint is called the vertex of the angle.

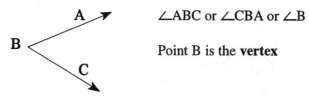

∠ABC or ∠CBA or ∠B

Point B is the **vertex**

► **Right angle** - A right angle is any angle that measures 90°. Four right angles are formed when two lines meet in a 90° angle.

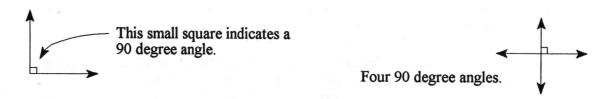

This small square indicates a 90 degree angle.

Four 90 degree angles.

The four 90° right angles add up to 360°. Halfway around would be two right angles or 180°. This is sometimes called a straight angle.

► **Straight angle** - A straight angle is an angle that measures 180°.

► **Acute angle** - An acute angle is an angle that measures less than 90°.

► **Obtuse angle** - An obtuse angle is an angle that measures more than 90° but less than 180°.

Perhaps it will help you remember which one is which if you notice that just as 90 comes before 180, acute comes before obtuse in the alphabet.

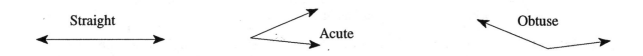

Straight

Acute

Obtuse

► **Complementary angles** - Two angles that add up to 90° are complementary angles.

► **Supplementary angles** - Two angles that add up to 180° are supplementary angles.

Notice that complementary (90°) and supplementary (180°) are in alphabetical order.

∠1 + ∠2 = 90

Complementary

∠3 + ∠4 = 180

Supplementary

► **Vertical angles** - are formed whenever two lines intersect. ∠1 and ∠3 are a vertical angle pair. ∠2 and ∠4 are also vertical angles.

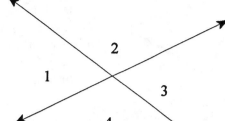

∠1 + ∠2 = 180˚   Supplemental
∠1 = 180˚ − ∠2
∠3 + ∠2 = 180˚   Supplemental
∠3 = 180˚ − ∠2
∠1 = ∠3

This is always the case with vertical angles. Vertical angles are always equal.

∠1 = ∠3 and ∠2 = ∠4

G1   **Practice. Find the missing angles.**

1. ∠1 = 42˚

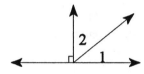

2. ∠3 = 34˚

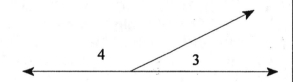

3. ∠5 = 40˚

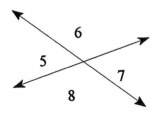

4. ∠a = 30˚, angles d and c are complementary.

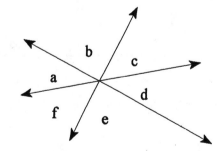

5. Which of the angles in problems 1 through 4 are acute? obtuse? right?

(Answers to all practices in Chapter Five are found on p.100.)

G2   TRIANGLES

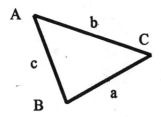

A triangle literally means three angles. A triangle is a three sided figure made up of three line segments. The shared endpoints of the segments are **vertices.** Vertices are denoted by capital letters. The sides opposite the vertices are denoted by lowercase letters that match the letters of the angle. In other words side "a" is opposite $\angle$ A (angle A). Triangles can be classified according to either the measures of the angles or the lengths of the sides.

CLASSIFICATION BY SIDES

Equilateral - All three sides are equal.

Isosceles - At *least* two sides are equal.

Scalene - No sides are equal.

If a triangle is equilateral, then it is equiangular. **Equiangular** means all angles are equal. Every equilateral triangle is isosceles, but every isosceles is not equilateral. The base angles of an isosceles triangle are equal.

CLASSIFICATION BY ANGLES

Acute - All angles are acute.

Right - One angle is a right angle.

Obtuse - One angle is obtuse.

THREE COOL FACTS ABOUT TRIANGLES

Triangle Angle Sum - The angles of any triangle will always add up to 180°.

Triangle Inequality Law - No side of a triangle can be larger than the sum of the other two sides.

$$a < b + c \qquad b < a + c \qquad c < a + b$$

Exterior Angles - An exterior angle is equal to the sum of the two remote interior angles. In the drawing below $\angle$1 and $\angle$2 are remote to $\angle$4.

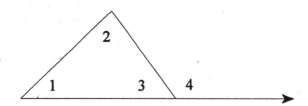

Proof of the Exterior Angle Theorem:

	Statement	**Justification**
1.	$\angle1 + \angle2 + \angle3 = 180°$	Triangle angle sum
2.	$\angle1 + \angle2 = 180° - \angle3$	Subtraction
3.	$\angle4 + \angle3 = 180°$	Supplemental angles
4.	$\angle4 = 180° - \angle3$	Subtraction
5.	$\therefore \angle1 + \angle2 = \angle4$	Substitution

The symbol $\therefore$ means "therefore." $\therefore$ is very useful when you are taking notes for just about any class.

AREA $A = \dfrac{1}{2} bh$

Memorize this formula. It says that the area of a triangle is equal to the product of the base and the height divided by 2. The height, h, is the perpendicular distance of a vertex from a side called b, the base.

Example 1
What is the area of this triangle?
Ignore the 17m and 25m.

$A = \dfrac{1}{2} \ (30)(15) = (15)(15) = 225m^2$

What is the perimeter?

$17 + 25 + 30 = 72m$

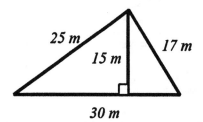

Notice that perimeter is a one dimensional measurement, so the unit of measure is m^1. Area is a two dimensional measurement, so the unit of measure is m^2. If we were looking for a volume measurement the unit of measure would be m^3. The exponent used in the unit of measure indicates the number of dimensions.

PYTHAGOREAN THEOREM
One of the oldest and perhaps the most famous of theorems is the Pythagorean Theorem.

In any right triangle, the square of the hypotenuse is equal to the sum of the squares of the other two sides.

$a^2 + b^2 = c^2$

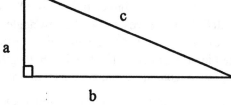

The side opposite the right angle is called the hypotenuse. It is always the longest side of a right triangle. The two shorter sides are called legs.

Example 2
Find the missing side in a right triangle. $a = 12$ and $c = 13$

$a^2 + b^2 = c^2$
$12^2 + b^2 = 13^2$
$144 + b^2 = 169$
$b^2 = 169 - 144$
$b^2 = 25$
$\sqrt{b^2} = \sqrt{25}$
$b = 5$

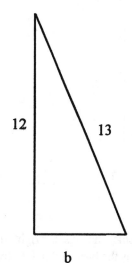

SPECIAL RIGHT TRIANGLES

45° − 45° − 90° Triangle

The diagonal of a square divides the square into two right isosceles triangles. The measures of the angles in these triangles is 45°–45°–90°. The hypotenuse of this triangle is always the product of the side and the square root of $\sqrt{2}$.

$$a^2 + b^2 = c^2$$
$$s^2 + s^2 = c^2$$
$$\sqrt{2(s)^2} = \sqrt{c^2}$$
$$s\sqrt{2} = c$$

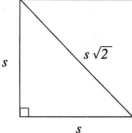

This means rather than using the Pythagorem Theorem next time you work with the diagonal of a square all you have to do is multiply a side by $\sqrt{2}$

30° − 60° − 90° Triangle

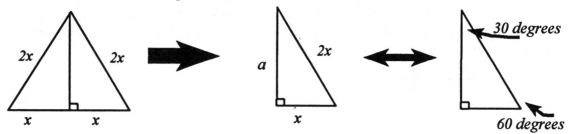

Take an equiangular triangle, where all the angles are equal to 60°, and bisect one of the angles. The bisected angle is 30° and the untouched angle is still 60°. That leaves 90° for the new angle. If the equilateral triangle measured 2x on each side, then the hypotenuse is still 2x. The shortest leg is a bisected side so it is x in length. The remaining leg can be found using the Pythagorean theorem.

$$a^2 + b^2 = c^2$$
$$a^2 + x^2 = (2x)^2$$
$$a^2 + x^2 = 4x^2$$
$$a^2 = 4x^2 - x^2$$
$$a^2 = 3x^2$$
$$\sqrt{a^2} = \sqrt{3x^2}$$
$$a = x\sqrt{3}$$

∴ The short leg of a 30°–60°–90° triangle is always half of the hypotenuse. The longest leg is the product of the shortest leg and the square root of three.

Example 3

Find the perimeter and the area of a 30°–60°–90° triangle with a hypotenuse of 10ft.

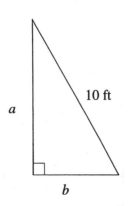

$$c = 10$$
$$b = 5$$
$$a = 5\sqrt{3}$$
Perimeter $= a + b + c$
$$= 5\sqrt{3} + 5 + 10$$
$$= (15 + 5\sqrt{3})\ \text{ft.}$$

Area $= \dfrac{1}{2}\ bh$

$$= (5)(5\sqrt{3})$$
$$= \dfrac{25\sqrt{3}}{2}\ \text{ft.}^2$$

Notice that since the legs of a right triangle meet in a 90° angle we can use them as the base and height for area computations.

A few words about the sides of triangles:

The longest side of a triangle is always opposite the largest angle. The smallest side is always is always opposite the smallest angle. So if side a is the shortest, ∠A is the smallest. If ∠B is the largest, side b is the longest.

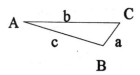

Equilateral triangles have all sides equal. Because all the sides are equal, all of the angles are equal as well. If all three angles are equal and they sum to 180°, then each must be equal to 60°. The "tick" marks indicate equal lengths.

Isosceles triangles have at least two sides equal. These two equal sides are opposite equal angles. The point that joins the two equal sides is called the vertex angle of the isosceles triangle. The other two equal angles are called base angles. The vertex angle has this relationship with the base angles: (vertex) = 180° − 2(1 base angle). So if you know one angle of an isosceles triangle you can figure out the other two.

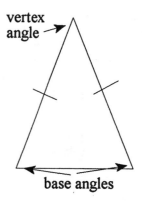

Example 4
What is the vertex angle of an isosceles triangle that has a base angle of 40°?

Because the two base angles are equal to 40°:
∠A + 40° + 40° = 180°
∠A + 80° = 180°
∠A = 180° − 80°
∠A = 100°

Or, using the formula:
(vertex) = 180° − 2(1 Base angle)
∠A = 180° − 2(40)°
∠A = 180° − 80° = 100°

SIMILAR TRIANGLES

Similar triangles are triangles that may or may not be different sizes, but have exactly the same angles. Similar triangles are proportional. This means that if we know that a pair of triangles are similar, then we can set up ratios and proportion statements about the triangles.

ΔABC ~ ΔA`B`C`

Read as "triangle ABC is similar to triangle A prime, B prime, C prime."

$$\frac{8}{12} = \frac{10}{y} = \frac{x}{18}$$

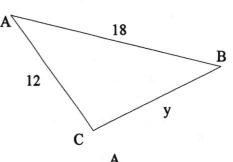

G2   Practice.

1.   If the legs of a right triangle are both equal to 4m, what are the measurements of the angles? What is the perimeter? What is the area?

2.   If one leg of a right triangle is 8 feet and the hypotenuse is 10 feet, then what is the area? What is the perimeter?

3.   If the short leg of a 30°-60°-90° is 5 cm., what is the perimeter? What is the area?

4. $\angle 1 = 130°$ $\angle 4 = 35°$. Find the missing angles.

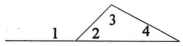

5. $\angle A = \angle BDE$
AB = 6, DB = 4, DE = 8, BE = 6
What is the perimeter of $\triangle ABC$?

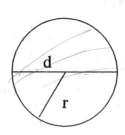

G3   CIRCLES

A circle is a collection of all points in a plane equidistant from the center. This distance, r, is called the radius. A segment that has endpoints on a circle and passes through the center is d, the diameter. d = 2r

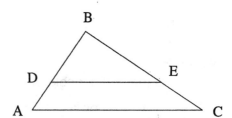

The perimeter of a circle is called C, the circumference. π, pi, is a Greek letter that represents an irrational number that is about 3.14159. π is defined to be the ratio of the circumference to the diameter.

So, to find the circumference of a circle, multiply the diameter by π. If you know the value of C, r, or d, you know the value of the others.

$$\frac{C}{d} = \pi$$

d = 2r

$$d\left(\frac{C}{d}\right) = (\pi)$$

$$C = d\pi = 2r\pi$$

C = 2π r

To find the area of a circle: **A = πr²**

A = πr²

94

Example 1

What is the circumference and the area of a circle with a diameter of 10 feet?

Circumference:

$$C = d\pi = 10\pi$$

$$C = 10\pi \text{ feet}$$

Area:

$$A = \pi r^2$$

$$2r = d = 10$$

$$r = 5$$

$$A = \pi(5)^2 = 25\pi$$

$$A = 25\pi \text{ square feet}$$

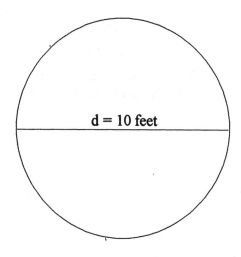

ARC

An arc is a portion of a circle. There are 360° of arc in a circle. 180° of arc is half of a circle, or a semi-circle.

$$\text{arc } \overparen{AC} = 120° \qquad \text{arc } \overparen{AXC} = 240°$$

$$\text{arc } \overparen{AC} + \text{arc } \overparen{AXC} = 360°$$

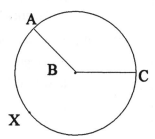

CENTRAL ANGLE

A central angle is defined by three points, two on the circle and the vertex at the center. The measure of an arc is equal to the central angle of that arc. Each side of the central angle passes through the endpoints of the arc. $\angle ABC$ is the central angle for arc $\overparen{AC}$.

$$\angle ABC = 86° \qquad \text{arc } \overparen{AC} = 86°$$

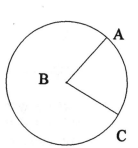

INSCRIBED ANGLES

An inscribed angle is defined by three points on a circle. The vertex of an inscribed angle is on the circle. The measure of an inscribed angle is half the measure of the central angle of the same arc. For a given arc there is one central angle but many different inscribed angles.

$$\text{Arc } \overparen{AC} = 86° \qquad \angle AXC = \angle AYC = \angle AZC = 43°$$

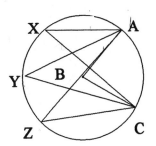

LINES AND CIRCLES

A line and a circle always fall into one of three possible cases.

1. They do not intersect.

2. They intersect exactly twice.

3. They intersect exactly once. In this case, they are said to be **tangent.**

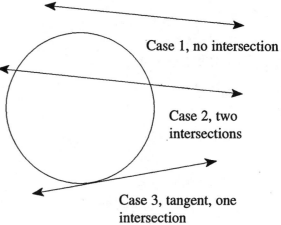

Case 1, no intersection

Case 2, two intersections

Case 3, tangent, one intersection

G3   Practice.

1. If the radius of a circle is 5 ft., what is the area? What is the circumference?

2. If the circumference of a circle is 12π meters, what is the area?

3. A circle with center B has a radius of 5". A, C and D are on the circle. Arc AC is 60°. What is the measure of line segment $\overline{AC}$? What is $\angle ADC$?

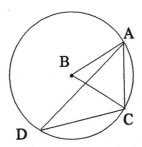

4. Circle A with center A has a diameter of 12. A second circle B with center B has a diameter of 6. Point A is on circle B. Point C is on both circles. If you subtract the area of the smaller circle from the area of the larger circle, how much area is left?

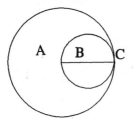

96

G4 OTHER GEOMETRIC FIGURES

QUADRILATERAL

A quadrilateral is a four-sided polygon. The interior angle sum (add up all of the angles inside) is 360°.

TRAPEZOID

A trapezoid is a quadrilateral with only one pair of sides parallel. It is like a triangle with the top cut off. Consecutive angles along a non-parallel side are supplemental.

$$A = \frac{1}{2}(b_1 + b_2)h$$

$\angle ABC + \angle BAD = 180°$

$\angle BCD + \angle ADC = 180°$

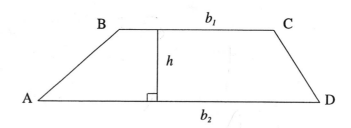

PARALLELOGRAM

A parallelogram is a quadrilateral with two pairs of parallel sides. Opposite sides are equal. Opposite angles are equal. Any consecutive angles are supplemental. The base (b) and the length (*l*) are the same.

$A = b \cdot h$

$P = 2l + 2w$

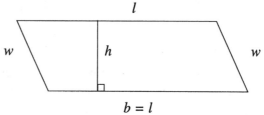

RECTANGLES

A rectangle is parallelogram with all angles equal. Every angle is 90°. Opposite sides are equal in length and parallel.

$A = l \cdot w$

$P = 2l + 2w$

The **diagonal** is the hypotenuse of a right triangle. $d^2 = l^2 + w^2$

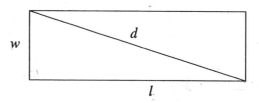

RHOMBUS

A rhombus is an equilateral parallelogram.

$A = b \cdot h$

$P = 4s$

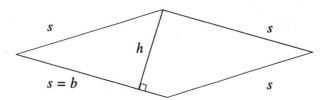

SQUARE

A square is an equilateral, equiangular quadrilateral. A square is a regular quadrilateral. A square is a rhombus. A square is a rectangle.

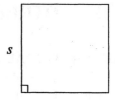

$A = s^2$

$P = 4s$

HIERARCHY CHART OF THE QUADRILATERAL FAMILY

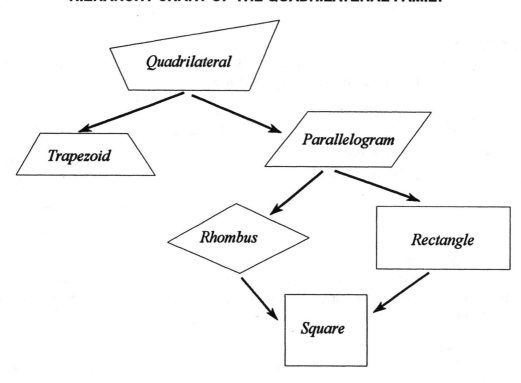

In this hierarchy chart, each quadrilateral has the characteristics of the quadrilaterals above it. For example, a square is always a rectangle, but a rectangle is not always a square.

COMPOSITE STRUCTURES

Composite Structures are two or more simple objects put together to make a more complex object.

Example 1 The figure below is constructed entirely with right angles. Find the area.

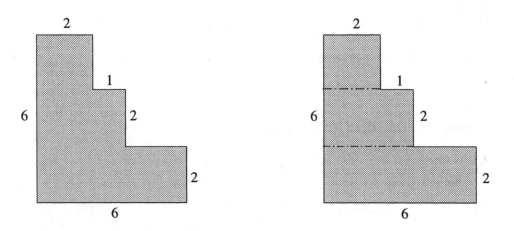

98

Try to find the simpler figures in the complex figure, and then add up the parts.

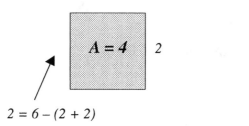

2 = 6 – (2 + 2)

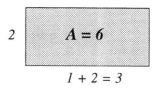

1 + 2 = 3

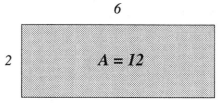

4 + 6 + 12 = 22

So, the area is 22 units.

G4   Practice.

1. The diagonals of a rhombus meet in right angles. What is the perimeter of a rhombus with one diagonal that measures 6 inches and the longer diagonal measures 8 inches?

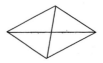

2. The trapezoid ABCD has an area of 66cm².
   Line AB is parallel to line CD ∠C = 90°.
   Segment AB = 10 cm.
   Segment BC = 6 cm.
   What is the measure of segment CD?
   What is the measure of ∠B? What is the measure of ∠A + ∠D?

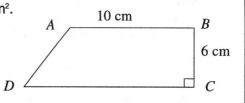

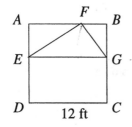

3. Square ABCD has sides that measure 12 feet each.
   E is the midpoint of segment AD
   Point F is collinear with points A and B
   G is the midpoint of segment BC
   What is the area of the square ABCD less the triangle EFG?

4. ABCD is a square.
   F is collinear with points C and D
   Point E is the midpoint of AD and is the center of circle E
   Segment AB is 8 inches in length
   Segment DF is 12 inches in length
   Point A and point D are on Circle E
   Find the area of the figure.

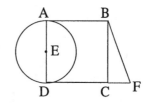

99

ANSWERS TO PRACTICES

G1 Answers
1. $\angle 2 = 48°$
2. $\angle 4 = 146°$
3. $\angle 6 = 140°$ $\angle 7 = 40°$ $\angle 8 = 140°$
4. $\angle a = 30°$ $\angle b = 90°$ $\angle c = 60°$ $\angle d = 30°$ $\angle e = 90°$ $\angle f = 60°$
5. Acute 1, 2, 3, 5, 7, a, c, d, f,
   Obtuse 4, 6, 8
   Right b, e

G2 Answers
1. 45°-45°-90°, $P = (8 + 4\sqrt{2})$m, $A = 8$m²
2. $A = 24$ ft.², $P = 24$ ft.
3. $P = (15 + 5\sqrt{3})$cm $\qquad A = \dfrac{25\sqrt{3}}{2}$ cm²
4. $\angle 2 = 50°$ $\angle 3 = 95°$
5. 27

G3 Answers
1. $A = 25\pi$ ft² $C = 10\pi$ft
2. $A = 36\pi$ m²
3. Segment $\overline{AC}$ measures 5"

   Segments $\overline{BA}$ and $\overline{BC}$ are both radii of the same circle, so they are equal so triangle ABC is isosceles. Since arc AC = 60°, then $\angle B = 60°$. The base angles of an isosceles triangle are equal. $\angle BAC = \angle BCA = 60°$. That means triangle ABC is an equilateral triangle with all sides equal. Therefore, segment $\overline{AC} = 5"$.

   $\angle ADC = 30°$

   $\angle ADC$ is an inscribed angle. Therefore it is half of arc AC which is 60°.

4. 27π

   The large circle has a radius of 6, therefore the large circle has an area of 36π. The smaller circle has a raduis of 3, therefore the small circle has an area of 9π. $35\pi - 9\pi = 27\pi$.

G4 Answers
1. 20 inches (Each right triangle measures 3, 4 and 5 inches on a side.)
2. Segment $\overline{CD} = 12$ cm. $\angle B = 90°$ $\angle A + \angle D = 180°$
3. Square ABCD area = 144 Triangle EFG = 36 $\quad$ 144 − 36 = 108ft.²
4. Semi-circle = 8π
   Square = 64
   Triangle = 16
   $8\pi + 64 + 16 = (80 + 8\pi)$ inches²

CHAPTER SIX

TRIGONOMETRY

The Trigonometry portion of the COMPASS exam covers the basics of functions and identities, right triangle problems, applications, trigonometric equations, and graphs of trigonometric functions.

This chapter is divided into 14 sections to help you review.

T1 Pythagorean Theorem
T2 Definition of Trigonometric Functions
T3 Signs of the Trigonometric Functions
T4 Reciprocal Identities
T5 The Pythagorean Identities
T6 Quotient Identities
T7 Right Triangle Trigonometry
T8 Cofunction Identities
T9 30° - 60° - 90° Triangles
T10 45° - 45° - 90° Triangles
T11 Law of Sines
T12 Law of Cosines
T13 Circular Function
T14 Applications

CALCULATORS

Before you take the trigonometry portion of the COMPASS test you should find out what calculator you can use on the test. Many of the questions can be answered without the aid of a calculator but some of the problems are much easier when you do use one. Different testing sites will have different rules about calculators. Some sites will furnish calculators or allow you to bring one of your own. Other testing sites will require that you use the one that is included on the computer you take the test on. If you are using the Windows calculator on the computer system make sure that you are in scientific mode.

Before you take the test make sure that you can use the calculator in radian and degree mode. You should practice with the calculator to make sure you are familiar with its operation.

T1 PYTHAGOREAN THEOREM

A right triangle is any triangle that contains a 90° angle.

Note that in the drawing the 90° angle is denoted with a small square at point C. The length of the sides are denoted by lower case letters that are the same as the uppercase letters used to name the points of the vertices of the angles that are opposite the sides. So the small c denotes the length of the side opposite the right angle. The side that is opposite the right triangle is called the hypotenuse. The sides that are not the hypotenuse are called the legs.

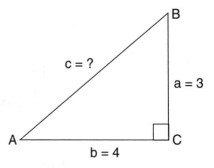

The Pythagorean theorem states that the sum of the square of the lengths of the legs of a right triangle is equal to the square of the length of the hypotenuse. Algebraically we can say the same thing much more efficiently:

$$a^2 + b^2 = c^2$$

If we apply the Pythagorean theorem to the drawing we can find the length of side c, the distance from point A to point B.

$$a^2 + b^2 = c^2$$
$$3^2 + 4^2 = c^2$$
$$9 + 16 = c^2$$
$$25 = c^2$$
$$\sqrt{25} = \sqrt{c^2}$$
$$5 = c$$

So the three sides of this triangle are the integers 3, 4, 5. An integer solution to a right triangle is called a Pythagorean triple. Once you have found one Pythagorean triple you can generate others by multiplying by any integer. So if we multiply the [3 4 5] by 2 we have the [6 8 10]. Pythagorean triples occur often on the COMPASS trigonometry exam. Other examples of Pythagorean triples include: [5 12 13], [7 24 25], [9 40 41] and [11 60 61].

Example 1
Suppose a right triangle has a hypotenuse that measures 15 feet and one of the legs measure 10 feet. How long is the remaining leg?

Solution Apply the Pythagorean theorem:

$$a^2 + b^2 = c^2$$
$$10^2 + b^2 = 15^2$$
$$100 + b^2 = 225$$
$$b^2 = 225 - 100$$
$$b^2 = 125$$
$$b = \sqrt{125}$$
$$b = \sqrt{25 \cdot 5}$$
$$b = 5\sqrt{5}$$
$$b \approx 11.2\, ft$$

DISTANCE FORMULA

As we saw in section A16 earlier in this book the distance formula is an alternate expression of the Pythagorean relationship.

$$d = \sqrt{(x_2 - x_1)^2 + (y_2 - y_1)^2}$$

The distance formula is particularly useful for finding the distance from the origin to a point in the plane.

Example 2
Find the distance from the origin (0, 0) to the point (4, 3) .

Solution Apply the distance formula

$$d = \sqrt{(x_2 - x_1)^2 + (y_2 - y_1)^2}$$
$$d = \sqrt{(4-0)^2 + (3-0)^2}$$
$$d = \sqrt{4^2 + 3^2}$$
$$d = \sqrt{16 + 9}$$
$$d = \sqrt{25} = 5$$

DEGREES AND RADIANS

When we measure temperature the two most popular scales to use are Fahrenheit and Celsius. Just as there are two scales to measure temperatures there are two different ways to measure angles. We have a choice of using degrees or radians.

The circumference, C, of a circle is given by the formula $C = \pi r$ where r is the radius.

Since a circle is 360° we can say:

$$360° = 2\pi \text{ radians}$$

When converting between degree and radian measures it is important to keep the proportion in mind:

$$\frac{\text{radian measure}}{\pi} = \frac{\text{degree measure}}{180}$$

Example 3

Convert 30° to radian measure.
Solution Apply the degree, radian proportion.

$$\frac{\text{radian measure}}{\pi} = \frac{\text{degree measure}}{180}$$
$$\frac{\text{radian measure}}{\pi} = \frac{30}{180}$$
$$\text{radian measure} = \frac{30\pi}{180}$$
$$\text{radian measure} = \frac{\pi}{6}$$

Example 4

Convert $\frac{\pi}{4}$ to a degree measure.

Solution Apply the degree, radian proportion.

$$\frac{\text{radian measure}}{\pi} = \frac{\text{degree measure}}{180}$$

$$\frac{\frac{\pi}{4}}{\pi} = \frac{\text{degree measure}}{180}$$

$$\frac{1}{4} = \frac{\text{degree measure}}{180}$$

$$\frac{180}{4} = \text{degree measure}$$

$$45° = \text{degree measure}$$

T1 Practice.

Find the missing side of the right triangles listed below. Assume that side c is always the hypotenuse.

1. a = 6, b = 8, c = ____   2. a = 24, b = ____ , c = 25   3. a = 1, b = 2 c = ____

4. A rectangle measures 5 feet by 12 feet. How long is the diagonal?

5. What is the distance from the origin to the point (9, 12)?

6. What is the exact distance from the origin to the point (3, 10)?

7. Convert 120° to radian measure.

8. Convert 2π to degree measure.

(Answers at the end of the chapter)

T2 DEFINITION OF TRIGONOMETRIC FUNCTIONS

If we place our 3, 4, 5 triangle on a graph so that point *A* is at the origin and point C is on the x-axis at the point (4,0) we end up with this useful reference triangle.

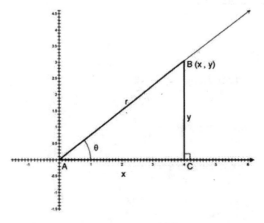

Note that in this drawing the angle A is labeled θ (Greek letter theta), the hypotenuse is labeled r as in radius, the length of side b which lines on the x-axis is labeled x and the length of the side a, opposite θ, is labeled y. The angle θ is said to be in standard position. The coordinate of point B is (x, y) in this case $(4, 3)$. The ray that begins at the origin and extends through point B is the terminal side of angle θ.

Now since we used the Pythagorean theorem to find that the length of $r = 5$, we can use our 3, 4, 5 triangle and this figure to define the six trigonometric functions.

Trigonometric Functions		
$\sin\theta = \dfrac{y}{r} = \dfrac{3}{5}$	$\csc\theta = \dfrac{r}{y} = \dfrac{5}{3}$	$y \neq 0$
$\cos\theta = \dfrac{x}{r} = \dfrac{4}{5}$	$\sec\theta = \dfrac{r}{x} = \dfrac{5}{4}$	$x \neq 0$
$\tan\theta = \dfrac{y}{x} = \dfrac{3}{4} \quad x \neq 0$	$\cot\theta = \dfrac{x}{y} = \dfrac{4}{3}$	$y \neq 0$

Knowing these definitions of the trigonometric functions allows us to answer many questions about angles.

Example 1

Consider a ray with a vertex at the origin that passes through the point $(15, 8)$. This ray and the x-axis form an angle we will call α (Greek letter Alpha). Find the values of the six trigonometric functions of angle α.

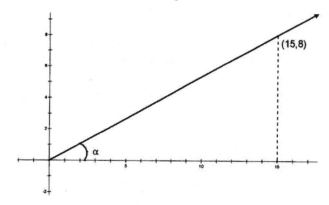

Solution The point $(15, 8)$ is 15 units to the right of the point of origin and 8 units above the origin, so $x = 15$ and $y = 8$. Now in order to find the value of r we apply the distance formula. This will find the distance from the origin $(0, 0)$ to the point $(15, 8)$.

$$r = \sqrt{(15-0)^2 + (8-0)^2}$$
$$r = \sqrt{15^2 + 8^2}$$
$$r = \sqrt{225 + 64}$$
$$r = \sqrt{289}$$
$$r = 17$$

Now since we know the three sides of the triangle we can write down the values of the six trigonometric functions of α.

$$\sin\alpha = \frac{y}{r} = \frac{8}{17} \qquad\qquad \csc\alpha = \frac{r}{y} = \frac{17}{8}$$

$$\cos\alpha = \frac{x}{r} = \frac{15}{17} \qquad\qquad \sec\alpha = \frac{r}{x} = \frac{17}{15}$$

$$\tan\alpha = \frac{y}{x} = \frac{8}{15} \qquad\qquad \cot\alpha = \frac{x}{y} = \frac{15}{8}$$

Example 2

The terminal side of angle β in standard position goes through point (-12,-5) as shown in the drawing below. Find the six trigonometric function values for the angle β.

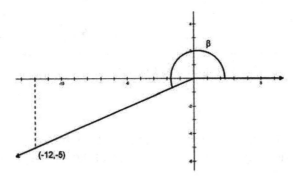

Solution The point $(-12, -5)$ is 12 units to the left of the origin and -5 units below the origin, so $x = -12$ and $y = -5$. To find the value of r we apply the distance formula.

$$r = \sqrt{(-12-0)^2 + (-5-0)^2}$$
$$r = \sqrt{(-12)^2 + (-5)^2}$$
$$r = \sqrt{144+25}$$
$$r = \sqrt{169}$$
$$r = 13$$

Now plug in $x = -12$, $y = -5$, and $r = 13$ to find the six trigonometric functions of β. Pay close attention to the signs.

$$\sin\beta = \frac{y}{r} = \frac{-5}{13} \qquad\qquad \csc\beta = \frac{r}{y} = \frac{13}{-5} = \frac{-13}{5}$$

$$\cos\beta = \frac{x}{r} = \frac{-12}{13} \qquad\qquad \sec\beta = \frac{r}{x} = \frac{13}{-12} = \frac{-13}{12}$$

$$\tan\beta = \frac{y}{x} = \frac{-5}{-12} = \frac{5}{12} \qquad\qquad \cot\beta = \frac{x}{y} = \frac{-12}{-5} = \frac{12}{5}$$

T2 Practice.

Suppose that θ is in standard position and that the point given is on the terminal side of θ. Give the exact values of the six trigonometric functions of θ.

1. (12, 5) 2. (3, -4) 3. (-12, 9)

(Answers at the end of the chapter)

T3 SIGNS OF THE TRIGONOMETRIC FUNCTIONS

Notice that the definition of tangent is very similar to slope $m = \dfrac{y_2 - y_1}{x_2 - x_1}$. This similarity can help you determine which sign is correct when dealing with the tangent and cotangent functions. If the slope of the terminal side of the angle is positive then tangent and cotangent will also be positive.

The signs of the other functions depend on the components of the function value. The r value is always positive. The x and y values depends upon where the terminal side of the angle is located.

T3 Practice

Complete the following table to find out more about the signs of the trigonometric functions. The point P is on the terminal side of the angle θ and is located at the point (a,b).

Signs of the Trigonometric Function Values						
Point P in quadrant	sin θ	cos θ	tan θ	cot θ	sec θ	csc θ
I (+, +)	+	+	+	+	+	+
II (-, +)	+					
III (-, +)	-	ι				
IV (+, -)	-					
x-axis (x, 0)	0			undefined		undefined
y-axis (0, y)	same as y					

(Answers at the end of the chapter)

T4 RECIPROCAL IDENTITIES

Notice that the sine and cosecant are reciprocals of each other.

$$\sin x = \frac{1}{\csc x} \quad \leftrightarrow \quad \csc x = \frac{1}{\sin x} \quad \leftrightarrow \quad (\sin x)(\csc x) = 1$$

This reciprocal relationship is also true of cosine and secant pair:

$$\cos x = \frac{1}{\sec x} \quad \leftrightarrow \quad \sec x = \frac{1}{\cos x} \quad \leftrightarrow \quad (\cos x)(\sec x) = 1$$

As well as for the tangent and cotangent pair:

$$\tan x = \frac{1}{\cot x} \quad \leftrightarrow \quad \cot x = \frac{1}{\tan x} \quad \leftrightarrow \quad (\tan x)(\cot x) = 1$$

Example 1
Find the function value of the sec θ if $\cos \theta = \sqrt{5}$.

Solution Since $\sec x = \frac{1}{\cos x}$, $\sec \theta = \frac{1}{\sqrt{5}}$

Now rationalize the denominator.

$$\sec \theta = \frac{1}{\sqrt{5}}\left(\frac{\sqrt{5}}{\sqrt{5}}\right) = \frac{\sqrt{5}}{5}$$

The reciprocal identities allow us to evaluate csc, sec, and cot using calculators that only have sin, cos, and tan buttons. So to find sec 60° you would enter this expression into your calculator $\frac{1}{\cos 60}$ and get the value 2 (make sure your calculator is in degree mode).

T4 Practice

1. Find the function value of sin θ if $\csc \theta = \sqrt{2}$.

2. Find the function value of tan θ if $\cot \theta = \frac{\sqrt{3}}{3}$.

3. Use a calculator to find the value of cot 30. Round your answer to the nearest tenth.

(Answers at the end of the chapter)

T5 THE PYTHAGOREAN IDENTITIES

Consider the point B, (x, y), on the terminal side of θ.

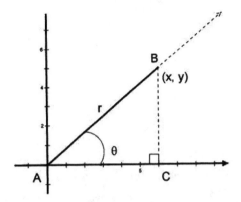

Application of the Pythagorean theorem to Δ ABC above and some algebra will reveal three important identities. These identities are known as the Pythagorean identities because they are derived from the Pythagorean relationship.

$$x^2 + y^2 = r^2$$

First divide both sides by x^2.

$$\frac{x^2}{x^2} + \frac{y^2}{x^2} = \frac{r^2}{x^2}$$

$$1 + \left(\frac{y}{x}\right)^2 = \left(\frac{r}{x}\right)^2$$

$$1 + (\tan\theta)^2 = (\sec\theta)^2$$

This identity is more commonly written as:

$$\tan^2\theta + 1 = \sec^2\theta$$

Alternately we could have divided by y^2 rather than by x^2.

$$\frac{x^2}{y^2} + \frac{y^2}{y^2} = \frac{r^2}{y^2}$$

$$\left(\frac{x}{y}\right)^2 + 1 = \left(\frac{r}{y}\right)^2$$

$$(\cot\theta)^2 + 1 = (\csc\theta)^2$$

This identity is more commonly written as:

$$1 + \cot^2\theta = \csc^2\theta$$

Finally if we divide by r^2.

$$\frac{x^2}{r^2} + \frac{y^2}{r^2} = \frac{r^2}{r^2}$$

$$\left(\frac{x}{r}\right)^2 + \left(\frac{y}{r}\right)^2 = 1$$

$$(\cos\theta)^2 + (\sin\theta)^2 = 1$$

Which is typically written as:

$$\sin^2\theta + \cos^2\theta = 1$$

Summary of the Three Pythagorean Identities

$$\tan^2\theta + 1 = \sec^2\theta \qquad 1 + \cot^2\theta = \csc^2\theta \qquad \sin^2\theta + \cos^2\theta = 1$$

Example 1
Find $\sin\theta$ if $\cos\theta = \dfrac{-\sqrt{5}}{3}$ with θ in the second quadrant.

Solution   Use the Pythagorean identity $\sin^2\theta + \cos^2\theta = 1$.

$$\sin^2\theta + \left(\frac{-\sqrt{5}}{3}\right)^2 = 1$$

$$\sin^2\theta + \frac{5}{9} = 1$$

$$\sin^2\theta = 1 - \frac{5}{9}$$

$$\sin^2\theta = \frac{9}{9} - \frac{5}{9}$$

$$\sin^2\theta = \frac{4}{9}$$

$$\sqrt{\sin^2\theta} = \sqrt{\frac{4}{9}}$$

$$\sin\theta = \frac{2}{3}$$

T5 Practice.

1. Find $\sin\theta$ if $\cos\theta = \dfrac{-4}{5}$ with θ in quadrant II.

2. Find $\tan\theta$ if $\sec\theta = \dfrac{13}{12}$ with θ in quadrant I.

3. Find $\cot\theta$ if $\csc\theta = \dfrac{-25}{24}$ with θ in quadrant IV.

(Answers at the end of the chapter)

T6 QUOTIENT IDENTITIES

The quotient identities are derived by dividing certain trigonometric functions and their reciprocals. For example if we divide the sin θ by cos θ, the result is another trigonometric function, tan θ.

$$\frac{\sin\theta}{\cos\theta} = \frac{\frac{y}{r}}{\frac{x}{r}} = \frac{y}{r} \div \frac{x}{r} = \frac{y}{r} \cdot \frac{r}{x} = \frac{y}{x} = \tan\theta$$

In a similar fashion, if we divide the cos θ by the sin θ, the result is cot θ which is the reciprocal of tan θ.

$$\frac{\cos\theta}{\sin\theta} = \frac{\frac{x}{r}}{\frac{y}{r}} = \frac{x}{r} \div \frac{y}{r} = \frac{x}{r} \cdot \frac{r}{y} = \frac{x}{y} = \cot\theta$$

Summary of the Quotient Identities

$$\frac{\sin\theta}{\cos\theta} = \tan\theta \qquad\qquad \frac{\cos\theta}{\sin\theta} = \cot\theta$$

Example 1

If $\cos\theta = \dfrac{-\sqrt{3}}{2}$ and θ is located in quadrant II, find all of the other trigonometric values.

Solution Use the trigonometric identity $\sin^2\theta + \cos^2\theta = 1$ and substitute the given information for cos θ.

$$\sin^2\theta + \cos^2\theta = 1$$

$$\sin^2\theta + \left(\frac{-\sqrt{3}}{2}\right)^2 = 1$$

$$\sin^2\theta + \frac{3}{4} = 1$$

$$\sin^2\theta = 1 - \frac{3}{4}$$

$$\sin^2\theta = \frac{1}{4}$$

$$\sin\theta = \sqrt{\frac{1}{4}} = \frac{1}{2}$$

To find tan θ we can apply the quotient identity $\tan\theta = \dfrac{\sin\theta}{\cos\theta}$

$$\tan\theta = \frac{\sin\theta}{\cos\theta} = \frac{\frac{1}{2}}{\frac{-\sqrt{3}}{2}} = \frac{1}{2} \div \frac{-\sqrt{3}}{2} = \frac{1}{2} \cdot \frac{2}{-\sqrt{3}} = \frac{-1}{\sqrt{3}} \cdot \left(\frac{\sqrt{3}}{\sqrt{3}}\right) = \frac{-\sqrt{3}}{3}$$

The value of cot θ can be found using the other quotient identity $\cot \theta = \dfrac{\cos \theta}{\sin \theta}$.

$$\cot \theta = \frac{\cos \theta}{\sin \theta} = \frac{\dfrac{-\sqrt{3}}{2}}{\dfrac{1}{2}} = \frac{-\sqrt{3}}{2} \div \frac{1}{2} = \frac{-\sqrt{3}}{2} \cdot \frac{2}{1} = -\sqrt{3}$$

Use the reciprocal identities to find the other two function values.

$$\csc \theta = \frac{1}{\sin \theta} = \frac{1}{\dfrac{1}{2}} = 2$$

$$\sec \theta = \frac{1}{\cos \theta} = \frac{1}{\dfrac{-\sqrt{3}}{2}} = \frac{-2}{\sqrt{3}}\left(\frac{\sqrt{3}}{\sqrt{3}}\right) = \frac{-2\sqrt{3}}{3}$$

T6 Practice

1. Find all six trigonometric function values if $\cos \theta = \dfrac{-4}{5}$ with θ located in quadrant III.

2. Find all six trigonometric function values if $\tan \theta = \sqrt{3}$ with θ located in quadrant III.

3. Find all six trigonometric function values if $\sin \theta = \dfrac{12}{13}$ with θ located in quadrant II.

(Answers at the end of the chapter)

T7 RIGHT TRIANGLE TRIGONOMETRY

In section T2 we defined the trigonometric functions using x, y and r. In this section we will develop synonyms for x, y and r that will allow us to apply trigonometric relationships to triangles and angles that are not in the standard position.

The figure shows a right triangle with angle θ in standard position. When speaking of θ in this triangle we call the short side *opposite*. The longer side that lies on the x-axis is called *adjacent*. The side labeled r is the *hypotenuse* just as it would be in any right triangle. Note the relationship of the (x, y) coordinates of point B to the lengths of these sides.

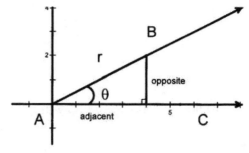

Point B (x, y) x = adjacent y = opposite

This relationship is only true when the angle in question is in standard position.

The trigonometric functions of angle A can be defined using the vocabulary of *adjacent*, *opposite*, and *hypotenuse*.

Definitions of Trigonometric Functions in a Right Triangle

$$\sin A = \frac{y}{r} = \frac{opposite}{hypotenuse} \qquad\qquad \csc A = \frac{r}{y} = \frac{hypotenuse}{opposite}$$

$$\cos A = \frac{x}{r} = \frac{adjacent}{hypotenuse} \qquad\qquad \sec A = \frac{r}{x} = \frac{hypotenuse}{adjacent}$$

$$\tan A = \frac{y}{x} = \frac{opposite}{adjacent} \qquad\qquad \cot A = \frac{x}{y} = \frac{adjacent}{opposite}$$

Example 1

Determine the values of all six trigonometric functions for angle A and angle B.

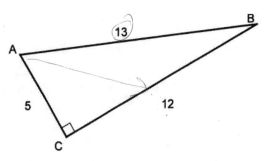

Solution For angle A

opposite = 12
adjacent = 5
hypotenuse = 13

$$\sin A = \frac{opposite}{hypotenuse} = \frac{12}{13} \qquad\qquad \csc A = \frac{hypotenuse}{opposite} = \frac{13}{12}$$

$$\cos A = \frac{adjacent}{hypotenuse} = \frac{5}{13} \qquad\qquad \sec A = \frac{hypotenuse}{adjacent} = \frac{13}{5}$$

$$\tan A = \frac{opposite}{adjacent} = \frac{12}{5} \qquad\qquad \cot A = \frac{adjacent}{opposite} = \frac{5}{12}$$

Solution For angle B

opposite = 5
adjacent = 12
hypotenuse = 13

$$\sin B = \frac{opposite}{hypotenuse} = \frac{5}{13} \qquad\qquad \csc B = \frac{hypotenuse}{opposite} = \frac{13}{5}$$

$$\cos B = \frac{adjacent}{hypotenuse} = \frac{12}{13} \qquad\qquad \sec B = \frac{hypotenuse}{adjacent} = \frac{13}{12}$$

$$\tan B = \frac{opposite}{adjacent} = \frac{5}{12} \qquad\qquad \cot B = \frac{adjacent}{opposite} = \frac{12}{5}$$

Note that in the previous example that $\sin A = \cos B = \dfrac{12}{13}$. This will be important in section **T8 Cofunction Identities**.

T7 Practice

1. In Example 1 on the previous page, what is the product of (tan *A*)(tan *B*)?

2. Find the exact values of the six trigonometric functions of α in the drawing below.

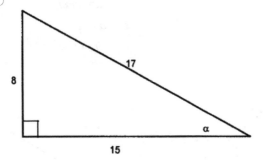

3. Find the exact values of the six trigonometric functions of β in the drawing below.

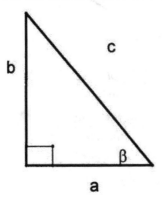

4. A triangle has sides that measure 20, 21 and 29 feet. Is this a right triangle? If it is what are values of the six trigonometric functions associated with the smallest angle?

(Answers at the end of the chapter)

T8 COFUNCTION IDENTITIES

The sum of the angles of any triangle in the plane is 180°. Complementary angles are angles that sum to 90°. Since a right triangle has one angle that is 90° then by definition the other two acute angles must sum to 90° and are thus complimentary to each other. Because of this complimentary relationship between the two acute angles the trigonometric functions can be related through co-function identities.

In example 1 from section T7 you may have noticed that $\sin A = \cos B = \dfrac{12}{13}$ and $\cos A = \sin B = \dfrac{5}{13}$. Such relationships are always true for complimentary angles.

Summary of Cofunction Identities **Degrees**	
If A is an acute angle.	
$\sin A = \cos(90° - A)$	$\csc A = \sec(90° - A)$
$\cos A = \sin(90° - A)$	$\sec A = \csc(90° - A)$
$\tan A = \cot(90° - A)$	$\cot A = \tan(90° - A)$

Summary of Cofunction Identities **Radians**

If A is an acute angle.

$$\sin A = \cos\left(\frac{\pi}{2} - A\right) \qquad \csc A = \sec\left(\frac{\pi}{2} - A\right)$$

$$\cos A = \sin\left(\frac{\pi}{2} - A\right) \qquad \sec A = \csc\left(\frac{\pi}{2} - A\right)$$

$$\tan A = \cot\left(\frac{\pi}{2} - A\right) \qquad \cot A = \tan\left(\frac{\pi}{2} - A\right)$$

Example 1

Write sin 28° in terms of its cofunction.

Solution sin 28° = cos (90° - 28°) = cos 62°

Example 2

Write $\cot\dfrac{\pi}{3}$ in terms of its cofunction.

Solution $\cot\dfrac{\pi}{3} = \tan\left(\dfrac{\pi}{2} - \dfrac{\pi}{3}\right) = \tan\left(\dfrac{3\pi}{6} - \dfrac{2\pi}{6}\right) = \tan\dfrac{\pi}{6}$

T8 Practice

1. Write cot 65° in terms of its cofunction.
2. Write sec 35° in terms of its cofunction.
3. Write sec $\dfrac{\pi}{3}$ in terms of its cofunction.
4. Write cos $\dfrac{\pi}{2}$ in terms of its cofunction.

(Answers at the end of the chapter)

T9 30° - 60° - 90° TRIANGLES

The 30° - 60° - 90° triangle is the first of two special triangles we will consider in this section and the next.

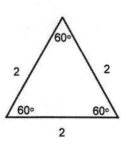

To construct the 30° - 60° - 90° we start first with an equilateral triangle that measures 2 on each side. Since the angle sum of any triangle is 180° we know that each angle measures 60°.

If we connect the vertex of one of the angles to the midpoint of the opposite side then we will have two smaller triangles. The midpoint divides the side into two equal segments of length 1. The original 60° angle is bisected into two equal 30° angles.

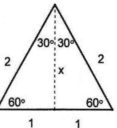

Now consider just one of the small triangles. Since the triangle already has angles of 30° and 60° we know that the last angle must measure 90° which makes this a right triangle. Since it is a right triangle we can apply the Pythagorean theorem to determine the length of the leg that is opposite the 60° angle.

$$a^2 + b^2 = c^2$$
$$x^2 + 1^2 = 2^2$$
$$x^2 + 1 = 4$$
$$x^2 = 4 - 1$$
$$x^2 = 3$$
$$\sqrt{x^2} = \sqrt{3}$$
$$x = \sqrt{3}$$

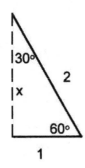

T9 Practice

1. What are the values of the six trigonometric functions of a 30° angle?

2. What are the values of the six trigonometric functions of a 60° angle?

3. If the hypotenuse of a 30° - 60° - 90° triangle is 4 feet, what is the perimeter?

(Answers at the end of the chapter)

T10 45° - 45° - 90° TRIANGLES

To construct our next special triangle we will start with a square and then construct the diagonal segment AB. We know that angle C is a right angle because it was part of the original square. Since the legs AC and BC of triangle *ABC* are equal then angle *A* is equal to angle *B*. Since we know the measure of angle C is a right angle and that angle A and angle B are equal we can find the exact measurement using the triangle angle sum.

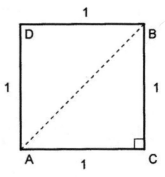

$$\angle A + \angle B + \angle C = 180°$$
$$\angle A + \angle A + 90° = 180°$$
$$2\angle A = 180° - 90°$$
$$2\angle A = 90°$$
$$\angle A = 45°$$

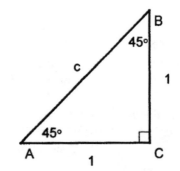

Now we can apply the Pythagorean theorem to find the length of the hypotenuse c. This will allow us to find the trigonometric function values for a 45° angle.

$$a^2 + b^2 = c^2$$
$$1^2 + 1^2 = c^2$$
$$2 = c^2$$
$$\sqrt{2} = \sqrt{c^2}$$
$$\sqrt{2} = c$$

Since we know the three sides of this triangle we can write down the function values for the 45° angle. Since the square root of 2 will be used for sine and cosine you should be prepared to rationalize the denominator.

$$\sin 45° = \frac{opposite}{hypotenuse} = \frac{1}{\sqrt{2}} = \frac{1}{\sqrt{2}}\left(\frac{\sqrt{2}}{\sqrt{2}}\right) = \frac{\sqrt{2}}{2}$$

$$\cos 45° = \frac{adjacent}{hypotenuse} = \frac{1}{\sqrt{2}} = \frac{1}{\sqrt{2}}\left(\frac{\sqrt{2}}{\sqrt{2}}\right) = \frac{\sqrt{2}}{2}$$

The table below summarizes the result of the previous two sections. If you memorize this table all of your friends will be impressed and your next math class will be easier.

Trigonometric Function Values of Special Angles						
θ	$\sin \theta$	$\cos \theta$	$\tan \theta$	$\cot \theta$	$\sec \theta$	$\csc \theta$
$30° = \dfrac{\pi}{6}$	$\dfrac{1}{2}$	$\dfrac{\sqrt{3}}{2}$	$\dfrac{\sqrt{3}}{3}$	$\sqrt{3}$	$\dfrac{2\sqrt{3}}{3}$	2
$45° = \dfrac{\pi}{4}$	$\dfrac{\sqrt{2}}{2}$	$\dfrac{\sqrt{2}}{2}$	1	1	$\sqrt{2}$	$\sqrt{2}$
$60° = \dfrac{\pi}{3}$	$\dfrac{\sqrt{3}}{2}$	$\dfrac{1}{2}$	$\sqrt{3}$	$\dfrac{\sqrt{3}}{3}$	2	$\dfrac{2\sqrt{3}}{3}$

T10 Practice

1. The perimeter of a square is 16 feet. What is the length of the diagonal?

2. If the area of an isosceles right triangle is 8 square feet then what is the length of the diagonal?

3. If the diagonal of a square is 5 feet long, what is the perimeter?

(Answers at the end of the chapter)

T11 LAW OF SINES

An oblique triangle is a triangle that is not a right triangle. So far our discussion has been limited to right triangles. The extension of trigonometry to oblique triangles can be accomplished by constructing right triangles in any arbitrary, oblique triangle.

We do this in triangle *ABC* by dropping a perpendicular from point *B*. This perpendicular intersects side *AC* at point *D* making two right triangles *ABD* and *CBD*. So now we can use *h* as the side opposite angle *A* and angle *C*.

$$\sin A = \frac{h}{c} \quad \text{and} \quad \sin C = \frac{h}{a}$$
$$c \sin A = h \qquad\qquad a \sin C = h$$

Now since ($c \sin A$) and ($a \sin C$) are both equal to *h* we can say $c \sin A = a \sin C$. Now divide both sides by ($\sin A$)($\sin C$).

$$\frac{c \sin A}{(\sin A)(\sin C)} = \frac{a \sin C}{(\sin A)(\sin C)}$$
$$\frac{c}{\sin C} = \frac{a}{\sin A}$$

In a similar way, if we had selected point A to drop the perpendicular from we would have found that $\frac{b}{\sin B} = \frac{c}{\sin C}$. The equality of all three ratios makes up the law of sines. This result allows us to apply trigonometry to oblique triangles.

Law of Sines

For any triangle *ABC* with angles *A, B,* and *C* and sides opposite *a, b,* and *c,*

$$\frac{a}{\sin A} = \frac{b}{\sin B} = \frac{c}{\sin C}$$

Example 1
Solve triangle *ABC* given $A = 94.87°$, $B = 50.36°$ and $c = 6.54$ cm.

Solution When we say solve a triangle that means to find all of the missing parts. The easiest part to find here is *C*, the missing angle, using the triangle angle sum.

$$A + B + C = 180°$$
$$94.87 + 50.36 + C = 180$$
$$C = 180 - 94.87 - 50.36$$
$$C = 34.77$$

Now to find the missing sides we will use the law of sines, substitute what we know, and then find the unknowns.

$$\frac{a}{\sin A} = \frac{b}{\sin B} = \frac{c}{\sin C}$$

$$\frac{a}{\sin 94.87} = \frac{b}{\sin 50.36} = \frac{6.54}{\sin 34.77}$$

So to find the length of side a we will solve the proportion: $\dfrac{a}{\sin 94.87} = \dfrac{6.54}{\sin 34.77}$.

$$a = \frac{6.54(\sin 94.87)}{\sin 34.77} \approx 11.43$$

In a similar fashion we can find side b using the proportion: $\dfrac{b}{\sin 50.36} = \dfrac{6.54}{\sin 34.77}$.

$$b = \frac{6.54(\sin 50.36)}{\sin 34.77} \approx 8.83$$

T11 Practice

Solve each of the following triangles.

1. B = 68.37°, C = 40.48°, a = 7.01 cm

2. B = 83.20°, b = 10.03 cm, C = 52.84°

3. C = 19.41°, B = 143.50°, c = 6.58 cm

(Answers at the end of the chapter)

T12 LAW OF COSINES

Consider triangle ABC in standard position with A at the origin $(0, 0)$ and B on the x-axis. Now take the coordinate position of point C to be (x, y). The coordinate location of point B is $(c, 0)$. The coordinates of point C can be expressed using the definition of sine and cosine.

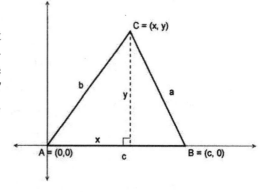

$$\cos A = \frac{x}{b}$$

$$b\cos A = x$$

$$\sin A = \frac{y}{b}$$

$$b\sin A = y$$

Now using the distance formula we find the distance from point B $(c, 0)$ to point C (x, y).

$$d = \sqrt{(x_2 - x_1)^2 + (y_2 - y_1)^2}$$

$$a = \sqrt{(x - c)^2 + (y - 0)^2}$$

$$a^2 = (x - c)^2 + (y - 0)^2$$

$$a^2 = (b\cos A - c)^2 + (b\sin A)^2$$

$$a^2 = b^2\cos^2 A - 2bc\cos A + c^2 + b^2\sin^2 A$$

$$a^2 = b^2(\cos^2 A + \sin^2 A) + c^2 - 2bc\cos A$$

Now since $(\sin^2 A + \cos^2 A) = 1$

$$a^2 = b^2 + c^2 - 2bc\cos A$$

In a similar fashion we could have placed point B or point C at the origin and found the following results:

Law of Cosines

$$a^2 = b^2 + c^2 - 2bc\cos A, \qquad b^2 = a^2 + c^2 - 2ac\cos B \qquad c^2 = a^2 + b^2 - 2ab\cos C$$

Example 1

In the drawing below angle $B = 109.81°$, $a = 7.06$ cm and $c = 6.58$ cm. Find the length of b.

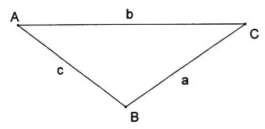

Solution Apply the law of cosines.

$$b^2 = a^2 + c^2 - 2ac\cos B$$

$$b^2 = (7.06)^2 + (6.58)^2 - 2(7.06)(6.58)\cos 109.81°$$

$$b^2 = 49.8436 + 43.2967 - 92.9096\cos 109.81°$$

$$b^2 \approx 93.14 - 92.9096(-0.3389)$$

$$b^2 \approx 124.627$$

$$b \approx \sqrt{124.627}$$

$$b \approx 11.16\,\text{cm}$$

T12 Practice

Solve the following triangles using the law of sines and cosines as needed.

1. $B = 73.58°$, $a = 11.34$ cm $c = 5.73$ cm

2. $B = 80.01°$, $a = 10.87$ cm $c = 16.23$ cm

3. $B = 30.03°$, $a = 11.56$ cm $c = 12.09$ cm

(Answers at the end of the chapter)

T13 CIRCULAR FUNCTION

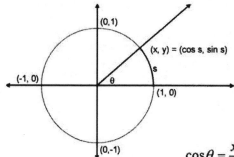

The unit circle has a radius of one and is centered at the origin. If we place angle θ in standard position so that it is a central angle of the unit circle then the terminal side of the angle will determine an arc s that is equal to θ. Since the radius of the circle is 1, the location of the point (x, y) can easily be described using the trigonometric definitions.

$$\cos\theta = \frac{x}{r} = \frac{x}{1} = x = \cos s$$

$$\sin\theta = \frac{y}{r} = \frac{y}{1} = y = \sin s$$

Once we know the (x, y) position of any point on the unit circle we can determine the values of all six trigonometric functions.

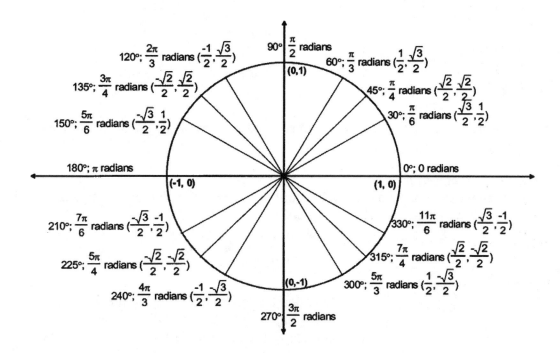

Example 1

Find exact values of the six trigonometric function of $\theta = \dfrac{5\pi}{6}$.

Solution from the unit circle chart above we can see that $\dfrac{5\pi}{6}$ corresponds to a 150° angle. The coordinates for this point is $\left(\dfrac{-\sqrt{3}}{2}, \dfrac{1}{2} \right)$, so the six trigonometric functions will have the following exact values:

$$\sin\theta = \frac{1}{2} \qquad\qquad \csc\theta = \frac{1}{\frac{1}{2}} = 2$$

$$\cos\theta = \frac{-\sqrt{3}}{2} \qquad\qquad \sec\theta = \frac{1}{\frac{-\sqrt{3}}{2}} = \frac{-2\sqrt{3}}{3}$$

$$\tan\theta = \frac{\frac{1}{2}}{\frac{-\sqrt{3}}{2}} = \frac{-\sqrt{3}}{3} \qquad\qquad \cot\theta = \frac{\frac{-\sqrt{3}}{2}}{\frac{1}{2}} = -\sqrt{3}$$

T14 APPLICATIONS

The following examples illustrate the type of application problems you might find on the COMPASS exam.

Example 1 Rectangle

A rectangle measures three feet by four feet. What is the cosine of the largest angle formed with the diagonal and a side?

a. $\dfrac{4}{5}$ b. $\dfrac{3}{5}$ c. $\dfrac{3}{4}$ d. $\dfrac{4}{3}$ e. undefined

Solution First draw the rectangle:

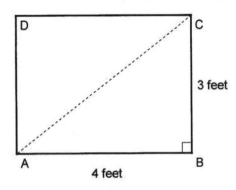

Now find the length of the hypotenuse. If you do not recognize the [3, 4,5] Pythagorean triple you can apply the Pythagorean theorem to find the length of the hypotenuse which is five feet.

The larger of the two angles of the triangle formed by the diagonal and a side will be opposite the larger side. So the larger of the two angles is angle *ACB* or angle *CAD*.

From our work with right triangles in section **T7** we know:

$$\cos\theta = \frac{adjacent}{hypotenuse} \qquad \text{so} \qquad \cos\angle ACB = \frac{3}{5}$$

So answer **b** is the correct choice.

Example 2 Altitude

An airplane is directly above a stadium. An observer at the airport which is five miles away notes that the angle of elevation to the airplane is 15°. What is the height of the airplane above the stadium?

Solution First make a sketch of the problem.

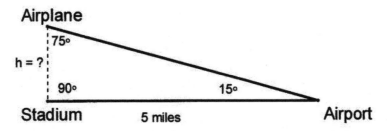

Now determine all of the angles. Since the ground and the height form a 90° angle we know that the other acute angle must be 75°.

Now using the law of sines from section **T13** we can write this proportion and then solve for *h*.

$$\frac{\sin 15°}{h} = \frac{\sin 75°}{5}$$

$$5(\sin 15°) = h(\sin 75°)$$

$$\frac{5(\sin 15°)}{\sin 75°} = h$$

$$1.34 \text{ miles} \approx h$$

Example 3 Ladder

A ladder of a certain length is placed ten feet away from a building such that it forms a 70° angle with the ground. How high does the ladder reach?

Solution Make a drawing.

Once again we can use the law of sines to find the height of the ladder.

$$\frac{\sin 20°}{10} = \frac{\sin 70°}{h}$$

$$h(\sin 20°) = 10(\sin 70°)$$

$$h = \frac{10(\sin 70°)}{\sin 20°}$$

$$h \approx 27.47 \text{ feet}$$

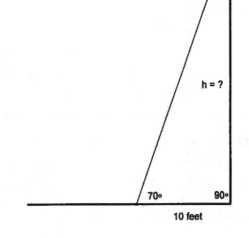

ANSWERS TO PRACTICES

T1 Answers

1. 10
2. 7
3. $\sqrt{5}$
4. 13 feet
5. 15
6. $\sqrt{109} \approx 10.4$
7. $\dfrac{2\pi}{3}$
8. 360°

T2 Answers

1. (12, 5)

$\sin\theta = \dfrac{y}{r} = \dfrac{5}{13}$ $\qquad$ $\csc\theta = \dfrac{r}{y} = \dfrac{13}{5}$

$\cos\theta = \dfrac{x}{r} = \dfrac{12}{13}$ $\qquad$ $\sec\theta = \dfrac{r}{x} = \dfrac{13}{12}$

$\tan\theta = \dfrac{y}{x} = \dfrac{5}{12}$ $\qquad$ $\cot\theta = \dfrac{x}{y} = \dfrac{12}{5}$

2. (3, -4)

$\sin\theta = \dfrac{y}{r} = \dfrac{-4}{5}$ $\qquad$ $\csc\theta = \dfrac{r}{y} = \dfrac{-5}{4}$

$\cos\theta = \dfrac{x}{r} = \dfrac{3}{5}$ $\qquad$ $\sec\theta = \dfrac{r}{x} = \dfrac{5}{3}$

$\tan\theta = \dfrac{y}{x} = \dfrac{-4}{3}$ $\qquad$ $\cot\theta = \dfrac{x}{y} = \dfrac{-3}{4}$

3. (-12, 9)

$\sin\theta = \dfrac{y}{r} = \dfrac{3}{5}$ $\qquad$ $\csc\theta = \dfrac{r}{y} = \dfrac{5}{3}$

$\cos\theta = \dfrac{x}{r} = \dfrac{-4}{5}$ $\qquad$ $\sec\theta = \dfrac{r}{x} = \dfrac{-5}{4}$

$\tan\theta = \dfrac{y}{x} = \dfrac{-3}{4}$ $\qquad$ $\cot\theta = \dfrac{x}{y} = \dfrac{-4}{3}$

T3 Answers

Signs of the Trigonometric Function Values						
Point P in quadrant	$\sin\theta$	$\cos\theta$	$\tan\theta$	$\cot\theta$	$\sec\theta$	$\csc\theta$
I (+, +)	+	+	+	+	+	+
II (-, +)	+	-	-	-	-	+
III (-, +)	-	-	+	+	-	-
IV (+, -)	-	+	-	-	+	-
x-axis (x, 0)	0	Same as x	0	Undefined	Same as x	Undefined
y-axis (0, y)	Same as y	0	Undefined	0	Undefined	Same as y

T4 Answers

1. $\sin\theta = \dfrac{1}{\sqrt{2}} = \dfrac{\sqrt{2}}{2}$

2. $\tan\theta = \dfrac{\frac{1}{1}}{\frac{\sqrt{3}}{3}} = \dfrac{3}{\sqrt{3}} = \sqrt{3}$

3. cot 30° ≈ 1.7 (make sure your calculator is in degree mode)

T5 Answers

1. $\sin\theta = \dfrac{3}{5}$

2. $\tan\theta = \dfrac{5}{12}$

3. $\cot\theta = \dfrac{-7}{24}$

T6 Answers

Values of the Trigonometric Function Values in problems 1-3						
	$\sin\theta$	$\cos\theta$	$\tan\theta$	$\cot\theta$	$\sec\theta$	$\csc\theta$
1.	$\dfrac{3}{5}$	$\dfrac{-4}{5}$	$\dfrac{-3}{4}$	$\dfrac{-4}{3}$	$\dfrac{-5}{4}$	$\dfrac{5}{3}$
2.	Use $\tan^2\theta + 1 = \sec^2\theta$ to find $\sec\theta = 2$					
	$\dfrac{-\sqrt{3}}{2}$	$-\dfrac{1}{2}$	$\sqrt{3}$	$\dfrac{\sqrt{3}}{3}$	-2	$-\dfrac{2\sqrt{3}}{3}$
3.	$\dfrac{12}{13}$	$\dfrac{-5}{13}$	$\dfrac{-12}{5}$	$\dfrac{-5}{12}$	$\dfrac{-13}{5}$	$\dfrac{13}{12}$

T7 Answers

1. Since angle *A* and angle *B* are complimentary angles the two tangents will be reciprocals of each other. The product of reciprocals is always 1.

2.
$$\sin\alpha = \frac{opposite}{hypotenuse} = \frac{8}{17} \qquad \csc\alpha = \frac{hypotenuse}{opposite} = \frac{17}{8}$$

$$\cos\alpha = \frac{adjacent}{hypotenuse} = \frac{15}{17} \qquad \sec\alpha = \frac{hypotenuse}{adjacent} = \frac{17}{15}$$

$$\tan\alpha = \frac{opposite}{adjacent} = \frac{8}{15} \qquad \cot\alpha = \frac{adjacent}{opposite} = \frac{15}{8}$$

3.
$$\sin\beta = \frac{opposite}{hypotenuse} = \frac{b}{c} \qquad \csc\beta = \frac{hypotenuse}{opposite} = \frac{c}{b}$$

$$\cos\beta = \frac{adjacent}{hypotenuse} = \frac{a}{c} \qquad \sec\beta = \frac{hypotenuse}{adjacent} = \frac{c}{a}$$

$$\tan\beta = \frac{opposite}{adjacent} = \frac{b}{a} \qquad \cot\beta = \frac{adjacent}{opposite} = \frac{a}{b}$$

4. Yes, it is a right triangle. Twenty-nine is the largest side so it is the hypotenuse. Since the question wants to know about the smallest angle, and 20 is the smallest side, then 20 is the side opposite the smallest angle. Twenty-one is the adjacent side to the smallest angle.

$$\sin\theta = \frac{opposite}{hypotenuse} = \frac{20}{29} \qquad \csc\theta = \frac{hypotenuse}{opposite} = \frac{29}{20}$$

$$\cos\theta = \frac{adjacent}{hypotenuse} = \frac{21}{29} \qquad \sec\theta = \frac{hypotenuse}{adjacent} = \frac{29}{21}$$

$$\tan\theta = \frac{opposite}{adjacent} = \frac{20}{21} \qquad \cot\theta = \frac{adjacent}{opposite} = \frac{21}{20}$$

T8 Answers

1. $\cot 65° = \tan(90° - 65°) = \tan 25°$
2. $\sec 35° = \csc(90° - 35°) = \csc 55°$

3. $\sec\dfrac{\pi}{3} = \csc\left(\dfrac{\pi}{2} - \dfrac{\pi}{3}\right) = \csc\dfrac{\pi}{6}$

4. $\cos\dfrac{\pi}{2} = \sin\left(\dfrac{\pi}{2} - \dfrac{\pi}{2}\right) = \sin 0 = 0$

T9 Answers

Trigonometric Function Values of Special Angles						
θ	$\sin\theta$	$\cos\theta$	$\tan\theta$	$\cot\theta$	$\sec\theta$	$\csc\theta$
1. $30° = \dfrac{\pi}{6}$	$\dfrac{1}{2}$	$\dfrac{\sqrt{3}}{2}$	$\dfrac{\sqrt{3}}{3}$	$\sqrt{3}$	$\dfrac{2\sqrt{3}}{3}$	2
2. $60° = \dfrac{\pi}{3}$	$\dfrac{\sqrt{3}}{2}$	$\dfrac{1}{2}$	$\sqrt{3}$	$\dfrac{\sqrt{3}}{3}$	2	$\dfrac{2\sqrt{3}}{3}$

3. If the hypotenuse is 4 feet, then the short leg is 2 feet an the long leg is $2\sqrt{3}$ feet. So the perimeter is the sum of the three sides: $4 + 2 + 2\sqrt{3} = 6 + 2\sqrt{3}$ feet.

T10 Answers

1. $4\sqrt{2}$ feet
2. Same sqaure as #1: $4\sqrt{2}$ feet
3. Since the diagonal is 5 the length of the side of the square is obtained by dividing the diagonal by the square root of 2. We multiply by 4 to find the perimeter.

$$4\left(\frac{5}{\sqrt{2}}\right) = \frac{20}{\sqrt{2}}\left(\frac{\sqrt{2}}{\sqrt{2}}\right) = \frac{20\sqrt{2}}{2} = 10\sqrt{2} \text{ feet}$$

T11 Answers

Solve each of the following triangles.
1. A = 71.15°, B = 68.37°, C =40.48°, a = 7.01 cm, b = 6.89 cm, c = 4.81 cm

2. A = 43.96°, B = 83.20°, C =52.84°, a = 7.01 cm, b = 10.03 cm, c = 8.05 cm

3. A = 17.09°, B = 143.50°, C =19.41°, a = 5.82 cm, b = 11.78 cm, c = 6.58 cm

T12 Answers

1. B = 73.58°, a = 11.34 cm c = 5.73 cm, A = 76.93°, C = 29.5°, b = 11.17 cm

2. B = 80.01°, a = 10.87 cm c = 16.23 cm, A = 36.75°, C = 63.25°, b = 17.9 cm

3. B = 30.03°, a = 11.56 cm c = 12.09 cm, A = 70.19°, C = 79.77°, b = 6.15 cm

CHAPTER SEVEN

MATHEMATICS PRACTICE TESTS

This chapter contains a practice test for Pre–algebra, Algebra, College Algebra, Geometry, and Trigonometry—five tests in all. Each test consists of twenty questions in no particular order. Make sure you know which tests to study for. Many people will not have to take the geometry or trigonometry tests at all, so may not want to spend any time practicing for it.

When you prepare for COMPASS using these tests on the following pages, work on them one question at a time. As soon as you select an answer, turn to the solution section at the end of each test and see how you did. Make sure you understand how to get the correct answer before you move on to another problem.

The tests in this book are longer than the one you will take for COMPASS, unless you take multiple mathematics test in your test session. Most COMPASS test sessions will be seventeen problems or less. Do not try to guess your score by the number of problems you take.

Look over the hints in the mathematics introduction at the beginning of Chapter 2, but always keep in mind the most important thing: TIME DOES NOT MATTER. Take as long as you want on any problem.

TEST ONE PRE–ALGEBRA

Select the best answer.

1. Simplify. $23 + (-8) + 22 - (-12) + 8$
   - ❍ A. 17
   - ❍ B. 33
   - ❍ C. 49
   - ❍ D. 57
   - ❍ E. 45

2. Compute. $\dfrac{3}{8} + \dfrac{4}{5}$
   - ❍ A. $\dfrac{7}{13}$
   - ❍ B. $\dfrac{3}{10}$
   - ❍ C. $\dfrac{7}{40}$
   - ❍ D. $\dfrac{11}{20}$
   - ❍ E. $\dfrac{47}{40}$

3. Divide. $\dfrac{5}{9} \div \dfrac{7}{18}$

   ○ A. $\dfrac{35}{162}$

   ○ B. $\dfrac{4}{9}$

   ○ C. $\dfrac{7}{10}$

   ○ D. $1\dfrac{3}{7}$

   ○ E. $2\dfrac{1}{7}$

4. Simplify. $\dfrac{4}{5} + \dfrac{5}{9} \cdot \dfrac{-4}{7} - \dfrac{4}{5}$

   ○ A. $1\dfrac{13}{35}$

   ○ B. $-\dfrac{20}{63}$

   ○ C. $\dfrac{8}{27}$

   ○ D. 0

   ○ E. $1\dfrac{16}{45}$

5. Jack is making pencil holders for a yard sale. Each pencil holder costs $1.20 to make. If he sells the pencil holders for $2.00 each, how many will he have to sell to make a profit of exactly $20.00?

   ○ A. 10
   ○ B. 15
   ○ C. 20
   ○ D. 25
   ○ E. 30

6. What is the average (arithmetic mean) of 10, 9, 5, 7, 7, 4, and 4?

   ○ A. $4\dfrac{6}{7}$

   ○ B. $5\dfrac{3}{4}$

   ○ C. $6\dfrac{4}{7}$

   ○ D. 6.5

   ○ E. $7\dfrac{2}{3}$

7. Simplify. 30 – 3 x 4 + 6

- ○ A. 0
- ○ B. 24
- ○ C. 52
- ○ D. 86
- ○ E. 270

8. Simplify. $\dfrac{14 - 9}{4^2 - 2^3}$

- ○ A. $\dfrac{5}{12}$
- ○ B. $\dfrac{1}{4}$
- ○ C. $\dfrac{5}{8}$
- ○ D. $\dfrac{23}{24}$
- ○ E. $2\dfrac{1}{2}$

9. 16 is 25% of what number?

- ○ A. 4
- ○ B. 40
- ○ C. 400
- ○ D. 32
- ○ E. 64

10. A shirt has been marked down 20% and now sells for $12.60. What was the original selling price?

- ○ A. $10.08
- ○ B. $11.80
- ○ C. $13.40
- ○ D. $15.12
- ○ E. $15.75

11. Pat charged $300 worth of goods on her credit card. On her first bill, she was not charged any interest, and she made a payment of $80. She then charged another $50 worth of goods. On her second bill, a month later, she was charged 3% interest on her entire unpaid balance. How much interest was Pat charged on her second bill?

- ○ A. $7.70
- ○ B. $8.10
- ○ C. $9.00
- ○ D. $9.70
- ○ E. $12.90

12. If four pounds of bananas cost $1.60, what is the cost of 10 pounds?

   ○ A. $0.40
   ○ B. $2.40
   ○ C. $3.20
   ○ D. $3.60
   ⊘ E. $4.00

13. The largest prime factor of 90 is

   ○ A. 2
   ○ B. 3
   ⊘ C. (5)
   ○ D. 6 ✗
   ○ E. 11 ✗

14. What is the least common multiple of 6, 8, and 12?

   ○ A. 12
   ○ B. 18
   ⊘ C. 24
   ○ D. 48
   ○ E. 72

15. How many yards of material remain from a 24-yard length after two pieces, each 2 1/2 yards long, and four pieces, each 3 1/4 yards long, are removed?

   ○ A. $5\frac{3}{4}$
   ⊘ B. 6
   ○ C. $6\frac{1}{4}$
   ○ D. 18
   ○ E. $18\frac{1}{4}$

16. What is the average (arithmetic mean) of 8, 12, 18, 13, 11, 14?

   ○ A. 7
   ○ B. 11
   ○ C. $11\frac{1}{3}$
   ○ D. 12
   ⊘ E. $12\frac{2}{3}$

17. What is the meaning of 3^5?

   ⊘ A. $3 \cdot 3 \cdot 3 \cdot 3 \cdot 3$

   ○ B. 15

   ○ C. $3 \cdot 5$

   ○ D. $5 \cdot 5 \cdot 5$

   ○ E. $\dfrac{3}{5}$

18. Multiply 1.2 x 8.5

   ○ A. .92

   ○ B. 9.2

   ○ C. .102

   ○ D. 1.02

   ⊘ E. 10.2

19. What is 40% of 70?

   ○ A. 18

   ○ B. 20

   ○ C. 24

   ⊘ D. 28

   ○ E. 35

20. Six pieces of wire are cut from a length of wire that is 50 feet long. Two of the pieces are each 12 $^1/_3$ feet long. Two of the pieces are 3 1/4 feet long each. Two of the pieces are 8 1/2 feet long each. How many feet of wire is left from the original length?

   ⊘ A. $1 \dfrac{5}{6}$

   ○ B. $1 \dfrac{1}{12}$

   ○ C. $25 \dfrac{11}{12}$

   ○ D. $24 \dfrac{1}{12}$

   ○ E. 4

Answers and solutions on next page

1. D
2. E
3. D
4. B
5. D
6. C
7. B
8. C
9. E
10. E
11. B
12. E
13. C
14. C
15. B
16. E
17. A
18. E
19. D
20. A

SOLUTIONS FOR TEST 1

1. Simplify. 23 + (–8) + 22 – (–12) + 8

Answer D

$$23 + (–8) + 22 – (–12) + 8$$
$$15 + 22 – (–12) + 8$$
$$15 + 22 + 12 + 8$$
$$37 + 12 + 8$$
$$49 + 8$$
$$57$$

▶ NOTE: The answers are in ascending order.

▶ Distractors, the incorrect answers, are computed with the same numbers with the wrong signs. This problem is about signed numbers. The only way to get it wrong is by adding wrong. Therefore, take your time. And do the problem several times before you select your answer.

2. Compute. $\dfrac{3}{8} + \dfrac{4}{5}$

Answer E

$$\frac{3}{8} + \frac{4}{5} = \frac{3}{8}\left(\frac{5}{5}\right) + \frac{4}{5}\left(\frac{8}{8}\right) = \frac{15}{40} + \frac{32}{40} = \frac{47}{40}$$

▶ Note that some of the distractors do not even have the common denominator.

▶ Some of the distractors have been reduced.

3.   **Divide.** $\dfrac{5}{9} \div \dfrac{7}{18}$

Answer D

$$\frac{5}{9} \div \frac{7}{18} = \frac{5}{9} \cdot \frac{18}{7} = \frac{5}{1} \cdot \frac{2}{7} = \frac{10}{7} = 1\frac{3}{7}$$

▶   Don't ask why, just flip and multiply.

4.   **Simplify** $\dfrac{4}{5} + \dfrac{5}{9} \cdot \dfrac{-4}{7} - \dfrac{4}{5}$

Answer B

▶   First notice 4/5 and – 4/5 wash out.

$$\frac{5}{9} \cdot \frac{-4}{7} = -\frac{20}{63}$$

5.   **Jack is making pencil holders for a yard sale. Each pencil holder costs \$1.20 to make. If he sells the pencil holders for \$2.00 each, how many will he have to sell to make a profit of exactly \$20.00.**

Answer D

Jack is making \$0.80 profit per sale. Divide 20 by 0.8.

$$\frac{20}{0.8} = \frac{200}{8} = \frac{100}{4} = 25$$

▶   Profit is the difference in revenue and costs.

6.   **What is the average (arithmetic mean) of 10, 9, 5, 7, 7, 4, and 4?**

Answer C

$$\frac{10 + 9 + 5 + 7 + 7 + 4 + 4}{7} = \frac{46}{7} = 6\frac{4}{7}$$

▶   Memorize this method; it will give you confidence.

7.   **Simplify. 30 – 3 x 4 + 6**

Answer B

     30 – 3 x 4 + 6
     30 – 12 + 6
     18 + 6
     24

▶   Order of Operations

8. **Simplify.** $\dfrac{14 - 9}{4^2 - 2^3}$

Answer C

$$\frac{14 - 9}{4^2 - 2^3} = \frac{14 - 9}{16 - 8} = \frac{5}{8}$$

▶ Exponents come first.

9. **16 is 25% of what number?**

Answer E

$$16 = 25\% \text{ of } w?$$
$$16 = 0.25(w)$$
$$\frac{16}{0.25} = w$$
$$w = \frac{16}{0.25} \cdot \frac{100}{100} = \frac{16 \cdot 100}{25} = 16 \cdot 4 = 64$$

10. **A shirt has been marked down 20% and now sells for \$12.60. What was the original selling price?**

Answer E

If a shirt has been marked down 20%, that means the current selling price is 80% of the original. In other words, \$12.60 is 80% of what?

$$\$12.60 = 80\% \text{ of } w?$$
$$12.6 = 0.8(w)$$
$$\frac{12.6}{0.8} = w$$
$$w = \frac{12.6}{0.8} \cdot \frac{10}{10} = \frac{126}{8} = \frac{63}{4} = \$15.75$$

11. **Pat charged \$300 worth of goods on her credit card. On her first bill, she was not charged any interest, and she made a payment of \$80. She then charged another \$50 worth of goods. On her second bill, a month later, she was charged 3% interest on her entire unpaid balance. How much interest was Pat charged on her second bill?**

Answer B

$300 - 80 = 220$	(1st month purchases) − (payment) = balance after first month
$220 + 50 = 270$	(balance brought forward) + (purchase) = unpaid balance
$270 \cdot 0.03 = 8.10$	(unpaid balance) • 3% = interest \$8.10

▶ Take a problem like this one step at a time.

▶ Write down what things mean.

12. **If four pounds of bananas cost \$1.60, what is the cost of 10 pounds?**

Answer E

$1.60 / 4 = \$0.40$. Each pound costs \$0.40. Ten pounds would cost \$4.00.

▶ Figure the cost per unit then multiply by the desired number of units.

▶ You could use a proportion to solve as well.

13. **The largest prime factor of 90 is**

Answer C

  A. 2
  B. 3
  C. 5
  D. 6
  E. 11

▶ Process of elimination. 11 will not divide into 90. 6 is not a prime.

▶ Numbers 13 and 14 are good examples of working backwards from the given answers.

14. **What is the least common multiple of 6, 8, and 12?**

Answer C

  A. 12
  B. 18
  C. 24
  D. 48
  E. 72

▶ Process of elimination. 8 will not divide into 12 or 18.

15. **How many yards of material remain from a 24-yard length after two pieces, each 2 1/2 yards long, and four pieces 3 1/4 yards long, are removed.**

Answer B

$$24 - 2(2\,\tfrac{1}{2}) - 4(3\,\tfrac{1}{4}) = 24 - 5 - 13 = 19 - 13 = 6$$

▶ Make sure you answer the question that is asked. Don't go for a distractor just because it is an answer in an intermediate step.

▶ Take your time, it is only a fraction.

16. **What is the average (arithmetic mean) of 8, 12, 18, 13, 11, 14?**

Answer E

$$\frac{8 + 12 + 18 + 13 + 11 + 14}{6} = \frac{76}{6} = 12\frac{2}{3}$$

17. **What is the meaning of 3^5?**

Answer A

$3 \cdot 3 \cdot 3 \cdot 3 \cdot 3$

▶ Repeat 3 five times as a factor.

18. **Multiply 1.2 x 8.5.**

Answer E

▶ Count the number of decimals behind the point.

▶ If you multiply by a number bigger than 1, 1.2 in this case, you must get a number bigger than what you started with. B and E are the only possibilities.

19. **What is 40% of 70?**

Answer D

$w = 40\% \cdot 70$
$w = 0.4 \cdot 70$
$w = 28$

▶ "**of**" means **x** (multiply), and "**is**" means **=** (equals)

20. **Six pieces of wire are cut from a length of wire that is 50 feet long. Two of the pieces are 12 1/3 feet long. Two of the pieces are 3 1/4 feet long. Two of the pieces are 8 1/2 feet long. How many feet of wire is left from the original length?**

Answer A

$50 - 2(12\,{}^1\!/_3) - 2(3{}^1\!/_4) - 2(8{}^1\!/_2) = 1\,{}^5\!/_6$

TEST TWO ALGEBRA

Select the best answer.

1. If x = –1 and y = 3, what is the value of the expression $3x^3 - 2xy$?

   ○ A. –9
   ○ B. –3
   ○ C. 3
   ○ D. 9
   ○ E. 21

2. Which of the following expressions represents the product of three less than x and five more than twice x?

   ○ A. $2x^2 + 11x + 15$
   ○ B. $2x^2 - 11x + 15$
   ○ C. $2x^2 + x - 15$
   ○ D. $2x^2 - x - 15$
   ○ E. $2x^2 + 22x + 15$

3. A student earned scores of 83, 78, and 77 on three of four tests. What must the student score on the fourth test to have an average (arithmetic mean) of exactly 80?

   ○ A. 80
   ○ B. 82
   ○ C. 84
   ○ D. 85
   ○ E. 86

4. What is the equation of the line that contains the points (2, 3) and (14, –6)?

   ○ A. $y = -\dfrac{3}{4}x + 5$

   ○ B. $y = -\dfrac{3}{4}x + \dfrac{9}{2}$

   ○ C. $y = \dfrac{3}{4}x + 5$

   ○ D. $y = -\dfrac{4}{3}x + \dfrac{17}{3}$

   ○ E. $y = -\dfrac{1}{2}x + \dfrac{5}{2}$

137

5. For all $x \neq \pm 4$, $\dfrac{x^2 - x - 20}{x^2 - 16} = ?$

- ○ A. $\dfrac{x + 5}{x - 4}$
- ○ B. $\dfrac{x + 4}{x - 4}$
- ○ C. $\dfrac{x - 5}{x + 4}$
- ○ D. $\dfrac{x + 5}{x + 4}$
- ○ E. $\dfrac{x - 5}{x - 4}$

6. A rope 36 feet long is cut into three pieces. The second piece is four feet longer than the first, and the last piece is three times as long as the second. If x represents the length of the first piece, then which equation determines the length of the first piece?

- ○ A. $36 = 5x + 8$
- ○ B. $36 = x + (x + 4) + (3x)$
- ○ C. $36 = 3x + 12$
- ○ D. $36 = x + (x + 4) + 3(x + 4)$
- ○ E. $36 = 3x + 16$

7. The product $(x^2 + 3)(x - 1)$ is

- ○ A. $x^3 + 3x^2 - x - 3$
- ○ B. $x^2 + 2x - 3$
- ○ C. $3x - 3$
- ○ D. $x^3 - 3$
- ○ E. $x^3 - x^2 + 3x - 3$

8. If n is an integer, which expression must be an even integer?

- ○ A. $2n + 1$
- ○ B. $2n - 1$
- ○ C. $n + 1$
- ○ D. $2n^2$
- ○ E. n^2

9. If $x = -3$, what is the value of $2x^2 + 3x - 5$?

- ○ A. -22
- ○ B. -6
- ○ C. -5
- ○ D. 4
- ○ E. 22

10.   Which of the following is the complete factorization of $2x^2 - 13x - 24$?

⭘ A. $(2x - 6)(x + 4)$

⭘ B. $(x - 6)(2x + 4)$

⭘ C. $(2x - 3)(x - 8)$

⭘ D. $(2x + 3)(x - 8)$

⭘ E. $2(x + 3)(x - 4)$

11.   Which of these is the product of $(a + 2b)$ and $(c - d)$?

⭘ A. $ac + ad + bc - 2bd$

⭘ B. $ac - ad + bc - 2bd$

⭘ C. $ac - ad + bc - 2bd$

⭘ D. $ac - ad + 2bc + 2bd$

⭘ E. $ac - ad + 2bc - 2bd$

12.   If $a = -2$ and $b = 3$, what is the value of the expression $3(a + b)(a - b)$?

⭘ A. -5

⭘ B. 5

⭘ C. 15

⭘ D. -15

⭘ E. 75

13.   This is a graph of which equation?

⭘ A. $y = -\dfrac{3}{2}x + 6$

⭘ B. $y = \dfrac{3}{2}x + 6$

⭘ C. $y = \dfrac{2}{3}x + 6$

⭘ D. $y = -\dfrac{2}{3}x + 6$

⭘ E. $y = -\dfrac{2}{3}x - 6$

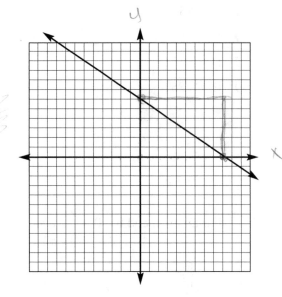

14.   What is the solution to the equation $2(x + 3) - 3(x + 5) = 13$?

⭘ A. -22

⭘ B. -12

⭘ C. -4

⭘ D. 5

⭘ E. 15

15. Peggy gets paid a weekly salary of D dollars a week plus a commission of 8% on her total sales S. Which expression below best describes Peggy's weekly pay?

  ○ A. D + S

  ○ B. 8D + S

  ○ C. D + 8S

  ○ D. D + .08S

  ○ E. .08(D + S)

16. Which of these is the product of $(D^3 + 2D^2 - 2D + 3)$ and $(D - 5)$?

  ○ A. $D^4 + 2D^3 - 2D^2 + 3D$

  ○ B. $D^4 - 3D^3 - 8D^2 + 13D - 15$

  ○ C. $D^4 - 3D^2 - 12D^2 + 13D + 15$

  ○ D. $D^4 + 7D^3 + 12D^2 + 13D + 15$

  ○ E. $D^4 - 3D^3 - 12D^2 + 13D - 15$

17. What is the distance from point A to point B?

  ○ A. 13

  ○ B. 85

  ○ C. $\sqrt{5}$

  ○ D. $\sqrt{13}$

  ○ E. $\sqrt{85}$

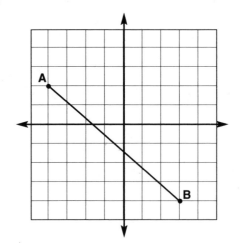

18. For all $a \neq 0$ and $b \neq 0$, $\dfrac{a^{-3}b^2}{a^5b^{-4}}$

  ○ A. $\dfrac{a^2}{b^2}$

  ○ B. $\dfrac{b^3}{a^4}$

  ○ C. $\dfrac{b^6}{a^2}$

  ○ D. $\dfrac{b^6}{a^8}$

  ○ E. $\dfrac{1}{a^2b^2}$

19. For all a, b, and c, $(a^3b^2c)^2$

   ○ A. $a^5b^4c^2$

   ○ B. $a^6b^4c^2$

   ○ C. $a^9b^4c^2$

   ○ D. $a^5b^4c^3$

   ○ E. $2a^3b^2c$

20. For all x, $3(2x + 5) - 4(x - 2) = 3(2x + 2) + 1$

   ○ A. $x = 9$

   ○ B. $x = -5$

   ○ C. $x = 4$

   ○ D. $x = 3$

   ○ E. $x = 0$

Answers and solutions on next page

ANSWERS FOR TEST 2

1.	C
2.	D
3.	B
4.	B
5.	E
6.	D
7.	E
8.	D
9.	D
10.	D
11.	E
12.	D
13.	D
14.	A
15.	D
16.	E
17.	E
18.	D
19.	B
20.	C

SOLUTIONS TO TEST 2

1. **If x = –1 and y = 3, what is the value of the expression $3x^3 – 2xy$?**

Answer C

$$3(-1)^3 - 2(-1)(3) =$$
$$3(-1) - 2(-1)(3) =$$
$$-3 - (-6) =$$
$$-3 + 6 =$$
$$3$$

2. **Which of the following expressions represents the product of three less than x and five more than twice x?**

Answer D

This question asks to multiply the binomials "3 less than x" $(x – 3)$ and "five more than twice x" $(2x + 5)$

$$(x - 3)(2x + 5) = 2x^2 + 5x - 6x - 15 = 2x^2 - x - 15$$

142

3. A student earned scores of 83, 78, and 77 on three of four tests. What must the student score on the fourth test to have an average (arithmetic mean) of exactly 80?

Answer B

$$\frac{83 + 78 + 77 + x}{4} = 80$$

$$4 \cdot \frac{83 + 78 + 77 + x}{4} = 80 \cdot 4$$

$$83 + 78 + 77 + x = 320$$

$$238 + x = 320$$

$$x = 320 - 238$$

$$x = 82$$

4. What is the equation of the line that contains the points (2, 3) and (14, –6)?

Answer B

► Note that all of the answers are presented in y = mx + b format. Find the slope first. This eliminates every answer except for A and B.

$$m = \frac{y_2 - y_1}{x_2 - x_1} = \frac{3 - (-6)}{2 - 14} = \frac{9}{-12} = -\frac{3}{4}$$

► Now we must find the value of b. We could plug either ordered pair into the equation. Let's choose (2, 3) since the numbers are smaller and we will not have to worry about negative signs.

$$y = mx + b$$

$$(3) = -\frac{3}{4}(2) + b$$

$$3 = -\frac{3}{2} + b$$

$$3 + \frac{3}{2} = b$$

$$\frac{6}{2} + \frac{3}{2} = b$$

$$\frac{9}{2} = b$$

► Therefore, the answer is B.

► Note that if you did not remember the slope formula and the slope intercept for the line, you could just plug in both points into all five choices until you eliminate four of them.

5.   For all $x \neq \pm4$, $\dfrac{x^2 - x - 20}{x^2 - 16}$ = ?

Answer E

▶ This problem is both a rational expression problem and a factoring problem.

Factor the numerator: Factor the denominator:
$x^2 - x - 20 = (x - 5)(x + 4)$ $x^2 - 16 = (x + 4)(x - 4)$

▶ The $(x + 4)$ cancel and you are left with answer E.

▶ Pay close attention to the signs. Every possibility is covered in the distractors.

6.   **A rope 36 feet long is cut into three pieces. The second piece is four feet longer than the first, and the last piece is three times as long as the second. If x represents the length of the first piece, then which equation determines the length of the first piece?**

Answer D

▶ Let x represent the first length. Then $(x + 4)$ represents the second. The third length is 3 times the second (not 3 times the first): $3(x + 4)$. Therefore, the equation is D.

$x + (x + 4) + 3(x + 4) = 36$

▶ If you have some alternate way of finding that the length of the shortest rope is 4, you can plug it in until you find the equation that works.

7.   **The product $(x^2 + 3)(x - 1)$ is**

Answer E

▶ This is just a binomial times a binomial, which is a FOIL problem.

$(x^2 + 3)(x - 1) = x^3 - x^2 + 3x - 3$

8.   **If n is an integer, which expression must be an even integer?**

Answer D

Most people will do a problem like this by process of elimination.

▶ If you plug any number into A or B you always get an odd number so we can eliminate them as possible answers.

▶ If you plug 3 into C you get an even number, but if you plug 4 into C you get an odd number, so eliminate it.

▶ If you plug any odd number into E you get an odd number.

▶ Therefore, the only possible answer is D.

Some people will think about the definition of even (any integer divisible by 2) and see that since $2n^2$ is a product of some number (n^2) and 2 that it will always be even.

9. **If x = –3, what is the value of 2x² + 3x – 5?**

Answer D

$$2(-3)^2 + 3(-3) - 5 =$$
$$2(9) + 3(-3) - 5 =$$
$$18 - 9 - 5 =$$
$$4$$

10. **Which of the following is the complete factorization of 2x² – 13x –24?**

Answer D

► If you cannot factor, just FOIL out each of the distractors.

11. **Which of these is the product of (a + 2b) and (c – d)?**

Answer E

$$FOIL(a + 2b)(c - d) = ac - ad + 2bc - 2bd$$

► Watch out for signs when you select your answer.

12. **If a = –2 and b = 3, what is the value of the expression 3(a + b)(a – b)?**

Answer D

$$3(a + b)(a - b)$$
$$3((-2) + (3))((-2) - (3)) =$$
$$3(1)(-5) =$$
$$3(-5) = -15$$

► Check your work carefully. Suppose you left the three off the beginning of the multiplication. Distractor A = –5 is there and would look very good to you. You could select that, think you had the correct answer, and never know it was wrong just because of that sneaky 3 in front of the FOIL.

13. **This is a graph of which equation?**

Answer D

► Do this problem by process of elimination.

► First, the slope is negative. That eliminates B and C. Second, the y intercept is +6, which eliminates E. So we must decide between A and D. Select any other point on the graph, (9, 0) for example, and plug it into both equations.

A. $0 = -\dfrac{3}{2}(9) + 6$

$0 = -\dfrac{27}{2} + \dfrac{12}{2}$

$0 = -\dfrac{15}{2}$ False

D. $0 = -\dfrac{2}{3}(9) + 6$

$0 = -\dfrac{18}{3} + 6$

$0 = -6 + 6$ True

14. **What is the solution to the equation 2(x + 3) – 3(x + 5) = 13?**

Answer A

$$2(x + 3) - 3(x + 5) = 13$$
$$2x + 6 - 3x - 15 = 13$$
$$-x - 9 = 13$$
$$-x = 22$$
$$x = -22$$

► Make certain in a distribution problem like this, that you distribute to every term with the correct sign. Many people miss the –3(5) multiplication in the second binomial and solve incorrectly as follows:

$$2(x + 3) - 3(x + 5) = 13$$
$$2x + 6 - 3x - 5 = 13$$
$$-x + 1 = 13$$
$$-x = 12$$
$$x = -12 \quad \text{INCORRECT}$$

► This happens to be distractor B. The other distractors contain similar small errors. Take your time and don't commit the small fatal error.

15. **Peggy gets paid a weekly salary of D dollars a week plus a commission of 8% on her total sales S. Which expression below best describes Peggy's weekly pay?**

    A.   D + S
    B.   8D + S
    C.   D + 8S
    D.   D + .08S
    E.   .08(D + S)

Answer D

► This is another process of elimination problem.

    A.   Does not work because there is no 8% involved.

    B.   Does not work because the 8% is on the D salary. Also, the % conversion is wrong.

    C.   Does not work because the % conversion is wrong.

    E.   Does not work because the 8% is on the D salary.

    D.   Does work.

16. **Which of these is the product of $(D^3 + 2D^2 - 2D + 3)$ and $(D - 5)$?**

Answer E

▶ The word "product" indicates that you need to multiply the polynomial by the binomial. This means that there will be a total of eight multiplications before you are finished. Make sure each term of the binomial is multiplied by each term of the polynomial.

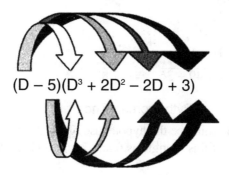

$$(D - 5)(D^3 + 2D^2 - 2D + 3)$$

▶ Sometimes it helps to rewrite this type of multiplication as a monomial times a polynomial plus a monomial times a polynomial:

$D(D^3 + 2D^2 - 2D + 3) = D^4 + 2D^2 + 3D$ (notice that each exponent went up by 1)

$+$

$(-5)(D^3 + 2D^2 - 2D + 3) = -5D^3 - 10D^2 + 10D - 15$ (notice that each term changed signs because of the negative 5)

▶ And carefully and watch signs.

$$\begin{array}{r} D^4 + 2D^3 - 2D^2 + 3D \\ + \quad\quad - 5D^3 - 10D^2 + 10D - 15 \\ \hline D^4 - 3D^3 - 12D^2 + 13D - 15 \end{array}$$

▶ Look carefully at the difference between the choices given. Choices B and E are almost identical:

B. $D^4 - 3D^3 - 8D^2 + 13D - 15$
E. $D^4 - 3D^3 - 12D^2 + 13D - 15$

▶ When selecting your answer, make sure you get the one that you want and not just the one that looks like the answer you want.

17. **What is the distance from point A to point B?**

Answer E

▶ There are two ways to do this problem: with the Distance Formula or the Pythagorean Theorem.

Distance Formula

▶ First you have to find out what the points are: A (–4, 2) and B (3, –4) then plug those points into the distance formula.

$$d = \sqrt{(x_2 - x_1)^2 + (y_2 - y_1)^2}$$
$$d = \sqrt{(3 - (-4))^2 + ((-4) - 2)^2}$$
$$d = \sqrt{(7)^2 + (-6)^2} \ = \ \sqrt{49 + 36} \ = \ \sqrt{85}$$

Pythagorean Theorem

▶ Notice that segment AB could be the hypotenuse of a right triangle with a vertex at (–4, –4). You can count the legs of this triangle as 6 and 7 units. Then plug this into the Pythagorean equation.

$$a^2 + b^2 = c^2$$
$$6^2 + 7^2 = c^2$$
$$36 + 49 = c^2$$
$$85 = c^2$$
$$\sqrt{85} = c$$

18. **For all a ≠ 0 and b ≠ 0,** $\dfrac{a^{-3}b^2}{a^5b^{-4}}$

Answer D

$$\frac{a^{-3}b^2}{a^5b^{-4}} \ = \ \frac{b^2b^4}{a^5a^3} \ = \ \frac{b^6}{a^8}$$

▶ First make all of the exponents positive, then add the exponents of like bases.

19. **For all a, b, and c, $(a^3b^2c)^2$**

Answer B

▶ When taking a power to a power, just multiply the exponents. Since we are raising the expression to the second power, each exponent gets doubled.

20. **For all x, 3(2x + 5) – 4(x –2) = 3(2x + 2) + 1**

Answer C

$$3(2x + 5) - 4(x - 2) = 3(2x + 2) + 1$$
$$6x + 15 - 4x + 8 = 6x + 6 + 1$$
$$2x + 23 = 6x + 7$$
$$23 - 7 = 6x - 2x$$
$$16 = 4x$$
$$4 = x$$

TEST THREE COLLEGE ALGEBRA

Select the best answer.

1. If $F(x) = 2x^2 + 3x - 8$, then $F(-2) = ?$
   - ○ A. -22
   - ○ B. -10
   - ○ C. -6
   - ○ D. -2
   - ○ E. $-4x^2 - 6x + 16$

2. If $g(3) = 9$ and $g(1) = 5$, which of the following could represent $g(x)$?
   - ○ A. $x + 4$
   - ○ B. $2x + 3$
   - ○ C. $3x$
   - ○ D. $4x - 3$
   - ○ E. $x^2 - 4x + 12$

3. If $\dfrac{y^{\frac{3}{2}}}{y^{\frac{1}{3}}} = y^k$, then $k =$
   - ○ A. 2
   - ○ B. -2
   - ○ C. $\dfrac{7}{6}$
   - ○ D. $-\dfrac{7}{6}$
   - ○ E. $\dfrac{1}{2}$

4. If $a = 3b + 2$ and $b = 7 - 2c$, express a in terms of c.
   - ○ A. $a = -6c + 23$
   - ○ B. $a = 6c - 23$
   - ○ C. $a = 21 - 6c$
   - ○ D. $a = 2c - 21$
   - ○ E. $a = 10b - c$

5. For $i = \sqrt{-1}$, if $2i(4 - 3i) = x + 8i$, then $x = ?$
   - ○ A. 6
   - ○ B. 8
   - ○ C. $6i$
   - ○ D. $-6i$
   - ○ E. $-8i$

6. Let $F(x) = 2x^2 + 3x - 5$ and $G(x) = x + 5$, then $F \circ G(x) =$

- A. 36
- B. $2x^2 + 3x$
- C. $2x^2 + 4x$
- D. $2x^2 + 23x + 60$
- E. $2x^3 + 13x^2 + 10x - 25$

7. For all x such that $x^2 + 25 = 0$, $x = ?$

- A. -25
- B. 5
- C. ± 5
- D. $5i$
- E. $\pm 5i$

8. For all x such that $\dfrac{18}{\sqrt{x^2 + 4}} = 6$, $x^2 = ?$

- A. 9
- B. 5
- C. $\sqrt{5}$
- D. $\dfrac{9}{4}$
- E. -13

9. If $F(x) = 2x + 5$ then $F^{-1}(x) = ?$

- A. $\dfrac{x + 5}{2}$
- B. $-2x - 5$
- C. $\dfrac{x - 2}{5}$
- D. $\dfrac{x - 5}{2}$
- E. $\dfrac{4x + 10}{2}$

10. For $a > 0$, $\sqrt{a} \cdot \sqrt[3]{a^2}$?

- A. $\sqrt[4]{a^3}$
- B. $\sqrt[4]{a^2}$
- C. $\sqrt[3]{a^5}$
- D. $\sqrt[6]{a^3}$
- E. $a\sqrt[6]{a}$

11. If $i = \sqrt{-1}$, then express $\sqrt{-72x^3}$ in terms of i and simplify.

- ○ A. $4x\sqrt{-18x}$
- ○ B. $4x\sqrt{18x^3}$
- ○ C. $6xi\sqrt{2x}$
- ○ D. $xi\sqrt{72x}$
- ○ E. $6x\sqrt{2xi}$

12. Simplify $9^{\frac{7}{10}} \cdot 9^{\frac{4}{5}}$

- ○ A. $9^{\frac{14}{25}}$
- ○ B. 3
- ○ C. 9
- ○ D. 27
- ○ E. 81

13. What are the roots, where the function equals zero, of the function $f(x) = x^3 - 3x^2 - 4x + 12$?

- ○ A. 4, 3
- ○ B. 4, –3
- ○ C. 2, 3
- ○ D. 2, –2, 3
- ○ E. 2, –2, –3

14. In which interval does the function $h(x) = -3x^2 + 12x - 9$ obtain its maximum value?

- ○ A. between –3.5 and –0.5
- ○ B. between –0.5 and 1.5
- ○ C. between 1.5 and 3.5
- ○ D. between 3.5 and 5.5
- ○ E. between 5.5 and 7.5

15. For $p \neq 0$, $\left(\dfrac{1}{P}\right)^{x^2} = P^{-4}$, for what values of x?

- ○ A. 4
- ○ B. ± 4
- ○ C. 0
- ○ D. 2
- ○ E. ± 2

16. If $i = \sqrt{-1}$, $i^2 + i^3 + i^4 + i^5 + i^6 =$

- ○ A. 0
- ○ B. 1
- ○ C. –1
- ○ D. i
- ○ E. –i

17. What is the sum of the solutions of $2x^2 = 7x + 15$?

    A. $-\dfrac{7}{2}$

    B. $-\dfrac{3}{2}$

    C. $\dfrac{3}{2}$

    D. $\dfrac{7}{2}$

    E. $\dfrac{13}{2}$

18. If $\dfrac{2x^2 + kx - 15}{x - 5} = 2x + 3$, then $k = ?$

    A.   7
    B. -7
    C.   0
    D.   2
    E. -2

19. The operation $\star$ is defined to be: $x \star y = 3x - 2y$. If $4 \star a = 8$, then $a = ?$

    A.   4
    B. -4
    C. -1
    D.   2
    E. -2

20. For what values of x is the equation $\log_2 x + \log_2 (x - 2) = 3$ true?

    A.   4
    B. ± 4
    C.   2
    D. ± 2
    E.   2, 4

Answers and solutions on next page

ANSWERS FOR TEST 3

1. C
2. B
3. C
4. A
5. A
6. D
7. E
8. B
9. D
10. E
11. C
12. D
13. D
14. C
15. E
16. C
17. D
18. B
19. D
20. A

SOLUTIONS FOR TEST 3

1. **If F(x) = 2x² + 3x − 8, then F(−2) = ?**

Answer C

$$2(-2)^2 + 3(-2) - 8$$
$$= 2(4) + 3(-2) - 8$$
$$= 8 + (-6) - 8$$
$$= -6$$

2. **If g(3) = 9 and g(1) = 5, which of the following could represent g(x)?**

Answer B

► Do this problem by process of elimination. Find the choice that will give you a 9 when you plug in a 3 and a 5 when you plug in a 1.

► When you plug in a 3, you get 9 for all choices except A. So eliminate choice A. When you plug 1 into the rest of the choices, B is the only one that will yield a 5. Therefore the answer is B.

3. If $\dfrac{y^{\frac{3}{2}}}{y^{\frac{1}{3}}} = y^k$, then k =

Answer C

▶ When dividing like bases, subtract exponents.

$$k = \frac{3}{2} - \frac{1}{3} = \frac{9}{6} - \frac{2}{6} = \frac{9-2}{6} = \frac{7}{6}$$

4. If a = 3b + 2 and b = 7 − 2c, express a in terms of c.

Answer A

▶ Substitute b = 7 − 2c into a = 3b + 2

a = 3(7 − 2c) + 2
a = 21 − 6c + 2
a = 23 − 6c   which is the same as a = −6c + 23

5. For $i = \sqrt{-1}$, if 2i(4 − 3i) = x + 8i, then x = ?

Answer A

2i(4 − 3i) = x + 8i
8i − 6i² = x + 8i
8i + 6 = x + 8i
6 = x

6. Let F(x) = 2x² + 3x − 5 and G(x) = x + 5, then F ∘ G(x) =

Answer D

F ∘ G(x) = 2(x + 5)² + 3(x + 5) − 5
         = 2(x² + 10x + 25) + 3(x + 5) − 5
         = 2x² + 20x + 50 + 3x + 15 − 5
         = 2x² + 23 x + 60

7. For all x such that x² + 25 = 0, x = ?

Answer E

x² + 25 = 0
x² = −25
$\sqrt{x^2} = \pm \sqrt{-25}$
x = ±5i

8. For all x such that $\dfrac{18}{\sqrt{x^2 + 4}} = 6,\ \ x^2 = ?$

Answer B

► Watch out! This problem does not want to know what x is. This problem is looking for the value of x^2.

$$\dfrac{18}{\sqrt{x^2 + 4}} = 6$$

$$\dfrac{18}{6} = \sqrt{x^2 + 4}$$

$$3 = \sqrt{x^2 + 4}$$

$$3^2 = \sqrt{x^2 + 4}^2$$

$$9 = x^2 + 4$$

$$5 = x^2$$

9. If $F(x) = 2x + 5$ then $F^{-1}(x) = ?$

Answer D

$$F(x) = 2x + 5$$

1.	Replace F(x) with y	$y = 2x + 5$
2.	Swap x and y	$x = 2y + 5$
3.	Solve for y	$x - 5 = 2y$

$$\dfrac{x - 5}{2} = \dfrac{2y}{2} = y$$

4. Replace y with $F^{-1}(x)$ $\qquad\qquad F^{-1}(x) = \dfrac{x - 5}{2}$

10. For $a > 0$, $\quad \sqrt{a}\ \sqrt[3]{a^2}\quad ?$

Answer E

$$\sqrt{a}\ \sqrt[3]{a^2} = a^{\frac{1}{2}} \bullet a^{\frac{2}{3}} = a^{\frac{1}{2} + \frac{2}{3}} = a^{\frac{3}{6} + \frac{4}{6}} = a^{\frac{7}{6}} = \sqrt[6]{a^7} = a\sqrt[6]{a}$$

11. If $i = \sqrt{-1}$, then express $\sqrt{-72x^3}$ in terms of i and simplify.

Answer C

► The negative sign inside the radical tells you that the answer will have have an i in it. This eliminates choices A, B, and E.

► We know that $\sqrt{72} = \sqrt{36 \bullet 2} = 6\sqrt{2}$. This eliminates choice D; therefore, the answer is C.

12. Simplify $9^{\frac{7}{10}} \cdot 9^{\frac{4}{5}}$

Answer D

$$9^{\frac{7}{10}} \cdot 9^{\frac{4}{5}} = 9^{\frac{7}{10} + \frac{4}{5}} = 9^{\frac{7}{10} + \frac{8}{10}} = 9^{\frac{7+8}{10}} = 9^{\frac{15}{10}} = 9^{\frac{3}{2}} \quad (\sqrt{9})^3 = 3^3 = 27$$

13. What are the roots, where the function equals zero, of the function
$f(x) = x^3 - 3x^2 - 4x + 12$?

Answer D

$$f(x) = x^3 - 3x^2 - 4x + 12$$
$$0 = x^3 - 3x^2 - 4x + 12$$
$$0 = x^2(x - 3) - 4(x - 3)$$
$$0 = (x - 3)(x + 2)(x - 2)$$

$$x = \{3, -2, 2\}$$

14. In which interval does the function $h(x) = -3x^2 + 12x - 9$ obtain its maximum value?

Answer C

► Recall that the vertex of a parabola always has an x value of $-b/2a$.

$$\frac{-b}{2a} = \frac{-12}{2(-3)} = \frac{-12}{-6} = 2$$

► This value, 2, is on the interval between 1.5 and 3.5.

15. For $p \neq 0$, $\left(\dfrac{1}{P}\right)^{x^2} = P^{-4}$, for what values of x?

Answer E

► Notice that the bases $1/P$ and P are reciprocals of each other. To make the bases exactly the same and thus make the exponents equal, change the sign of the (-4).

$$\left(\frac{1}{P}\right)^{x^2} = P^{-4}$$

$$\left(\frac{1}{P}\right)^{x^2} = \left(\frac{1}{P}\right)^{4}$$

$$x^2 = 4$$
$$\sqrt{x^2} = \pm\sqrt{4}$$
$$x = \pm 2$$

16. If $i = \sqrt{-1}$, $i^2 + i^3 + i^4 + i^5 + i^6 =$

Answer C

$\quad\quad i^2 = -1 \quad\quad\quad i^3 = -i \quad\quad\quad i^4 = 1 \quad\quad\quad i^5 = i \quad\quad\quad\quad i^6 = -1$

$\quad\quad i^2 + i^3 + i^4 + i^5 + i^6 = (-1) + (-i) + (1) + (i) + (-1) = -1$

17. **What is the sum of the solutions of $2x^2 = 7x + 15$?**

Answer D

$\quad\quad 2x^2 = 7x + 15$

$\quad\quad 2x^2 - 7x - 15 = 0$

$\quad\quad (2x + 3)(x - 5) = 0$

$\quad\quad x = \left\{\dfrac{-3}{2}, 5\right\}$

▶ Now add the solutions.

$\quad\quad 5 + \dfrac{-3}{2} = \dfrac{10}{2} + \dfrac{-3}{2} = \dfrac{7}{2}$

18. If $\dfrac{2x^2 + kx - 15}{x - 5} = 2x + 3$, then k = ?

Answer B

▶ This rational equation is just an unusual way to ask you to FOIL the binomials.

$\quad\quad \dfrac{2x^2 + kx - 15}{x - 5} = 2x + 3$

$\quad\quad 2x^2 + kx - 15 = (x - 5)(2x + 3)$

$\quad\quad 2x^2 + kx - 15 = 2x^2 + 3x - 10x - 15$

$\quad\quad 2x^2 + kx - 15 = 2x^2 - 7x - 15$

$\quad\quad kx = -7x$

$\quad\quad k = -7$

▶ Watch out for the sign! It would be a shame to do all that work and select A. +7, just because you were being careless.

19. **The operation $\star$ is defined to be: $x \star y = 3x - 2y$. If $4 \star a = 8$, then a = ?**

Answer D

▶ Plug in the values of 4 and a into $3x - 2y$.   8 is a result, not an argument.

$\quad\quad 3x - 2y =$

$\quad\quad 3(4) - 2a = 8$

$\quad\quad 12 - 2a = 8$

$\quad\quad 12 - 8 = 2a$

$\quad\quad 4 = 2a$

$\quad\quad 2 = a$

20. **For what values of x is the equation $\log_2 x + \log_2 (x - 2) = 3$ true?**

Answer A

$\log_2 x + \log_2 (x - 2) = 3$
$\log_2 (x^2 - 2x) = 3$
$x^2 - 2x = 2^3$
$x^2 - 2x = 8$
$x^2 - 2x - 8 = 0$
$(x - 4)(x + 2) = 0$

$x = \{4, -2\}$

▶ The negative 2 must be rejected since it is not in the domain of $\log_2 x$. Therefore, $x = 4$.

TEST FOUR GEOMETRY

Select the best answer.

1. In the figure below, $\overline{AB}$ and $\overline{CD}$ are perpendicular. If the measure of ∠EDB is 33°, what is the measure of ∠EDC?

- ○ A. 33°
- ○ B. 57°
- ○ C. 66°
- ○ D. 123°
- ○ E. 147°

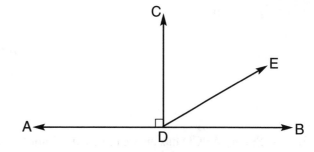

2. Line segments $\overline{AB}$ and $\overline{CD}$ intersect at point E. If ∠AEC is 142°, what is ∠AED?

- ○ A. 18°
- ○ B. 28°
- ○ C. 38°
- ○ D. 48°
- ○ E. 58°

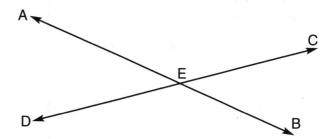

3. Lines $\overleftrightarrow{AB}$, $\overleftrightarrow{CD}$, and $\overleftrightarrow{EF}$ all intersect at the point G. $\overleftrightarrow{AB}$ is perpendicular to $\overleftrightarrow{CD}$. If ∠AGF is 27°, what is ∠CGE?

- ○ A. 33°
- ○ B. 43°
- ○ C. 53°
- ○ D. 63°
- ○ E. 153°

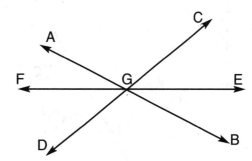

159

4. In the drawing point B is colinear with point A and point D. If ∠ACB is 100° and ∠CBD is 130°, what is ∠CAB?

  ○ A.   30°
  ○ B.   40°
  ○ C.   80°
  ○ D.   100°
  ○ E.   130°

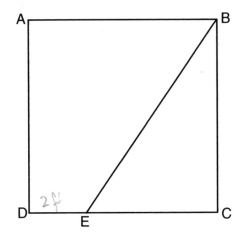

5. Square ABCD has an area of 64 ft². Point E is collinear with points C and D. Segment $\overline{DE}$ is 2 feet long. What is the perimeter of triangle BCE?

  ○ A.   5 feet
  ○ B.   10 feet
  ○ C.   14 feet
  ○ D.   24 feet
  ○ E.   48 feet

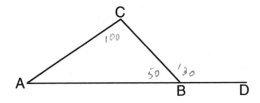

6. In the figure below ∠BAC = ∠BDE.   If $\dfrac{\overline{BE}}{\overline{EC}} = \dfrac{4}{1}$, then $\dfrac{\overline{BD}}{\overline{BA}}$ = ?

  ○ A.   1
  ○ B. $\dfrac{1}{4}$
  ○ C. $\dfrac{4}{1}$
  ○ D. $\dfrac{4}{5}$
  ○ E. $\dfrac{5}{4}$

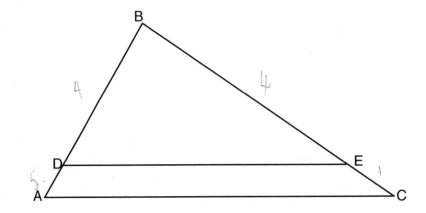

7. If both legs of a right triangle are 1 meter in length, what is the perimeter of the triangle?

○ A. $\sqrt{2}$ meters

○ B.   2 meters

○ C.   3 meters

○ D. $(2 + \sqrt{2})$ meters

○ E.   4 meters

8. A ladder 13 feet long is placed 5 feet away from the base of a wall and then leaned against the wall. How high up does the ladder reach?

○ A.   8 feet

○ B.   9 feet

○ C.   12 feet

○ D.   15 feet

○ E.   18 feet

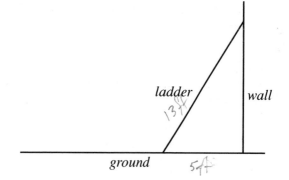

ladder   *wall*

ground

9. A rectangular hallway that measures 6 feet by 18 feet is to be tiled using square tiles that measure 9 inches on a side. What is the minimum number of tiles that can be used to cover this entire area?

○ A.   108

○ B.   136

○ C.   164

○ D.   192

○ E.   220

10. In the drawing below, lines $\overleftrightarrow{AB}$ and $\overleftrightarrow{CD}$ are parallel. Line $\overleftrightarrow{EH}$ intersects line $\overleftrightarrow{AB}$ at F. Line $\overleftrightarrow{EH}$ intersects line $\overleftrightarrow{CD}$ at G. If $\angle HGD$ is 125°, what is $\angle AFE$?

○ A.   25°

○ B.   55°

○ C.   90°

○ D.   125°

○ E.   180°

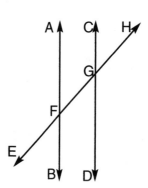

161

11. The vertex angle of an isosceles triangle is 120°. How much is one base angle?

- ○ A. 15°
- ○ B. 30°
- ○ C. 55°
- ○ D. 60°
- ○ E. 120°

12. If the diameter of a circle is 12 meters, how many square meters is the area?

- ○ A. 6π
- ○ B. 12π
- ○ C. 24π
- ○ D. 36π
- ○ E. 144π

13. In an isosceles triangle, one of the angles measures 70°. What other angles are possible in this triangle?

I.	55° and 55°
II.	110°
III.	40° and 70°

- ○ A. I
- ○ B. II
- ○ C. I, II
- ○ D. I, III
- ○ E. I, II, III

14. Points A, B, and C are on the circle with center O. Segment $\overline{AB}$ is a diameter. If ∠BOC is 40°, what is ∠ACO?

- ○ A. 10°
- ○ B. 20°
- ○ C. 40°
- ○ D. 60°
- ○ E. 140°

15. In the drawing below, segment $\overline{AB}$ is a radius of the large circle and a diameter of the small circle. If $\overline{AB}$ = 10 meters, how much area is left when the area of the small circle is subtracted from the area of the large circle?

- ○ A. 25π square meters
- ○ B. 50π square meters
- ○ C. 75π square meters
- ○ D. 100π square meters
- ○ E. 125π square meters

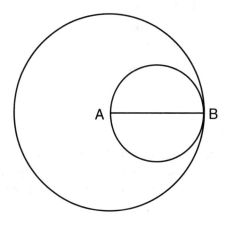

16. In the drawing below, the circle with center S is inscribed inside the square ABCD. The diameter of the circle is 8, the same length as the side of the square. If the area of the circle is subtracted from the area of the square, how much area is left?

- ○ A.   4
- ○ B. 8π
- ○ C. $8 - 4\pi$
- ○ D. $64 - 16\pi$
- ○ E.   64

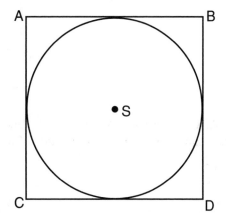

17. In the drawing below $\angle A = \angle D$ and $\angle E = \angle B$. If $\overline{AB}$ is 24 feet long, $\overline{BC}$ is 18 feet long, and $\overline{DE}$ is 8 feet long, how long is $\overline{EF}$?

- ○ A.   6 feet
- ○ B.   9 feet
- ○ C.   12 feet
- ○ D.   15 feet
- ○ E.   18 feet

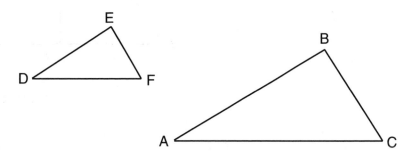

18. $\overline{AC}$ is the diagonal of rectangle ABCD. $\overline{AC}$ measures 15 units. $\overline{BC}$ measures 9 units. How many square units is the area of rectangle ABCD?

○ A. 54
○ B. 90
○ C. 108
○ D. 135
○ E. 180

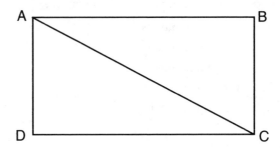

19. Square ABCD measures 8 units on a side. Point E is collinear with points C and D. Segment $\overline{ED}$ measures 4 units. $\overline{AB}$ is a diameter of the semicircle. How many square units is the area of the entire figure?

○ A. 88π
○ B. 80 + 8π
○ C. 80 − 16π
○ D. 96 + 8π
○ E. 96 + 16π

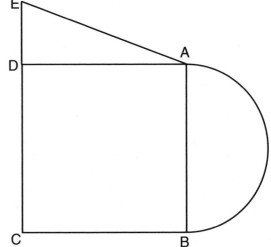

20. Triangle ABC is isosceles, $\overline{AB} = \overline{BC} = 8$ units. $\overline{BD}$ is perpendicular to $\overline{AC}$. $\overline{AD} = 4$ units. How many square units make up the area of triangle ABC?

○ A. 16 √3
○ B. 16 √5
○ C. 32 √3
○ D. 32 √5
○ E. 64

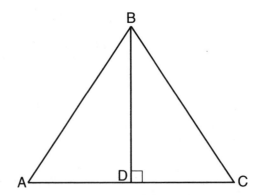

Answers and solutions on next page

ANSWERS FOR TEST 4

1.	B
2.	C
3.	D
4.	A
5.	D
6.	D
7.	D
8.	C
9.	D
10.	D
11.	B
12.	D
13.	D
14.	B
15.	C
16.	D
17.	A
18.	C
19.	B
20.	A

SOLUTIONS FOR TEST 4

1. **In the figure below, $\overline{AB}$ and $\overline{CD}$ are perpendicular. If the measure of $\angle EDB$ is 33°, what is the measure of $\angle EDC$?**

Answer B

> $\angle EDB$ and $\angle EDC$ are complimentary.
> $\angle EDB + \angle EDC = 90°$
> $33° + \angle EDC = 90°$
> $\angle EDC = 90° - 33° = 57°$

2. **Line segments $\overline{AB}$ and $\overline{CD}$ intersect at point E. If $\angle AEC$ is 142°, what is $\angle AED$?**

Answer C

> $\angle AEC$ and $\angle AED$ are supplementary.
> $\angle AEC + \angle AED = 180°$
> $142° + \angle AED = 180°$
> $\angle AED = 180° - 142° = 38°$

3. **Lines $\overleftrightarrow{AB}$, $\overleftrightarrow{CD}$, and $\overleftrightarrow{EF}$ all intersect at the point G. $\overleftrightarrow{AB}$ is perpendicular to $\overleftrightarrow{CD}$. If $\angle AGF$ is 27°, what is $\angle CGE$?**

Answer D

> $\angle AGF + \angle AGC + \angle CGE = 180°$
> $27° + 90° + \angle CGE = 180°$
> $117° + \angle CGE = 180°$
> $\angle CGE = 180° - 117° = 63°$

4. In the drawing point B is colinear with point A and point D. If $\angle ACD$ is $100°$ and $\angle CBD$ is $130°$, what is $\angle CAB$?

Answer A

$\angle A + \angle C = \angle CBD$ Exterior angle theorem

$\angle A + 100° = 130°$

$\angle A = 130° - 100° = 30°$

5. Square ABCD has an area of 64 ft². Point E is collinear with points C and D. Segment $\overline{DE}$ is 2 feet long. What is the perimeter of triangle BCE?

Answer D

▶ First use the Pythagorean theorem to find the length of $\overline{BE}$. Then add the three sides $\overline{EC} = 8 - 2 = 6$

$\overline{BC}^2 + \overline{EC}^2 = \overline{BE}^2$

$8^2 + 6^2 = \overline{BE}^2$

$64 + 36 = \overline{BE}^2$

$100 = \overline{BE}^2$

$10 = \overline{BE}$

Perimeter $8 + 6 + 10 = 24$

6. In the figure below $\angle BAC = \angle BDE$.   If $\dfrac{\overline{BE}}{\overline{EC}} = \dfrac{4}{1}$, then $\dfrac{\overline{BD}}{\overline{BA}} = ?$

Answer D

▶ As soon as we know two pairs of angles are equal we know these are similar triangles. This means you can set up ratios and proportions about the sides.

Take $\overline{BD}$ to be 4 and $\overline{BA}$ to be $(4 + 1) = 5$

7. If both legs of a right triangle are 1 meter in length, what is the perimeter of the triangle?

Answer D

▶ Find the hypotenuse and then add up all three sides.

$a^2 + b^2 = c^2$

$1^2 + 1^2 = c^2$

$1 + 1 = c^2$

$2 = c^2$

$\sqrt{2} = c$

Perimeter

$1 + 1 + \sqrt{2} = 2 + \sqrt{2}$

8.   A ladder 13 feet long is placed 5 feet away from the base of a wall and then leaned against the wall. How high up does the ladder reach?

Answer C

▶ This problem is 100% Pythagorean.

$a^2 + b^2 = c^2$
$5^2 + b^2 = 13^2$
$25 + b^2 = 169$
$b^2 = 169 - 25$
$b^2 = 144$
$\sqrt{b^2} = \sqrt{144}$
$b = 12$

9.   A rectangular hallway that measures 6 feet by 18 feet is to be tiled using square tiles that measure 9 inches on a side. What is the minimum number of tiles that can be used to cover this entire area?

Answer D

▶ First, convert feet to inches.
    $6 \times 12 = 72$ $18 \times 12 = 216$

▶ Now divide each dimension by 9 to find out how many tiles will fit on a side.
    $72 \div 9 = 8$ $216 \div 9 = 24$

▶ Now multiply the length by the width to get the number of tiles needed
    $8 \times 24 = 192$

10.   In the drawing below, lines $\overleftrightarrow{AB}$ and $\overleftrightarrow{CD}$ are parallel. Line $\overleftrightarrow{EH}$ intersects line $\overleftrightarrow{AB}$ at F. Line $\overleftrightarrow{EH}$ intersects line $\overleftrightarrow{CD}$ at G. If $\angle HGD$ is 125°, what is $\angle AFE$?

Answer D

    $\angle HGD$ and $\angle AFE$ are alternate exterior angles.

11.   The vertex angle of an isosceles triangle is 120°. How much is one base angle?

Answer B

▶ Two base angles plus the vertex angle = 180°

    $2B + V = 180°$
    $2B + 120° = 180°$
    $2B = 180° - 120°$
    $2B = 60°$
    $B = 30°$

12. **If the diameter of a circle is 12 meters, how many square meters is the area?**

Answer D

▶ Divide the diameter by 2 to get the radius. Then plug into the formula $A = \pi r^2$.

d = 12
r = 6
$A = \pi(6)^2 = 36\pi$

13. **In an isosceles triangle, one of the angles measures 70°. What other angles are possible in this triangle?**

I. 55° and 55°
II. 110°
III. 40° and 70°

Answer D

▶ Whenever you see a multiple case problem like this, try process of elimination.

Case I: 55° + 55° + 70° = 180°   True
Case II: 110 ° + 70° = 180°   But what about the third angle? False
Case III: 40° + 70° + 70° = 180°   True

▶ Therefore the answer is I and III, choice D.

14. **Points A, B, and C are on the circle with center O. Segment $\overline{AB}$ is a diameter. If ∠BOC is 40°, what is ∠ACO?**

Answer B

▶ ∠BOC = 40° means that ∠AOC = 140°

▶ Because triangle ∠AOC is isosceles, ∠ACO = ∠OAC. Since ∠AOC takes up 140° of the triangle, ∠ACO = ∠OAC = 20°.

▶ Or since ∠BAC is inscribed on a 40° arc, it measures 20°. Since ∠ACO is the other base angle of an isosceles triangle, it too must be 20°.

15. **In the drawing below, segment $\overline{AB}$ is a radius of the large circle and a diameter of the small circle. If $\overline{AB}$ = 10 meters, how much area is left when the area of the small circle is subtracted from the area of the large circle?**

Answer C

Large Circle
    $A = \pi r^2 = \pi(10)^2 = 100\pi$
Small Circle
    D = 2r = 10
    r = 5
    $A = \pi r^2 = \pi(5)^2 = 25\pi$
Area remaining
    $100\pi - 25\pi = 75\pi$

16. In the drawing below, the circle with center S is inscribed inside the square ABCD. The diameter of the circle is 8, the same length as the side of the square. If the area of the circle is subtracted from the area of the square, how much area is left?

Answer D

Square
$$A = s^2 = 8^2 = 64$$
Circle
$$A = \pi r^2 = \pi(4)^2 = 16\pi$$
Area remaining
$$64 - 16\pi$$

17. In the drawing below $\angle A = \angle D$ and $\angle E = \angle B$. If $\overline{AB}$ is 24 feet long, $\overline{BC}$ is 18 feet long, and $\overline{DE}$ is 8 feet long, how long is EF?

Answer A

▶ Similar triangles mean you can set up ratios and proportions. Reduce the ratio for ease in computation.

$$\frac{small\ triangle}{large\ triangle} = \frac{8}{24} = \frac{1}{3}$$
$$\frac{1}{3} = \frac{x}{18}$$
$$18 = 3x$$
$$\frac{18}{3} = \frac{3x}{3}$$
$$6 = x = EF$$

18. $\overline{AC}$ is the diagonal of rectangle ABCD. $\overline{AC}$ measures 15 units. $\overline{BC}$ measures 9 units. How many square units is the area of rectangle ABCD?

Answer C

▶ First use the Pythagorean Theorem to find the length of $\overline{AB}$.

$$\overline{AB}^2 + \overline{BC}^2 = \overline{AC}^2$$
$$\overline{AB}^2 + 9^2 = 15^2$$
$$\overline{AB}^2 + 81 = 225$$
$$\overline{AB}^2 = 225 - 81 = 144$$
$$AB = 12$$

▶ Find the area

$$12 \times 9 = 108$$

19. Square ABCD measures 8 units on a side. Point E is collinear with points C and D. Segment $\overline{CD}$ measures 4 units. $\overline{AB}$ is a diameter of the semicircle. How many square units is the area of the entire figure?

Answer B

Area of square
$$A = s^2 = 8^2 = 64$$
Area of triangle
$$A = (^1/_2)bh = (^1/_2)(8)(4) = 16$$
Area of semicircle
$$A = (^1/_2)\pi r^2 = (^1/_2)\pi(4)^2 = (^1/_2)\pi(16) = 8\pi$$
Sum the three areas for a grand total.
$$64 + 16 + 8\pi = 80 + 8\pi$$

20. Triangle ABC is isosceles, $\overline{AB} = \overline{BC} = 8$ units. $\overline{BD}$ is perpendicular to $\overline{AC}$. $\overline{AD} = 4$ units. How many square units make up the area of triangle ABC?

Answer A

▶ First use the Pythagorean theorem to find the length of $\overline{BD}$, it is the altitude of the triangle.

$a^2 + b^2 = c^2$
$4^2 + b^2 = 8^2$
$16 + b^2 = 64$
$b^2 = 64 - 16$
$b^2 = 48$
$b = \sqrt{48} = 4\sqrt{3}$

▶ If $\overline{AD} = 4$, then $\overline{AC} = 8$.

- Because triangle ABC is isosceles, $\angle A = \angle C$.
- Because $\overline{BD}$ is perpendicular to $\overline{AC}$, $\angle BDA = \angle BDC$.
- Therefore triangle BDA is similar to triangle BDC.
- Since $\overline{BD} = \overline{BD}$ in both triangles, then $\overline{AD} = \overline{AC}$.
  $\overline{AC} = 8$

$$A = \frac{1}{2} \ (b)(h) = \frac{1}{2} \ (8)(4\sqrt{3}) = 16\sqrt{3}$$

TEST FIVE TRIGONOMETRY

Select the best answer.

1. In the right triangle below what is cos θ?

    ○ A. $\dfrac{5}{12}$

    ○ B. $\dfrac{12}{5}$

    ○ C. $\dfrac{5}{13}$

    ○ D. $\dfrac{12}{13}$

    ○ E. $\dfrac{17}{13}$

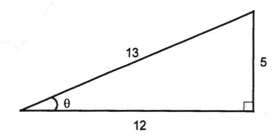

2. In ΔABC below ∠C is a right angle what is the sine of ∠B?

    ○ A. $\sqrt{3}$

    ○ B. $\dfrac{1}{2}$

    ○ C. $\dfrac{\sqrt{3}}{2}$

    ○ D. $\dfrac{2\sqrt{3}}{3}$

    ○ E. 2

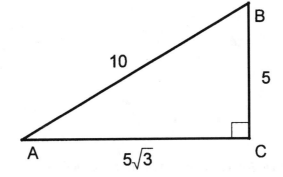

3. If $\sin \theta = \dfrac{1}{2}$ then tan θ = ?

    ○ A. $\dfrac{\sqrt{3}}{2}$

    ○ B. $\dfrac{\sqrt{3}}{3}$

    ○ C. $\dfrac{3}{4}$

    ○ D. $\dfrac{1}{3}$

    ○ E. $\dfrac{2\sqrt{3}}{3}$

4. If the point (-3, 4) is on the terminal side of angle θ in standard position as shown in the drawing below, what is the value of tan θ?

○ A. $\dfrac{-3}{5}$

○ B. $\dfrac{4}{5}$

○ C. $\dfrac{-3}{4}$

○ D. $\dfrac{-4}{3}$

○ E. $\dfrac{1}{5}$

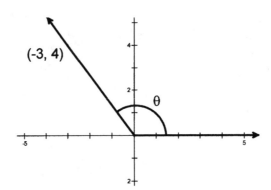

5. If $0° < x < 90°$ and $\sin x = \dfrac{3}{5}$ then $\tan x = ?$

○ A. $\dfrac{3}{5}$

○ B. $\dfrac{4}{5}$

○ C. $\dfrac{5}{3}$

○ D. $\dfrac{5}{4}$

○ E. $\dfrac{3}{4}$

6. Right triangle ΔABC has the angle measures and sides as marked below. What is the value of (tan A)(tan B)?

○ A. cot 90°
○ B. 1
○ C. tan 90°

○ D. $\dfrac{41}{90}$

○ E. $\dfrac{90}{41}$

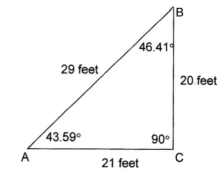

7. In the right triangle below the length of $\overline{AB}$ is 5 units and the length of $\overline{CB}$ is 4 units. What is the cotangent of $\angle$A?

- A. $\dfrac{4}{3}$

- B. $\dfrac{3}{4}$

- C. $\dfrac{3}{5}$

- D. $\dfrac{4}{5}$

- E. $\dfrac{9}{16}$

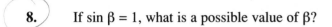

8. If $\sin \beta = 1$, what is a possible value of β?

- A. 0°
- B. 15°
- C. 30°
- D. 60°
- E. 90°

9. If $0° < x < 90°$ and $\tan x = \dfrac{5}{3}$ then $\cos x = $?

- A. $\dfrac{3}{5}$

- B. $\dfrac{4}{5}$

- C. $\dfrac{5\sqrt{34}}{34}$

- D. $\dfrac{5}{34}$

- E. $\dfrac{3\sqrt{34}}{34}$

10. If $\cos 45° = \dfrac{\sqrt{2}}{2}$ what is $\cos 135°$?

- A. $\dfrac{\sqrt{2}}{2}$

- B. $\dfrac{-\sqrt{2}}{2}$

- C. $\dfrac{\sqrt{3}}{2}$

- D. $\dfrac{-\sqrt{3}}{2}$

- E. $\dfrac{1}{2}$

11. In a rectangle that measures 5 feet by 12 feet, what is the cosine of the smallest angle formed by the diagonal and a side of the rectangle?

◯ A. $\dfrac{5}{13}$

◯ B. $\dfrac{12}{13}$

◯ C. $\dfrac{5}{12}$

◯ D. $\dfrac{13}{5}$

◯ E. $\dfrac{13}{12}$

12. In the triangle below angle *A* measures 25°, angle *C* measures 65°, and angle *B* measures 90°. The length of $\overline{BC}$ is 5 feet. How long is $\overline{AB}$?

◯ A. $\dfrac{5 \sin 25}{\sin 65}$ feet

◯ B. $5 \sin 25$ feet

◯ C. $\dfrac{\sin 5}{\sin 13}$ feet

◯ D. $\dfrac{5 \sin 65}{\sin 25}$ feet

◯ E. The answer cannot be determined from the given information.

13. If $0° < x < 90°$ and $\cos x = \dfrac{24}{25}$ then $\tan x = ?$

◯ A. $\dfrac{7}{24}$

◯ B. $\dfrac{24}{7}$

◯ C. $\dfrac{7}{25}$

◯ D. $\dfrac{24}{25}$

◯ E. $\dfrac{31}{25}$

14. If $\sin x = \dfrac{\sqrt{2}}{2}$ and $0° \leq x \leq 90°$ then what is $\sin 2x$?

    ○ A. $\sqrt{2}$
    ○ B. 2
    ○ C. 1
    ○ D. $\dfrac{\sqrt{3}}{2}$

    ○ E. $\dfrac{\sqrt{2}}{2}$

15. A ladder that is 20 feet long is leaned against a building so that the ladder and the ground form a 70° angle. How high does the top of the ladder reach?

    ○ A. $20 \sin \theta$

    ○ B. $\dfrac{\sin \theta}{20}$

    ○ C. $20 \cos \theta$

    ○ D. $\dfrac{\cos \theta}{20}$

    ○ E. The answer cannot be determined from the given information.

16. The diagonal of a square forms an angle with a side of the square. What is the tangent of this angle?

    ○ A. 2
    ○ B. $\dfrac{3}{2}$

    ○ C. $\sqrt{2}$
    ○ D. 1
    ○ E. $\dfrac{\sqrt{2}}{2}$

17. If β is an acute angle and $\cos \beta = \dfrac{5}{13}$ then what is $\tan \beta$?

    ○ A. $\dfrac{12}{13}$

    ○ B. $\dfrac{13}{5}$

    ○ C. $\dfrac{5}{12}$

    ○ D. $\dfrac{12}{5}$

    ○ E. 5

18. If the terminal side of α is in the second quadrant and sin $\alpha = \dfrac{\sqrt{7}}{4}$, then cos α = ?

○ A. $\dfrac{3}{4}$

○ B. $\dfrac{-3}{4}$

○ C. $\dfrac{3\sqrt{7}}{4}$

○ D. $\dfrac{-3\sqrt{7}}{4}$

○ E. $\dfrac{7}{16}$

19. If $\sin\theta = \dfrac{-3}{5}$, then tan θ = ?

○ A. Either $\dfrac{-4}{3}$ or $\dfrac{4}{3}$

○ B. Either $\dfrac{-3}{4}$ or $\dfrac{3}{4}$

○ C. Either $\dfrac{-4}{5}$ or $\dfrac{4}{5}$

○ D. Either 0 or undefined.

○ E. Either $\dfrac{5}{3}$ or $\dfrac{-5}{3}$

20. If an acute angle γ has a sine value of $\dfrac{5}{13}$ then what is the value of the cosine of γ?

○ A. $\dfrac{\sqrt{18}}{5}$

○ B. $\dfrac{\sqrt{18}}{12}$

○ C. $\dfrac{5}{13}$

○ D. $\dfrac{12}{13}$

○ E. $\dfrac{5}{12}$

ANSWERS FOR TEST 5

1. D
2. C
3. B
4. D
5. E
6. B
7. B
8. E
9. E
10. B
11. B
12. D
13. A
14. C
15. A
16. D
17. D
18. B
19. B
20. D

SOLUTIONS FOR TEST 5

1.   In the right triangle below what is cos θ?

Answer D

$$\cos\theta = \frac{adjacent}{hypotenuse} = \frac{12}{13}.$$

2.   In △ABC below ∠C is a right angle what is the sine of ∠B?

Answer C

$$\sin B = \frac{opposite}{hypotenuse} = \frac{5\sqrt{3}}{10} = \frac{\sqrt{3}}{2}$$

3. If $\sin \theta = \dfrac{1}{2}$ then $\tan \theta = ?$

Answer B

First find $\cos \theta$ using the Pythagorean identity $\sin^2 \theta + \cos^2 \theta = 1$.	Now apply the definition of tangent.
$$\sin^2 \theta + \cos^2 \theta = 1$$ $$\left(\frac{1}{2}\right)^2 + \cos^2 \theta = 1$$ $$\frac{1}{4} + \cos^2 \theta = 1$$ $$\cos^2 \theta = 1 - \frac{1}{4}$$ $$\cos^2 \theta = \frac{4}{4} - \frac{1}{4}$$ $$\cos^2 \theta = \frac{3}{4}$$ $$\sqrt{\cos^2 \theta} = \sqrt{\frac{3}{4}}$$ $$\cos \theta = \frac{\sqrt{3}}{2}$$	$$\tan \theta = \frac{\sin \theta}{\cos \theta}$$ $$\tan \theta = \frac{\frac{1}{2}}{\frac{\sqrt{3}}{2}} = \frac{2}{2\sqrt{3}} = \frac{1}{\sqrt{3}}$$ Now rationalize the denominator. $$\tan \theta = \frac{1}{\sqrt{3}}\left(\frac{\sqrt{3}}{\sqrt{3}}\right) = \frac{\sqrt{3}}{3}$$

4. If the point (-3, 4) is on the terminal side of angle θ in standard position as shown in the drawing below, what is the value of $\tan \theta$?

Answer D

► If we use the distance formula we can find that the distance from the origin to the point (-3, 4) is 5. So using the trigonometric definitions of sin, cos and tan we can find the following:

$$\sin \theta = \frac{4}{5}, \quad \cos \theta = \frac{-3}{5} \quad \text{so} \quad \tan \theta = \frac{\sin \theta}{\cos \theta} = \frac{\frac{4}{5}}{\frac{-3}{5}} = \frac{-4}{3}.$$

► Another way to look at this problem would be with the right triangle definition of tangent.

$$\tan \theta = \frac{opposite}{adjacent} = \frac{4}{-3} = \frac{-4}{3}$$

► A third way to look at tangent in this problem is as the slope of the line that connects the terminal point to the origin.

► Notice that the answers given are both positive and negative. When you see different signs in the answers think of it as a reminder to pay close attention to the sign of your answer.

3. If $\sin\theta = \dfrac{1}{2}$ then $\tan\theta = ?$

Answer B

First find $\cos\theta$ using the Pythagorean identity $\sin^2\theta + \cos^2\theta = 1$.	Now apply the definition of tangent.
$\sin^2\theta + \cos^2\theta = 1$ $\left(\dfrac{1}{2}\right)^2 + \cos^2\theta = 1$ $\dfrac{1}{4} + \cos^2\theta = 1$ $\cos^2\theta = 1 - \dfrac{1}{4}$ $\cos^2\theta = \dfrac{4}{4} - \dfrac{1}{4}$ $\cos^2\theta = \dfrac{3}{4}$ $\sqrt{\cos^2\theta} = \sqrt{\dfrac{3}{4}}$ $\cos\theta = \dfrac{\sqrt{3}}{2}$	$\tan\theta = \dfrac{\sin\theta}{\cos\theta}$ $\tan\theta = \dfrac{\frac{1}{2}}{\frac{\sqrt{3}}{2}} = \dfrac{2}{2\sqrt{3}} = \dfrac{1}{\sqrt{3}}$ Now rationalize the denominator. $\tan\theta = \dfrac{1}{\sqrt{3}}\left(\dfrac{\sqrt{3}}{\sqrt{3}}\right) = \dfrac{\sqrt{3}}{3}$

4. **If the point (-3, 4) is on the terminal side of angle θ in standard position as shown in the drawing below, what is the value of tan θ?**

Answer D

► If we use the distance formula we can find that the distance from the origin to the point (-3, 4) is 5. So using the trigonometric definitions of sin, cos and tan we can find the following:

$$\sin\theta = \frac{4}{5}, \quad \cos\theta = \frac{-3}{5} \quad \text{so} \quad \tan\theta = \frac{\sin\theta}{\cos\theta} = \frac{\frac{4}{5}}{\frac{-3}{5}} = \frac{-4}{3}.$$

► Another way to look at this problem would be with the right triangle definition of tangent.

$$\tan\theta = \frac{opposite}{adjacent} = \frac{4}{-3} = \frac{-4}{3}$$

► A third way to look at tangent in this problem is as the slope of the line that connects the terminal point to the origin.

► Notice that the answers given are both positive and negative. When you see different signs in the answers think of it as a reminder to pay close attention to the sign of your answer.

14. If $\sin x = \dfrac{\sqrt{2}}{2}$ and $0° \le x \le 90°$ then what is sin 2x?

- A. $\sqrt{2}$
- B. 2
- C. 1
- D. $\dfrac{\sqrt{3}}{2}$
- E. $\dfrac{\sqrt{2}}{2}$

15. A ladder that is 20 feet long is leaned against a building so that the ladder and the ground form a 70° angle. How high does the top of the ladder reach?

- A. 20 sin θ
- B. $\dfrac{\sin\theta}{20}$
- C. 20 cos θ
- D. $\dfrac{\cos\theta}{20}$
- E. The answer cannot be determined from the given information.

16. The diagonal of a square forms an angle with a side of the square. What is the tangent of this angle?

- A. 2
- B. $\dfrac{3}{2}$
- C. $\sqrt{2}$
- D. 1
- E. $\dfrac{\sqrt{2}}{2}$

17. If β is an acute angle and $\cos\beta = \dfrac{5}{13}$ then what is tan β?

- A. $\dfrac{12}{13}$
- B. $\dfrac{13}{5}$
- C. $\dfrac{5}{12}$
- D. $\dfrac{12}{5}$
- E. 5

18. If the terminal side of α is in the second quadrant and $\sin \alpha = \dfrac{\sqrt{7}}{4}$, then $\cos \alpha = ?$

A. $\dfrac{3}{4}$

B. $\dfrac{-3}{4}$

C. $\dfrac{3\sqrt{7}}{4}$

D. $\dfrac{-3\sqrt{7}}{4}$

E. $\dfrac{7}{16}$

19. If $\sin \theta = \dfrac{-3}{5}$, then $\tan \theta = ?$

A. Either $\dfrac{-4}{3}$ or $\dfrac{4}{3}$

B. Either $\dfrac{-3}{4}$ or $\dfrac{3}{4}$

C. Either $\dfrac{-4}{5}$ or $\dfrac{4}{5}$

D. Either 0 or undefined.

E. Either $\dfrac{5}{3}$ or $\dfrac{-5}{3}$

20. If an acute angle γ has a sine value of $\dfrac{5}{13}$ then what is the value of the cosine of γ?

A. $\dfrac{\sqrt{18}}{5}$

B. $\dfrac{\sqrt{18}}{12}$

C. $\dfrac{5}{13}$

D. $\dfrac{12}{13}$

E. $\dfrac{5}{12}$

176

ANSWERS FOR TEST 5

1. D
2. C
3. B
4. D
5. E
6. B
7. B
8. E
9. E
10. B
11. B
12. D
13. A
14. C
15. A
16. D
17. D
18. B
19. B
20. D

SOLUTIONS FOR TEST 5

1. **In the right triangle below what is cos θ?**

Answer D

$$\cos \theta = \frac{adjacent}{hypotenuse} = \frac{12}{13}.$$

2. **In △ABC below ∠C is a right angle what is the sine of ∠B?**

Answer C

$$\sin B = \frac{opposite}{hypotenuse} = \frac{5\sqrt{3}}{10} = \frac{\sqrt{3}}{2}$$

177

5. If $0° < x < 90°$ and $\sin x = \frac{3}{5}$ then $\tan x = ?$

Answer E

▶ The inequality $0° < x < 90°$ tells you that the angle is acute. If the angle is acute then we are confined to Quadrant I and every value will be positive.

Use the Pythagorean identity to find $\cos x$ first.

$\sin^2 x + \cos^2 x = 1$ $\left(\dfrac{3}{5}\right)^2 + \cos^2 x = 1$ $\dfrac{9}{25} + \cos^2 x = 1$ $\cos^2 x = 1 - \dfrac{9}{25}$ $\cos^2 x = \dfrac{25}{25} - \dfrac{9}{25}$ $\cos^2 x = \dfrac{16}{25}$ $\cos x = \dfrac{4}{5}$	Now apply the definition of tangent. $\tan\theta = \dfrac{\sin\theta}{\cos\theta}$ $\tan\theta = \dfrac{\frac{3}{5}}{\frac{4}{5}} = \dfrac{3}{4}$ Answer E

Another way to find this answer is to use a calculator. First find the inverse of $\sin x = \frac{3}{5}$.

This is also called arcsin x. This will give an approximate value of $x \approx 36.8989765°$. Now input $\tan 36.8989765°$ and the result is 0.75 which is a match for answer E.

6. **Right triangle △ABC has the angle measures and sides as marked below. What is the value of (tan A)(tan B)?**

Answer B

▶ Since angle A and angle B are complimentary the tangents will be reciprocals of each other. The product of reciprocals is always 1.

▶ You could also enter tan(43.59)tan(46.41) = into a calculator. Try this computation with the calculator you will use on the test. Make sure you get 1.

7. **In the right triangle below the length of $\overline{AB}$ is 5 units and the length of $\overline{CB}$ is 4 units. What is the cotangent of ∠A?**

Answer B

▶ Since this is a right triangle we can use the Pythagorean theorem to find that the length of side $\overline{AC} = 3$. Note the orientation of the angle in question. In particular angle A is located "above" the opposite side.

Now use the definition of cotangent $\cot A = \dfrac{adjacent}{opposite} = \dfrac{3}{4}$.

8. **If sin β = 1, what is a possible value of β?**

Answer E

▶ If you do not have the unit circle memorized you could use a calculator to enter sin 0, sin 15, sin 30, sin 60, and sin 90 until you found that E was the correct choice.

9. **If $0° < x < 90°$ and $\tan x = \dfrac{5}{3}$ then cos x = ?**

Answer E

▶ The angle is acute so our answer will be positive. Use the Pythagorean identity to find sec x first. The sec x is the reciprocal of cos x.

$\tan^2 x + 1 = \sec^2 x$ $\left(\dfrac{5}{3}\right)^2 + 1 = \sec^2 x$ $\dfrac{25}{9} + 1 = \sec^2 x$ $\dfrac{25}{9} + \dfrac{9}{9} = \sec^2 x$ $\dfrac{34}{9} = \sec^2 x$ $\sqrt{\dfrac{34}{9}} = \sqrt{\sec^2 x}$ $\dfrac{\sqrt{34}}{3} = \sec x$	Now since cos x is the reciprocal of sec x we can write down the cos x. $\cos x = \dfrac{1}{\sec x}$ $\cos x = \dfrac{1}{\dfrac{\sqrt{34}}{3}}$ $\cos x = \dfrac{3}{\sqrt{34}}$ $\cos x = \dfrac{3}{\sqrt{34}}\left(\dfrac{\sqrt{34}}{\sqrt{34}}\right)$ $\cos x = \dfrac{3\sqrt{34}}{34}$ Answer E

A calculator approach to this problem would be to find the inverse of $\tan x = \dfrac{5}{3}$.

This will give us an approximate value for x. Once you have this angle measure take the cosine. The problem here is that our answer is irrational and hard to recognize. You will need to be skilled with the use of the calculator to arrive at the correct answer ≈ 0.5144957554 and then match it to the values given in the answers.

$$\arctan \frac{5}{3} \approx 59.03624347$$

$$\cos 59.03624347 \approx 0.5144957554$$

$$\frac{3\sqrt{34}}{34} \approx 0.5144957554$$

10. If $\cos 45° = \dfrac{\sqrt{2}}{2}$ what is $\cos 135°$?

Answer B

▶ If you have the unit circle memorized you can just write down the answer.

▶ Another approach would be to enter cos 45 into a calculator. The display will read .7071067812 which is approximately equal to $\dfrac{\sqrt{2}}{2}$.

Then try it for cos 135. The display will read -.7071067812 which is approximately equal to $-\dfrac{\sqrt{2}}{2}$. So the answer is B.

11. **In a rectangle that measures 5 feet by 12 feet, what is the cosine of the smallest angle formed by the diagonal and a side of the rectangle?**

Answer B

▶ First make a sketch of the rectangle and diagonal. Use the Pythagorean theorem to find the length of the diagonal. The smallest angle is the one that is across from the shortest side (5).

Now use the definition of cosine to find the desired value.

$$\cos x = \frac{adjacent}{hypotenuse} = \frac{12}{13}$$

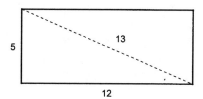

12. In the triangle below angle A measures $25°$, angle C measures $65°$, and angle B measures $90°$. The length of $\overline{BC}$ is 5 feet. How long is $\overline{AB}$?

Answer D

▶ Use the law of sines. Note that side $\overline{AB}$ is opposite angle C so $\overline{AB} = c$.

$$\frac{\sin A}{a} = \frac{\sin C}{c}$$
$$\frac{\sin 25}{5} = \frac{\sin 65}{x}$$
$$x \sin 25 = 5 \sin 65$$
$$x = \frac{5 \sin 65}{\sin 25} \text{ feet}$$

13. If $0° < x < 90°$ and $\cos x = \dfrac{24}{25}$ then $\tan x = ?$

Answer A

▶ Again the phrase "If $0° < x < 90°$" means that the angle is acute and all trigonometric values will be positive. Since all of the answer choices for this question are positive this information is not much help for this particular question.

Since the $\cos x = \dfrac{24}{25}$ then $\sec x = \dfrac{24}{25}$. We can substitute this value into the

Pythagorean identity and solve for $\tan x$.

$$\tan^2 x + 1 = \sec^2 x$$
$$\tan^2 x + 1 = \left(\frac{25}{24}\right)^2$$
$$\tan^2 x + 1 = \frac{625}{576}$$
$$\tan^2 x = \frac{625}{576} - 1$$
$$\tan^2 x = \frac{625}{576} - \frac{576}{576}$$
$$\tan^2 x = \frac{49}{576}$$
$$\sqrt{\tan^2 x} = \sqrt{\frac{49}{576}}$$
$$\tan x = \frac{7}{24}$$

14. If $\sin x = \dfrac{\sqrt{2}}{2}$ and $0° \le x \le 90°$ then what is $\sin 2x$?

Answer C

▶ If you have the unit circle memorized you know that $\sin 45° = \dfrac{\sqrt{2}}{2}$ so $2x = 90°$. Then the value of $\sin 90° = 1$.

▶ In a similar fashion on a calculator you would take the inverse sin of $\left(\dfrac{\sqrt{2}}{2}\right)$ and get $45°$. Double that and then find $\sin 90° = 1$. Practice with the calculator and it can help you memorize important values on the unit circle.

15. A ladder that is 20 feet long is leaned against a building so that the ladder and the ground form a 70° angle. How high does the top of the ladder reach?

Answer A

▶ Make a drawing and then use the law of sines.

$$\frac{\sin A}{a} = \frac{\sin C}{c}$$
$$\frac{\sin 90}{20} = \frac{\sin 70}{h}$$
$$h = 20 \sin 70$$

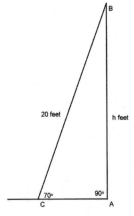

16. The diagonal of a square forms an angle with a side of the square. What is the tangent of this angle?

Answer D

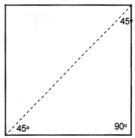

▶ First make a drawing.

The angles formed by the diagonal and the sides of a square are always 45° angles.

tan 45° = 1

17. If β is an acute angle and cos $\beta = \dfrac{5}{13}$ then what is tan β?

Answer D

Make a sketch of cos β. Use the Pythagorean theorem to find the side of the triangle marked y.

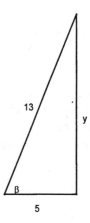

$$a^2 + b^2 = c^2$$
$$5^2 + y^2 = 13^2$$
$$25 + y^2 = 169$$
$$y^2 = 169 - 25$$
$$y^2 = 144$$
$$y = 12$$

Since we know the value of y we can write tan β.

$$\tan \beta = \frac{opposite}{adjacent} = \frac{12}{5}$$

This same result could be obtained using a calculator. Find the inverse of cos β which is about 67.38. Then find the tangent of this value which is 2.4. Convert 2.4 to a fraction and you have answer D.

18. If the terminal side of α is in the second quadrant and sin $\alpha = \dfrac{\sqrt{7}}{4}$, then cos α = ?

Answer B

Since the terminal side of the angle is in the second quadrant we know that the x values will be negative. So the cos α will also be negative.

We have several options for the solution of this particular problem including: make a drawing like we did in the previous solution, use a Pythagorean identity, or just use a calculator. This time I will use the Pythagorean identity as we did with problem #5.

(contiued on the next page)

$$\sin^2 x + \cos^2 x = 1$$

$$\left(\frac{\sqrt{7}}{4}\right)^2 + \cos^2 x = 1$$

$$\frac{7}{16} + \cos^2 x = 1$$

$$\cos^2 x = 1 - \frac{7}{16}$$

$$\cos^2 x = \frac{16}{16} - \frac{7}{16}$$

$$\cos^2 x = \frac{9}{16}$$

$$\cos x = \frac{3}{4}$$

Once we have found 3/4 we have to remember that the sign will be negative since the terminal side is in quadrant II.

19. **If sin $\theta = \dfrac{-3}{5}$, then tan θ = ?**

Answer B

► At this point you should recognize the [3, 4, 5] triangle and know that cos $\theta = \frac{4}{5}$ since we do not know which quadrant the terminal side of the angle is located in we do not know the sign of the cosine. Fortunately the answers provided cover both the positive and negative case and we just need to know the correct ratio for the tangent of θ.

$$\tan\theta = \frac{\sin\theta}{\cos\theta} = \frac{\frac{3}{5}}{\frac{4}{5}} = \frac{3}{4}$$

20. **If an acute angle γ has a sine value of $\dfrac{5}{13}$ then what is the value of the cosine of γ?**

Answer D

► Once again at this point you should recognize the [5, 12, 13] triangle and know that

$$\cos \gamma = \frac{12}{13} .$$

If you do not recognize the [5, 12, 13] triangle then you can use the Pythagorean identity like we did in problems 5 and 18 or make a drawing and apply the Pythagorean theorem like we did in problem 17.

COMPOSITION

The COMPASS Writing Skills Test is used by schools to help decide whether your writing and editing skills are advanced enough to place you in regular studies courses or if you would benefit from remedial work. The test consists of several essays of about two hundred words each. Your task is to revise each essay to its most correct form. The essays are divided into segments, or parts. There may be errors of usage, mechanics, or rhetorical skills in the essay. You are asked to use the mouse or the keyboard's arrow keys to move a pointer on the screen and select a segment. You then will be presented with options for making changes to the selected segment. Your task is to choose the best correction from among those given. If the segment is correct as written, no change is needed. Choice "A" is always the same as the uncorrected text. You also may be asked to determine where a sentence would logically fit or to change the order of the sentences. Additionally, there may be one or two other multiple choice items to answer once you finish revising the essay. After you make your revisions, ALWAYS read the essay again with the changes you have made. This is very important because once you confirm your choices, you will not be able to go back and change your answers.

THE CRAFT OF WRITING

Essays usually are not completed in one draft. All writing can be improved with careful proofreading and editing. Writing is a process, and revisions are common and necessary. The COMPASS Writing Test assesses your ability to proofread and revise writing. This includes the following skills: recognizing and correcting errors in grammar, punctuation, usage and style.

Assume you have been asked to proofread and revise the essay that follows. Cross through the errors and make corrections directly on the page. Use the checklist provided after the essay to help you identify errors.

Its time for me to plan my life. The decision of what to do after high school is an important one. The pressure is on. Everyone is asking me what I'm going to do next. Graduation is almost here and it feels like constant pressure. You see, I am undecide about my career choice. I know I need further schooling. High school are just not enough anymore. But where do I go?

Undecided, technical schools seem to be a good choice. Some are even called technical colleges now. It's not quite the same as college some people say. A college degree would give me a real education, they think, and a technical school will give me a practical education. From a technical school I would go write to work earning a good salary at a job I'd like. That would be perfect if I knew what I'd like, auto mechanics or computers or nursing or something.

And, if I went to college I'd be educated, but what would I do? If I major in education I might find I hate teaching. A lot of major's require you to go to graduate sc hools or professional schools for more education. I don't think I could stand more than four more years of school for four more years. Well, there you go; that's something I know. Maybe I should stop missing those appointments with the career counselor and try to find out what's best for me. Maybe than the pressure will stop. My life will all be planned out. And someone else will be responsible for it. And, that's all I have to say about that.

ESSAY CHECKLIST

      ____   1.   The sentences seem to be in the right order.

      ____   2.   Transitional words are appropriate.

      ____   3.   There are enough supporting facts and details.

      ____   4.   There is an opening and a conclusion.

      ____   5.   There is no wordiness or redundancy.

      ____   6.   Tone and style remain consistent.

      ____   7.   The essay appears to be well organized.

      ____   8.   Sentences are varied and interesting.

      ____   9.   Spelling is correct.

      ____ 10.   Capitalization is correct.

      ____ 11.   The writer uses parallel structure.

      ____ 12.   Modifiers are used correctly.

      ____ 13.   There are no inappropriate shifts in tense.

      ____ 14.   Pronouns are correctly used.

      ____ 15.   Verb forms are correct.

      ____ 16.   There is correct punctuation.

THE CRAFT OF WRITING AND COMPASS

The COMPASS Writing Skills Test will present you with an essay such as the one on the previous page. You will be asked to highlight segments you think have problems. Then you will be given options to correct the problems. The practice exercises in this book have numbered segments for you to consider just as you would consider parts of essays on the actual test.

The essay you have just edited is presented below with numbered segments. Each refers to an item with editing choices. Choose the option you believe is correct for each segment. Then, check your answers on page 233.

PRACTICE ESSAY

1/ Its time for me to plan my life. The decision of what to do after high school is an important one. 2/ The pressure is on. Everyone is asking me what I'm going to do next. Graduation is almost here and it feels like constant pressure. 3/ You see, I am undecide about my career choice. I know I need further schooling. 4/ High school are just not enough anymore. But where do I go?

5/ Undecided, technical schools seem to be a good choice. Some are even called technical colleges now. It's not quite the same as college some people say. 6/ A college degree would give me a real education, they think, and a technical school will give me a practical education. 7/ From a technical school I would go write to work earning a good salary at a job I'd like. 8/ That would be perfect if I knew what I'd like, auto mechanics or computers or nursing or something.

9/ And, if I went to college I'd be educated, but what would I do? If I major in education I might find I hate teaching. 10/ A lot of majors require you to go to graduate sc hools or professional schools for more education. 11/ I don't think I could stand more than four more years of school for four more years. 12/ Well, there you go; that's something I know. 13/ Maybe I should stop missing those appointments with the career counselor and try to find out what's best for me. 14/ Maybe than the pressure will stop. My life will all be planned out. And someone else will be responsible for it. 15/ And, that's all I have to say about that.

1/

- ○ A. Its time for me
- ○ B. Its' time for me
- ○ C. It's time for you
- ○ D. It's time for me
- ○ E. Its' time for you

2/

- ○ A. The pressure is on.
- ○ B. The pressure was on.
- ○ C. The pressure is being on.
- ○ D. The pressure be on.
- ○ E. The pressures on.

3/

- A. You see, I am undecide about my career choice.
- B. You see, I was undecide about my career choice.
- C. You see I will be undecide about my career choice.
- D. You see, I am undecided about my career choice.
- E. You see, I am being undecided about my career choice.

4/

- A. High school are just not enough anymore.
- B. High school just are not enough anymore,
- C. High school diplomas are just not enough anymore.
- D. High school just not enough anymore.
- E. High school just were not enough anymore.

5/

- A. Undecided, technical schools seem to be a good choice.
- B. Undecided, a good choice seems to be technical schools.
- C. Technical schools, while undecided, seem to be a good choice.
- D. Although I am still undecided, technical schools seem a good choice to be.
- E. Although I am still undecided, technical schools seem to be a good choice.

6/

- A. A college degree would give me a real education, they think, and a technical school will give me a practical education.
- B. A college degree would give me a real education, they think, and a technical school would give me a practical education.
- C. A college degree will give me a real education, they will think, and a technical school would give me a practical education.
- D. A college degree would grant me a real education, they think, and a technical school will give me a practical education.
- E. A college degree would have given me a real education, they think, and a technical school was giving me a practical education.

7/

- A. From a technical school I would go write to work earning a good salary at a job I'd like.
- B. From a technical school I would go right to work earning a good salary at a job I'd like.
- C. From a technical school I would write to work earning a good salary at a job I'd like.
- D. From a technical school writing to work earning a good salary at a job I'd like.
- E. From a technical school right to work earning a good salary at a job I'd like.

8/

- ○ A. what I'd like, auto mechanics, or computers, or nursing or something.
- ○ B. what I'd like is auto mechanics, or computers, or nursing or something.
- ○ C. what I'd like: auto mechanics, or computers, or nursing or something.
- ○ D. what I'd like, "auto mechanics, or computers, or nursing or something.
- ○ E. what I'd like auto mechanics, or computers, or nursing or something.

9/

- ○ A. And, if I went to college I'd be educated, but what would I do?
- ○ B. Nevertheless, if I went to college I'd be educated, but what would I do?
- ○ C. Additionally, if I went to college I'd be educated, but what would I do?
- ○ D. On the other hand, if I went to college I'd be educated, but what would I do?
- ○ E. In conclusions, if I went to college I'd be educated, but what would I do?

10/

- ○ A. A lot of major's require you to go to graduate school...
- ○ B. A lot of majors' require you to go to graduate school...
- ○ C. A lot of majors require you to go to graduate school...
- ○ D. A lots of majors requires you to go to graduate school...
- ○ E. A lot of majors required you to go to graduate school...

11/

- ○ A. I don't think I could stand four more years of school for four more years.
- ○ B. I don't think I could stand more than four more years of school for four more years.
- ○ C. I don't think I could stand for four more years of school.
- ○ D. I don't think four more years of school I could stand.
- ○ E. I don't think I could stand four more years of school.

12/

- ○ A. Well, there you go; that's something I know.
- ○ B. Well, there you go; thats something I know.
- ○ C. Well there you go; that's something I know.
- ○ D. Well there you go that's something I know.
- ○ E. Well, there you go that's something I know.

13/

 ○ A. Maybe I should stop missing those appointments with the career counselor and try to find out what's best for me.

 ○ B. Maybe I should stop missing those appointments with the career counselor or try to find out what's best for me.

 ○ C. Maybe I should stop missing those appointments with the career counselor also finding out what's best for me.

 ○ D. Maybe I should stop missing those appointments with the career counselor while she finds out what's best for me.

 ○ E. Maybe those appointments with the career counselor can find out what's best for me.

14/

 ○ A. Maybe than the pressure will stop.

 ○ B. Maybe then the pressure will stop.

 ○ C. Maybe, however, the pressure will stop.

 ○ D. Maybe also the pressure will stop.

 ○ E. Maybe therefore the pressure will stop.

15/

 ○ A. And, that's all I have to say about that.

 ○ B. And, that's all I have to say about that. The end.

 ○ C. And, for my ending, that's all I have to say about that.

 ○ D. This sentence would be more logical at the end of the first paragraph.

 ○ E. This sentence should be left out.

CHAPTER EIGHT

MECHANICS AND USAGE

The COMPASS Writing Test assesses your ability to write in what is called Standard English. This is English that follows certain rules. These rules are in categories referred to as **MECHANICS** and **USAGE.**

Mechanics refers to the ability to format your writing and use correct spelling, capitalization, and punctuation. Your ability to understand parts of sentences and create interesting and varied essays depends on your knowledge of mechanics. The COMPASS Writing Test assesses your ability to determine how to use mechanics to clearly express your ideas.

Usage refers to the ability to use correct grammar in constructing sentences. Topics in this area include subject-verb agreement, pronoun-antecedent, noun forms, verb forms, adjectives, adverbs, articles, and so on. The COMPASS Writing Test assesses your ability to recognize errors in usage and correct them.

Mechanics and usage help make sense of the written word. You would not be able to understand pages of words without punctuation. Tenses and cases help you understand the who, what, when, where, and how of writing. Proper use of pronouns, verbs, adjectives, adverbs, and prepositions is essential. You must be able to find and correct errors in your writing to make it understandable. COMPASS items in this category make up approximately 70% of the writing skills test. Read the following review of usage and mechanics and complete the exercises.

MECHANICS

SPELLING

The ability to spell correctly is important in writing and in proofreading. You may think that because you use a word processing program with the ability to check your spelling you do not have to worry about spelling. However, a word processing program will not correct an incorrect word choice such as a homonym that is spelled correctly. Spelling is more than simply knowledge of phonics. Read the following rules for spelling and be especially careful of spelling demons.

1. I before E except after C or when sounding like A: **achieve, receive, sleigh.**

2. Words ending in Y change it to I before adding endings: **happy/happiness.**

3. Some words referring to a particular person or persons are hyphenated: **mother-in-law/sisters-in-law.**

4. Numbers from **twenty-one** to **ninety-nine** are hyphenated.

5. If a word ends with a vowel then consonant, and its suffix begins with a vowel, sometimes the consonant is doubled: **commit/committed.**

6. Words ending in silent E drop the E before adding an ending unless the suffix begins with a consonant. Consider **concentrate/concentration** and **taste/tasteless.**

7. Some words need to be learned by their meanings and construction. These are sometimes called "**spelling demons.**"

COMMON SPELLING DEMONS

exercise	psychology	it's/its
prejudice	tragedy	wait/weight
magic	across	occur
write/right	discipline	to/two/too

Exercise 1

Find ten spelling errors in the following paragraph.

My first day in colege it became immediatly aparent that I was going to succeed. We were asked to right an essay on the topic My Most Embarassing Moment. A Commitee read the essays and gave us feedback at the end of the day. The coments on mine read, "good job," "a little to brief, but interesting," "you're write on topic," and "I can't weight to have you in class."

(*Answers* to all exercises in Chapter Eight are found on pp.233-236.)

CAPITALIZATION

Always capitalize the following:

1. Days: weekdays, months, Holy Days and holidays
2. Places: streets, towns, cities, states, countries, mountains, rivers, parks, planets
3. Names: people, pets, relatives when they are used as names, I (first person singular)
4. Titles of people, books, movies, songs, stories, poems
5. Academic courses
6. Events
7. Organizations
8. Companies, buildings, corporations, institutions
9. Races and religions
10. Brand names

Exercise 2

Correct any capitalization errors in the following paragraph by crossing out the incorrect letter and replacing it.

My summer vacation officially starts on the fourth of july. The last day of june we head for the beach and our cottage in martha's vineyard. That is in massachusetts, and it is a beautiful spot for relaxing, swimming, and fishing. We prepare for vacation kickoff for nearly a week. Mother and father go to cheri's bakery and order a special cake. Dad prepares the steak marinade and checks the stash of fireworks. We purchase all our groceries for the vacation month. My brother, nate, has to decide whether the vacation cereal this year will be cheerios or kix. Once vacation starts we don't venture beyond the beach at the end of hiawatha road unless we have to.

PUNCTUATION

Writers use punctuation to indicate breaks in thought and relationships of words, phrases, clauses, and sentences. Use of correct punctuation is essential in order to make the writer's material clear. Items in this category of COMPASS test your ability to identify punctuation that is omitted, unnecessary, or in the wrong place. Knowing the basics of correct punctuation will help you identify what you should change.

COMMAS

There are many uses for the comma: to separate items in a series, introductory elements, interrupters, independent clauses (which can stand on their own) joined by a coordinating or subordinating conjunction, quotations, correspondence, numbers, parenthetical expressions, nonessential clauses, coordinate adjectives, sharply contrasting coordinate elements, appositives, and direct address. They are also used to prevent misreading of a sentence. Here is a quick review of comma usage:

▶ **Series**   The artist limited her landscapes to rivers, lakes, and seashores.

▶ **Introductory element**   After removing his coat, my father would whistle for our two border collies.

▶ **Interrupter**   It is snowing. The sun, however, is shining.

▶ **Independent clauses**   Kate is currently performing in a play, so she must budget her time wisely.

▶ **Quotations**   "Heather," he said, "perhaps you should consult the map before heading to Columbus."

▶ **Correspondence**   Dear Susan, *or* 101 West Peachtree Road, Atlanta, Georgia

▶ **Numbers**   10,000

▶ **Parenthetical expression/nonessential clause**   Mrs. LaTulippe, who was always my favorite, baked delicious birthday cakes.

▶ **Coordinate adjectives**   The abandoned children became starved, violent savages.

▶ **Sharply contrasting coordinate adjectives**   The old sports car was rusty, yet charming in that way old things can be.

▶ **Appositive**   Our boat, a leaky old tub, was no match for the shiny new runabout.

▶ **Direct address**   Help me with the groceries, David, and I'll get dinner started.

▶ **Preventing misreading**   As Hamlet, David would cry out for his father's ghost.

Hint: Most people have trouble with commas because they use them too frequently. Make sure you are following a comma rule whenever you place one.

COLONS

Colons are used after a clause introducing a list, after a statement introducing an explanation or amplification, after a statement introducing a long quotation, in the salutation of a formal letter, to separate hour and minute, in Bible verses, and to separate title and subtitle.

▶ **A list**   This course will cover the following topics: first aid, CPR, nutrition, exercise, and stress management.

▶ **Explanation or amplification** (you could also use a dash)   There was one explanation for his success: luck.

▶ **Long quotation**   Benjamin Franklin once wrote:

▶ **Formal correspondence**   Dear Sir:

▶ **Bible reference**   John 3:16

▶ **Time**   10:45 p.m.

▶ **Title/Subtitle**   *Why Some Stay and Some Don't: An Analysis of First–Year College Students*

SEMICOLONS

A semicolon is used to separate independent clauses when there is no conjunction or to separate those that have a conjunction but also have heavy internal punctuation.

▶ **Independent clauses with no conjunction**   We went to see a movie; then we had lunch and did some shopping in the mall.

▶ **Heavy internal punctuation with coordinate elements**   The tour group visited museums in Vienna, Austria; Paris, France; Florence, Italy; Madrid, Spain; and London, England.

APOSTROPHES

The apostrophe (') is used for two purposes: to show possession and to form contractions. Writers use an apostrophe (') or an apostrophe s ('s) added to nouns or some adjectives to indicate possession. In deciding whether an apostrophe is correctly placed or not, ask yourself whether the noun or adjective is singular or plural.

Add apostrophe s ('s) to singular nouns and some possessive adjectives to indicate possession in this way:

the King**'s** horses   Joe**'s** new car   a day**'s** work   the cat**'s** claw

Add only the apostrophe (') to the end of a plural noun ending in s. If the plural noun does not end in s, however, add the apostrophe s ('s) just as you would for a single noun. Add apostrophe s to singular nouns ending in s (especially proper nouns) unless it would be too difficult to read (such as Athens's citizens).

the cats**'** toys   the women**'s** offices   Charles**'s** home   two months**'** vacation

MORE ON APOSTROPHES

Contractions are combinations of words. They are appropriate only in informal writing and conversation. Apostrophes are used to indicate what letters are left out when contractions are formed. Place them **only** where the letters are missing and **not** between the two words (wasn't **not** was'nt).

you are you're   we are we're   we will we'll   they are they're

Finally, use apostrophes with letters, numbers, and symbols that are plural and used as words:

Your **1's** look like **6's,** so I made the check out incorrectly.

PERIODS

Periods are used at the end of a declarative sentence, an imperative sentence, or an indirect question.

▶ **Declarative**   John hosted a dinner party for twelve after his daughter's dance recital.

▶ **Imperative**   Move to the middle of the transit car.

▶ **Indirect question**   Quintilla asked whether she could borrow the lawn mower.

QUESTION MARKS

Question marks are used only after directly stated questions. They are not used with politely stated requests or indirect questions.

▶ **Directly stated question**   What time does her flight arrive from Hong Kong?

▶ **Indirect**   He asked if the attorney had prepared her witnesses.

▶ **Business (politely stated request)**   Would you please review my resume.

EXCLAMATION POINTS

An exclamation mark is ending punctuation used after a statement of strong feeling.

▶ I have never been so angry!

DASHES

Dashes are used for emphasis when the writer wants the reader to pause a length of time somewhere between a comma and a period. Like parentheses, dashes should be used infrequently.

▶ My sister – may she be covered in freckles and peeling skin – was invited to the beach for our spring vacation.

PARENTHESES

Information that is extra or incidental to the sentence is set off by parentheses. A common use of parentheses is to indicate dates. Parentheses should not be used often.

▶ Susan (my oldest sibling) is writing a biography of our family.

▶ Tinto (1993) discusses the reasons why students leave college.

Exercise 3

Complete the following exercise by inserting the correct punctuation.

1. I like <u>Runaway Jury</u> the best of all the books John Grisham has written.

2. Have you read, <u>The Client</u>, his book about a female attorney?

3. "Do you want to go. Joseph asked, "or would you prefer to stay a little longer?"

4. I just cannot do mathematics!

5. Hey, don't drink out of my water glass!

6. Kate's birthday is July 4, 1979.

7. Because, we ran out of money, we went home early.

8. We were seventeen, attractive, and foolish the year we rented the house at the beach.

9. The Jungle, a book by Upton Sinclair, exposed the evils of the Chicago stockyards.

10. Tiramisu, on the other hand, is a dessert worth wasting the calories.

11. Atlanta, Georgia has been the site of many conferences, the Superbowl, and the Olympics.

12. Frank, I thought I asked you to pick up my registration booklet.

13. My favorite all–time movies are the following, *Diner Pulp, Fiction,* and *The Holy Grail.*

14. I finish classes at 4:00 p.m.; consequently, I cannot attend a 3:45 p.m. meeting.

15. New Jersey and Delaware are mid–Atlantic states, Maryland is as well.

SENTENCE CONSTRUCTION

Sentence construction may take several forms. Clauses may stand alone or be connected in many different configurations. The rule is, however, that a sentence must express a complete thought and have the elements of subject and verb to stand alone. Be careful of fragments and fused sentences, comma–splices, or run–ons.

Fragments are pieces of sentences. They have a capital letter at the beginning and a period at the end but cannot stand alone. Fragments are constructed in four main ways: dependent clauses made to look like sentences, –ing ending verbs that stand alone, sentences that are split by capitalization and punctuation, and modifiers that are set up as sentences although they have no subject. Study these examples:

▶ **Dependent clause** When I learned to drive at the age of fifteen.

▶ **–ing form** The mayor standing up on the platform.

▶ **Split sentence** Jimmy Carter, who lost the 1980 Presidential election. Is probably best known for his humanitarian work.

▶ **Modifying phrase set up like a sentence** Because he is the most famous living President. Ronald Reagan attracts attention wherever he goes.

Comma–splices, run–ons, or fused sentences occur when two complete thoughts that could be two separate sentences are incorrectly combined. Here are several such sentences:

▶ When she was first diagnosed with breast cancer, she tried to hide it she had never been so frightened in her life.

▶ **When she was first diagnosed with breast cancer, she tried to hide it because she had never been so frightened in her life.**

▶ He lied she believed him.

▶ **He lied, and she believed him.**

▶ The Olympic Games in Georgia will be dangerous for athletes they will be subjected to very high temperatures and soaring humidity.

▶ **The Olympic Games in Georgia will be dangerous for athletes; they will be subjected to very high temperatures and soaring humidity.**

Hint: You could correct the last three examples easily by making each into two separate sentences. Beginning writers should do that. Mature writers (college level) should learn to correct them in other ways, by rewriting the sentences or with punctuation.

AGREEMENT

VERBS AND THEIR SUBJECTS

A verb must agree in number with its subject. A singular subject requires a singular verb. A plural subject requires a plural verb. It's not quite as simple as it sounds, however. The first step in determining subject and verb agreement is identifying the subject and verb. Try not to be concerned with other words in the sentence as they may confuse you.

► The Tooth Fairy always paid well for the pearly white nuggets under the pillow. **(Tooth Fairy/paid)**

► The characters make the play come to life. **(characters/make)**

Be careful of plural words that come between subject and verb.

► Our concern for the young, the elderly, and the ill causes us to volunteer frequently. **(concern/causes)**

Sometimes verbs come before subjects. Watch for this when the following words precede the subject: there, here, which, who, what, where.

► Across the window ledge stretches the cat to her fullest length. **(stretches/cat)**

► There are your slippers. **(slippers/are)**

Sometimes the subject is compound. Nouns, noun phrases, or pronouns connected by **and** are compound subjects that usually take a plural verb.

► Tammy, Mandy, and I are all wearing blue to the winter formal. **(Tammy, Mandy, and I/are)**

Subjects that are combined using "either...or," "neither...nor," or "not only...but also" require the verb that agrees with the subject closest to the verb.

► Either a ring or bangle bracelets are what I want for my birthday. **(bracelets/are)**

Sometimes the subject is a collective noun. A collective noun takes a singular verb when the members are treated as a unit and a plural verb when they are treated as individuals.

► The class is attending the play tomorrow. **(acting as a unit)**

► The class are writing their autobiographies. **(acting as individuals)**

ADJECTIVES AND ADVERBS

Adjectives are used for comparison. They have three forms: absolute or positive, comparative, and superlative. The comparative form can be made by adding –er or the adverb "more," and the superlative can be made by adding –est or "most." Comparative form is used when comparing one thing to another. Superlative is used when comparing to three or more persons or things. Additionally, some adjectives (usually with two or more syllables) must use "more" and "most" to form the comparative and superlative forms. Also, some adjectives are absolute. For example, you cannot have degrees of **final, complete, empty, dead, full,** or **perfect.** Finally, look at the close relationship between adjectives and adverbs as represented by **good/well** and **bad/badly.** These pairs have the same comparative and superlative forms.

POSITIVE	COMPARATIVE	SUPERLATIVE
fine	finer	finest
short	shorter	shortest
dumb	dumber	dumbest
happy	happier	happiest
foolish	more foolish	most foolish
nervous	more nervous	most nervous
good	better	best
well	better	best
bad	worse	worst
badly	worse	worst

▶ Stan is **tall**. He is **taller** than his twin brother. He is the **tallest** player on the team.

Adjectives modify only nouns and pronouns and adverbs modify verbs, adjectives, and adverbs. A common mistake people make is using an adjective instead of an adverb after a verb.

Note the following examples:

▶ He rode the horse **easy**. (should be **easily**)

▶ The moose ran **aggressive** toward the boat. (should be **aggressively**)

Hint: Do not confuse the use of **well (an adverb)** and **good (an adjective.)** Some words may be adjectives or adverbs. Their use is determined by the word they modify.

Exercise 4

Complete the following exercise by underlining the correct choice, changing incorrect words, or rewriting sentences.

1. The dolphins (was, were) swimming along with the boat.

    were

2. Neither the captain nor his first mate (seem, seems) concerned that we are taking on water.

    seems

3. One of the Senatorial contenders was our (most best, best) friend.

    best

4. The subject of the course (is, are) the political process in the United States.

    is

5. Is he the man (who, whom) is running for office?

    who

6. (Who, whom) did you see at the tennis match?

    whom

7. It was (he, him) who stole the money and ran.

    he

8. (We, us) girls appreciate a night out once in awhile.

    We

9. This demonstration, with signs, people shouting, and police barricades, (remind, <u>reminds</u>) me of the 60's.

    reminds

10. At the age of six, Mozart's father gave him a harpsichord.

11. Kate read the play about overcoming hardships while riding the exercise bicycle.

12. While fixing dinner, the hamburger burned.

13. It was a present from her grandmother, the antique.

14. When Bill and Tom came in, I told him about the case.

    them

15. The seagulls were diving at the shellfish which scared the children.

PRONOUNS

Pronouns usually substitute for nouns and, as such, may be subjects, objects, or possessives. You must check the pronoun/antecedent relationship and watch for singular plural status. Consider:

Personal Pronouns: *I, you, he, she, it, we, you,* and *they* are used as subjects. *Me, you, him, her, it, us,* and *them* are used as objects. *My, mine, your, yours, his, her, hers, its, our, ours, their,* and *theirs* are used to show possession.

Reflexive Pronouns: *Myself, yourself, himself, herself, ourselves, yourselves, themselves,* and *itself* are all reflexive pronouns used to reflect the sentence action back to the subject. They are frequently misused, so it is a good idea to avoid them.

Relative Pronouns: *Who, whom, which, that, whatever,* and *whomever* are relative pronouns used to join subordinate clauses to sentences. Clauses containing relative pronouns are not complete sentences. Students often confuse *who* with *whom* and *that* with *which*. Use *who* as a subject form and *whom* as an object form. Use *that* when the clause is essential and *which* if the clause could be left out without changing the meaning of the sentence.

Demonstrative Pronouns: *That, this, these,* and *those* are demonstrative pronouns and are used to clarify what you are talking about.

Interrogative Pronouns: *Which, who, whom,* and *what* can all be used as interrogatives asking a question.

Indefinite Pronouns: *Everything, everybody, many, more, much, plenty, several, some, enough, someone, any, anybody, anything, both, either, each, one, none, nothing, few, less,* and *neither* may all be indefinite pronouns. Understanding whether they are used as singular or plural is important to be able to match them to the appropriate verb. Requiring the plural verb are: *all, many, plenty, few, both,* and *several*. Singular verbs are required by: *anything, anybody, everybody, everything, nothing, either, neither, much, one, someone, somebody, something, each,* and *every*. The following are singular if treated as a group and plural otherwise: *none, some, and most*.

> **Hint:** Commonly confused possessive pronouns: it's, its; your, you're; who's, whose; their, they're.

Here is a brief word about gender usage and pronouns. Writing that requires consistent use of "he or she" or "him/her" or "(s)he" can be strengthened by using gender neutral words. Could the word "students," "people," or "workers" substitute for male- or female-specific words in your paper? Instead of fireman, policeman, businessman, or chairman, how about firefighter, police officer, business professional, or chair? As an added bonus such substitutions may help you avoid pronoun problems.

AGREEMENT: PRONOUNS AND ANTECEDENTS

A pronoun must agree in number with the word it replaces. The word replaced is called the **antecedent.** Pronouns include: I, you (singular and plural), he, she, it, they, and their declensions.

▶ Herman could not understand why he didn't make the team. (**Herman/he**)

Pronouns must clearly refer and relate to what they modify.

▶ Jane's husband works **downtown**, but she isn't interested in **it. (unclear)**

▶ Jane's husband works **downtown**, but she isn't interested in working **there. (clear)**

One mistake students frequently make in pronoun usage is shifting point of view. Pronouns must not present a shift in view.

▶ **I** love acting and being able to interpret characters on stage. It's more to **you** than just a job. (**shifts from I to you**)

▶ **I** love acting and being able to interpret characters on stage. It's more to **me** than just a job. (**no shift**)

▶ I hate the parts of school such as tests, quizzes, and writing assignments that stress you out. (**shifts from I to you**)

▶ I hate the parts of school such as tests, quizzes, and writing assignments that stress me out. (**no shift**)

Hint: Keep modifiers as close to the word they modify as possible.

Exercise 5

Match the following pronoun uses to a description:

1. **We** asked Sherry to prepare the holiday meal.

2. Sherry sent **us** an email asking for menu suggestions.

3. I sent her **my** list of favorites.

4. I **myself** volunteered to bring the wine.

5. Dan said that we needed to prepare for fifty, **whatever** the actual responses were.

6. Gloria said, "**That** is a winner apple pie!"

7. "**Who** is bringing the stuffing?"

8. The cranberry sauce, **which** is my personal favorite, was left behind in Melba's fridge.

9. The one thing **that** we all forgot was rolls.

10. I had one helping of mashed potatoes. Jake and **several** others had more.

Hint: Try leaving out parts of the sentence when deciding what pronoun form to use.

FORMING VERBS

We use different tenses of verbs to indicate time. Verb tenses are based on three parts of the verb: present, past and past participle. From these it is easy to form the past, present, and future tenses, along with the past, present, and future perfect tenses. Regular verbs are those that form the past and past participle by adding –d or –ed to their endings. These are usually not difficult to use. Here are some common verbs in the six tenses:

present	wash	eat	put	complete
present perfect	has washed	has eaten	has put	has completed
past	washed	ate	put	completed
past perfect	had washed	had eaten	had put	had completed
future	will wash	will eat	will put	will complete
future perfect	will have washed	will have eaten	will have put	will have completed

---

Present describes something happening right now.

Present perfect indicates something has started and is continuing.

Past indicates something happened and is completed.

Past perfect indicates something happened before the past tense.

Future is for those things that have not happened yet.

Future perfect is for something from the past and the future that has happened and will go on and end at a certain point.

IRREGULAR VERBS

Some verbs are irregular and form tenses differently. Study the following:

present	swim	dive	hang (painting)	hang (execute)
past	swam	dived	hung	hung
past participle	swum	dived	hanged	hanged

Notice the verb TO BE:

present	past	past participle
am, is, are	was, were	been
I am	I was	I have been
we are	we were	we have been
you are	you were	you have been
he, she, it is	they were	they have been

Hint: Remember, the past participle form takes the helping word (has, have, had) and the past form does not.

SENTENCE STRUCTURE

RELATING CLAUSES

When writing sentences, it is important to structure the parts of a sentence to show equality or inequality of ideas. We show equality with what we call **parallelism** or **coordinate construction.** To do this, balance nouns with nouns, adjective clauses with adjective clauses, and prepositional phrases with prepositional phrases. When using the following conjunctions in parallel construction, always use them in pairs: **either/or; neither/nor; both/and; not only/ but also.**

► **Correct parallelism** During summer vacation I am going to swim, to sail, and to sleep late every day.

► **Incorrect parallelism** During summer vacation I am going to swim, sailing, and to sleep late every day.

► **Correct parallelism** **Both** Jeff **and** Choi are tied in their checkers match.

► **Incorrect parallelism** (needs **"but also"** to make parallel) I am **not only** the best all around athlete.

► **Correct parallelism** **Neither** the player **nor** the coach would give interviews.

► **Incorrect parallelism** (needs **"neither/nor"**) **Neither** the postmaster **or** the mail carrier could tell me where my package went.

When you are using ideas that are not equal you must use what is called **subordination.** In this type of sentence construction, the main idea is an independent clause (it can stand alone). The lesser or subordinate ideas are dependent clauses (cannot stand alone). Subordination is useful to keep short sentences from sounding choppy. The writer identifies the main idea and subordinates other ideas. Punctuate with a comma if the sentence is introduced by the dependent (cannot stand alone) clause. If the dependent clause is not introductory, then no comma is needed.

► If I score highly enough on the exam, I can exempt a college course. (**comma needed**)

► I can exempt a college course if I score highly enough on the exam. (**no comma needed**)

USING MODIFIERS

It is important that modifiers be placed correctly in a sentence to avoid ambiguity and to keep from splitting infinitives.

► At the end of the book, the characters begin to deliriously laugh.
(**misplaced modifier splitting an infinitive**)

► At the end of the book, the characters begin to laugh deliriously.
(**correctly placed modifier**)

Good writing is consistent in **voice and tense.** Voice indicates whether the subject is acting or being acted upon. Active voice is the stronger and preferred use of the two. Avoid passive voice as much as possible.

▶ **Passive voice**   Data **were collected** by members of the research team.

▶ **Active voice**   The research team **collected** data.

▶ **Passive voice**   The computer **was used** by the criminals to identify potential victims.

▶ **Active voice**   The criminals **used** the computer to identify potential victims.

Tense of verbs must be a logical indication of time.

▶ **Tense shift**   Harry **was wondering** if he should make a sandwich or not when the doorbell **rang** and his best friend **walks** in.

▶ **Consistent tense**   Harry **was wondering** if he should make a sandwich or not when the doorbell **rang** and his best friend **walked** in.

▶ **Tense shift**   College students need to **manage** their time wisely so they **didn't** have an unrealistic amount of work at the end of the semester.

▶ **Consistent tense**   College students need to **manage** their time wisely so they **don't** have an unrealistic amount of work at the end of the semester.

STANDARD IDIOMS

Idioms are figurative language that are used most often in speaking. They are a type of slang found in speech patterns of people of certain age, place, and culture. While they may be used in popular casual writing, they are inappropriate for formal academic writing. Consider the following:

▶ I remember my childhood and the family gatherings with great fondness because now I only see my relatives **once in a blue moon.**

▶ I remember my childhood and the family gatherings with great fondness because now I only see my relatives **occasionally.**

▶ I need to go home before we go to dinner and get rid of my **five-o'clock-shadow.**

▶ I need to go home and **shave** before we go to dinner.

Exercise 6

Edit the following sentences by making changes where necessary.

1. A person who likes fast food should watch their fat intake.

2. When the members of the team fell behind it lost the desire to win.

3. Yellow and dried Susan kept the corsage from the prom for months.

4. Hanging on the hook we forgot to grab our coats.

5. Eating leaves from the top branches we enjoyed photographing the giraffes.

6. Information about the terrorist threats was received by the news bureau chiefs.

7. She was neither the best.

8. Having my birthday cake.

9. Mini–blinds have been shown to cause a lead hazard to children. Which is why they will no longer be sold in the United States.

10. So I can get into a better college I am taking Advanced Placement courses.

11. We had walk ten miles before he said anything.

12. We had agreed to never argue about that issue again.

13. Some students do not realize that it is difficult to go to school and to be working.

14. The boat, quickly taking on water, sunk by the time help arrived.

15. All of us decided to consciously ignore the speaker who had insulted our intelligence.

CHAPTER NINE

RHETORICAL SKILLS

STRATEGY

APPROPRIATENESS FOR AUDIENCE AND PURPOSE

Whenever you write something, there are two things you must consider: **audience** and **purpose.** By **audience** we mean who will be reading what you write. If you are writing a letter to a friend, then you will use slang expressions and other informal usage. You might even use incomplete sentences. If, however, you are writing to a different audience, such as a prospective employer, you would want to use a formal style because that would make a good first impression. Compare the following two examples:

Hi,

    I am a high school student and I need to find a college. Could you please tell me what it's like at Yale? I guess I need to know how much it costs also. If you have some pictures could you send some?

Dr. Smith:

    I am a high school junior, and I am interested in learning more about Yale University. Your reputation for academics, opportunity for pre–law advisement, and resident college program are three areas that make me feel Yale may be the right choice for me.

The **purpose** for writing is an important consideration also. If you are writing directions for someone, you will want to describe steps in a chronological order. If you are describing the way something looks, you might want to use spatial order. If you are trying to persuade someone, you might want to make your points from most important to least important.

SUPPORTING FACTS AND DETAILS

Effective writing makes use of details to support a topic. Those details must be relevant to the subject and not stray from the topic. There should be enough detail to completely cover the topic for the intended audience. Someone who is very familiar with the subject of your writing will not need as many details as someone who is not. Consider the audience for the following paragraph. Note the irrelevant detail.

    My mother is a doctor. She is not just any doctor, though. She is the best. As she has her morning coffee, she looks over her patient list and tries to recall something about every person she is going to see that day. **She cooks a really good breakfast too. (This is not a relevant detail. It strays from the topic.)** Her patients always stay with her a long time because she cares so much about them.

OPENINGS, TRANSITIONS, AND CLOSINGS

These are all devices that help your writing to be cohesive, that is, flow smoothly from opening to closing with logical order and transitions. An opening is important because it is an opportunity to "hook" the reader and make the reader want to know more about your topic. In your attempt to find an interesting beginning, however, avoid such things as clichés, statements of what you are to write about, or apologies for any lack of knowledge. Notice the differences between these two openings.

"As God is my witness, I'll never be hungry again," said Scarlett O'Hara, and this is how I feel about my latest diet. I'm going to tell you how to achieve that skinny-minny Scarlett's eighteen inch waist. **(inappropriate reference, cliché, states what will follow)**

How can you lose weight and not endure hunger? My latest diet provides all the nutrients I need to feel satisfied, and yet I burn enough calories to lose two pounds per week. **(attention-getting and yet not chatty and cliché-ridden)**

Closings are also important for the same reason. You want to leave the reader with a good, strong ending. Generally, avoid the same problems as in your opening. Avoid clichés, statements about what you just said, and excuses. Never introduce material in a conclusion that you have not previously discussed. Consider the following:

So, I dare you to come see the new me. I'll be the skinny one in the teeny weeny bikini. I'll be thin as a rail, and I'll also have a new hairstyle. **(clichés, new material)**

So, if you're interested in a nutritionally balanced diet that allows you to eat good food and still lose weight, this is a plan you might want to try. **(concludes what was written about and makes a strong statement)**

ORGANIZATION

LOGICAL ORDER

The order in which you arrange ideas in your writing depends on the way you decide to develop your essays. You should always be sure your arrangement is logical. Consider the following paragraph:

1/ Planning a meeting can be a stressful experience if you've never done it before. **2/** The site needs to include enough meeting space. **3/** Good food can make even a poor meeting a pleasure. **4/** The committee must research the needs of members who have special needs. **5/** When considering the site, the meeting place is the most important consideration. **6/** You should discuss the purpose for the meeting before considering a site. **7/** Then there are several other considerations. **8/** Finally, the program planners should devise a varied and interesting series of activities for all the members of the organization.

What would be a better arrangement of these sentences? _____

(*Answers* to Logical Order and Chapter
Nine exercises are found on p.236.)

STYLE

MANAGING SENTENCE ELEMENTS/SUBORDINATION AND COMBINATION

As we have seen before, coordinate and subordinate construction are used to combine sentences. It is a mark of mature writing to be able to combine short, choppy sentences into longer, more effective sentences. In subordinate construction you determine the less important part of the sentence and place a subordinate conjunction before it. Coordinate construction (and coordinating conjunctions) is used when sentence elements are equal in importance.

▶ Coordinate conjunctions include: **or, nor, for, so, and, but,** and **yet.**

▶ Subordinate words include: **since, because, although, even though, though, when, where, how, after, as,** and **before.**

AVOIDING WORDINESS AND REDUNDANCY

Wordiness is the use of too many words to express your thoughts. Don't use more words than you need. Immature writers often do the following: string too many ideas together with *and*'s; use euphemisms; use worn out words; use the incorrect form of a word; use passive voice; use unnecessary words; repeat words.

MAINTAINING STYLE AND TONE

Be sure you maintain the same style, tone, and diction throughout writing. Notice how the following piece shifts in style.

Dr. Smith:

I was pleased to receive your invitation to interview for the faculty position in Biochemistry. Friday the thirteenth of August at 3:00 p.m. is a convenient time for me. I will be driving to Atlanta so I would appreciate it if you would provide a parking space. Maybe after the interview we could get a beer and take in a Braves game. I look forward to meeting you in August.

Sincerely,

Hardly A. Chance, Ph.D.

Exercise 7

Each of the following pieces of writing contains an error discussed in this section. Choose the letter of the corresponding fault for each sentence.

A. appropriateness for audience   F. wordiness

B. poor opening   G. redundancy

C. poor closing   H. maintaining style and tone

D. logical order   I. subordination/coordination

E. supporting facts and details

E 1. The rain was just what we needed. For weeks we had suffered under an unbearable burden of heat. All of our gardens were parched. Television programming was terrible.

C 2. As you can see, John F. Kennedy was a real "hear no evil, see no evil" kind of guy. The end.

A 3. Mr. James: I would like you to give me a job for the summer. I'm a really hard worker and I like being downtown.

H 4. Dear Sammi, It has been one week since we left on our vacation, and I have never had so much fun. We have visited museums, an aquarium, and other sites of interest. We have played miniature golf. I don't think Deborah is the best choice of girlfriend for James, do you?

D 5. The horses went galloping across the field. Over the stream and toward the hills, they raced. Two men had run to the barn and saddled horses.

I 6. I am going to see the Olympics so I don't have tickets yet.

G 7. In my honest opinion, if you know what I mean, and I'm sure you do, Cathy was one of the troublemakers.

F 8. Half a century has gone by since that happened fifty years ago.

B 9. Ghandi was a real people person and that's what this paper will be about.

CHAPTER TEN

PRACTICE TESTS

TEST ONE

Read the following paragraph carefully. For each numbered section, look at the choices that follow. Decide whether the section would be better with one of the changes or if it should remain unchanged. The choice "A" is always "no change." When you take the actual COMPASS test on the computer, the sections will not be numbered. You will have to move the cursor to the section you wish to change and highlight it. Then you will choose the letter of the change you would like to make. The item will be changed, and you will have the opportunity to see the changed text before going on.

1/ Hanging on the top of Faneuil Hall, in the market district, we always get excited when we see the grasshopper. **2/** Symbol of Boston. **3/** It's aged copper body is beloved by children and adults alike as one of the most famous landmarks of the city. **4/** Distinctively large as the gigantic grasshopper weathervane may be, however, it is one of **5/** many such easy identifiable Boston icons. **6/** Some others included the Statue of Paul Revere, the Public Gardens, the Old North Church, and the band shell on the Charles River.

The statue of Paul Revere is a famous reminder of the silversmith **7/** patriot which rode through the villages and **8/** warn of the approach of the British during the Revolutionary War. **9/** Much stories and poems have been written about him. **10/** The Old North Church which is where the **11/** lantern was hanged in the window, is another place worth visiting. **12/** Its graveyard is that very same place where many famous people are buried. **13/** The Public Gardens, across the street from the Common, has beautiful flowers and the famous Swan paddle boats. **14/** If you readed the story *Make Way for Ducklings* you have seen pictures of the Gardens and the Common. **15/** The famous band shell on the Charles River; that is where fans of the Boston Pops Orchestra have enjoyed summertime concerts for many years. It is located on an esplanade where you can see the crew teams of the many nearby colleges and **16/** sailboats bobbing for the river.

17/ Boston is such a historic city filled with such history. **18/** Everyone should plan to take his vacation there. **19/** Where else could you find such a mix of old and new.

1/

○ A. Hanging on the top of Faneuil Hall, in the market district, we always get excited

○ B. We always get excited when we see the grasshopper hanging on the top of Faneuil Hall

○ C. Hanging on the top of Faneuil Hall, the grasshopper always gets excited when we see

○ D. Hanging on the top of Faneuil Hall, we see the grasshopper and we always get excited

○ E. We always see the grasshopper hanging on the top of Faneuil Hall, very excited

2/

- ○ A. Symbol of Boston.
- ○ B. Symbols of Boston.
- ○ C. It is a symbol of Boston.
- ○ D. Symbolic of Boston.
- ○ E. Symbols in Boston.

3/

- ○ A. It's aged copper body is beloved
- ○ B. Its aged copper body is beloved
- ○ C. Its's aged copper body is beloved
- ○ D. It aged copper body is beloved
- ○ E. Its' aged coped body is beloved

4/

- ○ A. Distinctively large as the gigantic grasshopper weathervane may be, however,
- ○ B. Distinctively large as the gigantic weathervane may can be, however,
- ○ C. Distinctively large as the weathervane may be, however,
- ○ D. Distinctively as large as can be, however,
- ○ E. Distinctive large as can be, however,

5/

- ○ A. many such easy identifiable
- ○ B. many such easier identifiable
- ○ C. many such more easier identifiable
- ○ D. many such easily identifiable
- ○ E. many much easily identifiable

6/

- ○ A. Some others included the Statue of Paul Revere
- ○ B. Some others include; the Statue of Paul Revere
- ○ C. Some others includes the Statue of Paul Revere
- ○ D. Some others includes: the Statue of Paul Revere
- ○ E. Some others include: the Statue of Paul Revere

7/

- ○ A. patriot which rode through
- ○ B. patriot who rode through
- ○ C. patriot whose rode through
- ○ D. patriot that rode through
- ○ E. patriot who's rode through

8/

   ○ A. warn of the approach of
   ○ B. warned of the approach that
   ○ C. warned of the approach for
   ○ D. warned for the approach of
   ○ E. warned of the approach of

9/

   ○ A. Much stories and poems have
   ○ B. Much stories and poem have
   ○ C. Much story and poem have
   ○ D. Many stories and poems have
   ○ E. Many story and poem have

10/

   ○ A. The Old North Church which is where
   ○ B. The Old North Church, which is where
   ○ C. The Old North Church; which is where
   ○ D. The Old North Church: which is where
   ○ E. The Old North Church, which is that where

11/

   ○ A. lantern was hanged in the window
   ○ B. lantern was hanged; in the window
   ○ C. lantern was; hanged in the window
   ○ D. lantern was hung in the window
   ○ E. lantern which was hung in the window

12/

   ○ A. Its graveyard is that
   ○ B. It's graveyard is that
   ○ C. Its' graveyard is that
   ○ D. His graveyard is that
   ○ E. His' graveyard is that

13/

   ○ A. The Public Gardens, across the street from the Common, has beautiful flowers
   ○ B. The Public Gardens, across the street from the Common, have beautiful flowers
   ○ C. The Public Gardens, across the street from the Common, having beautiful flowers
   ○ D. The Public Gardens, across the street from the Common, they have beautiful flowers
   ○ E. The Public Gardens, across the street from the Common, are having beautiful

14/

   ○ A. If you read the story
   ○ B. If you have read the story
   ○ C. If you had read the story
   ○ D. If you read the story
   ○ E. If you have reading the story

15/

   ⊘ A. The famous band shell on the Charles River; that is where

   ⊘ B. The famous band shell on the Charles River: that is where

   ◯ C. The famous band shell on the Charles River was the place that

   ⊘ D. The famous band shell on the Charles River, that is where

   ◯ E. The famous band shell on the Charles River is where

16/

   ◯ A. sailboats bobbing for the river.

   ◯ B. sailboats bobbing on the river.

   ◯ C. sailboats bobbing in the river.

   ◯ D. sailboats bobbing to the river.

   ◯ E. sailboats bobbing over the river.

17/

   ◯ A. Boston is such a historic city filled with such history.

   ◯ B. Boston is such a historic city, filled with such history.

   ◯ C. Boston is such a historic city.

   ◯ D. Boston is such a filled with history city.

   ◯ E. Boston is such a city filled with history.

18/

   ◯ A. Everyone should plan to take his vacation here.

   ◯ B. Everybody should plan to take his vacation here.

   ◯ C. Everybody should plan to take one's vacation here.

   ◯ D. Everyone should plan to take one's vacation here.

   ◯ E. Everyone should plan to take a vacation here.

19/

   ◯ A. Where else could you find such a mix of old and new.

   ◯ B. Where else could you find such a mix of old and new?

   ◯ C. Where else could you find such a mix of old and new!

   ◯ D. Where? Else could you find such a mix of old and new.

   ◯ E. Where! Else could you find such a mix of old and new?

20/

If the following sentence needs to be inserted, where should it logically go?

For more information about visiting Boston, call your travel agent.

   ◯ A. after sentence 6

   ◯ B. at the end

   ◯ C. at the beginning

   ◯ D. before sentence 17

   ◯ E. before sentence 15

TEST TWO

1/ There have been a lot of research done on what makes students successful in college. 2/ The general belief is that if you work hard, study, and make good grades he will complete a degree. 3/ Studies show that; students most often leave college for reasons unrelated to grades. 4/ Girlfriends, boyfriends, homesickness, finances, lack of support, isolation. 5/ Would you like to know the most importantest thing you can do to increase your chances of remaining in college? 6/ No, its not study, although that is also essential. You need to bond with the institution. 7/ Thats the single most effective thing a student can do. 8/ What do we mean by bond, and how do you do it. 9/ We mean you need to really connect with a professor, 10/ make some friends, and attending some campus activities. 11/ Students who travel home each weekend to see their families and old friends do not make the important connections you need at college. 12/ Their not making the transition you make by connecting with a professor, 13/ you go to office hours, engage in conversation, and seek advice from professionals on campus. In this way you get in the groove. You also need to make some friends or at least acquaintances on campus. 14/ You will be much more satisfied with your choice of college and yet less likely to leave when things do not go smoothly. 15/ A good way to make friends is to immediately start a study group. 16/ We all think we captured all of the lecture notes and read all the important material also when we get together with others we find out everybody has information to contribute. 17/ Study groups help academically; and, can also lead to lasting friendships. 18/ Finally, get out of your dorm room and attend some campus events. 19/ Colleges and universities, take my word for it, provide many recreation opportunities from feature movies to sporting events to weekend camping trips. Relaxation is important to students; and, these activities could have provided some of the most worthwhile experiences of your college career.

1/

- ○ A. There have been a lot of research done
- ○ B. There have been many research done
- ○ C. There has been a lot of research done
- ○ D. There had been many researches done
- ○ E. There are many researches done

2/

- ○ A. if you work hard and study and make good grades he will complete
- ○ B. if you work hard and study and make good grades he will have completed
- ○ C. if you work hard and study and make good grades you complete
- ○ D. if you work hard and study and make good grades you will complete
- ○ E. if you work hard and study and make good grades you completed

3/

- ○ A. Studies show that; students most often leave
- ○ B. Studies show that students most often leave
- ○ C. Studies show: that students most often leave
- ○ D. Studies show that students: most often leave
- ○ E. Studies show that students most oftenest leave

4/

    ○ A. grades. Girlfriends, boyfriends, homesickness, finances, lack of support, isolation.

    ○ B. grades; girlfriends, boyfriends, homesickness, financed, lack of support, isolation.

    ○ C. grades, girlfriends, boyfriends, homesickness, finances, lack of support, isolation.

    ○ D. grades: girlfriends, boyfriends, homesickness, finances, lack of support, and isolation.

    ○ E. grades. Girlfriends and boyfriends and homesickness and finances and lack of support and isolation.

5/

    ○ A. Would you like to know the most importantest

    ○ B. Would you like to know the more importantest

    ○ C. Would you like to know the most important

    ○ D. Would you like to know the much more importantest

    ○ E. Would you like to know the importanter

6/

    ○ A. No, its not study, although that is also essential.

    ○ B. No, it's not study, although that is also essential.

    ○ C. No, it not study, although that is also essential.

    ○ D. No, its' not a study, although that is also essential.

    ○ E. No, it's not a study, although that is also essential.

7/

    ○ A. Thats the single most effective

    ○ B. That the single most effective

    ○ C. That's the single most effective

    ○ D. That's the single mostest effective

    ○ E. Thats the single more effectiver

8/

    ○ A. What do we mean by bond, and how do you do it.

    ○ B. What do we mean by bond, and who do you do it.

    ○ C. What do we mean by bond, and how do you do it?

    ○ D. What do you mean by bond, and how does it do it?

    ○ E. What do you mean by bond, and how did it do it?

9/

○ A. We mean you need to really connect with a professor,

⊘ B. We mean you really need to connect with a professor,

○ C. We mean you need to connect really with a professor,

○ D. We mean really, you need to connect with a professor,

○ E. We mean you need to connect with a real professor,

10/

○ A. make some friends, and attending some campus activities

○ B. make some friends, and be attending some campus activities

○ C. make some friends, and attended some campus activities

○ D. make some friends, who attended some campus activities

⊘ E. make some friends, and attend some campus activities

11/

○ A. Students who travel home each weekend to see their families and old friends do not make

○ B. Students who travel home each weekend to see his families and old friends do not make

○ C. Students who travel to home each weekend and see their family and old friends do not make

⊘ D. Students who travels home each weekend to see their families and old friends do not make

○ E. Student who travel home each weekend to see their families and old friends do not make

12/

○ A. Their not making the transition you need to make

○ B. They not making the transition you need to make

⊘ C. They're not making the transition you need to make

○ D. Theyre not making the transition you need to make

○ E. There not making the transition you need to make

13/

○ A. you go to office hours, engage in conversation, and seek advice from professionals

○ B. going to office hours, engaging in conversation, and seeking advice from professionals

⊘ C. go to office hours, engage in conversations, and seek advice from professionals

○ D. you going to office hours, you engaging in conversation, and you seeking advice from professionals

○ E. went to office hours, engaged in conversation, and sought advice from professionals

14/

○ A. You will be much more satisfied with your choice of college and yet less likely to leave

○ B. You will be much more satisfied with your choice of college but less likely to leave

○ C. You will be much more satisfied with your choice of college; nevertheless less likely to leave

○ D. You will be much more satisfied with your choice of college but likely to leave

○ E. You will be much more satisfied with your choice of college and less likely to leave

15/

   ○ A. A good way to make friends is to immediately start a study group

   ○ B. A good way to make friends is immediately to start a study group.

   ○ C. A good way to make friends is to start immediately a study group.

   ○ D. A good way to make friends is to start a study group immediately.

   ○ E. A good way to make friends is to start an immediate study group.

16/

   ○ A. important material also when we get together with others

   ○ B. important material; however, when we get together with others,

   ○ C. important material however when we get together with others

   ○ D. important material and also when we get together with others

   ○ E. important material so when we get together with others

17/

   ○ A. academically; and, can also lead

   ○ B. academically, and, can also lead

   ○ C. academically and can also

   ○ D. academically. And can also

   ○ E. academically, and: can also lead

18/

   ○ A. Finally, get out of your dorm room

   ○ B. Finally get out of your dorm room

   ○ C. Finally: get out of your dorm room

   ○ D. Finally; get out of your dorm room

   ○ E. Finally, get out of your: dorm room

19/

   ○ A. Colleges and universities, take my word for it,

   ○ B. Colleges and universities, you can take my word for it

   ○ C. Colleges and universities, why not take my word for it

   ○ D. Colleges and universities provides

   ○ E. Colleges and universities provide

20/

If you were asked to read about how to study in college, would this article fit that assignment?

   ○ A. Yes, because it talks about studying to make good grades.

   ○ B. Yes, because it focuses on studying in a group.

   ○ C. Yes, because anything you can read is helpful.

   ○ D. No, because it doesn't give you specific study techniques.

   ○ E. No, because it says study is not too important.

TEST THREE

1/ The period we know as the Industrial Revolution lasted approximately one hundred and fifty years from 1700 to 1850. 2/ Wow, that's a long time for a revolution! 3/ Inventions that changed lives forever and inspired future development. 4/ For example the steam engine led to mining improvements because water could be pumped out of coal mines. These coal mines were dark, and one never knew when one would step into an abyss. 5/ The steam engine yet powered the first steamship to cross the Atlantic, the kiln used to develop Wedgewood china, and the early locomotive. 6/ Communication was improved by the invention of the telegraph. Transportation by the macadam roadway.   7/ Early laws to protect workers including young children began to be developed.

8/ Although other countries made strides in technology and manufacturing, England is credited with leadership in the Industrial Revolution. 9/ There are several reasons for this: geography, capital, labor, management, and government. 10/ The government fostered, helped, and assisted the growth of the middle class through an expansion of the House of Commons. 11/ Thus, there was a middle class that was a part of the government and not in opposition to it. 12/ England had a financial stable government. 13/ It's banks could loan money and many citizens had investment capital. 14/ Feudal society was in decline. Workers could move about and establishs urban enclaves of factory workers. 15/ Agriculture could support an industrialize urban population. 16/ Additionally the educated middle class provided upwardly mobile management. 17/ Geographically England had ports useful for the shipping trade. 18/ Canals and the railroads provided transportation options throughout the country. 19/ Native raw materials, specifically, coal and iron meant that heavy industry and manufacturing did not have to depend on foreign assistance.

1/

- ○ A. The period we know as the Industrial Revolution lasted approximately one hundred and fifty years from 1700 to 1850.

- ○ B. The period we know as the Industrial Revolution lasted approximately one hundred and fifty years, from 1700 to 1850.

- ○ C. The period we know, as the Industrial Revolution, lasted approximately one hundred and fifty years, from 1700 to 1850.

- ○ D. The period we know as the Industrial Revolution; lasted approximately one hundred and fifty years from 1700 to 1850.

- ○ E. The period we know as the Industrial Revolution last approximately one hundred and fifty years, from 1700 to 1850.

2/

- ○ A. Wow, that's a long time for a revolution!
- ○ B. That's too long to be called a revolution.
- ○ C. In those years revolutions were long.
- ○ D. Wow! That's a long time for a revolution!
- ○ E. That is a long period of time for a revolution.

3/

- ○ A. Inventions that changed lives forever and inspired future development.
- ○ B. Inventions that changed lives forever inspired development.
- ○ C. Inventions that changed lives; forever, inspired future development.
- ○ D. Inventions came about that changed lives forever and inspired future development.
- ○ E. Inventions come about and changing lives forever inspired future development.

4/

- ○ A. For example
- ○ B. For: example
- ○ C. For example,
- ○ D. Four example
- ○ E. For examples

5/

- ○ A. yet powered . . .
- ○ B. also powered . . .
- ○ C. and also power . . .
- ○ D. and yet powers . . .
- ○ E. and has powered . . .

6/

- ○ A. invention of the telegraph. Transportation by the
- ○ B. invention of the telegraph; transportation by
- ○ C. invention of the telegraph, transportation by the
- ○ D. invention of the telegraph and transportation by the
- ○ E. invention of the telegraph, and transportation by the

7/

- ○ A. Early laws to protect workers including young children
- ○ B. Early laws to protect workers, including young children,
- ○ C. Early laws to protect workers including young children;
- ○ D. Early laws to protect workers including young children:
- ○ E. Early laws to protect, workers including young children

8/

- ○ A. technology and manufacturing, England is
- ○ B. technology and manufacturing. England is
- ○ C. technology and manufacturing; England is
- ○ D. technology and manufacturing, England was
- ○ E. technology and manufacturing. England was

9/

- ○ A. reasons for this: geography
- ○ B. reasons for this; geography
- ○ C. reasons for this. Geography
- ○ D. reasons for this, geography
- ○ E. reasons for this geography

10/

- ○ A. fostered, helped, and assisted the growth
- ○ B. fostered helped, and assisted the growth
- ○ C. fostered and assisted the growth
- ○ D. fostered the growth of the middle class and assisted in their growth
- ○ E. fosters and assists the growth

11/

- ○ A. Thus,
- ○ B. Thus'
- ○ C. Thus
- ○ D. Thus's
- ○ E. Thus:

12/

- ○ A. a financial stable
- ○ B. a financial, stable
- ○ C. a financially stable
- ○ D. a financially, stable
- ○ E. a financially, stabler

13/

- ○ A. It's banks
- ○ B. Its banks
- ○ C. Its' banks
- ○ D. Its's banks
- ○ E. It banks

14/

- ○ A. and establishes
- ○ B. and establish
- ○ C. and established
- ○ D. and establishing
- ○ E. and would establish

15/

    ◯ A. an industrialize

    ◯ B. and industrialize

    ◯ C. an industrialized

    ◯ D. and industrialized

    ◯ E. and industrializing

16/

    ◯ A. Additionally

    ◯ B. Additionally:

    ◯ C. Additionally,

    ◯ D. Additional information is

    ◯ E. Additionally and all,

17/

    ◯ A. Geographically England

    ◯ B. Geographically, England

    ◯ C. Geographically: England

    ◯ D. Geographical

    ◯ E. Geographical,

18/

    ◯ A. Canals and the railroads

    ◯ B. Canals, railroads

    ◯ C. Canals and railroads

    ◯ D. Canals, also railroads

    ◯ E. Canals also railroads

19/

    ◯ A. raw materials, specifically, coal and iron

    ◯ B. raw materials specifically coal and iron

    ◯ C. raw materials specifically: coal and iron

    ◯ D. raw materials, specifically: coal and iron

    ◯ E. raw materials, specifically coal and iron,

20/

    If you were asked to write an essay discussing the social effects of the Industrial Revolution would this essay fulfill that?

    ◯ A. Yes, because sentence 7 mentions a social problem.

    ◯ B. Yes, because it mentions people moving about.

    ◯ C. No, because it focuses on the inventions and conditions in England.

    ◯ D. No, because the English work very hard and are not very social.

    ◯ E. No, because there were no social effects. It was industrial only.

TEST FOUR

1/ Multiple Sclerosis is a nervous system disorder. 2/ Sclerosis means plaque, and multiple means many; hence, plaque in many sites. 3/ MS affect mostly people aged fifteen to fifty. 4/ More women contract MS than men, and those who live in the northern parts of the United States, Europe, and Canada are most likely to be affected. 5/ Caucasians have a greater chance of developing MS than people of other races. 6/ The cause of MS is not known, but a combination of factors–heredity, a suppressed immune system, and a virus–are all suspected. 7/ Many people are diagnosed after been seen by a doctor for another symptom. 8/ Diagnosis of MS is difficult but MRI and CT scans sometimes show the plaque formations. 9/ These formations develop, as science clearly has demonstrated in other diseases that are difficult to diagnose, when the myelin lining of the nerve axons is destroyed and plaque is left behind.

10/ Patients may experience weakness, numbness, dizziness, and hearing loss. 11/ They should know what cause their condition to worsen: stress, infection, and changes in climate. 12/ Emotional stability is sometimes affected. 13/ There is no cure for MS treatment is aimed at relieving symptoms. 14/ These treatment may include drug therapy, electrical stimulus, or surgery. 15/ These attempt to keep the patient active and functionally. 16/ The life expectancy of patients with MS is usually twenty–five years after you are diagnosed. 17/ Death is usually caused by infection that kills you. 18/ MS may be steadily progressive, or a patient could have episodes of progression and remission. 19/ Even, if there are steady periods of remission, each period of progression advances the disease.

1/

- ○ A. Multiple Sclerosis is a nervous system disorder.
- ○ B. Multiple Sclerosis being a nervous system disorder.
- ○ C. Multiple Sclerosis is being a nervous system disorder.
- ○ D. Multiple Sclerosis is becoming a nervous system disorder.
- ○ E. Multiple Sclerosis, a nervous system disorder.

2/

- ○ A. many; hence,
- ○ B. many, hence,
- ○ C. many hence;
- ○ D. many hence:
- ○ E. many, hence

3/

- ○ A. Multiple Sclerosis affect
- ○ B. Multiple Sclerosis have affect
- ○ C. Multiple Sclerosis will be affecting
- ○ D. Multiple Sclerosis do affect
- ○ E. Multiple Sclerosis affects

4/

   ○ A. More women contract MS than men,

   ○ B. More women contracts MS than men,

   ○ C. More women than men contract MS,

   ○ D. More women, men contract MS,

   ○ E. More women contract men than MS,

5/

   ○ A. have a greater chance of developing MS than people of other races.

   ○ B. are having greater chances of developing MS.

   ○ C. have been having greater chances of developing MS than people of other races.

   ○ D. will be having greater chances

   ○ E. would have had a greater chance of developing MS.

6/

   ○ A. and a virus—are all suspected.

   ○ B. and a virus are all suspected.

   ○ C. and a virus, are all suspected.

   ○ D. and, a virus, are all suspected.

   ○ E. and: a virus are all suspected.

7/

   ○ A. after been seen by a doctor for another symptom.

   ○ B. after seeing a doctor for another symptom.

   ○ C. after seen a doctor for another symptom.

   ○ D. after being saw by a doctor for another symptom.

   ○ E. after being sawn by a doctor for another symptom.

8/

   ○ A. difficult but MRI

   ○ B. difficult, but MRI

   ○ C. difficult, but; MRI

   ○ D. difficult; but, MRI

   ○ E. difficult: but, MRI

9/

   ○ A. develop, as science has clearly demonstrated in other diseases that are difficult to diagnose, when

   ○ B. develop, as science has shown us in other cases where it was difficult to diagnose, when

   ○ C. develop when the myelin

   ○ D. develop in similar ways to those in which scientists have a hard time diagnosing when

   ○ E. develop, not that they aren't easy to spot if you are a scientist, when

10/

- ○ A. Patients may experience weakness, numbness, dizziness, and hearing loss.
- ○ B. Patients may experience weakness numbness dizziness, and hearing loss.
- ○ C. Patients maybe experience weakness, numbness, dizziness, and hearing loss.
- ○ D. Patients may experiencing weakness, numbness, dizziness, and hearing loss.
- ○ E. Patients maybe are experiencing weakness, numbness, dizziness, and hearing loss.

11/

- ○ A. what cause their condition to worsen:
- ○ B. what causes their condition to worsen:
- ○ C. what causes their condition to worsen whereby
- ○ D. what causes their condition to worsen such as
- ○ E. what cause your condition to worsen:

12/

The best order of sentences 10, 11, 12, and 13 would be

- ○ A. 10, 11, 12, 13
- ○ B. 10, 12, 11, 13
- ○ C. 10, 13, 12, 11
- ○ D. 11, 13, 12, 10
- ○ E. 11, 12, 13, 10

13/

- ○ A. no cure for MS treatment
- ○ B. no cure for MS; treatment
- ○ C. no cure for MS, treatment
- ○ D. no cure for MS as treatment
- ○ E. no cure for MS: treatment

14/

- ○ A. These treatment
- ○ B. Anyway, treatments
- ○ C. Thus, treatments
- ○ D. Because these treatments
- ○ E. These treatments

15/

- ○ A. These attempt to keep the patient active and functionally.
- ○ B. These attempt to keep the patient actively and function.
- ○ C. These attempt to keep the patient actively and functionally.
- ○ D. These attempt to keep the patient activity and functional.
- ○ E. These attempt to keep the patient active and functional.

16/

◯ A. The life expectancy of patients with MS is usually twenty–five years after you are diagnosed.

◯ B. The life expectancy of patients with MS is usually twenty–five years after diagnosis is made of you.

◯ C. The life expectancy of patients with MS is usually twenty–five years after they can diagnose you.

◯ D. The life expectancy of patients with MS is usually twenty–five years after diagnosis.

◯ E. The life expectancy of patients with MS is usually twenty–five years after they diagnose.

17/

◯ A. Death is usually caused by infection that kills you.

◯ B. An infection usually causes death that kills you.

◯ C. Death is usually caused by an infection.

◯ D. An infection causing death usually kills you.

◯ E. Death causes an infection that kills you.

18/

◯ A. progressive, or a patient could have episodes of

◯ B. progressive thus, a patient could have episodes of

◯ C. progressive and so a patient could have episodes of

◯ D. progressive and so a patient could have had episodes of

◯ E. progressive and so a patient could have been episodes of

19/

◯ A. Even, if there are steady periods of remission

◯ B. Even if, as far as we know from patients we have studied, there are steady periods of remission

◯ C. Even if, there are steady periods of remission,

◯ D. Even if there are steady periods of remission,

◯ E. Even though we have studied and there are steady patients with periods of remission

20/

If the author wants to insert the following sentence, where would it be best to place it?

Some MS patients become so frustrated by their disease that they commit suicide.

◯ A. At the beginning to grasp the reader's attention

◯ B. At the end as a summation

◯ C. After sentence 12 because this is an example of emotional instability

◯ D. After sentence 14 because it contrasts with attempts to keep people alive

◯ E. After sentence 4 because Canadians have a higher rate of suicide

TEST FIVE

1/ Arthur Miller's *Death of a Salesman* was published in 1949 but the Loman family has all the elements of a contemporary dysfunctional family. **2/** Considered a modern tragedy, *Salesman* tells the story of Willy Loman, a salesman, who failed at life and paid the ultimate price. **3/** Female characters in Miller's play can be said to be used yet victimized. **4/** They are Willy's mistress, his wife, and the women son Happy is continually acquiring. **5/** The male characters exhibit the real tragedy in the play, however. **6/** Willy aspires to be success. **7/** In the process he accumulates debt, loses his job, and loses the respect of the son he favors. **8/** Biff is Willy's most favoritest son. **9/** Indeed, he ignores Happy who he pays no attention to. **10/** Biff, Willy's oldest son, and by all accounts the son with the brighter future, the high school football star. **11/** He has many university scholarship offers to play football in college in exchange for free tuition. **12/** However, he failed math and doesn't graduate from high school. **13/** Having an affair, Willy is seen by Biff when he travels to New England to seek his guidance. **14/** He leaves home, turns to compulsive stealing, and is fired from several jobs. **15/** Happy is the neglected Loman brother. **16/** He makes up for the inattention of his family by pursued women. **17/** A major theme of *Salesman* is dreams unfulfill. **18/** Willy is a man of dreams while his reality is crumbling around him. **19/** He even dreams his funeral will be a successfully event.

1/

    ◯ A. was published in 1949 but the Loman family

    ◯ B. was published in 1949, but the Loman family

    ◯ C. was published in 1949 but, the Loman family

    ◯ D. was published in 1949; but, the Loman family

    ◯ E. was published in 1949, and the Loman family

2/

    ◯ A. Considered a modern tragedy, *Salesman* tells the story of Willy Loman,

    ◯ B. Considered a modern tragedy; *Salesman* tells the story of Willy Loman,

    ◯ C. Considered a modern tragedy. *Salesman* tells the story of Willy Loman,

    ◯ D. Considering a modern tragedy, *Salesman* tells the story of Willy Loman,

    ◯ E. Consider a modern tragedy. *Salesman* tells the story of Willy Loman,

3/

    ◯ A. can be said to be used yet victimized.

    ◯ B. can be said to be used but victimized.

    ◯ C. can be said to be used and also to be victimized.

    ◯ D. can be said to be used up and victimized.

    ◯ E. can be said to be victimized.

4/

    ○ A. They are Willy's mistress, his wife, and the women son Happy is continually acquiring.

    ○ B. They are Willys' mistress, his wife, and the women son Happy is continually acquiring.

    ○ C. They are Willys's mistress, his wife, and the women son Happy is continually acquiring.

    ○ D. There are Willy's mistress, his wife, and the women son Happy is continually acquiring.

    ○ E. They are: Willy's mistress, his wife, and the women son Happy is continually acquiring.

5/

    ○ A. The male characters exhibit the real tragedy in the play, however.

    ○ B. The male character exhibit the real tragedy in the play, also.

    ○ C. The male characters exhibit the realest tragedy in the play, however.

    ○ D. The male characters exhibits the greatest tragedy in the play, however.

    ○ E. The male characters exhibit the greatest tragedy in the play however.

6/

    ○ A. Willy aspires to be success.

    ○ B. Willy aspires to be successful.

    ○ C. Willy aspires to achieve successful.

    ○ D. Willy aspires to be a successful.

    ○ E. Willy aspire to be successful.

7/

If you wanted to combine sentences 6 and 7 which of the following would be the best way?

    ○ A. to be successful, and in the process

    ○ B. to be successful, but in the process

    ○ C. to be successful so in the process

    ○ D. to be successful because in the process

    ○ E. to be successful; because, in the process

8/

    ○ A. Willy's most favoritest son.

    ○ B. Willy's son's most favorite.

    ○ C. Willy's favorite son.

    ○ D. Willy's son's favorite.

    ○ E. his most favoritest son.

9/

    ○ A. Indeed, he ignores Happy, who he pays no attention to.

    ○ B. Indeed, he ignores Happy, who he pays no attention with.

    ○ C. Indeed, he ignores Happy.

    ○ D. Indeed, he ignores Happy who he pays no attention to.

    ○ E. Indeed, he ignore Happy.

10/

- ○ A. son with the brighter future, the high school football star.
- ○ B. son with the brighter future, will be the high school football star.
- ○ C. son with the brighter future, the one who will be the high school football star.
- ○ D. son with the brighter future, the one who is being the high school football star.
- ○ E. son with the brighter future, is the high school football star.

11/

- ○ A. university scholarship offers to play football in college in exchange for free tuition.
- ○ B. university scholarship offers to play football.
- ○ C. university scholarship offers to play football in college.
- ○ D. university scholarship offers to play football in exchange for free.
- ○ E. university offers to play football for free.

12/

- ○ A. However, he failed math and doesn't graduate from high school.
- ○ B. However, he fails math and doesn't graduate from high school.
- ○ C. However he is failing math, he does graduate from high school.
- ○ D. However he fails math and doesn't graduate from high school.
- ○ E. However, he fail math and doesn't graduate from high school.

13/

- ○ A. Having an affair, Willy is seen by Biff when he travels to New England.
- ○ B. Having an affair, Biff sees Willy when he travels to New England to seek his guidance.
- ○ C. To seek his guidance, Biff travels to New England where Willy is having an affair.
- ○ D. Biff travels to New England to seek Willy's guidance, and he finds Willy is having an affair.
- ○ E. Biff travels to New England for guidance; Willy is having an affair.

14/

- ○ A. turns to compulsive stealing, and is
- ○ B. turns to compulsive stealing and be
- ○ C. turned to compulsive stealing and is
- ○ D. turns to compulsive stealing; and is
- ○ E. turned to compulsive stealing and was

15/

- ○ A. Happy is the neglected Loman brother.
- ○ B. The neglected Loman brother is happy.
- ○ C. Happy, the neglected Loman brother.
- ○ D. Happy, is the neglected Loman brother.
- ○ E. Neglected Happy is the Loman brother.

16/

○   A.   He makes up for the inattention of his family by pursued women.

○   B.   He makes up for the inattention of his family by pursuing women.

○   C.   Pursued by women he makes up for the inattention of his family.

○   D.   His family, pursued by women , make up for the inattention.

○   E.   Women he pursued make up for his family's inattention.

17/

○   A.   A major theme of *Salesman* is dreams unfulfill.

○   B.   A major theme of *Salesman* is dreams unfilled.

○   C.   A major theme of *Salesman* is dream unfulfill.

○   D.   A major theme of *Salesman* is dreamers unfulfilled.

○   E.   A major theme of *Salesman* is dreams unfulfilled.

18/

○   A.   dreams while his reality is crumbling around him.

○   B.   dreams and his reality is crumbling around him.

○   C.   dreams, yet his reality is crumbling around him.

○   D.   dreams so his reality is crumbling around him.

○   E.   dreams also his reality is crumbling around him.

19/

○   A.   a successfully event.

○   B.   a success event.

○   C.   a success of an event.

○   D.   a successful event.

○   E.   a success, for an event.

20/

If the author wants to add the following sentence, where would it logically go?
He dreams in superlatives of success for himself and his sons.

○   A.   between 6 and 7

○   B.   conclusion

○   C.   opening

○   D.   between 5 and 6

○   E.   between 11 and 12

ANSWER KEY FOR THE WRITING
SKILLS SECTION

Practice Essay

1. **D**   2. **A**   3. **D**   4. **C**   5. **E**   6. **B**   7. **B**   8. **C**

9. **D**   10. **C**   11. **E**   12. **A**   13. **A**   14. **B**   15. **E**

Exercise 1

1. college
2. immediately
3. apparent
4. write
5. Embarrassing
6. Committee
7. comments
8. too
9. right
10. wait

Exercise 2

1. Fourth of July
2. June
3. Martha's Vineyard
4. Massachussetts
5. Father
6. Cheri's Bakery
7. Nate
8. Cheerios
9. Kix
10. Hiawatha Road

Exercise 3

1. I like <u>Runaway Jury</u> the best of all the books John Grisham has written.   **(period)**

2. Have you read <u>The Client</u>, his book about a female attorney?   **(comma and question mark)**

3. "Do you want to go," Joseph asked, "or would you prefer to stay a little longer?"   **(commas and quotation marks)**

4. I just cannot do mathematics!   **(exclamation or period)**

5. Hey, don't drink out of my water glass!   **(comma and exclamation)**

6. Kate's birthday is July 4, 1979.   **(comma)**

7. Because we ran out of money, we went home early.   **(comma)**

8. We were seventeen, attractive, and foolish the year we rented the house at the beach.   **(commas)**

9. <u>The Jungle</u>, a book by Upton Sinclair, exposed the evils of the Chicago stockyards.   **(commas)**

10. Tiramisu, on the other hand, is a dessert worth wasting the calories.   **(commas)**

(continued on next page)

11. Atlanta, Georgia has been the site of many conferences, the Superbowl, and the Olympics. **(commas)**

12. Frank, I thought I asked you to pick up my registration booklet. **(comma)**

13. My favorite all–time movies are the following: *Diner, Pulp Fiction,* and *The Holy Grail.* **(colon and commas)**

14. I finish classes at 4:00 p.m.; consequently, I cannot attend a 3:45 p.m. meeting. **(semi–colon, comma, period)**

15. New Jersey and Delaware are mid–Atlantic states; Maryland is as well. **(semi–colon or period)**

Exercise 4

1. The dolphins (was, **were**) swimming along with the boat.

2. Neither the captain nor his first mate (seem, **seems**) concerned that we are taking on water.

3. One of the Senatorial contenders was our (most best, **best**) friend.

4. The subject of the course (**is**, are) the political process in the United States.

5. Is he the man (**who**, whom) is running for office?

6. (Who, **whom**) did you see at the tennis match?

7. It was (**he**, him) who stole the money and ran.

8. (**We**, us) girls appreciate a night out once in awhile.

9. This demonstration, with signs, people shouting, and police barricades, (remind, **reminds**) me of the 60's.

10. At the age of six, Mozart's father gave him a harpsichord.
    (answers may vary – be sure the reader can tell who was six)

11. Kate read the play about overcoming hardships while riding the exercise bicycle.
    (answers may vary – what does riding the exercise bicycle modify?)

12. While fixing dinner, the hamburger burned.
    (answers may vary – was the hamburger fixing dinner?)

13. It was a present from her grandmother, the antique.
    (answers may vary – was the present the antique or was the grandmother the antique?)

14. When Bill and Tom came in, I told him about the case.
    (change him to them – pronoun reference)

15. The seagulls were diving at the shellfish which scared the children
    (answers may vary – did the seagulls diving scare the children or did the seashells scare them?)

234

Exercise 5

1. PERSONAL PRONOUN as subject

2. PERSONAL PRONOUN as object

3. PERSONAL PRONOUN to show possession

4. REFLEXIVE PRONOUN

5. RELATIVE PRONOUN

6. DEMONSTRATIVE PRONOUN

7. INTERROGATIVE PRONOUN

8. RELATIVE PRONOUN

9. RELATIVE PRONOUN

10. INDEFINITE PRONOUN

Exercise 6

1. A person who likes fast food should watch their fat intake.
    (change "their" to "his" or "her" – or – say "people who...should,"– or –eliminate the pronoun entirely)

2. When the members of the team fell behind it lost the desire to win.
    (change "it" to "they")

3. Yellow and dried, Susan kept the corsage from the prom for months.
    (answers may vary – what was yellow and dried?)

4. Hanging on the hook, we forgot to grab our coats.
    (answers may vary – what was hanging on the hook?)

5. Eating leaves from the top branches, we enjoyed photographing the giraffes.
    (answers may vary – who was eating the leaves from the branches?)

6. Information about the terrorist threats was received by the news bureau chiefs.
    (passive voice – change to the news bureau chiefs received the information...)

7. She was neither the best.
    (fragment – answers may vary)

8. Having my birthday cake.
    (fragment – answers may vary)

(continued on next page)

(Exercise 6, continued)

9. Mini–blinds have been shown to cause a lead hazard to children which is why they will no longer be sold in the United States.
   (combine – subordinate independent first)

10. So I can get into a better college, I am taking Advanced Placement courses.
    (comma – subordinate construction)

11. We had walked ten miles before he said anything.
    (walked – verb form)

12. We had agreed to never argue about that issue again.
    (split infinitive – change to "never to argue")

13. Some students do not realize that it is difficult to go to school and to be working.
    (verb form not parallel; change to and to work)

14. The boat, quickly taking on water, sunk by the time help arrived.
    (verb form – sank)

15. All of us decided to consciously ignore the speaker.
    (split infinitive – to ignore the speaker consciously)

Answers to ORGANIZATION: Logical Order, p.210
1, 6, 5, 2, 7, 4, 3, 8

Exercise 7

1.	E		6.	I
2.	C		7.	F
3.	A		8.	G
4.	H		9.	B
5.	D			

ANSWERS FOR THE WRITING SKILLS
PRACTICE TESTS

Question #	Test 1	Test 2	Test 3	Test 4	Test 5
1.	B	C	B	A	B
2.	C	D	E	B	A
3.	B	B	D	E	D
4.	C	D	C	C	E
5.	D	C	B	A	A
6.	E	B	D	A	B
7.	B	C	B	B	B
8.	E	C	A	B	C
9.	D	B	A	C	C
10.	B	E	C	A	E
11.	D	A	A	D	B
12.	A	C	C	B	B
13.	B	B	B	B	D
14.	D	E	B	E	A
15.	E	D	C	E	A
16.	B	B	C	D	B
17.	C	C	B	C	E
18.	E	A	C	A	C
19.	B	E	E	D	D
20.	B	D	C	C	A

READING

PASSAGES

The Reading portion of **COMPASS** consists of passages similar to what you may have read on other traditional comprehension tests, such as the SAT. The average length of a passage is 215 words, and reading level of all passages is equal to that encountered in the first year of college. The material for the passages comes from textbooks, essays, journals, and magazines commonly used in entry-level college courses. There are five types of passages:

Practical Reading	These passages address everyday situations and experiences.
Prose Fiction	These passages focus on narration of events or telling a story and providing information about characters.
Humanities	These passages describe or analyze ideas or works of art.
Social Sciences	These passages present information gathered by research in areas such as Psychology, Sociology, and History.
Natural Sciences	These passages present a science topic along with an explanation of its significance.

Before each passage, you will see a screen that provides the following information about that passage:

    a)   a question that will help you focus your reading,

    b)   the source from which the reading text was excerpted, *and*

    c)   the author, copyright date, and publisher.

All of this information has been provided before each passage in the two practice tests located in Chapter 13.

QUESTIONS

COMPREHENSION ITEMS

There are five reading comprehension items that accompany each passage. Three of the five items are called **referring items**, and they pose questions about material directly stated in a passage. The reader can find the answer to the referring items in the information given in the passage. The remaining two items are **reasoning items,** which pose questions about material that is not directly stated in the passage. The reader must infer the answers to the reasoning items from the information given.

After you answer all the questions about a passage, you will be able to go back and change your answers. Since the test requires that you answer all of the questions about a passage before allowing you to go back and make changes, we recommend that you follow this same procedure when taking the practice tests in Chapter 13.

Your institution may elect to include a supplement to the reading comprehension items called **prior-knowledge items.** These six items measure what you already know about the subject matter of the passage. These items are easier than the referring and reasoning items, and they can be answered without reading the passage. In fact, reading the passage would not provide any information to help you answer the prior-knowledge items. The questions are presented after you have finished the test and when you can no longer refer back to the passage. These items do not contribute to your reading score.

ITEM FORMATS

There are two formats for items on COMPASS: multiple choice and text-highlighting. Multiple choice items require you to select the correct answer from five alternatives, and you need to read through the passage to determine which alternative is correct. Multiple choice items on COMPASS may be answered in one of two ways:

1) Press the up/down arrows to choose the bubble beside A, B, C, D, or E. Then press ENTER to select this answer.

2) Type the letter (A, B, C, D, or E) of the answer you think is correct. Then press ENTER . to select this answer.

You may choose the method of anwering you like best. Remember, you can go back and see the passage by pressing the S key.

Text-highlighting items ask you to locate within the passage a specific segment of the text that answers a question. This is done by highlighting a section of the passage. Sometimes, only a single word must be highlighted. Other questions may ask you to highlight several words or a sentence. For example, a text-highlighting item for a passage about abstract art might read:

Highlight the sentence in which the author sums up her feelings about abstract art.

CHAPTER ELEVEN

REFERRING ITEMS

As mentioned before, three of the five comprehension items following the passage will be referring items. Referring items test your skill level in identifying the stated main idea, recognizing the details, and understanding relationships presented in the passage. They also test your ability to think critically about the information in the passage. A definition for each of these subcategories of referring items, along with strategies for answering items correctly and exercises that allow you to practice these strategies, are presented below.

MAIN IDEA OF A PARAGRAPH

DEFINITION

The main idea is the central or most important thought in the paragraph. Every other sentence and idea in the paragraph is related to the main idea.

STRATEGY 1

One strategy for recognizing a main idea that is directly stated in a paragraph is to know the difference between the topic and the main idea. The topic is the one thing the paragraph is about and can usually be stated in one or two words. The topic may often be stated in the title. Establishing the topic will allow you to start locating the main idea efficiently. To determine the topic, try asking yourself simply, "Who or what is this paragraph about?" Students typically can identify the topic with little difficulty but struggle with verbalizing the main idea of what they read. The main idea is what the author is trying to communicate about the "who or what," or the key idea being expressed by the author. Once you have established the topic, you can identify the main idea by asking yourself, "What is the author communicating about the topic?" Then answer your question with a complete sentence! (This will help structure your thinking.)

Exercise 1

Read the paragraph below and answer the questions for identifying the main idea.

Psychology is relevant to our daily lives. We might get an argument from biologists, chemists, physicists, geologists, and even some astronomers, but I'm willing to make the claim that no other science has more practical, useful application in the real world than does the science of psychology. In everyday life, people can get by without thinking about physics or geology or biology, but they cannot get by without thinking psychologically. They must take into consideration a multitude of sensations, perceptions, memories, feelings, and consequences of their actions if they are going to survive, and certainly if they are going to prosper. [1]

1. Who or what is this paragraph about? _How Psychology_ _be used in our daily life_

2. What is the author trying to communicate to me about this who or what? _____ _We have to think our way, how_ _it's important to our daily life._

(Answers on next page)

These questions should have structured your thinking. The paragraph is about psychology and the author is trying to communicate the importance of psychology. Thus, the main idea is stated in the first sentence: *Psychology is relevant to our daily lives.*

STRATEGY 2

Another strategy for identifying a main idea explicitly stated in a paragraph is to visualize the possible locations of the main-idea sentence. Very often the main-idea sentence may be at the beginning of the paragraph, followed by the supporting information. You could think of the paragraph as information presented in the shape of an upside-down triangle: ▼

Or the supporting information may be presented first, with the concluding sentence stating the main idea. Picture the paragraph as a right-side up triangle: ▲

A paragraph may also present information, state the main idea in the middle of the paragraph, and then present additional information. Of course, a diamond shape would best represent this paragraph: ◆

Finally, both the introduction and concluding sentence of a paragraph may state the main idea. Visualize this format: ▼▲

Exercise 2

Read the following paragraphs and locate the main-idea sentences. Underline these sentences and then draw the shape (▼, ▲, ◆, ▼▲) that best fits the paragraph.

A. Foods that supply "empty calories"—calories without many nutrients—are not considered nutrient-dense. Soft-drinks, potato chips, candy bars, and cookies are not very nutrient-dense and are sometimes called "junk foods." However, many foods labeled as junk foods supply more than calories even if they are not considered traditional sources of nutrients. For instance, cookies are made with flour, usually enriched, which provides some nutrients. Also, some people need calories, just as some people need to limit calories. Foods that supply just calories are not inherently bad. It is the overeating of these foods, precluding or limiting the intake of more nutritionally valuable foods, that can create problems. Within the framework of sound nutritional practices, the consumption of these so-called junk foods is, and should be, permitted. Therefore, the term junk food is considered by most nutritionists to be inappropriate. All foods supply some nutrients, albeit sometimes in limited amounts.[2]

Shape that best fits this paragraph: _____

(*Answers* to exercises in Chapter Eleven are found on pp. 301-302.)

B.   Sounds are heard not only through the outer and middle ear, but also through the direct conduction of vibrations through the bones in the head. The clicking of one's teeth and chewing sounds from the mouth may be heard in this way. If a vibrating tuning fork is placed on the teeth, some of the vibrations are conducted directly to the cochlea of the inner ear. This kind of conductive hearing is very important when trying to determine whether a person has a hearing loss in the middle ear or has nerve damage in the inner ear. If a person has experienced a hearing loss and can hear a tuning fork placed on the teeth, the hearing loss has probably occurred in the outer or middle ear. If the tuning fork cannot be heard well using this method, the hearing loss is probably located in the inner ear. [3]

Shape that best fits this paragraph: _____

C.   Within eight years after Moliere's death, Louis XIV combined all French companies in one troupe, calling it the Comedie-Francais to differentiate it from the Comedie-Italian (commedia dell'arte). In 1689, a playhouse, the Theatre Francais, was built for the Comedie-Francais and the first national theatre in modern Europe was born. Sometimes known as the House of Moliere, the Theatre Francais was a symbol, in two important ways, of the emerging dominance of the middle class in the upcoming century. First, the repertoire of the Theatre Francais was based heavily on the comedies of Moliere, peopled with middle-class characters and their concerns. Second, the architectural shape of the Theatre Francais was more of a horseshoe than a semicircle. This subtle change commenced the process of eliminating the worst seats in the proscenium theatre and making more good seats available for the general public. That general public was the middle class who came to see themselves in Moliere's plays.[4]

Shape that best fits this paragraph: _____

D.   Before assessing someone's nutritional status, his family's medical history must be known. A history of heart disease, diabetes, obesity, or high blood pressure in a family can all be indicators of an increased risk for these diseases. Of course if an individual has problems such as diabetes, hypertension, kidney problems, and heart disease, nutritional status could be affected. A person's drug history is also important because many prescription drugs interfere with nutrient absorption, metabolism and excretion. The average elderly person takes three to eight prescription medicines per day. Many antibiotics such as penicillin interfere with the absorption of certain vitamins. A person may have an adequate intake of a nutrient, but because of interactions with a prescription drug, still develop symptoms of deficiency of that nutrient. For such reasons, you can fully evaluate someone's nutritional status only after assessing the complete medical history of that person.[5]

Shape that best fits this paragraph: _____

STRATEGY 3

Another strategy for identifying the main idea is to consider "directional" words. For example, *in general, generally, above all,* and *of great importance* are "directional" words that direct you to the main idea of the paragraph. The author may come out and explicitly say, *the main idea is, the main point* or *the main feature is, the key point is,* etc.

Exercise 3

Read the following paragraphs and circle the directional words that point you to the main-idea sentence.

A.　　Structure begins when one enters a classroom. As soon as people get together, even under a tree, structure begins. When they start talking we have even more structure. If it rains and we build a shelter to get in out of the rain even more structure emerges. And if there are too many people to meet all in the same room then other kinds of structure arise. Structure starts as soon as two people get together and continues as people continue. The crucial point is that some people persist in talking about unstructured education when they ought to be thinking about how much and what kind of structure.[6]

B.　　Techniques for aging skeletons rely on the appearance and structure of the skeleton and teeth. For aging young individuals, anthropologists rely on changes in the skeleton and teeth during growth and development, such as the age of tooth development and eruption, and the closure of epiphyses. Skeletal aging is generally less accurate in adults than in children, but there are a number of reliable methods available. These include the extent of wear or attrition of the teeth, the fusion of sutures of the skull, and appearance of the pubic symphysis. In general, the best approach to adult skeletal aging is to use as many indicators of age from a skeleton as are available for estimating age at death. A single indicator will not be as accurate as the combination of a number of age indicators or sites.[7]

C.　　It is clear that much of technology does come from the discoveries of science. It is also clear that a lot of technology doesn't. New "superconducting" materials are being made today. They conduct electricity with no resistance at relatively high temperatures, but we don't know how they work. The point is that it is technology that changes our lives, with the changes coming faster and faster. Given this tremendous impact, is it the case that students study technology in school? Do well educated people understand how microwave ovens work? Televisions? Automobile transmissions?[8]

MAIN IDEA OF A PASSAGE

DEFINITION

The main idea of a passage is an expanded version of the main idea of a paragraph. The main idea of a passage is the central or most important thought in the passage. Every other sentence and idea is related to the main idea.

STRATEGY 1

The same strategies you learned for determining the main idea for a paragraph can be applied for determining the main idea of a passage. Again, know the difference between topic and main idea. With a passage, the topic is sometimes referred to as the "general subject" and the main idea is sometimes referred to as the "central thought." The general subject would answer the question "Who or what the passage is about?" The central thought would answer the question "What is the author trying to communicate to me about the who or what?" Don't forget to answer these questions (in your mind) with complete sentences!

Exercise 4

Read the following passage, and answer the questions for identifying a main idea (or central thought) explicitly stated in a passage.

A.   A recent general theory of attitude change claims that there are two factors, or routes, involved in changing one's attitudes (Petty & Checkup, 1986; Teaser & Staffer, 1990). One factor of concern is the central route: the nature and quality of the message itself. The other factor is the peripheral route: issues above and beyond the content of the message, or its source. There are several factors involved in source credibility (e.g., such factors as vocal pleasantness and facial expressiveness) (Burgeon, Birk, & Pfau, 1990), but the two that seem especially important are expertise and trustworthiness.

Several studies (e.g., Aronson et al., 1963; Hovland & Weiss, 1951) suggest that the greater the perceived expertise of the communicator, the greater the persuasion. People convinced that they are listening to an expert are much more likely to be persuaded than they would be if they thought the speaker knew little about the subject matter—even if the messages were exactly the same.

Another factor that enhances a communicator's credibility is a high degree of trustworthiness (Cooper & Croyle, 1984). Studies by Walster and Festinger (1962), for example, demonstrated that more aided change resulted when subjects overheard a persuasive communication than when they believed the communication was directed at them. Trustworthiness and credibility were enhanced by a perceived lack of intent to persuade ("Why should they lie; they don't even know I can hear them?").[9]

1. Who or what is this passage about? _____

2. What is the author trying to communicate to me about this who or what?

    <u>Several factors are source of credibility</u>

Again, these questions may help to structure your thinking. The passage is about communication. The author is trying to communicate to the reader that: "There are several factors involved in source credibility, . . . but the two that seem especially important are expertise and trustworthiness."

STRATEGY 2

The strategy for visualizing the possible locations of a main-idea sentence is helpful for determining the main idea of a passage. Remember, the main-idea sentence can be at the beginning, at the end, in the middle, or at the beginning and at the end of the passage.

Exercise 5

Read the following passage, underline the main-idea sentence, and then draw the shape that best fits the passage.

A.   The word science is derived from the Latin word scientia meaning knowledge, and, indeed, science is a way of understanding that leads to a particular type of knowledge. Much of our world is understandable as a sequence of causes and effects. For example, we see a broken egg on the kitchen floor and several eggs near the edge of the kitchen counter. The broken egg can be seen as an effect, and we surmise that the cause was the egg rolling off the counter. The placement of the egg near the edge of the counter may also be seen as an effect, and its cause may be some one placing it there. Thus causes and effects occur in sequential chains of events. Science is our way of understanding such causal relationships.

Science should be contrasted with the humanities, which is a way of understanding aspects of the world that are not necessarily related to cause and effect. Judging the beauty of a picture or the morality of war are questions properly addressed within the humanities, but not through science. Both types of understanding are integral parts of our lives. A painter understands the science of pigments and light and the aesthetics of the painting being created. Both ways of understanding are necessary for human fulfillment.[10]

Shape that best fits the passage: _____

DETAILS

DEFINITION

The details of a passage are the information provided by the author as proof, explanation, or support of the main idea. The details can be described as the evidence provided to support the argument.

STRATEGY 1

The strategy for answering detail items is to shuttle back to the passage to find the information. Remember that detail items are explicitly stated information in the passage. It may help to tell yourself that the answer to a detail item is in the passage; all you have to do is locate it. It may be stated somewhat differently in the passage than in the question, but the material is substantively the same.

Exercise 6

Read the paragraph below and underline the details provided to support the main idea.

A.   Teachers use a wide array of rewards. Some give students candy or toys to reward desirable behaviors. Others use films, free time, extra outdoor periods, permitting a child to be first in the lunch line and other such positive actions as rewards to reinforce desirable behaviors. Frequently tokens, or paper "chips" are given to students that may later be redeemed for physical rewards or favors.[11]

STRATEGY 2

Another strategy for answering detail items correctly is to recognize directional words. In the same way that directional words can "direct" you to the main idea, they can "direct" you to the details and help you distinguish between major details and minor details. Major details provide proof, explanation, or support of the main ideas, and minor details provide proof, explanation, or support of the major details. In other words, the major details contribute directly to the main idea, and the minor details usually elaborate on some other detail that supports the main idea. Some directional words for major details are *one, first, another, further, also, finally,* etc. Some directional words for minor details are *for example, to be specific, that, this means,* etc.

Exercise 7

Read the following paragraphs, circle the directional words, and note on the blank line whether the directional words point you to a major or minor detail.

A.   It seems that the need to achieve is learned, usually in childhood. Children who show high levels of achievement motivation are generally those who have been encouraged in a positive way to excel ("Leslie, that grade of B is very good. You must be proud of yourself" as opposed to, "What! Only a B?"). High-nAch (need to achieve) children are generally encouraged to work things out for themselves, independently, perhaps with parental support and encouragement ("Here, Leslie, you see if you can do this" as opposed to "Here, dummy, let me do it; you'll never get it right!"). Further, McClelland is convinced that achievement motivation can be specifically taught and acquired by almost anyone, of any age, and he has developed training programs designed to increase achievement motivation levels (e.g., McClelland & Winter, 1969).[12]

(continued on next page)

Exercise 7 (continued)

B.   During and after the 1950's, physical anthropologists became more concerned with hypothesis testing and understanding evolutionary processes. Measurement, therefore, became a method by which to test hypotheses rather than the primary objective of research. Accurate measurements of skeletal material are still necessary today for (1) describing skeletons from archaeological sites, (2) comparing primate fossil remains with extant primates, and (3) investigating cases in forensic anthropology. For example, accurate measurements allow the physical anthropologist to estimate stature. This information is useful to both the description of skeletons from an archaeological site and in the investigation of skeletal material involved in a criminal case.[13]

RELATIONSHIPS

COMPASS includes items that test your skill in recognizing three different types of relationships: sequential relationships, cause and effect relationships, and comparative relationships.

DEFINITION

Sequential relationships are relationships in which the order is important and changing that order changes the meaning.

STRATEGY

A strategy for recognizing sequential relationships is to recognize signal words often used to indicate order. Some of these signal words include: *first, second, third, after, before, when, until, at last, next, later,* etc.

Exercise 8

Read the following paragraph and circle the signal word or words that indicate a sequential relationship.

A.   Experimental design begins with the difficult problem of asking the right question from which a testable hypothesis can be derived. Predictions are made based on the hypothesis, and methods for testing those predictions are designed. The experiment is conducted and data (sing. datum) are gathered. Finally, data are interpreted with respect to the perceived "correctness" of the explanation offered through the hypothesis.[14]

248

DEFINITION

    Cause and effect relationships are patterns where one element is seen as producing another element.

STRATEGY

    A reader can recognize cause and effect relationships by understanding signal words and phrases often used to indicate this type of relationship. Following are cause and effect signal words and phrases to be on the lookout for: *for this reason, consequently, on that account, therefore, because, hence,* etc.

Exercise 9

Read the following paragraph and circle the signal word or words that indicate a cause and effect relationship.

A.   One possible mechanism for triggering star formation from gas clouds has been recently suggested on theoretical grounds. Violent explosive events are not unusual in the universe. Stars can literally explode, sending off up to about ten percent of their mass into space along with a great deal of radiation. One consequence of such an explosion is a shock wave, which is a rapid change in pressure traveling as a pulse through space in much the same way that a "sonic boom" would travel. There are many of these shock waves traveling through space and observations have found stars forming at the edges of these waves.[15]

DEFINITION

    Recognizing **comparative** relationships involves an ability to see how two elements are similiar.

STRATEGY

    Again, look for key words that may indicate a comparative relationship. Signal words that are often used in this type of comparison are *greater than, less than, bigger than, similar, parallels,* etc.

Exercise 10

Read the following paragraph and circle the signal word or words that indicate a comparative relationship.

A.   Mars, midway in size between the Earth and the Moon, is also midway in many characteristics. It has an older surface with less activity than the Earth, but a younger and a more active surface than the Moon does. Martian lithosphere is thicker than the Earth's, indicating more rapid cooling, but not as thick as the Moon's. The Martian atmosphere is thin, but the Moon has none. But there does not seem to be intermediate life on Mars. Apparently physical conditions may once have been favorable for the beginning of life, but tests performed by the Viking Landers have not given results indicating life there today. The results do indicate a complex chemistry on the Martian surface so life on Mars is perhaps best left as an unanswered question.[16]

CRITICAL THINKING

Thinking critically may be described as an effort to make sense of our world by carefully examining our thinking and the thinking of others. Two types of items on COMPASS assess your ability to evaluate the thinking of others. These items are designed to determine your ability to recognize explicit evidence presented in support of a claim and your ability to recognize stated assumptions.

DEFINITION

Recognizing **explicit evidence** involves identifying the author's support for the idea or issue in question.

STRATEGY

A strategy for recognizing explicit evidence presented by the author is to be aware that evidence can be presented in a variety of forms. The author may provide evidence by relating a personal experience, describing observations, providing statistical data, discussing analogies (comparisons with similar situations), providing historical documentation, or explaining experimental evidence.

Exercise 11

Read the following paragraphs and write on the blank line the form of the evidence provided by the author to support the main idea.

A.   The world's petroleum use . . . is growing. While the growth rate varies somewhat, it is instructive to consider what will happen if we look at a simple calculation. From 1948 to 1973 oil consumption doubled in the U.S. In 1974 the world was consuming 56 million barrels of oil daily. Using these figures as a guide, a calculation can be made based on exponential growth. Starting in 1974, using 2×10^{10} barrels of oil and doubling every 22 years, in 784 years the earth would consume in one year a volume of oil equal to the volume of the earth![17]

_____ *Providing Data* _____

B.   When he was an MIT graduate student in industrial management, James Stoner gave subjects in his research a series of dilemmas to grapple with (Stoner, 1961). The result of each decision was to be a statement of how much risk the fictitious character in the dilemma should take. Much to his surprise, Stoner found that the decisions rendered by groups were much riskier than those individual group members had made prior to the group decision. Stoner called this move away from conservative solutions a risky shift. For example, doctors, if they were asked individually, might express the opinion that a patient's problem (whatever it might be) could be handled with medication and a change in diet. If these very same doctors were to get together to discuss the patient's situation, they might very well end up concluding that what was called for here was a new and potentially dangerous (risky) surgical procedure.[18]

_____

C.   Two flank eruptions of Kilauea volcano covered the village of Kapoho with lava. Between March 1 and 6, 1955, 36 million cubic yards of lava and cinders were erupted from vents west of the Kapoho prehistoric cone. Lavas covered 1,100 acres south of Kapoho. Between January 13 and February 20, 1960, 156 million cubic yards of lava flowed from vents north and east of Kapoho. Lavas covered 2,000 acres of land and formed 500 acres of new land when it flowed into the sea.[19]

Procedures   Data

D.   For hundreds of years, well into the eighteenth century, the attitude toward the mentally ill continued to be that they were in league with the devil or that they were being punished by God for sinful thoughts and deeds. They were witches who could not be cured except by confession and a denunciation of their evilness. When such confessions were not forthcoming, the prescribed treatment was torture. If torture failed to evoke a confession, death was the only recourse, often death by being burned at the stake. It has been estimated that between the fourteenth and mid-seventeenth centuries, nearly 200,000 to 500,000 "witches" were put to death (Ben-Yehuda, 1980).[20]

E.   I have attempted only one experiment that involved young children: a study of word associations. The procedure was simple: present a stimulus word and have a child respond with the first thing that came to mind. My first discovery was that 8 percent of the children simply did not want to play. They just walked away, back to the sandbox or some other activity. When children did agree to "play," they did some peculiar things. "I'm going to say a word, and then you tell me the first word you think of when you hear my word. Okay? My first word is black." After a moment's pause, a child looked up and responded, "My Mommy has a black dress and she wears it to church sometimes." The word association procedure is one of the most straightforward techniques in all of psychology. But "playing the game" is a task that some children may do with their own set of rules, and some may not be ready to play the game at all. I had failed to take into account the cognitive level of my "research participants."[21]

— Experimental Experiment

251

DEFINITION

Recognizing stated assumptions involves identifying an idea or principle that the writer states as true with no effort to prove the idea. When the author states an assumption with no proof or evidence, he assumes the reader will agree with what is being said. A critical reader does not believe something is true simply because it is in print or simply because it is in a textbook. However, a critical reader may decide to accept a statement without evidence, based on the author's qualifications or the quality of the publication.

STRATEGY

A strategy for recognizing stated assumptions is to identify any proof or evidence provided by the author to support what is being said. If proof or evidence is lacking, ask yourself questions such as, "Who wrote the article?" "What are the author's qualifications?" "Where was the article published?" "What seems to be the purpose of the publication?"

Exercise 12

Read the following paragraphs. Which paragraphs have stated assumptions by the author with no proof or evidence?

A.   Sadly enough, phobic disorders are far from uncommon. Estimates place prevalence rates at between 7 and 20 percent of the population; that's tens of millions of people (Marks, 1986; Robins et al., 1984). Phobias seldom extinguish on their own. Why don't they? There are many reasons, but one is that someone with a phobia is usually successful at avoiding the conditioned stimulus that elicits the fear. Someone with a fear of flying may get by driving or taking a bus or train.[22]

B.   Family therapy is based on the assumptions that (1) family members can be seen as a part of a system in which one member (and one member's problem) affects all of the others, and that (2) many psychological problems arise because of faulty communication, and that this is particularly critical within a family.[23]

C.   There are several potential advantages to group therapy. (1) The basic problem may be an interpersonal one and thus will be better understood and dealt with in an interpersonal situation. (2) There is value in realizing that one is not the only person in the world with a problem and that there are others who may have an even more difficult problem of the same nature. (3) There is therapeutic value in providing support for someone else. (4) The dynamics of intragroup communication can be analyzed and changed in a group setting.[24]

Which paragraphs have stated assumptions?_____C_____

252

CHAPTER TWELVE

REASONING ITEMS

As mentioned before, two of the five comprehension items following the passage will be reasoning items. Reasoning items test your skill level in making appropriate inferences about the main idea, thinking critically about the information in the passage, and determining meanings of words based on context. A definition for each of these subcategories of reasoning items, along with strategies for answering items correctly and exercises that allow you to practice these strategies, are presented below.

INFERENCES

DEFINITION

A basic level of reading comprehension is the literal level, where information is explicitly or directly stated in the passage. Chapter 11 provides strategies and exercises for the literal level of comprehension, or what we call referring items. You can go back to the passage and refer to what is actually stated in the passage to answer referring items. This is sometimes called "reading the lines." This chapter addresses a more advanced level of reading comprehension, the inference level. Rather than finding information directly stated in the passage, reading at the inferential level requires inferring the correct information from what the author suggests in his/her writing. This is sometimes called "reading between the lines."

Making appropriate inferences is a two-step process: first, you must be aware of the clues, or suggestions provided, and second, you must consider what you already know about the subject, or your background knowledge. For instance, imagine that you are walking down the street, and you notice a man walking toward you on the sidewalk. You realize certain things about this individual: he is walking in an unsteady manner and carrying a small brown bag that looks like it may contain a bottle of some kind. He is mumbling something to himself, and he looks unkempt with dirty, torn clothing. You decide, based on these clues or evidence, that this man is most likely drunk. He has not directly told you this, but because of his clothes, manner of walking, appearance, etc., you infer that he is drunk. You also make this inference based on what you know about behavior of individuals who are intoxicated. You have either experienced being intoxicated yourself, been around other individuals who were intoxicated, or you have read about behavior of individuals under the influence of alcohol. So, based on the evidence provided and your background knowledge, you make an inference. However, there could be other explanations for his behavior: perhaps this individual is sick, and that is why he is walking in an unsteady manner, or perhaps this person is playing a joke on you and trying to make you think he is intoxicated. You may consider these alternative explanations and discard them, or you may adjust your inference.

This same process is employed to make correct inferences with written material. Consider the clues, or evidence, provided by the author. These clues, together with your background knowledge, lead you to the appropriate inference. If your background knowledge about the subject is limited, you must rely more heavily on your reading skills, or your ability to understand the clues or evidence provided by the author.

STRATEGY 1

The following process is helpful in considering the clues or evidence provided by the author:

1) Understand the information on the literal level first. Before a reader can make correct inferences he has to understand what the author is directly telling him.

2) Become conscious of the connotative meaning of words, or the emotions surrounding words. Authors select words very carefully with a great deal of thought in an effort to make a reader feel or think a certain way. For instance, describing where one lives as "a home" creates different feelings than describing where one lives as a "house" or "shack." A reader feels differently toward a character described as a "guest" versus one described as a "boarder." Describing sleepwear as "lingerie" makes one feel more positive than does a description of "pajamas." The connotative meaning of words is important evidence to support an inference.

3) Consider the author's tone. Word choice and the connotative meaning of words will determine if the author is generally positive, negative, or neutral regarding the issues. Have you ever had anyone tell you, "Don't use that tone of voice with me!" Perhaps you were communicating more with your tone than with your actual words. The same may be true of written text. From word choice, one can determine whether the author is being sarcastic, angry, sympathetic, funny, etc.

4) Understand the author's point of view. Word choice, along with the general manner of description, will help the reader know "where the author is coming from." A student may describe a recent tuition increase in a different manner than a university official. It is perfectly acceptable for one's point of view to influence the manner in which information is presented. It is the reader's responsibility to be sensitive to various points of view and to decide for himself where he stands on the issue.

5) Determine the author's purpose. If the author's purpose is to explain or inform, which is often the case with textbook material, the author will likely present factual material. If the author's purpose is to persuade, the material may be presented in a more subjective, opinionated manner. A sophisticated reader is sensitive to the difference between facts (something that can be proven true or false) and opinions (that which cannot be proven true or false) and realizes that the author's purpose influences how the information is presented.

Exercise 1

Read the following paragraphs, and, in your own words, write the main idea in a complete sentence in the space provided. Write the clues or suggestions provided by the author as the support for inferring this main idea.

A.   Overpraise tends to create an environment in which student actions are largely designed to please the teacher and are less likely to be products of student judgment. Students who are given a high level of overt praise are less adventurous in their thinking, choosing the safe answer over the creative one. A pattern of frequent overt teacher praise also reduces subject matter related interactions among students. Students tend to guard their responses so they can acquire the praise. In a high praise classroom, students listen less to one another and seldom react to another student's statement except to disagree. The use of overt praise can result in discipline problems as students compete to be called on by the teacher.[1]

Main Idea: _____

Clues:_____

_____

_____

_____

B.   Industrial production creates air and water pollution. Acid rain has been killing trees and the life in lakes in Europe since the 1800s. The smog from burning coal in London in the nineteenth century was so thick that sunlight couldn't get through. Human skin needs some sunshine to produce vitamin D. Unless the skin produces this, or it is present in the diet (many foods are fortified with vitamins today), a deficiency disease called rickets occurs. Rickets results in a softening and bending of growing bones, and children in London were often found to have it.

Conditions in early factories were often horrible. People worked fourteen hours a day or more, in ill lit and poorly ventilated factories. The equipment was dangerous, and there were no provisions for injury. Children had to work as much as adults. In some cases, such as with weaving machines, children were preferred over adults because they were smaller and were able to reach into the machines and make repairs. (The machines were usually not stopped to do this.)[2]

Main Idea: _____ Negative result _____

Clues: _____ Negative tone _____

_____

_____

_____

255

CRITICAL THINKING

Thinking critically about what you are reading involves actively examining the validity of the information presented by the author. **COMPASS** determines if you have a critical understanding of the text with reasoning items that focus on recognizing assumptions made by the author and recognizing logical fallacies.

DEFINITION

Assumptions by the author are ideas, beliefs, or information recognized by the author as valid. A critical reader is sensitive to the assumptions made by the author, and a critical reader questions information presented to support a particular position.

STRATEGY 1

The critical reader asks, "What is left unstated?" and "What are the underlying assumptions?" The author is assuming certain things are true, but has the author presented actual evidence to support what is being said? One strategy is to evaluate whether the author is presenting facts (information that can be proven to be true or false) or opinions (information that can not be proven to be true or false).

Exercise 2

Read the following paragraphs and write the assumptions made by the author.

A. The complaint journalism teachers hear most often from employers is that graduates cannot spell. "Why don't you teach them how to spell?" is the universal question. The answer possibly is that no one can teach students how to spell. All that can be taught is the necessity of spelling words correctly. Correct spelling is achieved as other journalistic demands are achieved—by diligent attention to detail. Spelling correctly is just a matter of accuracy, as are other areas of reporting and writing.[3]

Assumptions:

No one can teach a student how to spell

B. Effective teaching takes much practice. Similar to other pursuits in life, the rewards of teaching seem both proportional to, and contingent on, thoughtful involvement, structured action, and continuous learning and evaluation. Hopefully, the end product of this teaching will be a person who is informed, who is individually productive and socially responsible, who has the ability to analyze, criticize, and choose alternatives, and who has a compelling system of values whereby he may actualize his life in a manner consistent with ever-increasing knowledge—in a word, a person who evidences discipline.[4]

Assumptions:

DEFINITION

An author may present **fallacious arguments** that appeal for support to factors that have little or nothing to do with the argument. A critical reader is able to recognize fallacious thinking even though the material may sound quite convincing.

STRATEGY 1

The best strategy for recognizing fallacious thinking is to become aware of the more commonly used arguments. The following represent different false appeals that often substitute for sound reasoning:

Appeal to authority: The author attempts to persuade the reader of the value of a product, or position on an issue, through the appeal of an authority figure. A critical reader considers whether these authorities offer any legitimate expertise about the issue or product.

Appeal to pity: The author provides irrelevant reasons to support a conclusion. The reasons may be true and they are often effective in eliciting sympathy, but the reasons do not support the conclusions, and therefore the argument is not sound. A critical reader is aware that evidence must be relevant to the argument.

Appeal to fear: The author more or less threatens an unpleasant consequence if the reader does not agree with his position. A critical reader recognizes that appeals to fear do not provide support for conclusions.

Appeal to ignorance: The author takes the position that if you cannot disprove what is being said, then the conclusion is true. A critical reader realizes that the inability to disprove a conclusion is not evidence that the conclusion is in fact justified.

Appeal to personal attack: The author ignores the issues of the argument and focuses instead on the personal qualities of the person with whom he is arguing. A critical reader understands that discrediting the person does not discredit the argument.

Exercise 3

Read the following paragraphs and write in the space provided the type of fallacious arguments presented by the author.

A. At present rates of consumption we have enough coal to last for thousands of years. The problem with this is that we don't continue to consume at our present rate. If we continue to increase our consumption, then sooner or later, we will be in the "last minute." The consequences of running low on petroleum, natural gas, and coal would be devastating.[5]

Appeal to __Fear__

B. I admit that my client embezzled money from the company, your honor. However, I would like to bring several facts to your attention. He is a family man, with a wonderful wife and two terrific children. He is an important member of the community. He is active in the church, coaches a little league baseball team, and has worked very hard to be a good person who cares about people. I think that you should take these things into consideration in handing down your sentence.[6]

Appeal to _____

C. "With me, abortion is not a problem of religion. It's a problem of the Constitution. I believe that until and unless someone can establish that the unborn child is not a living human being, then that child is already protected by the Constitution, which guarantees life, liberty, and the pursuit of happiness to all of us." Ronald Reagan, October 8, 1984.[7]

Appeal to __ignorance case of religion__

D. Hi. You've probably seen me out on the football field. After a hard day's work crushing halfbacks and sacking quarterbacks, I like to settle down with a cold, smooth Maltz beer.[8]

Appeal to _____

E. "Well, I guess I'm reminded a little bit of what Will Rogers once said about Hoover. He said it's not what he doesn't know that bothers me, it's what he knows for sure just ain't so." Walter Mondale characterizing Ronald Reagan, Oct. 8, 1984.[9]

Appeal to __Personal Attack__

258

WORD MEANINGS

COMPASS includes vocabulary items to assess your ability to determine, based on context, the specific meaning of difficult, unfamiliar, or ambiguous words.

DEFINITION

The **context** of a word refers to the sentence or paragraph in which the word appears. The information offered in the context helps the reader determine the word's definition. There are limitations in relying on the context for determining the meaning of a word, since often the context does not provide enough information. Also, the context will provide information only on the meaning of the word as used in this setting, and often words have several different meanings.

STRATEGY 1

The strategy for using the context to determine word meaning is to be aware of the typical manner in which this information is presented. Often called "context clues," the different types are as follows:

Definition or Synonym Clues - A writer may give a brief definition or synonym for a word. A synonym is another word with the same meaning. The definition or synonym usually appears in the same sentence as the word being defined, and it may be set apart from the key idea with commas, dashes, or parentheses. Some directional words for recognizing definitions or synonyms are *such as, including, for instance, to illustrate,* and *for example.*

Contrast Clues - A writer may use a word opposite in meaning of the word being defined. A writer may also present a word or phrase indicating that the opposite or contrasting situation exists. Some direction words for recognizing contrast clues are *rather than, but, however, despite, rather, while, yet,* and *nevertheless.*

Inference Clues - A writer may rely on the logical reasoning of the reader or expect the reader to draw on his or her own knowledge and experience. In other words, the general sense of the paragraph or passage, or the main idea, may provide clues to the meaning of the word.

Exercise 4

Read the following paragraphs and answer the vocabulary item based on the surrounding context of the word. In the space provided, identify the type of clue provided by the surrounding context.

A.   As waves approach the shore, they begin to "feel bottom," which causes an increase in height and steepness. If the offshore zone is of variable depth, the section of a wave passing over shallow water will be retarded more than the section in deeper water. As a result, the wave front will be bent, or **refracted**. Shallow water in front of rocky headlands and deeper water in adjacent bays cause refraction and concentrate wave energy on the headlands, which are rapidly eroded.[10]

Refracted means _____

Type of context clue _____

(continued on next page)

Exercise 4 (continued)

B. So, exactly how does the process of genetic transmission work in humans? You probably recognize that the process is very complex, even though the basics are straightforward. The nuclei of all human cells normally contain 23 pairs of chromosomes, except for the sex cells (the sperm in males, the ovum in females), which hold only half of each of the 23 possible pairs. At **conception**, the male and female sex cells unite to form a new cell, producing a new mixture of 23 chromosome pairs (and genes), half from the father and half from the mother.[11]

Conception means _____

Type of context clue _____

C. Wegener proposed that the supercontinent, which he called Pangaea, was made up of all the present continents and had existed about 200 million years ago. Pangaea broke apart, and the pieces, which form today's continents, moved apart, creating new oceans between them. Wegener cited a variety of evidence for his theory, including similarities of rocks, fossils, and geological structures on separate continents. The evidence wasn't bad, but it was not **compelling**, especially since no one could come up with a plausible mechanism for the motion of huge continents. There didn't seem to be any force large enough to do this. While some scientists speculated on the possibility of "continental drift," most ignored it. There simply wasn't enough hard evidence.[12]

Compelling means _____

Type of context clue _____

D. One could say that vicarious learning is not only important but also represents the future hope for our civilization. Certainly we hope that a child does not need to participate in violence to learn that it is destructive, nor be prejudiced in order to learn about racial, religious, or sexual discrimination, nor engage in war to learn of desolation and death. Many things, because of their permanence or harmfulness, are better learned vicariously.[13]

Vicarious means _____

Type of context clue _____

CHAPTER THIRTEEN

PRACTICE TEST ONE

PASSAGE ONE

You may use the following question to help you focus your reading:

How did the use of tokens influence the development of writing?

(The following text is adapted from R. A. Roy, Physical Science: An Integrated Approach © 1991 by Contemporary Publishing.)

One scenario for the development of writing uses four stages. In the first stage merchants used the tokens to represent commodities such as sheep, jugs of oil, or clothing materials. This allowed them to keep track of their "inventory." In the second stage merchants began to use the tokens in actual trading. When they shipped goods, they would enclose the appropriate tokens in sealed clay balls called bullae. When the goods arrived, the recipient would break the bullae open and check the shipment against the tokens which acted as an invoice. Thus the bullae were the first bills of lading. In the next stage, merchants made token marks on the outside of the bullae before firing them so there was a record inside and outside. Finally merchants realized they could more easily just make all the token marks on a clay tablet and dispense with lots of tokens and sealed balls. Thus, "pictographs," the shapes and marks on the tokens began to represent real objects. Then the pictographs would easily represent, in a more abstract way, a work, the name of the object. As symbols began to represent sounds, which could be put together to make words, alphabets were developed. Because writing was tied in with trade, it developed and spread rapidly. (Using symbols to represent objects also led to another useful invention: money.)[1]

1.   The best title for the above passage is

   ○ A. Trade and The Development of Writing.

   ○ B. Tokens, Bullae, and Pictographs.

   ○ C. The Invention of Writing and Money.

   ○ D. Writing.

   ○ E. Trade and Inventory.

2. At what stage in the development of writing did merchants make token marks on the outside of the bullae before firing them so there was a record inside and outside?

○ A. the second stage
○ B. the third stage
○ C. the final stage
○ D. the stage where symbols represent sounds
○ E. the first stage

3. Bullae were used by merchants for what purpose?

○ A. The bullae held the tokens, which acted as the merchant's invoice.
○ B. Pictographs, the shapes and marks that began to represent real objects, were written on the bullae.
○ C. The bullae represented commodities such as sheep, jugs of oil, or clothing materials.
○ D. Bullae was the name given to the clay tablet used as the invoice for shipment of goods.
○ E. Bullae were used by merchants in place of tokens.

4. The best statement of the main idea of the above passage is:

○ A. writing developed as merchants of trade began using symbols to represent objects.
○ B. bullae and tokens were the base of our alphabet.
○ C. marks on a clay tablet, bullae, and tokens played important roles in the trade process.
○ D. the inventions of writing and money were based on using symbols to represent objects.
○ E. bullae were the first bills of trading.

5. The author discusses the four stages in the development of writing through

○ A. cause and effect.
○ B. demonstrating a comparative relationship among the stages.
○ C. sequential order of the stages.
○ D. a pattern where one element is seen as causing another element.
○ E. comparison and contrast.

PASSAGE TWO

You may use the following question to help you focus your reading:

What are the two different methods used by anthropologists to determine the sex of a skull?

(The following passage is adapted from L.D. Wolfe, L.S. Lieberman & d.L. Hutchinson, Laboratory Textbook for Physical Anthroplogy. © 1994 by Contemporary Publishing.)

There are differences in the male and female human skeleton. In general, the skeletons of males are larger and more **robust** than the skeletons of females. There are also specific differences between women and men in skulls and pelves, which can be used to determine sex. Physical anthropologists and forensic anthropologists use two different methods to determine the sex of a skull. One method, which is qualitative, depends on a visual inspection of the skull. That is, the skull is inspected and its traits noted. Subsequently, the observed traits are compared to those of skulls of known sex.

There is also a quantitative method to sex skulls. This method involves measuring skulls of known sex from anatomical collections and generating discriminant function scores that best characterize the samples. Giles and Elliott (1963) examined crania from American Blacks and American Whites in order to identify the discriminant functions that could be used to determine the sex of a skull. Giles (1970) later incorporated a similar study of the Japanese by Hanihara (1959).[2]

6.   From the above passage, one can conclude that
  ○ A.   the quantitative method to sex skulls involves numerical analysis.
  ○ B.   the skulls of men are more pristine than the skulls of women.
  ○ C.   it is more difficult to sex skulls by the qualitative method.
  ○ D.   it is necessary to use both qualitative and quantitative methods to sex skulls accurately.
  ○ E.   the skeletons of females are more robust than the skeletons of males.

7.   The main idea of the above passage is:
  ○ A.   there are no differences in the male and female human skeleton.
  ○ B.   there is a qualitative and quantitative method for determining the sex of a skull.
  ○ C.   studies by Giles (1970) and Hanihara (1959) determined that the ethnic origin of the skull was important in determining sex.
  ○ D.   qualitative research methods rely on observations and quantitative research methods rely on measurement.
  ○ E.   there are specific differences between women and men in skulls.

8.   As it is used in the passage, the word **robust** most nearly means

    ○   A.   more delicate.

    ○   B.   smaller.

    ○ (C.) stronger.

    ○   D.   masculine.

    ○   E.   feminine.

9.   The quantitative method to sex skulls involves

    ○   A.   a visual inspection of the skull.

    ○   B.   measuring skulls of known sex from anatomical collections and generating discriminant function scores that best characterize the samples.

    ○   C.   a determination that the skeletons of males are larger and more robust than the skeletons of females.

    ○   D.   measurement of specific differences between pelves of women and men.

    ○   E.   notation of typical traits.

10.   Both qualitative and quantitative methods for determining the sex of skulls

    ○   A.   were used in studies by Giles and Elliot (1963).

    ○ (B.) are used by physical and forensic anthropologists.

    ○   C.   involve measuring skulls.

    ○   D.   involve the statistical procedure of discriminant function.

    ○   E.   were used in a study of the Japanesse by Hanihara (1959).

PASSAGE THREE

You may use the following question to help you focus your reading:

Why are sedimentary rocks important to Historical Geology?

(The following passage is adapted from R.A. Gastaldo, C.E. Savrda, & R.D. Lewis, Deciphering Earth History. © 1996 by Contemporary Publishing.)

Rocks of all types—igneous, metamorphic, and sedimentary—have stories to tell about Earth history. Sedimentary rocks, however, are most important to Historical Geology. Sedimentary rocks have grossly similar origins; most are born at the Earth's surface by weathering of pre-existing rock, the transport of solid or dissolved weathering products by various agents (e.g., water, wind, ice), and eventual deposition or precipitation in one of a multitude of settings ranging from glaciated mountain peaks to the deepest ocean basins. Despite their general genetic similarities, sediments and sedimentary rocks differ broadly in composition, texture, and other features. These differences reflect **variations** in physical and chemical conditions at the Earth's surface and help us recognize temporal and spatial changes in the magnitude of weathering, mechanisms of transport, and environments in which sediments accumulated. This type of information, in turn, allows us to reconstruct aspects of the geologic past, including ancient climates, geographies, and tectonic events. Moreover, sedimentary rocks contain the great majority of fossils, and hence, provide the basis for our understanding of the history of life on Earth.[3]

---

11. Although sedimentary rocks are similar in genetic origin, they differ broadly in

   ○ A. tectonic events.

   ○ B. fossil density.

   ○ C. composition.

   ○ D. environmental sediments.

   ○ E. geologic past.

12. The author believes that rocks of all types—igneous, metamorphic, and sedimentary—

   ○ A. are important to Historical Geology.

   ○ B. allow us to reconstruct aspects of the geologic past.

   ○ C. have stories to tell about Earth history, but sedimentary rocks are the most important to Historical Geology.

   ○ D. are born at the Earth's surface by weathering of pre-existing rock.

   ○ E. differ broadly in composition.

13. The best statement of the main idea of the above passage is

   ○ A. sedimentary rocks are important for understanding historical geology.

   ○ B. rocks of all types have stories to tell about Earth history.

   ○ C. differences in composition and texture help us to understand sedimentary rocks.

   ○ D. sedimentary rocks reflect differences in chemical conditions at the Earth's surface.

   ○ E. sedimentary rocks contain the great majorigy of fossils.

14. The author supports his position on the importance of sedimentary rock through

   ○ A. objective facts.

   ○ B. subjective experience.

   ○ C. comparisons of the three types of rocks.

   ○ D. experimental evidence.

   ○ E. anecdotal evidence

15. In the above passage, **variations** means

   ○ A. similarities.

   ○ B. consistencies.

   ○ C. viscosity.

   ○ D. dissimilarities.

   ○ E. conditions.

PASSAGE FOUR

You may use the following question to help you focus your reading:

How is the brightness of a variable star different than a comparison star?

(The following passage is adapted from J.W. Wilson, Astronomy: A laboratory Textbook. © 1996 by Contemporary Publishing.)

In general, most stars have a constant brightness. However, certain very young stars and some aging stars become unstable and vary in brightness and are known as variable stars. The oldest observations of variable stars come from China. The star Omicron Ceti was discovered in 1596 as the first periodic variable star. It was named Mira, The Wonderful, and has been studied by astronomers ever since.

Modern day astronomers know that many stars are variable and have classified them into groups. One type is called the Mira variables because they exhibit the same characteristics as Mira. These Mira variables are known to be red giant stars near the end of their evolutionary lives. Their amplitudes vary over several stellar magnitudes and over hundreds of days.

When astronomers observe a variable star they usually compare the brightness of the variable to the brightness of a nearby star which has a constant brightness, the "comparison star." A comparison star may be chosen **at random**, and it is possible that, by chance, it is also some type of variable star. In this case, the astronomer is comparing one variable star to another variable star and the observations are meaningless. In order to make sure the comparison star is constant, its brightness is compared to yet another star called the "check star" (because it is used to check for variations of the comparison star).[4]

---

16. According to the author, variable stars

   ○ A. have the same brightness as the "comparison star."
   ○ B. are very young stars and aging stars that have become unstable and vary in brightness.
   ○ C. may be chosen at random, which makes observations of variable stars a meaningless process.
   ○ D. originated in China in 1596.
   ○ E. have a constant brightness.

17. In paragraph three, the author is describing

   ○ A. the process involved in observing a variable star.
   ○ B. how the science of astronomy is based on chance.
   ○ C. how and why variable stars are at the end of their evolutionary lives.
   ○ D. the role played by the comparison star when observing the variable star.
   ○ E. the star called Omicron Ceti, discovered in 1596.

18. According to the author, the star Omicron Ceti

    ○ A. is periodically different than a variable star.

    ○ B. has a constant brightness and is often used as a "comparison star."

    ○ C. was discovered in 1596 as the first variable star.

    ○ D. was named Mira, The Wonderful, by modern-day astronomers.

    ○ E. is often called the "check star."

19. According to the passage, the "check star" is

    ○ A. more important than the variable or comparison star for understanding constellations and brightness.

    ○ B. used to check for variations of the comparison star.

    ○ C. used to check for variations of the variable star.

    ○ D. one type of red giant star.

    ○ E. was named Mira, the Wonderful.

20. In the above passage, **at random** means

    ○ A. by design.

    ○ B. according to a plan.

    ○ C. with certainty.

    ○ D. arbitrarily.

    ○ E. purposefully.

PASSAGE FIVE

You may use the following question to help you focus your reading:

What is one explanation for phobic disorders?

(The following passage is adapted from R. Gerow, Psychology: An Introduction. © 1995 by Addison-Wesley Educational Publishers.)

Some people are intensely afraid of flying, of elevators, of heights, of small closed-in areas, of spiders, or of the dark. Psychologists say that these people are suffering from a phobic disorder—an intense, irrational fear of an object or event that leads a person to avoid contact with it. There are many explanations for how phobic disorders, or phobias, occur, but one clear possibility is classical conditioning.

This explanation goes as follows: a person experiences an intense, natural emotional response to a powerful, emotion-producing stimulus—perhaps a traumatic event, such as a severe injury or an accident. When an emotion-producing stimulus occurs in the presence of another, neutral stimulus, the pairing may result in the formation of a conditioned fear response to the originally neutral stimulus. A child at a local carnival becomes separated from his parents and gets swept away by a large crowd into a tent where clowns are performing. The youngster is (sensibly) frightened by the separation from his parents, and after they are reunited, requires considerable reassurance before he settles down. Should we be terribly surprised if this child—even much later, as an adolescent or an adult—appears to be irrationally afraid of carnivals, circuses, or clowns? Not if one believes that classical conditioning can account for the formation of phobias.[5]

21.   According to the author, classical conditioning is

    ◯   A.   the only logical explanation for fear of flying.

    ◯   B.   one explanation for phobic disorders.

    ◯   C.   when an emotion-producing stimulus occurs in the presence of another emotion-producing stimulus.

    ◯   D.   involves the separation of certain stimuli.

    ◯   E.   unrelated to the formation of phobias.

22.   According to the passage, a phobic disorder is

    ◯   A.   when an emotion-producing stimulus occurs in the presence of a neutral stimulus.

    ◯   B.   an intense, irrational fear of an object or event that leads a person to avoid contact with it.

    ◯   C.   experienced by most first-time airplane passengers.

    ◯   D.   a traumatic event, such as a severe injury or an accident.

    ◯   E.   when a child becomes separated from his parents.

23. The author explains classical conditioning and phobic disorders through

- ○ A. personal experience.
- ○ B. psychological experiments.
- ○ C. examples.
- ○ D. scientific data.
- ○ E. historical evidence.

24. From the above passage, one can conclude that

- ○ A. there is only one explanation for phobic disorders.
- ○ B. classical conditioning is one explanation of phobic disorders.
- ○ C. many children experience phobic disorders.
- ○ D. phobic disorders are treatable.
- ○ E. most people are afraid of heights.

25. According to the above passage, a conditioned fear response may be evoked by an originally

- ○ A. emotion-producing stimulus.
- ○ B. natural emotional response.
- ○ C. neutral stimulus.
- ○ D. intense emotional response.
- ○ E. positive stimulus.

PASSAGE SIX

You may use the following question to help you focus your reading:

What are Francie's feelings about the librarian?

(The following passage is adapted from B. Smith, <u>A Tree Grows in Brooklyn.</u> © 1943 by Harper Collins Publishers.)

She stood at the desk a long time before the librarian **deigned** to attend to her.

"Yes?" inquired the lady pettishly.

"This book. I want it." Francie pushed the book forward opened at the back with the little card pushed out of the envelope. The librarians had trained the children to present the books that way. It saved them the trouble of opening several hundred books a day and pulling several hundred cards from as many envelopes.

She took the card, stamped it, pushed it down a slot in the desk. She stamped Francie's card and pushed it at her. Francie picked it up, but she did not go away.

"Yes?" The librarian did not bother to look up.

"Could you recommend a good book for a girl?"

"How old?"

"She is eleven."

Each week Francie made the same request and each week the librarian asked the same question. A name on a card meant nothing to her and since she never looked up into a child's face, she never did get to know the little girl who took a book out every day and two on Saturday. A smile would have meant a lot to Francie and a friendly comment would have made her so happy. She loved the library and was anxious to worship the lady in charge. But the librarian had other things on her mind. She hated children anyhow.

Francie trembled in anticipation as the woman reached under the desk. She saw the title as the book came up: <u>If I Were King</u> by McCarthy. Wonderful! Last week it had been <u>Beverly of Graustark</u> and the same two weeks before that. She had the McCarthy book only twice. The librarian recommended these two books over and over again. Maybe they were the only ones she herself had read; maybe they were on a recommended list; maybe she had discovered that they were surefire as far as eleven-year old girls were concerned.[6]

---

26. **Deigned**, as used in the above passage, most likely means

- ○ A. designed.
- ○ B. decided.
- ◉ C. condescended.
- ○ D. deliberately.
- ○ E. with kindness.

27. The above passage indicates that Francie

- A. wanted to please the librarian.
- B. found reading very tedious and boring.
- C. had an excellent rapport with the librarian.
- D. often misbehaved in the library.
- E. was often disrespectful to her elders.

28. Francie is requesting the library book for

- A. her friend.
- B. herself.
- C. the librarian.
- D. the lady in charge.
- E. a twenty-year-old girl.

29. The librarians trained the children to present their books in a certain way because

- A. there was a good amount of book theft.
- B. the same books were requested each week.
- C. they checked out hundreds of books.
- D. they wanted children to respect them.
- E. the children did not respect books.

30. The explanations for why the librarian recommends the same books over and over again indicate Francie's

- A. desire to think well of others.
- B. sarcastic nature.
- C. caustic wit.
- D. ability to see people for what they are.
- E. negative outlook.

PASSAGE SEVEN

You may use the following question to help you focus your reading:

Would speaking more than one language help Americans in foreign trade?

(The following passage is adapted from L. Lauder, "The Language of Foreign Trade." © 1985 by The New York Times Co.)

Why has no one raised the fact that so many Americans engaged in foreign trade can speak no language but their own? It's getting late in the day to realize that the language of international trade is not English. The language of international trade is the language of the customer.

It is self-evident that you can't sell unless there is a demand for the product. It is also self-evident that you can't begin to understand what a people demand if you can't talk to them on their own terms. Their own terms, of course, means their own language.

As far as business is concerned, our national **parochialism** is growing worse. A study commissioned by the National Council on Foreign Language and International Studies questioned 1,690 young men and women in 564 business schools working toward their doctoral degrees in business in the spring of 1984. The study found only 17 percent of these students were taking one or more courses in international affairs and foreign languages. In 1976, that figure was 25 percent.[7]

---

31.   **Parochialism,** as used in the above passage, most likely means

   ○   A.   provincialism.
   ○   B.   openness.
   ○   C.   perspective.
   ○   D.   viewpoint.
   ○   E.   attitude.

32.   "It's getting late in the day" as used in the above passage most likely means it is

   ○   A.   late afternoon or early evening.
   ○   B.   long past overdue.
   ○   C.   late in the year.
   ○   D.   insulting.
   ○   E.   inappropriate.

33. The author states that the language of internal trade is

○ A. not entirely practical.

○ B. speaking English.

○ C. most prevalent in doctoral programs.

○ D. essential for success.

○ E. the language of the customer.

34. The passage indicates that the study of foreign language in business schools

○ A. is on the decline.

○ B. will increase in the future.

○ C. is more important in foreign trade schools.

○ D. is the responsibility of the faculty.

○ E. rose from 17 to 25 percent.

35. According to the author, understanding what a people demand

○ A. depends on the product you are selling.

○ B. requires proficiency in English.

○ C. is self-evident.

○ D. is taught in business schools.

○ E. requires talking to them in their own language.

PASSAGE EIGHT

You may use the following question to help you focus your reading:

How do the Agricultural and Industrial Revolution differ in terms of energy used?

(The following passage is adapted from R.A. Roy, Physical Science: An Integrated Approach. © 1991 by Contemporary Publishing.)

After the Agricultural Revolution, growth and change took place, but at a slower pace. One way to describe this growth is by the energy available for work. At the beginning of the Agricultural Revolution, human energy was used, along with fire. As people learned how to make hotter fires, **pyrotechnology** led to fired clay, to smelted metals, and to cooking and preserving foods. The domestication of large animals like horses and oxen allowed more work to be done like plowing larger fields and transporting more goods. Early sailboats harnessed the wind.

As the Dark and Middle Ages proceeded, larger, more powerful animals were bred. (This development, as today, was often tied to war. Large horses were used to carry armored knights, the military "tanks" of their day.) Wind was used more effectively by "fore and aft" rigs on sailboats, allowing a vessel to tack into the wind. Windmills and waterwheels were also developed. Around 1750 in England, however, changes began to occur that led to revolutionary changes in energy use. The changes, termed the Industrial Revolution, involve using mechanical devices, machines, which can apply energy to perform useful work. We are still in this revolution. Machines are used in agriculture, mining, commerce, and other areas, even in the home. Large factories, by concentrating machines, raw materials, labor, and energy can mass produce huge amounts of manufactured goods: automobiles, clothes, steel chemicals, and the rest of the modern cornucopia of technology.[8]

---

36. **Pyrotechnology**, as used in the above passage, means

   O A. pottery.

   O B. clay work.

   O C. art of fire.

   O D. fireworks.

   O E. smelted metals

37. The time frame discussed in the above passage is

   O A. the Agricultural Revolution to the Industrial Revolution.

   O B. the Dark Ages.

   O C. around 1750 in England.

   O D. the Industrial Revolution.

   O E. the Middle Ages.

38.   The author states that the military "tanks" of their day were the

    ○ A. large horses.

    ○ B. rigs on sailboats.

    ○ C. windmills and waterwheels.

    ○ D. oxen.

    ○ E. armored knights.

39.   The Industrial Revolution occurred

    ○ A. before the Agricultural Revolution.

    ○ B. at the same time as the Dark Ages.

    ○ C. during the Middle Ages.

    ○ D. around 1750.

    ○ E. only in England.

40.   According to the passages, the Industrial Revolution involved

    ○ A. machines that could apply energy to perform useful work.

    ○ B. human energy and pyrotechnology.

    ○ C. harnessing the wind.

    ○ D. the domestication of large animals like horses and oxen that allowed more work to be done.

    ○ E. the "fore" and "aft" rigs on sailboats.

PASSAGE NINE

You may use the following question to help you focus your reading:

What are dramatic artists trying to achieve through "entertaining"?

(The following passage is adapted from a.W. Staub, Varieties of Theatrical Art. © 1994 by Contemporary Publishing.)

The verb "to entertain" comes from the Latin words meaning "to hold between," and that is what entertainment attempts to do: hold someone's attention from a beginning to an end. But there are many ways to hold a person's attention between two points in time or space. Most people, for instance, are attentive when threatened with a weapon, though most will not feel entertained. **Coercion** is not entertaining. Entertainment is agreeable; coercion is not. "Let me entertain you" means "let me hold your attention in an agreeable manner from the moment I take hold until the moment I let go." Why should anyone want to hold another's attention agreeably? Because it is satisfying to be the center of attention. To be so placed is like being loved. Indeed, many entertainers have been literally adored. Moreover, persons being entertained often find the experience so pleasant that they are willing to pay the entertainer well, sometimes extravagantly. For many performers, however, a third motivation is equally important; the entertainment arts provide performers a means to create beauty and communicate ideas about the human experience. In fact, the theatrical arts are an ideal medium of communication, for when people are in an agreeable mood they are more likely to be receptive to another's thoughts and feelings. That is why dramatic artists are first and foremost communicators; they create beauty and express ideas and attitudes about life while holding an audience's attention within an agreeable form or artistic metaphor.[9]

41. According to the passage, people entertain

   ○ A. to be the center of attention.

   ○ B. for money.

   ○ C. to create beauty and communicate ideas.

   ○ D. to hold someone's attention.

   ○ E. for all of the above reasons.

42. The author describes dramatic artists as first and foremost

   ○ A. attention seekers.

   ○ B. mercenaries.

   ○ C. individuals seeking love.

   ○ D. communicators.

   ○ E. attention givers.

43.   **Coercion**, as used in the above passage, means

　○　A.　volition.

　○　B.　freedom.

　○　C.　free will.

　○　D.　force.

　○　E.　threatening.

44.   The author states that dramatic arts are an ideal medium of communication because

　○　A.　people are agreeable when they are being entertained and therefore open to ideas.

　○　B.　people communicate more effectively when they have paid a great deal of money to be entertained.

　○　C.　the theater is the best place to discuss ideas and attitudes about life.

　○　D.　people will listen more to individuals they adore.

　○　E.　the theater often intimidates people.

45.   What is the author's central point about entertainment?

　○　A.　Artists entertain primarily for attention.

　○　B.　There is no clear definition of what it means "to entertain."

　○　C.　The opportunity to make money is not important to artists.

　○　D.　Artists are communicators that create beauty and express ideas about life.

　○　E.　Most artists expect to be paid extravagantly well.

PASSAGE TEN

You may use the following question to help you focus your reading:

Is information from an "authority" more readily accepted?

The following passage is adapted from R.A. Roy, Physical Science: An Integrated Approach. © 1991 by Contemporary Publishing.)

Ordinary people accept most of their information from an "authority." We accept what we read in the newspapers, what our teachers and friends tell us; rarely are we skeptical. Many human activities are based on authority. Law is one example. In a criminal or civil proceeding, the outcome is determined by what statutes say and by the outcomes of earlier, similar cases. The judges, juries, and attorneys do not make up new laws for the specific case, but accept the authority of preceding cases.

Religion is also based on authority. This might be found in a document such as the Bible or the Koran, or in a hierarchy of church officers such as the College of Cardinals or a presbytery.

Scientists do not accept information from authority. In our everyday lives we are usually not skeptical; but, when doing science, skepticism is required. No matter how carefully the information is collected, scientists check it rigorously before accepting it.[10]

46. The above passage focuses on the relationship between

   ○ A. ordinary people and scientists.
   ○ B. law and religion.
   ○ C. religion and scientists.
   ○ D. authority and science.
   ○ E. criminal and civil.

47. The author states that the outcome of a criminal or civil proceeding is determined by

   ○ A. new laws made up for specific cases.
   ○ B. the hierarchy of church officers.
   ○ C. the authority of documents such as the Bible.
   ○ D. the Koran.
   ○ E. what statutes say.

48.   All of the following accept information from authority except

   ◯ A. ordinary people.

   ◯ B. lawyers.

   ◯ C. scientists.

   ◯ D. priests.

   ◯ E. teachers.

49.   As it is used in the passage, the word **skeptical** most nearly means

   ◯ A. silly.

   ◯ B. made up.

   ◯ C. unaccepting.

   ◯ D. accepting.

   ◯ E. smart.

50.   When doing science, according to the passage,

   ◯ A. most information comes from an "authority."

   ◯ B. we accept what we read in the newspaper.

   ◯ C. we rely heavily on teachers, family, and friends.

   ◯ D. skepticism is required.

   ◯ E. reference is made to the College of Cardinals.

PRACTICE TEST TWO

You may use the following question to help you focus your reading:

Do individuals have the right to decide when to die?

(The following passage is adapted from N. Cousins, "The Right to Die," The Saturday Review. © 1975 by General Media International.)

The world of religion and philosophy was shocked recently when Henry P. Van Dusen and his wife ended their lives by their own hands. Dr. Van Dusen had been president of Union Theological Seminary; for more than a quarter-century he had been one of the **luminous** names in Protestant theology. He enjoyed world status as a spiritual leader. News of the self-inflicted death of the Van Dusens, therefore, was profoundly disturbing to all those who attach a moral stigma to suicide and regard it as a violation of God's laws.

Henry and Elizabeth Van Dusen had lived full lives. In recent years, they had become increasingly ill, requiring almost continual medical care. Their infirmities were worsening, and they realized they would soon become completely dependent for even the most elementary needs and functions. Under these circumstances, little dignity would have been left in life. They didn't like the idea of taking up space in a world with too many mouths and too little food. They believed it was a misuse of medical science to keep them technically alive.

They therefore believed they had the right to decide when to die. In making that decision, they weren't turning against life as the highest value; what they were turning against was the notion that there were no circumstances under which life should be discontinued.

An important aspect of human uniqueness is the power of free will. In his books and lectures, Dr. Van Dusen frequently spoke about the exercise of this uniqueness. The fact that he used his free will to prevent life from becoming a caricature of itself was completely in character. In their letter, the Van Dusens sought to convince family and friends that they were not acting solely out of despair or pain.[11]

1.   The author of the above passage probably

   O A. agrees with the moral stigma attached to suicide.

   O B. regards suicide as a violation of God's life.

   O C. believes suicide is turning against life as the highest value.

   (D) D. supports the Van Dusens' decision to end their lives.

   O E. believes life should continue under any circumstances.

2. The passage states that Dr. Van Dusen's position in the world of theology was

   A. that of a world spiritual leader.

   B. undeserved since he committed suicide.

   C. profoundly disturbing.

   D. a hardship as his medical problems worsened.

   E. controversial.

3. **Luminous**, as used in the above passage, means

   A. recognized.

   B. obscure.

   C. little known.

   D. infamous.

   E. enlightened.

4. The author states that Dr. Van Dusen's books and lectures revealed his belief that

   A. humans are unique in their ability to exercise free will.

   B. humans need to avoid becoming dependent on others.

   C. family and friends should support their decision.

   D. theology and philosophy are unique disciplines.

   E. life should be valued above everything.

5. The statement that Van Dusen used "his free will to prevent life from becoming a caricature of itself" most likely means he committed suicide

   A. to avoid people taking advantage of his illness.

   B. so that others would not belittle him.

   C. so that his status as a spiritual leader would not be threatened.

   D. so that his illness would not make a mockery of his life.

   E. to avoid dependency on family and friends.

PASSAGE TWO

You may use the following question to help you focus your reading:

What evidence supports the Big Bang theory on how the universe began?

(The following passage is adapted from P.G. Hewitt, "The Origin of the Universe and Solar System," Conceptual Physics. © 1985 by Scott, Foresman, and Company.)

No one knows how the universe began. Evidence suggests that about 15 to 20 billion years ago most of the matter-energy of the universe was highly concentrated at an unimaginably high temperature and underwent a primordial explosion, usually referred to as the **Big Bang**, which was accompanied by a high-powered blast of high-frequency radiation that we call the primeval fireball. The universe is the remnant of this explosion, and we view it as still expanding. Radiation from the dying embers of the primeval fireball now permeate all space in the form of the presently observed long-wavelength microwaves, which have been lengthened by the expansion of the universe. The present expansion of the universe is evident in a Doppler red shift in the light from other galaxies, which is greater than gravitation would account for. This red shift indicates a recession of the galaxies. All galaxies are getting farther away from our own. This does not, as a first thought may indicate, place our own galaxy in a central position. Consider a balloon with ants on it: as the balloon is inflated, every ant will see every neighboring ant getting farther away, which certainly doesn't suggest a central position for each ant. In an expanding universe, every observer sees clusters of all other galaxies receding.

If you throw a rock skyward, it slows down due to its gravitational attraction to the earth below. Similarly, matter blown away in the primordial explosion is gravitationally attracted to every other bit of matter, which results in a continual slowing down of the overall expansion.[12]

6. The best title for the above passage is

○ A. The Expanding Balloon.

○ B. The Big Bang and The Expanding Universe.

○ C. The Big Bang.

○ D. Recession of the Galaxies.

○ E. The Doppler Red Shift.

7. The author provides the example of the balloon with ants on it to explain

○ A. how you throw a rock skyward.

○ B. how the Earth can be compared to the balloon.

○ C. that matter in the explosion is centrally located.

○ D. that although galaxies are getting further away, it does not place our galaxy in a central position.

○ E. the gravitational attraction of the Earth.

8. The author states that the Big Bang was, in essence,

○ A. high-frequency radiation.

○ B. an explosion.

○ C. a Doppler red shift.

○ D. a primeval fireball.

○ E. long-wavelength microwaves.

9. The author most likely views the Big Bang Theory as

○ A. the only explanation for the beginning of the universe.

○ B. an incorrect explanation for the beginning of the universe.

○ C. a theory on the beginning of the universe proven by evidence.

○ D. a theory on the beginning of the universe suggested by evidence.

○ E. a ridiculous theory.

10. The author states that the present expansion of the universe is evident in a(n)

○ A. Doppler red shift in the light from other galaxies.

○ B. Doppler red shift being less than gravitation would account for.

○ C. primeval fireball.

○ D. presently observed long-wavelength microwaves.

○ E. inflated balloon with ants on it.

PASSAGE THREE

You may use the following question to help you focus your reading:

What has delayed industrialization of certain regions in the world?

(The following passage is adapted from R.A. Roy, Pysical Science: An Integrated Approach. © 1991 by Contemporary Publishing.)

Why haven't all regions in the world undergone industrialization? Agriculture occurs everywhere; why not industry? Various answers have been given for this, many of them **invidious**. People are described as lazy, or unintelligent, or lacking in the cultural values required to run industries. The real answer is that large amounts of energy are simply not available to all countries. Not everyone is lucky enough to have deposits of petroleum, oil, coal, and natural gas, to say nothing of ore deposits, rich soils, and good weather. There is another reason also, which goes back to the early days of the Industrial Revolution. In Europe there arose an economic policy called mercantilism. This emphasized the economic development of the home country at the expense of trading partners such as colonies. By passing laws and regulations, a home country, such as England or Spain, could benefit greatly. England imported raw materials from its colonies, made the finished goods in its factories and sold them back to the colonies at a profit. The colonies were forbidden by law to make their own finished products, or even to make factories. The colonies were also forbidden to trade with other countries, so that they were economic "captives." It is asserted, with some justification, that this system greatly delayed industrialization in many areas. Needless to say, these repressive economic policies led to real revolutions, the American Revolution being the first of several.[13]

---

11. From the above passage, one can conclude that the author

   ○ A. supports the economic policy of mercantilism.

   ○ B. believes people delayed industrialization in many countries.

   ◉ C. believes mercantilism is an unjust economic policy.

   ○ D. supported home countries' efforts to control colonies.

   ○ E. believes mercantilism promoted industrialization.

12. The purpose of the above passage is to

   ○ A. discuss the importation of raw materials from colonies.

   ◉ B. discuss the reasons industrialization was delayed in many areas.

   ○ C. explain the process of colonization.

   ○ D. support people in nonindustrialized nations.

   ○ E. note the importance of petroleum, oil, coal, and natural gas for industrialization.

13. The passage attributes delayed industrialization to

- ○ A. the lack of motivation of the people.
- ○ B. the abundance of energy.
- ○ C. the amount of coal and petroleum.
- ○ D. revolutions.
- ○ E. mercantilism.

14. **Invidious**, as used in the above passage, means

- ○ A. industrious.
- ○ B. insulting.
- ○ C. divisive.
- ○ D. insubstantial.
- ○ E. substantial.

15. Home countries enforced mercantilism by

- ○ A. laws and regulations making colonies "economic captives."
- ○ B. preventing cultural values.
- ○ C. teaching cultural values.
- ○ D. preaching motivation and ambition.
- ○ E. using large amounts of energy.

PASSAGE FOUR

You may use the following question to help you focus your reading:

What factors affect an individual's basal metabolic rate (BMR)?

(The following passage is adapted from W.A. Forsythe, Nutrition and You With Readings. © 1995 by Contemporary Publishing.)

Much of the energy you use each day maintains the basal metabolic rate (BMR). Energy used for basal metabolism is the minimum energy used to keep a person alive. Some of the body processes that use energy for BMR are...[those] that would continue if you are to stay alive. Think of them as the processes that would continue if a person were in a coma. Any activity or movement above this is not truly basal.

Your BMR is directly affected by your body size. The larger a person is, the greater the BMR. A larger body size means more tissue to keep functioning and therefore more energy expended in the BMR. Men, on average, have a higher BMR than women, in part because men are bigger than women. BMR also increases as lean body mass increases. Lean body mass is a person's weight minus the weight of his adipose (fat) tissue. The more bone and muscle you have, the greater the amount of energy needed to maintain the BMR. Again, because men generally have more lean body mass than women, their BMR will be greater. It is easy to understand that a 230-pound person would have a higher BMR than a 150-pound person. However, if a man and a woman each weigh 150 pounds, the man, having a greater lean body mass than the woman, would have a higher BMR. It takes much more energy to keep muscle and bone functioning than it does to keep adipose (fat) tissue functioning.

A last factor that affects one's BMR is age. The BMR decreases as one gets older. It is estimated that a person's BMR decreases by about 10% per decade of life after age forty. That means that a person at age 75 needs only about one-half as much energy to support the BMR as when he was 25 years old.[14]

16.   Examples of body processes that use energy for basal metabolic rate are

○   A. beating of the heart.

○   B. body-temperature regulation.

○   C. liver and kidney function.

○   D. pumping of blood.

○   E. all of the above.

17. According to the passage, if a man and a women each weigh 150 pounds, the one with a lower BMR is the

○ A. person with the greater lean body mass.

○ B. man.

○ C. woman.

○ D. person with less fat.

○ E. person with more bone and muscle.

18. According to the passage, lean body mass

○ A. is the same as the weight of fat tissue.

○ B. is the opposite of bone and muscle.

○ C. needs less energy.

○ D. is a person's weight minus the weight of fat tissue.

○ E. is adipose tissue.

19. The factors, according to the passage, that affect one's BMR are

○ A. body size, lean body mass, and age.

○ B. activities or movements that are not truly basal.

○ C. body processes and age.

○ D. sex and energy level.

○ E. age and metabolism.

20. According to the passage, BMR increases as

○ A. lean body mass increases.

○ B. one gets older.

○ C. the weight of fat tissue increases.

○ D. body size decreases.

○ E. bone and muscle decreases.

PASSAGE FIVE

You may use the following question to help you focus your reading:

What is the explanation for the Doppler phenomenon?

(The following passage is adapted from J. Wagner, Introductory Musical Acoustics. © 1994 by Contemporary Publishing.)

> When a police car or ambulance approaches and passes, the frequency and the amplitude of the siren increase as the vehicle approaches, reach a peak level at the closest point, and then decrease as the vehicle passes. This seemingly odd acoustical phenomenon is called the Doppler effect.
>
> It may seem that the nearer we are to a sound, the higher its pitch. Although we know this is not true, if either the sound source or the listener is moving at a sufficient rate, the Doppler phenomenon will be perceived.
>
> The explanation is quite simple. Pitch depends upon the number of vibrations per second that reach the ear. If one moves rapidly toward a sound source or it toward us, the rate at which those vibrations reach us increases. That is, more vibrations reach the ear per second than if both sound source and listener were stationary. The natural consequence of this phenomenon is that a higher pitch is perceived, i.e., one with more vibrations per second.
>
> As the sound source moves away from the listener (or the listener from the sound source), fewer vibrations reach the listener per second and the pitch becomes lower. The relative speed of the sound source or listener is all-important. The distance between the two is not a factor. Distance may seem to play a part because as the sound source and listener get closer and closer, amplitude increases.
>
> To review, the faster the speed that the sound source and listener travel toward or away from each other, the greater the rise or fall in pitch. The rate of movement toward or away from the source of sound is all-important. Distance has only to do with the amplitude of the sound.[15]

21. According to the passage, the rise or fall in pitch depends on the

   ○ A. speed that the sound source and listener travel toward or away from each other.

   ○ B. distance between the sound source and listener.

   ○ C. increase in amplitude of the sound.

   ○ D. increase in frequency of the sound.

   ○ E. decrease in frequency of the sound.

22. According to the passage, the Doppler effect explains why it may seem that the nearer we are to a sound,

    ○ A. the lower its pitch.

    ○ B. the higher its pitch.

    ○ C. the fewer vibrations reach the ear per second.

    ○ D. the lower its amplitude.

    ○ E. the fewer vibrations reach the listener.

23. The best title for the above passage is

    ○ A. Acoustical Phenomena.

    ○ B. Sound Effects.

    ○ C. Frequency and Amplitude of Sound.

    ○ D. Pitch and The Doppler Effect.

    ○ E. Sound Vibrations and the Ear.

24. The author explains the Doppler effect through

    ○ A. objective facts.

    ○ B. comparison and contrast.

    ○ C. scientific experiments.

    ○ D. analogies.

    ○ E. historical evidence.

25. The best statement of the main idea of the above passage is:

    ○ A. the Doppler phenomenon is explained by the speed that the sound source and listener travel toward or away from each other.

    ○ B. amplitude is as important as pitch in the Doppler effect.

    ○ C. amplitude depends upon the number of vibrations per second that reach the ear.

    ○ D. more vibrations reach the ear per second when sound source and listener are moving than when they are stationary.

    ○ E. sound vibrations cause pitch to be higher.

PASSAGE SIX

You may use the following question to help you focus your reading:

What kinds of thoughts and actions are controlled by the cerebral cortex?

(The following passage is adapted from J. Wagner, Introductory Musical Acoustics. © 1994 by Contemporary Publishing.)

The cerebral cortex (covering of the cerebrum) or "grey matter" is possibly the most interesting of the brain's components because it contains distinctive electrical properties, which can be monitored to give clues about sensory input and thought processes. The cortex contains over ten billion nerve cells and, through synaptic routing, there are more possible combinations of neural pathways than there are atoms in the universe! This intricate organ shows both a continuous and rhythmic alteration of electrical potential and a variety of more localized, larger microvoltage responses. The continuous flow of electrical output is called "spontaneous" activity because it is always present in living organisms. The localized responses are called "evoked" because their presence seems closely associated with the input of the senses.

A closer examination of the physical makeup of the cerebral cortex will reveal the nature of these brainwaves. The cortex of the cerebrum is divided into two hemispheres (halves)—a right hemisphere and a left hemisphere. Each hemisphere is divided into four lobes—frontal, parietal, temporal and occipital. Together, these four lobes make up one hemisphere of the cerebral cortex. Each of the brain's hemispheres is nearly a mirror of the other, yet the brain hemispheres seem to specialize in controlling certain kinds of thoughts and actions.

To state accurately all the functions of each of the four lobes would be impossible, since the human brain is still in the early stages of being mapped. It may generally be said that areas of the occipital lobes are associated with the input of visual stimuli, parts of the parietal lobes with speech and motor activities, and portions of the frontal lobes with complex thought processes.[16]

26.   The number of lobes in the cerebral cortex is

○ A. two.

○ B. four.

○ C. eight.

○ D. impossible to state accurately.

○ E. six.

27.   The author believes the cerebral cortex is probably the most interesting of the brain's components because of the

   ◯ A. information it provides about sensory input and thought processes.
   ◯ B. number of atoms in the brain.
   ◯ C. ten billion nerve cells.
   ◯ D. possibilities of electrical potential.
   ◯ E. larger microvoltage responses.

28.   The author refers to localized "evoked" responses as

   ◯ A. electrical responses closely associated with the input of the senses.
   ◯ B. the continuous flow of electrical output.
   ◯ C. very similar to the spontaneous activity.
   ◯ D. continuous alteration of electrical potential.
   ◯ E. rhythmic alteration of electrical potential.

29.   The best title for the above passage is

   ◯ A. The Cerebral Cortex.
   ◯ B. Input and Output of Electrical Activity.
   ◯ C. The Right Hemisphere of the Brain.
   ◯ D. Frontal, Parietal, Temporal and Occipital Lobes.
   ◯ E. Occipital Lobes and Visual Stimuli.

30.   By stating that "the human brain is still in the early stages of being mapped" the author means

   ◯ A. there is more to be learned about the functions of the brain.
   ◯ B. each lobe of the brain has a specific job to do.
   ◯ C. we have yet to distinguish between "spontaneous" and "evoked" electrical output.
   ◯ D. we need a closer examination of the physical makeup of the cerebral cortex.
   ◯ E. it is extremely difficult to monitor electrical properties.

PASSAGE SEVEN

You may use the following question to help you focus your reading:

What are the beliefs of Hinduism?

(The following passage is adapted from R. Eshleman & B.G. Cashion, Sociology: An Introduction. © 1985 by Scott Foresman and Company.)

The great majority of the 457 million Hindus in the world live in India and Pakistan. In India, approximately 85 percent of the population is Hindu. Hinduism has evolved over about 4,000 years and comprises an enormous variety of beliefs and practices. It hardly corresponds to most Western conceptions of religion since organization is minimal and there is no religious hierarchy.

Hinduism is so closely intertwined with other aspects of the society that it is difficult to describe it clearly, especially in the case of castes. Hindus sometimes refer to the ideal way of life as fulfilling the duties of one's class and station, which means obeying the rules of the four great castes of India: the Brahmins, or priests; the Ksatriyas, warriors and rulers; the Vaisyas, merchants and farmers; and the Sudras, peasants and laborers. A fifth class, the Untouchables, includes those whose occupations require them to handle "unclean" objects.

To Hindus, the word "dharma" means the cosmos or the social order. Hindus practice rituals that uphold the great cosmic order. They believe that, to be righteous, one must strive to behave in accordance with the way things are. In a sense, the Hindu sees life as a ritual. The world is regarded as a great dance determined by one's Karma, or personal destiny, and the final goal of the believer is liberation from this cosmic dance. Hindus also believe in transmigration of souls. After one dies one is born again in another form, as either a higher or lower being, depending on whether the person was righteous or evil in the previous life. If one becomes righteous enough, one will cease to be reborn.[17]

---

31. An example of a member of the fifth class would be a

○ A. priest in a respected holy order.

○ B. carpenter in a small village.

○ C. shop owner in India.

○ D. nurse in a leper colony.

○ E. great warrior.

32. Transmigration of souls, according to Hindus, involves

○ A. reincarnation.

○ B. one's Karma.

○ C. one's personal destiny.

○ D. striving to behave in accordance with the way things are.

○ E. the social order.

33. The author states that Hinduism "hardly corresponds" to most Western religions. He most likely means

- ○ A. it is difficult to write about with Western influences.
- ○ B. there is a great deal of similarity between Hinduism and Christianity.
- ○ C. the two religions have many followers.
- ○ D. there are very few similarities between Hinduism and Western religions.
- ○ E. that Hinduism and Western religions need stronger leadership.

34. The author of the above passage

- ○ A. is most likely Jewish.
- ○ B. has little respect for Hinduism.
- ○ C. presents the information in an objective manner.
- ○ D. thinks the beliefs of Hinduism are very strange.
- ○ E. is most likely Christian.

35. According to the above passage, Hindus

- ○ A. should strive for upward social mobility.
- ○ B. will achieve Karma if they better themselves.
- ○ C. achieve righteousness through acceptance.
- ○ D. strive to be continually reborn.
- ○ E. strive for transmigration of souls.

PASSAGE EIGHT

You may use the following question to help you focus your reading:

How did Helen Keller discover the meaning of language?

(The following passage is adapted from H. Keller, The Story of My Life. © 1976 by Buccaneer Books.)

She brought me my hat and I knew I was going out into the warm sunshine. This thought, if a wordless sensation may be called a thought, made me hop and skip with pleasure.

We walked down the path to the well-house, attracted by the fragrance of the honey-suckle with which it was covered. Some one was drawing water and my teacher placed my hand under the spout. As the cool stream gushed over one hand she spelled into the other the word water, first slowly, then rapidly. I stood still, my whole attention fixed upon the motion of her fingers. Suddenly I felt a misty consciousness as of something forgotten—a thrill of returning thought; and somehow the mystery of language was revealed to me. I knew then that w-a-t-e-r meant the wonderful cool something that was flowing over my hand. That living word awakened my soul, gave it light, hope, joy, set it free! There were barriers still, it is true, but barriers that could in time be swept away.

I left the well-house eager to learn. Everything had a name, and each name gave birth to a new thought. As we returned to the house every object which I touched seemed to quiver with life. That was because I saw everything with the strange, new sight that had come to me.[18]

---

36. After her experience at the well, Helen

   ○ A. was aware that her eyesight was greatly improved.

   ○ B. was extremely discouraged.

   ○ C. worried about the barriers she had yet to overcome.

   ○ D. connected language and thought.

   ○ E. experienced deep depression.

37. The experience by the well most likely occurred

   ○ A. during spring or summer.

   ○ B. after school.

   ○ C. during winter.

   ○ D. before school.

   ○ E. during a rainstorm.

38.   Helen's attitude toward learning could best be described as

○   A. enthusiastic.

○   B. discouraged.

○   C. realistic.

○   D. cynical.

○   E. critical.

39.   The above passage is describing

○   A. how the mystery of language was revealed to Helen Keller.

○   B. the relationship between Helen and her teacher.

○   C. how Helen Keller overcame barriers.

○   D. how we all connect language and objects.

○   E. Helen's relationship with her family.

40.   The author makes her point about the importance of language through

○   A. description.

○   B. analogy.

○   C. critical analysis.

○   D. sequential events.

○   E. comparison and contrast.

PASSAGE NINE

You may use the following question to help you focus your reading:

What skills are important for an education?

(The following passage is adapted from R.A. Roy, Physical Science: An Integrated Approach. © 1991 by Contemporary Publishing.)

In school we learn two kinds of things. One kind of thing is learning to read and write. (Yesterday's new technology is today's basic skill.) We learn arithmetic and algebra, how to write a business letter and how do to chemistry. These skills certainly help us with jobs and with life. But there is another kind of learning. It is more basic and more important. It is the skill of learning itself. We learn how to learn. If we are good learners, we will be able to keep up. If we are poor learners, we will be passed by.

Most of us realize that there are some skills, like algebra perhaps, that we won't need very much. "Why bother?" we ask ourselves. The answer is that if we can learn how to master new and difficult material, then we will be able to master the new skills necessary to get a better job and to have a richer life. (It will probably also turn out that the algebra was useful after all.)

One big part of making the American Dream a reality is to get an education. Our economic and political way of life depends so much on educated citizens that educational opportunity is guaranteed to everyone through high school; and, most can go to college with some individual effort. No one is forced to learn, but the opportunity is there for everyone.[19]

41. The two kinds of things learned in school, according to the author, are

- ○ A. reading and writing.
- ○ B. reading and algebra.
- ○ C. algebra and arithmetic.
- ○ D. basic skills and the skill of learning itself.
- ○ E. writing and listening.

42. The author believes

- ○ A. algebra is an impractical skill.
- ○ B. educational opportunity is readily available.
- ○ C. basic skills are unimportant.
- ○ D. the American Dream is far from reality.
- ○ E. reading and writing are the most important skills

43. Statements in the above passage are primarily

   ◯ A. facts.

   ◯ B. opinions.

   ◯ C. supported by data.

   ◯ D. common sense.

   ◯ E. backed by scientific evidence.

44. The best title for the above passage is

   ◯ A. The Importance of Learning to Learn.

   ◯ B. Writing and Education.

   ◯ C. Education.

   ◯ D. Basic Skills.

   ◯ E. Algebra.

45. The author believes the American Dream

   ◯ A. is difficult to achieve.

   ◯ B. can be achieved through education.

   ◯ C. is only possible for a select few.

   ◯ D. is a hoax.

   ◯ E. will pass us by.

PASSAGE TEN

You may use the following question to help you focus your reading:

How is the theme of an advertisement related to the theme of a news story?

(The following passage is adapted from E.D. Yates, The Writing Craft. © 1985 by Contemporary Publishing.)

Just as in a news story, the advertisement must have a theme, a unity provided by using only material that will reflect the theme. You arrive at a theme in an ad usually by choosing a specific benefit that the particular product will provide for the reader/listener/ viewer. Once you have selected a theme, the material you select to use in the ad must advance and enhance that theme. You should put nothing in the ad that would detract from the theme or divert the attention of the consumer from the theme.

The theme can be anything that is likely to persuade the reader/listener/viewer to purchase the product being advertised or to use the service being advertised. The benefit can be anything that appeals to the reader/listener/viewer's need or desire for amusement, good health, recognition, food or drink, security, comfort, approval of the opposite sex and friends of the same sex, a chance to make or save money, a chance to save time, a chance to gain relief from labor, etc. In other words, anything that will improve life or the perception of life.

The theme of an advertisement, unlike the theme of a news story, is more likely to be an appeal to an emotional response than it is an intellectual response. Thus, the need to create a desire for the item or service advertised and the need to move the reader/ listener/viewer to action often will take precedence in determining the theme than the need to attract attention and gain interest.[20]

---

46.   The author discusses advertisements by

○ A. comparing an advertisement to a news story.

○ B. chronological events.

○ C. sequential developments.

○ D. description.

○ E. scientific evidence.

47.   According to the author, the theme of a news story

○ A. is less likely to be an appeal to an emotional response.

○ B. is unrelated to an advertisement.

○ C. has less of a theme than an advertisement.

○ D. may detract from the theme of an advertisement.

○ E. may enhance advertisements.

48. The author believes that the benefit of what is being advertised can be

○ A. security.

○ B. desire or need for amusement.

○ C. need for recognition.

○ D. comfort.

○ E. any or all of the above.

49. According to the author, an advertisement and news story must both

○ A. have a theme.

○ B. appeal to an emotional response.

○ C. have benefits that improve life.

○ D. create a need for action.

○ E. offer a chance to make or save money.

50. According to the author, in determining the theme in an advertisement, the need to create a desire for the item is

○ A. more important than the need to attract attention.

○ B. less important than the need to gain interest.

○ C. less important than the need to take action.

○ D. impossible without a strong interest.

○ E. less important than the need to attract attention.

ANSWERS KEY FOR THE READING SKILLS SECTION

Chapter 11 *Answers*

EXERCISE 2

Paragraph A

Main idea sentence: All foods supply some nutrients, albeit sometimes in limited amounts.

Shape: ▲

Paragraph B

Main idea sentence: Sounds are heard not only through the outer and middle ear, but also through the direct conduction of vibrations through the bones in the head.

Shape: ▼

Paragraph C

Main idea sentence: Sometimes known as the House of Moliere, the Theatre Francais was a symbol, in two important ways, of the emerging dominance of the middle class in the upcoming century.

Shape: ◆

Paragraph D

Main idea sentences: Before assessing someone's nutritional status, his family's medical history must be known. For such reasons, you can fully evaluate someone's nutritional status only after assessing the complete medical history of that person.

Shape: ▼

EXERCISE 3

Paragraph A

Directional words: The crucial point is

Paragraph B

Directional words: In general

Paragraph C

Directional words: The point is

EXERCISE 5

Paragraph A

Main idea sentence: Both ways of understanding are necessary for human fulfillment.

Shape: ▲

EXERCISE 6

Paragraph A

Details: candy, toys, films, free time, extra outdoor periods, first in the lunch line, tokens, "chips"

EXERCISE 7

Paragraph A
　　Directional word: Further, major
Paragraph B
　　Directional words: therefore, major; For example, minor

EXERCISE 8

Paragraph A
　　Signal word(s): Finally

EXERCISE 9

Paragraph A
　　Signal word(s): One consequence of

EXERCISE 10

Paragraph A
　　Signal word(s): older, younger, thicker

EXERCISE 11

Paragraph A
　　Form: providing data
Paragraph B
　　Form: explaining experimental evidence
Paragraph C
　　Form: providing data
Paragraph D
　　Form: providing historical documentation
Paragraph E
　　Form: describing observations

EXERCISE 12

　　Stated assumptions in Paragraph B and C

Chapter 12 *Answers*

EXERCISE 1

Paragraph A
> Main idea: Overpraise may have negative effects on students.
> Clues: Author's tone is negative.

Paragraph B
> Main idea: There are many negative results of industrial production.
> Clues: Author's tone is negative.

EXERCISE 2

Paragraph A
> Assumptions: Author assumes that spelling cannot be taught and that attention to detail will lead to correct spelling.

Paragraph B
> Assumptions: Author assumes rewards of teaching are proportional to effort.

EXERCISE 3

Paragraph A
> Appeal to fear

Paragraph B
> Appeal to pity

Paragraph C
> Appeal to ignorance

Paragraph D
> Appeal to authority

Paragraph E
> Appeal to personal attack

EXERCISE 4

Paragraph A
> Refracted means bent
> Type of context clue: synonym

Paragraph B
> Conception means male and female sex cells unite
> Type of context clue: definition

Paragraph C
> Compelling means strong
> Type of context clue: contrast

Paragraph D
> Vicarious means indirect
> Type of context clue: inference

ANSWERS FOR THE READING SKILLS
PRACTICE TESTS

Practice Test One		**Practice Test Two**	
1. A	26. C	1. D	26. C
2. B	27. A	2. A	27. A
3. A	28. B	3. A	28. A
4. A	29. C	4. A	29. A
5. C	30. A	5. D	30. A
6. A	31. A	6. B	31. D
7. B	32. B	7. D	32. A
8. C	33. E	8. B	33. D
9. B	34. A	9. D	34. C
10. B	35. E	10. A	35. C
11. C	36. C	11. C	36. D
12. C	37. A	12. B	37. A
13. A	38. E	13. B	38. A
14. A	39. D	14. B	39. A
15. D	40. A	15. A	40. A
16. B	41. E	16. E	41. B
17. D	42. D	17. C	42. B
18. C	43. D	18. D	43. B
19. B	44. A	19. A	44. A
20. D	45. D	20. A	45. B
21. B	46. D	21. A	46. A
22. B	47. E	22. B	47. A
23. C	48. C	23. D	48. E
24. B	49. C	24. A	49. A
25. C	50. D	25. A	50. A

ACKNOWLEDGEMENTS

Chapter 11

1   Gerow, R. *Psychology: An Introduction*, 4th Edition. Addison-Wesley Educational Publishers, Inc., Reading, MA, (1995). p. 42.

2   Forsythe, W.A., III. *Nutrition and You With Readings*, 3rd Edition. Contemporary Publishing Company of Raleigh, Inc., Raleigh, NC, (1995). p. 7.

3   Wagner, J. *Introductory Musical Acoustics*, 3rd Edition. Contemporary Publishing Company of Raleigh, Inc., Raleigh, NC, (1994). p. 62.

4   Staub, A.W. *Varieties Of Theatrical Art*, 3rd Edition. Contemporary Publishing Company of Raleigh, Inc., Raleigh, NC, (1994). p. 212.

5   Forsythe, W.A., III. *Nutrition and You With Readings*, 3rd Edition. Contemporary Publishing Company of Raleigh, Inc., Raleigh, NC, (1995). p. 41.

6   Madsen, C.K. & Kuhn, R.L. *Contemporary Music Education*, 2nd Edition. Contemporary Publishing Company of Raleigh, Inc., Raleigh, NC, (1994). p. 70.

7   Wolfe, L.D., Lieberman, L.S. & Hutchinson, D.L. *Laboratory Textbook for Physical Anthropology*, 4th Edition. Contemporary Publishing Company of Raleigh, Inc., Raleigh, NC, (1994). p. 10-35.

8   Roy, R.A. *Physical Science: An Integrated Approach*. Contemporary Publishing Company of Raleigh, Inc., Raleigh, NC, (1991). p. 369.

9   Gerow, R. *Psychology: An Introduction*, 4th Edition. Addison-Wesley Educational Publishers, Inc., Reading, MA, (1995). p. 690–691.

10 Curry, K.J. *Biology Experience*, 2nd Edition. Contemporary Publishing Company of Raleigh, Inc., Raleigh, NC, (1995). p. 1.

11 Esler, W.K. & Sciortino, P. *Methods for Teaching: An Overview of Current Practices*, 2nd Edition. Contemporary Publishing Company of Raleigh, Inc., Raleigh, NC, (1991). p. 72.

12 Gerow, R. *Psychology: An Introduction*, 4th Edition. Addison-Wesley Educational Publishers, Inc., Reading, MA, (1995). p. 514.

13 Wolfe, L.D., Lieberman, L.S. & Hutchinson, D.L. *Laboratory Textbook for Physical Anthropology*, 4th Edition. Contemporary Publishing Company of Raleigh, Inc., Raleigh, NC, (1994). p. 10-1.

14 Curry, K.J. *Biology Experience*, 2nd Edition. Contemporary Publishing Company of Raleigh, Inc., Raleigh, NC, (1995). p. 5.

15 Roy, R.A. *Physical Science: An Integrated Approach*. Contemporary Publishing Company of Raleigh, Inc., Raleigh, NC, (1991). p. 250.

16 Roy, R.A. *Physical Science: An Integrated Approach*. Contemporary Publishing Company of Raleigh, Inc., Raleigh, NC, (1991). p. 186.

17 Roy, R.A. *Physical Science: An Integrated Approach*. Contemporary Publishing Company of Raleigh, Inc., Raleigh, NC, (1991). p. 380.

18 Gerow, R. *Psychology: An Introduction*, 4th Edition. Addison-Wesley Educational Publishers, Inc., Reading, MA, (1995). p. 714.

19 Brook, G. & Heyl, R.J. *Introduction to Landforms*, 3rd Edition. Contemporary Publishing Company of Raleigh, Inc., Raleigh, NC, (1993). p. A-7.

20 Gerow, R. *Psychology: An Introduction*, 4th Edition. Addison-Wesley Educational Publishers, Inc., Reading, MA, (1995). p. 637.

21 Gerow, R. *Psychology: An Introduction*, 4th Edition. Addison-Wesley Educational Publishers, Inc., Reading, MA, (1995). p. 353.

22 Gerow, R. *Psychology: An Introduction*, 4th Edition. Addison-Wesley Educational Publishers, Inc., Reading, MA, (1995). p. 216–217.

23 Gerow, R. *Psychology: An Introduction*, 4th Edition. Addison-Wesley Educational Publishers, Inc., Reading, MA, (1995). p. 674–675.

24 Gerow, R. *Psychology: An Introduction*, 4th Edition. Addison-Wesley Educational Publishers, Inc., Reading, MA, (1995). p. 674.

Chapter 12

1   Esler, W.K. & Sciortino, P. *Methods for Teaching: An Overview of Current Practices*, 2nd Edition. Contemporary Publishing Company of Raleigh, Inc., Raleigh, NC, (1991). p. 72.

2   Roy, R.A. *Physical Science: An Integrated Approach*. Contemporary Publishing Company of Raleigh, Inc., Raleigh, NC, (1991). p. 377.

3   Yates, E.D. *The Writing Craft*, 2nd Edition. Contemporary Publishing Company of Raleigh, Inc., Raleigh, NC, (1985). p. 122.

4   Madsen, C.H., III & Madsen, C.K. *Teaching/Discipline: A Positive Approach For Educational Development*, 3rd Edition. Contemporary Publishing Company of Raleigh, Inc., Raleigh, NC, (1983). p. 77.

5   Roy, R.A. *Physical Science: An Integrated Approach*. Contemporary Publishing Company of Raleigh, Inc., Raleigh, NC, (1991). p. 381.

6   Chaffee, J. *Thinking Critically*, 3rd Edition. Copyright © 1991 by John Chaffee. Reprinted with permission of Houghton Mifflin Company, Boston, MA. p. 571.

7   Chaffee, J. *Thinking Critically*, 3rd Edition. Copyright © 1991 by John Chaffee. Reprinted with permission of Houghton Mifflin Company, Boston, MA. p. 571.

8   Chaffee, J. *Thinking Critically*, 3rd Edition. Copyright © 1991 by John Chaffee. Reprinted with permission of Houghton Mifflin Company, Boston, MA. p. 570.

9   Chaffee, J. *Thinking Critically*, 3rd Edition. Copyright © 1991 by John Chaffee. Reprinted with permission of Houghton Mifflin Company, Boston, MA. p. 572.

10 Brook, G. & Heyl, R.J. *Introduction to Landforms*, 3rd Edition. Contemporary Publishing Company of Raleigh, Inc., Raleigh, NC, (1993). p. 14-2.

11 Gerow, R. *Psychology: An Introduction*, 4th Edition. Addison-Wesley Educational Publishers, Inc., Reading, MA, (1995). p. 355.

12 Roy, R.A. *Physical Science: An Integrated Approach*. Contemporary Publishing Company of Raleigh, Inc., Raleigh, NC, (1991). p. 356.

13 Madsen, C.K. & Kuhn, R.L. *Contemporary Music Education*, 2nd Edition. Contemporary Publishing Company of Raleigh, Inc., Raleigh, NC, (1994). p. 17.

Chapter 13

1   Roy, R.A. *Physical Science: An Integrated Approach*. Contemporary Publishing Company of Raleigh, Inc., Raleigh, NC, (1991). p. 374.

2   Wolfe, L.D., Lieberman, L.S. & Hutchinson, D.L. *Laboratory Textbook for Physical Anthropology*, 4th Edition. Contemporary Publishing Company of Raleigh, Inc., Raleigh, NC, (1994). p. 10-47.

3   Gastaldo, R.A., Savrda, C.E. & Lewis, R.D. *Deciphering Earth History*. Contemporary Publishing Company of Raleigh, Inc., Raleigh, NC, (1996). p. 1-1.

4   Wilson, J.W., *Astronomy: A Laboratory Textbook*, 2nd Edition. Contemporary Publishing Company of Raleigh, Inc., Raleigh, NC, (1996). p. 25.1.

5   Gerow, R. *Psychology: An Introduction*, 4th Edition. Addison-Wesley Educational Publishers, Inc., Reading, MA, (1995). p. 216.

6   Smith, B. *A Tree Grows In Brooklyn*. HarperCollins Publishers, Inc., New York, NY, (1943). p. 25.

7   Lauder, L. "The Language of Foreign Trade," © 1985 by *The New York Times Co.*, New York, NY, (October 7, 1985). p. 136–137.

8   Roy, R.A. *Physical Science: An Integrated Approach*. Contemporary Publishing Company of Raleigh, Inc., Raleigh, NC, (1991). p. 375.

9   Staub, A.W. *Varieties of Theatrical Art*, 3rd Edition. Contemporary Publishing Company of Raleigh, Inc., Raleigh, NC, (1994). p. 19.

10 Roy, R.A. *Physical Science: An Integrated Approach*. Contemporary Publishing Company of Raleigh, Inc., Raleigh, NC, (1991). p. 3.

11 Cousins, N. "The Right To Die," *The Saturday Review*, © 1975, General Media International, Inc., New York, NY, (June 14, 1975). p. 258–260.

12 Hewitt, P.G. "The Origin of the Universe and Solar System," in *Conceptual Physics*, 5th Edition, Scott, Foresman and Company, Glenview, IL, p. 591, from *Academic Reading*, Scott, Foresman/Little, Brown Higher Education, Glenview, IL, (1985).

13 Roy, R.A. *Physical Science: An Integrated Approach*. Contemporary Publishing Company of Raleigh, Inc., Raleigh, NC, (1991). p. 375.

14 Forsythe, W.A., III. *Nutrition and You With Readings*, 3rd Edition. Contemporary Publishing Company of Raleigh, Inc., Raleigh, NC, (1995). p. 46.

15 Wagner, J. *Introductory Musical Acoustics*, 3rd Edition. Contemporary Publishing Company of Raleigh, Inc., Raleigh, NC, (1994). p. 48.

16 Wagner, J. *Introductory Musical Acoustics*, 3rd Edition. Contemporary Publishing Company of Raleigh, Inc., Raleigh, NC, (1994). p. 82.

17 Eshleman, R. & Cashion, B.G. Adapted from *Sociology: An Introduction*, 2nd Edition. Scott Foresman, and Company, p. 353–4 from *Academic Reading*, Scott, Foresman/Little, Brown Higher Education, Glenview, IL (1985).

18 Keller, H. *The Story Of My Life*. Buccaneer Books, New York, 1976. Ed. by John Albert Macy, Cambridge, Mass. (1903). p. 36.

19 Roy, R.A. *Physical Science: An Integrated Approach*. Contemporary Publishing Company of Raleigh, Inc., Raleigh, NC, (1991). p. 382.

20 Yates, E.D. *The Writing Craft*, 2nd Edition. Contemporary Publishing Company of Raleigh, Inc., Raleigh, NC, (1985). p. 71.

raising, and recruiting environment, the problem is generally not a lack of options but determining which ones are most likely to succeed or provide the greatest return in the shortest time. If you have $10,000 to buy advertising aimed at nontraditional students, you can use research to pinpoint the media to which they are most likely to respond.

Fourth, research allows you to test ideas. With research, you can evaluate publication concepts, logo ideas, even signage. Using research in this way can often prevent you from making expensive and very public mistakes.

And finally, research helps monitor your environment. It can quickly pinpoint problems while they are still manageable. At the same time, research can highlight opportunities that you might otherwise miss.

Not data but information

It is not difficult to generate research data. Chances are you have volumes of data sitting on a shelf somewhere in your office. Rather than just data, successful research must generate information upon which you can act. In other words, it is not the collection of data that matters most but the interpretation and application of data.

Each year, college administrators send my company multivolumed studies done by nationally known research companies. Accompanying the studies is a question: "What did we learn—would you mind going over the numbers for us and letting us know what we found out?"

Good research, research that can be used to support a marketing plan, must do more than gather data. It must provide answers to real questions. It must provide clear direction. And it must set out options in priority order.

A necessary vocabulary

Like any specialized endeavor, market research has its own vocabulary. It is important to understand some key terms before we begin a more detailed discussion.

Primary research and secondary research

Essentially, there are two sources of research data: primary and secondary. Primary research uses data that originate with your specific study. Secondary research uses existing data from a completed study that may be applicable to yours.

Suppose, for example, you want to know why alumni give to your institution. If you conduct a survey to find out, you are engaged in primary research. On the other hand, if you use data from a study completed by a colleague at another institution, you are using secondary research.

The difference is important for several reasons. First, because primary research involves designing an original study, it is more expensive and time-consuming. Secondary research is usually less expensive or even free and is usually available quickly.

The second major difference involves the quality, suitability, and integrity of the

Innovation community college. She noted that her institution sets clear goals before launching new programs. If a program does not meet these goals, it is cut or reconfigured. This must be the model for all of higher education in the future, just as it is the model for marketing.

Good research must do more than gather data. "

4

"Data, d
data. I
make
withou
—Sherlo

Market Research

A foundation built on research

Solid marketing plans rest on a foundation of research. In fact, any marketing plan that does not include research at its base is almost surely flawed. It either will fail or will take more time and money to execute. This reality is reflected in a basic definition of market research: the systematic design, collection, analysis, and reporting of data and findings relevant to a specific marketing situation an institution faces. In short, market research involves finding specific answers to specific questions—information that is used to refine marketing goals and to help develop the overall marketing plan.

Market research can help you in a variety of ways. First, you can use it to gather perceptual data. Because people act on their perceptions, learning how different audiences perceive and sometimes misperceive you is critical.

Second, you can use research to provide answers. A recent client was interested in knowing which of two academic programs would attract the most students. A survey of prospective students, an analysis of competing curricula, and an evaluation of short- and long-term regional job and employment trends provided the necessary data. Another client wanted to know which message strategies prospective donors might best respond to. A survey of donors quickly pinpointed some strategies the client had not previously considered.

Third, research helps you clarify and set priorities. In today's marketing, fund-

data. A well-designed primary research study should offer high-quality data. With secondary data, you are inferring conclusions from someone else's research, so you must take extra care to ascertain the data's relevance, examine the impartiality of the study's sponsor, and ensure that correct methodology was followed.

Quantitative research and qualitative research

Just as there are two broad sources of research, there are two broad types of research: quantitative and qualitative.

Quantitative research uses a statistically valid and randomly generated sample to represent a larger population. Validity is important because you want to project data obtained from a relatively small sample to the larger population. Quantitative research requires a carefully designed methodology. For this reason, it is usually fairly expensive and may take some time. Done correctly, mail surveys and telephone surveys are two forms of quantitative research.

Qualitative research, on the other hand, is not statistically valid, and data cannot be projected to larger populations with any degree of certainty. Because qualitative research uses a much less strict methodology, it can usually be conducted more quickly and at lower cost. Focus groups and in-depth interviews are two forms of qualitative research.

Qualitative Research ⟷ Quantitative Research

The key difference between quantitative and qualitative research is really how you wish to use the data. Qualitative research is descriptive, but it is not projectionable. In other words, you cannot project the findings from a focus group of six students to predict how other students might react to your new viewbook. However, with a well-done quantitative study, you can project the findings to a larger population with a high degree of reliability. If 73 percent of your sample responded a certain way to a question, you can be reasonably sure that 73 percent of the larger population would respond in the same manner.

Populations and samples

A population is the group of people to be studied. You may have a population of faculty, staff, donors, alumni, current students, prospective students, parents, or community residents.

A sample is a small subset of that population. In statistical or projectionable studies, the sample must be of a certain size, representative of the larger population, and randomly generated to be considered valid.

Sampling is important for three reasons. First, it is much less expensive to survey a sample of 370 than a population of 10,000. Second, correctly drawn samples are highly representative. And third, it takes less time to survey a sample than an entire population.

Quick Glance

Sources of Secondary Data
Sometimes secondary data can provide the insight and information you need. For sources of exceptional data, see Appendices A, B, and C.

Reliability

Reliability, often called confidence or validity, is usually expressed as a percentage. A study that is reliable at the 95 percent level has a range of error of five percent. If 68 percent of respondents say yes to a particular question, the assumption for the population as a whole could range from 63 percent (68 percent minus five percent) to 73 percent (68 percent plus five percent). The greater the reliability, the more valid the findings.

However, as in many things, there is a tradeoff. Although many factors affect reliability, one of the most important is sample size. The more reliability you want, the greater the sample must be. Table 4-1 illustrates this point.

For example, suppose you have a population of 4,000 alumni (see arrow in left column of Table 4-1). If you want 95 percent reliability, you must survey 350 of them (see ✓ in right column of Table 4-1). A confidence level of 95 percent is very good. Note, however, how much larger the sample would be if you wanted a confidence level of 98 percent. Instead of 350 alumni in your sample, you would need 1,500.

As you can see, moving from 95 percent to 98 percent means sampling four times as many alumni. Of course, this will have a tremendous impact on the cost of the research. Clients often begin projects with the hope of achieving 99 percent reliability. However, 95 percent is really a much better goal. This level is a good balance between cost and validity.

Table 4-1
Reliability and Sample Size

Size of Population	Sample +/-1%	Size +/-2%	for +/-3%	Reliability +/-4%	+/-5%
1,000	**	**	**	375	278
2,000	**	**	696	462	322
3,000	**	1,334	787	500	341
➤ 4,000	**	1,500	842	522	350 ✓
5,000	**	1,622	879	536	357
10,000	4,899	1,936	964	566	370
20,000	6,489	2,144	1,013	583	377
50,000	8,057	2,291	1,045	593	381
100,000	8,763	2,345	1,056	597	383
500,000	9,423	2,390	1,065	600	384

Types of research

Focus groups

Focus groups are designed to focus discussions around a specific topic so people's attitudes, perceptions, and language can be captured and analyzed. This makes focus groups ideal for exploring opinions and attitudes held by students, donors, parents, and others.

Typically, focus groups involve 10 to 12 people, are about 60 minutes in length, and are directed by a moderator. Respondents are selected and screened so they are relatively homogeneous, thereby minimizing both conflicts among group members on issues not relevant to the study and wide-ranging differences in perceptions, experiences, and verbal skills. During the discussion, the moderator follows a guide, a pre-established list of questions and topics to address during the session. Sessions are usually audiotaped. The tape transcriptions and the moderator's notes are the raw data to be analyzed and presented in the final report.

Mail surveys

Mail surveys are widely used in research for examining dispersed populations such as

Quick Glance

Focus Group Guidelines

To make your focus groups as successful as possible, consider the following suggestions:

Length: About 60 minutes per session. Can usually be adjusted so a session will fit during a dinner or a class period.

Number of participants: Ten to 12 per session. It is extremely difficult to control the discussion with more than 12, and the quality of the data will suffer.

Screening participants: Where possible, screen participants so they are as similar/homogeneous as possible. The participants should closely match the profile of the target audience.

Location: Almost any room will do as long as it is comfortable. Because the sessions are usually recorded, the room should be fairly quiet. Ideally, chairs and tables should be movable.

In-depth examination of a single publication: If participants will examine one publication in depth, they should receive a copy ahead of time so they can examine it before the session begins. Remember, it takes time to scrutinize a publication, so you will usually have time for only one or two during the session.

Mounting publication samples: If you are interested in comparing the covers of different publications (for example, you want to compare your viewbook cover with those of your competition), mount each one securely on identical, numbered mat boards.

Displaying publications: If you want to compare covers, have enough tables or easels so all are easily seen at the same time.

Refreshments: When available, it is appropriate to serve soda or coffee. However, avoid messy finger foods such as pizza at sessions where people will handle publications.

alumni, community residents, or—if you use campus mail—students or faculty. As you write and pretest the survey instrument, draw a representative sample of the population, or audience, to be investigated. In some cases, a presurvey postcard should notify your sample that it will be part of an important research project. The survey goes out with a cover letter that explains the need for research. Depending on the audience, these surveys may include some sort of incentive to increase response.

After a short period, you may send a follow-up letter to people who have not returned the survey. This, too, helps increase response. As the surveys come in, you or your researcher will review them for completeness and validity. The actual analysis involves frequency counts (percentages) of how each question was answered and cross-tabulations (comparisons of how different groups answered the same question). In some cases more sophisticated statistical analyses may be applied.

Telephone surveys

Telephone surveys are actually a combination of in-depth interviews and mail surveys. Their methodology is largely similar to that of mail surveys, except the interview is conducted over the phone. Because the interviewer reads all the questions, telephone surveys tend to be less sophisticated and shorter than mail surveys.

Table 4-2. **Strengths and Weaknesses of Types of Market Research**	**Type of Research** *Focus groups*	**Strengths** 1. Informal 2. Often uncover ideas never anticipated by researcher 3. Great for capturing anecdotal data useful for illustration, for comparisons, or to gather insight before developing a quantitative research instrument 4. Often spontaneous	**Weaknesses** 1. Require an experienced moderator 2. Group dynamics can be problematic 3. Can turn into gripe sessions 4. Heavily anecdotal and nonquantitative 5. Often difficult to arrange 6. Relatively expensive for the quality of data obtained	**Best Use** 1. Early in the research process to provide initial direction 2. For testing concepts, especially visuals 3. For testing and comparing messages and media from competing institutions
	Mail surveys	1. Relatively inexpensive if an adequate sample can be obtained 2. Can be longer 3. Can ask complex or sensitive questions 4. Can show/use illustrations and graphics 5. No geographic limitations	1. Take longer to complete 2. Less control over response rate 3. Can be perceived as impersonal 4. Less control over timing 5. Depend heavily on quality of mailing list 6. May require an incentive	1. For audiences that have a great affinity for you (alumni, parents) so are more likely to respond 2. To gather comprehensive data 3. To survey audiences that are dispersed geographically
	Telephone surveys	1. Much more control over response rates 2. Can be completed quickly 3. Some respondents prefer anonymity 4. Can be highly representative	1. Must be shorter and less complex 2. Difficult to establish initial rapport 2. Sometimes difficult to gather sensitive or personal data 3. Relatively expensive 4. Cannot show/use illustrations and graphics 5. Telephone numbers of respondents may not be available	1. Audiences that may not respond to a mail survey 2. When surveys are short 3. When you need a great deal of data in a short time
	In-depth interviews	1. Can probe and follow lead of respondent 2. Good for highly political audiences 3. Doesn't always strike respondent as "research" 4. Often used to both gather data and build bridges with the audience 5. Difficult to be representative	1. Very expensive 2. Depends heavily on skill of interviewer 3. More potential for interviewer bias 4. Can take a great deal of time 5. Difficult to input; data often subject to multiple interpretations	1. Best for high-profile audiences not available through other means 2. When validity is not a big issue or when population is very small

In-depth interviews

Lasting 30 to 45 minutes, in-depth, or one-on-one, interviews are designed to elicit information and opinions from people who are unable or unwilling to be approached through other research techniques. Like other forms of research, in-depth interviews follow an interview guide, a series of questions that serve to direct the discussion. Most in-depth interviews are conversational in nature.

See Table 4-2 for a breakdown of strengths and weaknesses of the various types of market research.

Understanding the importance of trend data

Though any research project can provide important information, at best it is a snapshot that gathers data on how people think at a specific time. This is useful, but it is often much more useful to know how those data have changed over time. Suppose your research revealed that 23.5 percent of alumni do not read any portion of your quarterly magazine. Many people would find this distressing. However, you know that two years ago this number was 31.4 percent. Rather than being distressed, you are elated because you are making progress. Trend data provide an important perspective: Rather than a snapshot, they are an ongoing movie.

To collect trend data, you must routinely survey the same audience and ask that audience the same question. These steps are the only way to make meaningful comparisons.

Designing a research study

Undertaking a research study involves completing seven distinct yet sequential steps:
1. Develop the research agenda.
2. Design the research methodology.
3. Write the research instrument.
4. Draw the sample.
5. Complete the study.
6. Input and analyze data.
7. Present the results.

Step 1: Develop the research agenda

The research agenda is a guide to action. It provides direction, clarifies options, and keeps things on track.

Developing a research agenda involves answering four questions: Why are you doing the research? What do you hope to learn? What audiences have the answers? And finally, what decisions will you make as a result?

It is important to know why you are undertaking research. Perhaps you are responding to changes in your institution or your marketplace. Perhaps you have a new president who needs to be acclimated or you just want to keep a finger on the pulse of your environment. All of these are good reasons to conduct research.

At the beginning of your research project, it is important to clarify exactly what it is you wish to learn. We sometimes call this the "big question." Big questions might be these:

■ Why do so few (or many) alumni give to the annual fund?
■ Why don't former donors give again?
■ How do parents perceive our institution?
■ Why do some students withdraw?

The big question serves as a sort of thesis statement and helps direct the creation of the survey instrument. As you develop individual survey questions, keep the big question in mind. If survey questions don't help answer the big question, don't use them.

As you define the big question, keep in mind who is most likely to have the answers you seek. Often this is self-evident, but not always. For example, when exploring who influences students in choosing a college, some administrators automatically survey guidance counselors, parents, high school teachers, and others. A better strategy is to survey prospective students about who most influenced their decision. Then survey the people the students identified as important.

The final question that helps shape your research agenda is one of the most important: How are you going to apply the results; what are you going to do with the data? What policy and program changes do you anticipate making? The very best research keeps this outcome firmly in mind. Knowing how you will use the data helps you not just shape the questionnaire but decide how to analyze the data and present the results.

At this point in the project, it is important to establish the range of possibilities. You must determine how receptive your senior administrators and other groups will be to the data. It is very frustrating to gather results that provide insight and direction—and then have the president or chief administrators ignore them. Ascertain the range of possibilities before starting the project. If the president really doesn't want to change the curriculum or move the campus, don't explore these issues.

Step 2: Design the research methodology

Now that the research agenda is beginning to take shape, you must decide which

Table 4-3. **Research Strategy Grid**	**Research Question**	**Audience**	**Methodology**	**Population**	**Validity Sought**	**Sample Size**
	How do parents perceive the institution?	Parents	Telephone survey	2,000	95 percent	322
	Why do major donors give to the institution?	Major donors	Personal interviews	95*	100 percent	All
	How do alumni feel about the institution?	Alumni	Mail survey	12,000	95 percent	375

*Because this population is so small, you must survey the entire universe (everyone in the population).

Integrated Marketing for Colleges, Universities, and Schools

method(s) are most practical for the study you envision. You might choose different research methods for different audiences. As you develop the strategy, you must also address issues of reliability and confidence.

To help guide your overall research project, you might want to create a Research Strategy Grid that links the important components of each study. As you can see in Table 4-3, such a grid is a useful way to keep things organized.

In this grid, the first column contains the "big question." The second column defines the target audience. The third indicates the chosen methodology. At this point some judgment comes into play.

As you choose a method, you must weigh several factors:

- Audience size
- Audience importance or status
- Amount of money available for research
- Level of validity sought
- Time frame for completing the survey
- Geographic distribution of the audience
- Survey length
- Survey complexity
- Sensitivity of survey questions

In the example in Table 4-3, we chose a telephone survey for parents because of their geographic distribution and because the survey will be relatively short. However, we chose personal interviews for the donors because of their status and the small size of their population. Finally, we chose a mail survey for alumni because of the size of the sample and because the intended alumni survey is long, complex, and covers several sensitive issues.

The fourth column gives the population size. You must determine this before you can establish the sample size. Next, establish the level of reliability you want. At this point you must ask yourself three key questions: In relation to the rest of the audiences being studied,

- How important is this particular audience?
- How important are these data?
- What major decisions will we make as a result?

Because of the direct relationship between cost and reliability, use these questions to guide your thinking about the level of validity you should seek.

The final column, sample size, comes from computing the reliability level sought and the size of the population.

Consider three rules as you choose your research strategy. First, there is a relationship between the significance of the decision to be made and the amount of time and money you should spend on research to support it. In other words, decisions that will have far-reaching implications warrant more research.

Second, as the complexity of the project increases, balance quantitative research methods (surveys) with qualitative research methods (interviews and focus groups). This will improve the overall quality and validity of the final data.

When designing your strategy, make sure you begin discussing the type of research after isolating the questions and the audience. It can be disastrous to begin a market research study by saying "let's do a focus group" before deciding what and whom you want to examine.

Finally, remember that a good research methodology protects not only the subject and the data but the credibility of the researcher.

Step 3: Write the research instrument

For many people, writing the survey instrument is the hardest part of the research process. Although experience plays an important part, these guidelines will help you get off to a quick start.

First, consider the methodology. Telephone surveys are generally shorter and less complex; mail surveys, because the recipients will read them, can be longer and cover more complex issues. Focus groups and personal interviews are usually more conversational in nature.

Second, concentrate on the research agenda. Why are you doing this? What do you hope to learn? What decisions will you make as a result? Your survey must focus on answering these three questions; if a potential question does not, don't include it.

Remember to move from general questions to specific questions, from safe questions to sensitive ones. As in any good interview, save the most difficult questions for later; open with those that are easy to answer and that gain the respondents' trust.

Open-ended and close-ended questions

Most surveys use two different kinds of questions. Open-ended questions allow respondents to answer in their own words; close-ended questions ask respondents to choose from a list of possible answers.

Sample open-ended question:
What is your favorite part of the alumni magazine?

There are several kinds of close-ended questions:
- Dichotomous (no measure of intensity)
  Do you remember receiving the homecoming announcement?
  ☐ Yes   ☐ No

- Multiple choice (no measure of intensity or direction)
  Do you prefer to take classes in
  ☐ the morning   ☐ the weekend   ☐ the afternoon
  ☐ no preference   ☐ the evening   ☐ don't know

- Scaled (used to measure intensity or direction)
  How important was the net cost (after aid) of this college in your decision to attend?
  Very important __ __ __ __ __ Not important at all

There is a great deal of debate about which types of questions are best. With close-ended questions, the respondents must choose from the answers offered, so you must take great care that the answers cover the full range of possibilities. There is also some loss of detail. However, close-ended questions take less space on the instrument, are easier for respondents to complete, are less likely to be misinterpreted, and are less expensive to tabulate and analyze.

Whereas open-ended questions allow a much greater variety of answers, they are also less likely to be interpreted properly and completed and are much more expensive to analyze.

Generally, the best surveys use both kinds. The majority of the survey questions are close-ended, and open-ended questions are used to gather data for which you have developed no succinct set of responses. Open-ended questions are also useful in gathering anecdotal data that might be used to illustrate other data.

As you develop your questions, remember . . .

- Seek only information that is not available elsewhere.
- Test both directions and questions to make sure they are clear and simple.
- Use examples to illustrate any questions that may be confusing.
- Place personal or sensitive questions later in the survey.
- Ask important questions more than once and in more than one way.
- Do not put the most important questions at the end of the survey.
- Clarity is essential. All items must mean the same thing to all respondents. Avoid terms like "several," "most," and "usually."
- Vary the types of questions.
- Do not talk down to respondents.
- Do not assume too much knowledge on their part.
- Avoid hypothetical questions; they will get you hypothetical answers.
- Avoid negative questions; respondents often misread them. For instance, people may overlook the negative word, then give an answer opposite to their real opinion.
- Avoid questions that contain stereotypes, slang, or emotionally loaded words.
- Avoid technical terms, abbreviations, jargon, and "big words" that some respondents may not understand.
- Avoid items that require people to respond to two separate ideas with a single answer.
- Avoid biased or leading questions. If you hint at the type of answer you prefer, respondents may tell you what you want to hear.
- Avoid questions that embarrass respondents or make them defensive.
- Use close-ended questions where possible, but go for answers that are more revealing than yes and no.
- People are less likely to complete long surveys than short ones, so construct as few items as your objectives will allow.
- Take advantage of desktop publishing and laser printers so the survey is visually appealing.

Quick Glance

Asking Better Questions
There is as much art as science to writing good research questions. Two helpful sources are Ken Metzler's *Creative Interviewing* and Stanley Payne's *The Art of Asking Questions.*

Table 4.4.
Sources for Statistical Software

StatPac
(612) 925-0159

SPSS
(800) 543-5815

Minitab
(800) 448-3555

Survey Pro
(800) 478-7839

P-Stat
(609) 466-1688

Table 4-5.
Breakdown of Donor Pool

Donor Pool	Size of Donation	Pop. of Donors
1	$10,000 or more	275
2	$3,000 to $9,999	450
3	Less than $3,000	1,275

Software considerations

Keep in mind the statistical software you will use to analyze the data. There is nothing more frustrating than having a box of 375 surveys that your software cannot analyze. When you've finished the first draft of the instrument, ask your resident statistics-software expert to evaluate the suitability of your question formats.

Chances are someone in the department of psychology, sociology, or education already has statistical software you can borrow. However, if you need to buy software, check out the packages listed in Table 4-4.

Check each software choice for the following:
- Will it help you develop the survey?
- How easily can you input and verify data?
- Does it provide the analyses you need?
- Does it include a graphics package?
- Will it easily export data to Excel, QuattroPro, or Lotus?

Conduct a pretest

There is no survey instrument anywhere that wouldn't be improved with a pretest. To conduct it, ask a subset of your sample to complete the survey. Afterward, have the subjects evaluate and comment on its apparent purpose, its contents and length, the order and construction of the questions, and the instructions. This will greatly improve the quality of your instrument.

Step 4: Draw the sample

To be statistically valid and projectionable, you must draw the sample correctly. Correct sampling means that everyone in the population has an equal chance to be chosen for the study.

Assume, for example, that you are completing a survey of potential donors. There are 2,000 people in this population, and you want a reliability level of 95 percent. To achieve this level of confidence, you will need a sample of 322.

If the population is homogeneous, you can use a basic random sample. This is sometimes called "nth name sampling" because you choose every nth name from the larger population. Divide your sample population of 2,000 by 322, and draw every sixth name from a randomly generated list. (Never choose the first 322 people. Most lists are organized alphabetically, geographically, or chronologically, and taking the sample from the first part of the list would make the names not representative. Fortunately, database software often includes provisions for randomly generating lists, so it should not be difficult to develop a truly representative sample.)

If the population is heterogeneous, use a stratified random sample. This means you actually break the larger population into subpopulations that you have determined are important, then sample each subpopulation separately. For example, you might break the larger group of 2,000 potential donors into three segments according to the size of the gift they are able to give.

Consider arranging the prospective-donor pool as we have done in Table 4-5.

A stratified random sample would require you to treat each subpopulation as a separate study. In other words, you would have to draw a specific number of names randomly from each of the three pools. The level of validity you seek, of course, would determine the number of names.

If you are completing a survey of prospective students, you might want to divide your larger sample into several smaller ones to categorize students by ethnicity, household income, distance from the institution, or some other characteristic or quality you feel is important.

Of course, it is possible to stratify every large population into smaller subsets. However, you must always balance the need to stratify with expediency and economy. Stratified studies are more complicated, take longer, and cost more. In most cases you should never go beyond two or three levels of stratification.

At this stage in the project, you must also begin to think about probable response rates. This is especially true for mail surveys because responses have consistently slipped over the past decade. Response rate is less of an issue for telephone surveys because you generally keep calling until you complete an adequate number.

When you assign levels of reliability to a study, you assume a response rate of at least 50 percent for each sample. If the response rate is less, you have what is called nonresponse bias; more people didn't respond than did.

There are three basic strategies for dealing with nonresponse bias. First, oversample your population. For example, if your study calls for a sample of 370, you should consider surveying twice or even three times that many. This oversampling will help boost response rates.

Second, include incentives with your survey. Mail surveys often include incentives such as cash, the opportunity to win a larger sum of cash or a prize through a drawing, or a small gift such as a calendar, booklet, or coupon.

A third strategy to reduce nonresponse bias is to use ART, an acronym that reminds you to

- ■ Announce the study with a postcard.
- ■ Remind participants to complete the survey (use another postcard or perhaps a second survey).
- ■ Thank respondents for their help.

ART is especially suited for mail surveys, though the basic strategy works for all kinds of research.

All of these strategies must be implemented *a priori*. There is nothing you can do to salvage a study after it suffers from nonresponse bias.

Step 5: Complete the study

Follow the research methodology and timelines you have developed. Monitor return rates. For important studies, be prepared to oversample or send reminders when the response rate fails to meet projections.

Quick Glance

Conducting a Pretest
A pretest can dramatically improve the quality of your research instrument. Draw a sample of 10 to 15 people and have them complete the survey. Ask them to think about:

- ■ Clarity of the opening instructions
- ■ Clumsy or unclear wording
- ■ Order of questions
- ■ Clarity of instructions on skipping certain questions
- ■ Lack of alternatives such as "don't know" or "does not apply"
- ■ Inadequate space for writing responses to open-ended questions
- ■ Leading or confusing questions
- ■ Confusing scale devices
- ■ Their own fatigue, tendency to skip questions, or loss of interest

When they are done, hold a group discussion about the experience and take notes on problem areas and suggestions for improvement.

Quick Glance

Increasing Response Rates

Nonresponse is a growing problem in mail surveys. To help increase your response rate, consider the following strategies:

- Use the 2x rule (mail twice as many surveys as you need to achieve your sample size).
- Place a short announcement in an appropriate newsletter about the study's importance.
- Use monetary, emotional, or tangible incentives.
- Send participants a presurvey announcement postcard.
- Time the survey to avoid holidays and calendar conflicts.
- Use a personalized cover letter from a prestigious person.
- Use quality reproduction of all written surveys and cover letters.
- Mail it first class (hand-stamped).
- Include return postage on pre-addressed envelopes.
- Send a thank-you/reminder postcard a few days after mailing the survey.
- Send a second survey and cover letter to people who have not returned the first survey.

Step 6: Input and analyze data

As surveys are returned or interviews done, check them for validity and completeness. Before entering each survey into the computer, number it so you can later compare or verify randomly selected surveys against the data to assure the input's accuracy.

Inputting the data from close-ended questions is usually just a matter of typing in the responses. Handling data from open-ended questions is more problematic. All responses must first be read, then categorized, and then entered. This process converts open-ended data to close-ended data so that you can analyze it with the other close-ended responses.

In most cases, analysis is relatively straightforward and includes descriptive statistics such as percentages (frequency counts) and statistics that highlight central tendencies and the shape of distributions such as mean, median, mode, and standard deviation. In a few cases, you might want to use more sophisticated techniques such as analysis of variance (ANOVA) or regression analysis.

The crosstab, an extremely useful method, allows you to look at a relationship between two variables. For example, suppose you have the questions listed in Table 4-6.

Table 4-6.
Crosstab of the Relationship Between Two Variables

		Number	Percent
What year are you?	freshman	40	40 percent
	sophomore	24	24 percent
	junior	20	20 percent
	senior	16	16 percent
	TOTAL	100	100 percent
Do you live:	on campus	60	60 percent
	off campus	40	40 percent
	TOTAL	100	100 percent

A crosstab, as in Table 4-7, would allow you to examine the relationship between where students live and their year in college. Crosstabs allow you to pinpoint relationships between different questions and responses.

Analysis of qualitative research is usually not very sophisticated. It typically involves preserving and categorizing comments drawn from in-depth interviews and focus groups and, within context, using these comments to support quantitative data. The result will be a highly representative picture of the data.

Step 7: Present the results

Presenting the findings actually involves two steps: writing a detailed final report and deciding which parts of it you want to present. The written report is the document of record. If your research and its conclusions are to be accepted, they must be well-written. At the very least, the report should include the following:

- Introduction
- Statement of the problem
- Goals and purpose of research
- Brief overview of the methodology

A more detailed methodology should be in the appendix of the final report.

- Analysis of all data
- Executive summary
  - Review of key data
  - Relevant cross-tabulations
  - Implications
  - Strategies for implementation
  - Areas of further research
  - Conclusion
- Appendices
  - Detailed methodology
  - Sample of instruments
  - Hard copy of all analyses

The tone of the report is important. It must be authoritative yet nontechnical. The report should include a clear table of contents so readers can focus on the parts most important to them. The methodology section should include information on survey design and pretesting, the timeline for the study's execution, response rates, and a description of the statistical software and analyses used.

The best reports often open with a demographic snapshot of the people who completed the surveys. This helps provide perspective on the findings.

As you write the report, avoid the tendency to focus only on the negative findings. In fact, it is often useful to stress positive findings early in the report to increase support for the research.

The presentation of your research is also extremely critical. The integrity of your study, and your reputation, may rest on the quality of this presentation.

Table 4-7.
Where Students Live, by Percentage

	On Campus	Off Campus
Freshmen	85.0	15.0
Sophomores	70.8	29.2
Juniors	30.0	70.0
Seniors	18.8	81.2

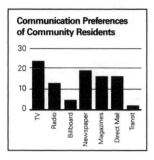

Figure 4-1.
Sample Graph

The goal of market research is to present information on which people can act—to make that information accessible and understandable. Most people are not interested in raw data. Instead, they want real answers to their tough questions.

When designing the presentation, remember three cardinal rules. First, by emphasizing everything, you actually emphasize nothing. Be judicious in deciding how much of your data to present. Second, people can absorb only so much information, and most have trouble dealing with endless columns of numbers. Take the time to present the most salient bits of data in high-quality graphs such as the one in Figure 4-1.

Finally, remember that you exercise enormous power when you decide what elements of the research to present and how to present them. The simple act of graphing a data element can make it appear more important than data you did not graph.

Develop a research cycle

Because there is no shortage of potential research studies and audiences, it is often useful to develop a research cycle. This allows you to survey key audiences systematically. Although the nature of your institution, its budgetary commitment to market research, and its specific marketing challenges will affect the design of your research cycle, the cycle represented in Table 4-8 offers some initial direction and insight as to the frequency of oft-undertaken studies.

Do it yourself or go outside?

Whether to conduct market research yourself or seek outside help is an important question you must answer fairly early. A few guidelines should help your thinking.

Staying inside

Undertaking the research yourself may save you money. Additionally, your intimate familiarity with your institution is a bonus. Of course, you are also aware of in-house research resources upon which you can depend.

Going outside

Hiring outside help will save you time. This is especially true when you are conducting multiple studies or when your internal resources are tight. Also, outside companies often have more expertise. They can correctly match the research question, the audience, and the type of study to be undertaken.

In addition, an outside researcher has no stake in the findings—no hidden agenda—and is not trying to use data to prove something. This impartiality and objectivity is especially important if you are examining a sensitive issue. Finally, go outside when you need perspective on the findings. Good research is more than collecting data; it uses data to provide direction for improving programs and strategies. One of the biggest reasons colleges and universities go to a company that specializes in higher education research is that they realize the importance of data interpretation and application. It is one thing to collect data but quite another to know what to do with it.

Options to lower research costs

For some institutions, the biggest obstacle to market research is its cost. Here are some ideas to increase cost-effectiveness.

Check secondary sources

Before you begin a primary research project, see if secondary research is available from an association or consortium to which you belong. The World Wide Web is also a good source of secondary data.

Develop a central research registry

It is not unusual for more than one office at a college to initiate research projects. This can mean duplicate studies or portions of studies, missed opportunities to piggyback, and wasted dollars and time. To avoid this problem, consider developing a central research registry that keeps track of who is doing what study.

Involve faculty experts

For a sophisticated study, seek guidance from faculty experts in statistics or research design. Their input and direction may save you time and money. Take care, however, that the topic of study will have no impact on any faculty involved. For example, you would not want a psychology professor to participate in the evaluation of publications produced by her husband working in campus public relations.

Scale down the study's size

Some colleges and universities insist on trying to survey an entire population when a representative sample would do fine. Instead of trying to see how all 18 of your constituent publics perceive you, rank-order these publics and seek information from the most important five or six. There are options for scaling down a research project that will not affect its quality.

Choose a less expensive type of research

There is an enormous difference in the costs of doing 370 mail surveys and 370 phone surveys. With minor modifications, less expensive strategies may gain the same information.

When possible, use close-ended questions

Questions that ask respondents to choose from an established series of answers (yes or no; very good, good, or not very good; and the like) are much easier and cheaper to tabulate.

Pretest your instruments

A solid pretest can uncover questions that need rewording or a word here and there that is not universally understood. Revising your survey will increase its validity.

Table 4-8.
Research Cycle

Annually
Survey of nonmatriculants
Survey of nonapplicants
Survey of prospective students

Every two years
Survey of prospective students
Survey of current students
Survey of noninquirers
Survey of high school influencers
Survey of donors
Survey of community leaders

Every three years
Survey of parents
Survey of general community
Survey of alumni
Survey of former donors
Survey of faculty and staff

Develop a research cycle

A research cycle involves doing smaller studies each year rather than one massive study every three years. Not only will you have more control over the research, you will also be able to focus on current problems and opportunities. In addition, you will be able to monitor your market continually, probably pay less for the research, and assimilate data more easily.

Balance what you need to know with what would be interesting to know

One quick way to cut your costs is to reduce the size of the survey. I have seen three-page surveys burgeon to eight or more pages after everyone in the administration has a chance to add a few favorite questions. When looking over the questions, ask yourself, "How can I realistically use these data to improve my marketing and communication effort?"

Use sound methodology

A solid, balanced research methodology will increase the integrity and vitality of your research data. Don't cut corners and be forced to redo the study.

Standardize your instruments

Writing the survey instrument is one of the most expensive components of a research project. If possible, standardize your instruments and get all possible life out of them. This is extremely important if you are trying to create longitudinal data.

When to conduct research

Among the many times when it is important to conduct research, five are probably most important.

First, conduct research when you are making million-dollar decisions. A few years ago I was asked to complete a study for an Eastern college that had four regional campuses but, following a budget crisis, could afford to operate only three. Sound research provided the information needed about which campus should be closed and how to consolidate the other three.

Second, conduct research when you want to test a new idea or concept. Spending a few thousand dollars on research can prevent you from making very costly and very public advertising or publication mistakes.

Third, conduct research when you sense that your marketplace or target audiences are changing. You might want to undertake research if you are facing more competition for each donated dollar, struggling to recruit students, or finding that fewer and fewer people have a good idea of what you are all about.

Fourth, conduct research if you are new, are working in a new area, or have lost your perspective. Research can quickly clarify and prioritize the issues and options before you. Early in my career, a college president hired me to complete a study because he had lost faith in a senior administrator. He felt he was not being adequately informed about an issue and wanted to find out what was happening.

> "A solid, balanced research methodology will increase the integrity and vitality of your research data."

Integrated Marketing for Colleges, Universities, and Schools

Finally, conduct research when you cannot afford to be wrong. When dollars are tight, time is critical, or public opinion is shaky, research can keep you from making costly, and often very public, mistakes.

The politics of research

It is important to recognize at the outset that market research can become political. Generally, this occurs for three reasons.

First, data can upset existing, perhaps widely held, paradigms. Second, research often reveals data about performance and productivity. For instance, if alumni are dissatisfied with the alumni magazine, it is reasonable to focus some attention on the editor's abilities. And third, research often results in a reallocation of funds. Undertaking a marketing plan, creating a video for major donors, or sending the president out on an eight-city tour all cost money—and more often than not, money to fund these activities will be reallocated from other sources. Henry Kissinger once said that the reason politics in academics is so intense is because the stakes are so small. Well, the stakes may not be small, but some administrators' provincial outlook may be.

Dealing with the potential political fallout of market research involves five strategies.

Win support from the top

First and foremost, you must get demonstrated support from the top: Your president and senior administrators must actively support the research project. Part of their support must be a willingness not only to conduct the research but to act on the results.

Get your ducks in a row

Having the administration on your side is half the battle. Now you must spread ownership to colleagues, potential adversaries, and subordinates by
- Demonstrating the need for the research
- Explaining why these data must be collected now
- Showing how these data will be used
- Citing ways the research may save institutional dollars

Stewart Dyke, a colleague at Denison University, used to remind me that if I didn't involve people in the takeoffs, they wouldn't be around for the crash landings. In other words, seek people's advice and input at the beginning of the project so they'll be there if you need their help later on. His advice was good 10 years ago, and it is even better now.

Use correct methodology

An indirect way of attacking you and your recommendations is to attack the methodology of your research. In my experience, scrutiny is most likely to focus on sampling

> "Henry Kissinger once said that the reason politics in academics is so intense is because the stakes are so small."

procedure and response rates. So take great care to follow a correct methodology and sampling process.

Make it work the first time

Your first study must succeed. If it doesn't, you may not be given an opportunity to conduct research in the future. With that in mind . . .

- Don't promise more than you can deliver.
- Have a consultant or campus expert help with your first study.
- Begin with a small study and proceed slowly until you gain experience.
- Make your first study as nonpolitical as possible. Don't study faculty workloads—this is too political. Instead, study something both useful and that faculty will support. Later, when you have learned more about research and earned their trust, it might be more appropriate to study something a bit more controversial.

Explain and apply results in an understandable way

One of the quickest ways to lose institutional support for market research is to fail to explain the results or show how those results will be applied. Everyone can point to a research study that sits on a shelf somewhere because the data either couldn't be applied or were not applied.

Conclusion

The goal of market research is to present information on which you can act. I hope this chapter will allow you to create or refine your market-research strategies so they will do a better job providing the information you need to guide your programs. As you create your questions and design your strategies, keep in mind some guiding principles of market research:

- Don't ask a question if you can't do anything with the answer.
- Ask important questions as often and of as many different people as possible.
- Remember, it always takes longer than you think.
- Balance your research methods.
- Separate what you need to know from what you are interested in knowing.
- Have an idea of what you hope to learn, but expect some surprises.

5

Image *Is* Everything

Image. The very word conjures up fears of superficiality and lack of depth. But astute administrators have borrowed a page from business's playbook and learned that their institution's image or reputation is one of their most precious and powerful marketing tools.

Let me offer a few thoughts to support this point. First, it is well established that people are more influenced by prior knowledge than by new knowledge. We interpret each day, and each day's messages, in light of the days and messages that have gone before. We see fractions of messages and flesh them out on the basis of what we already know.

For instance, a few months ago I had the opportunity to conduct a series of focus groups for a client on the West Coast. As part of this research, I asked groups of high school juniors to give their impressions of viewbook covers from eight different colleges. In one group of covers, the college names were not masked. All the students picked one well-known college as the most academic, the most prestigious, and the institution they would most like to attend. For the second group of students I masked the names of the colleges. The students responded only to how the covers looked and were not biased by the institution's name. The viewbook that had fared so well with the first group was ignored by the next.

Second, image has a tremendous and often underappreciated effect on college choice. Each year, Stamats Communications asks thousands of high school students and first-year college students why they chose the college they did. Just as routinely, they offer a handful of reasons: image or reputation, location, cost, the availability of a specific major, and safety. And when asked to choose their top reason, they often choose image.

Fred Gehrung, president of Gehrung and Associates, a media-relations company in Keene, N.H., affirms this point: "In today's uncertain economy and intensely competitive environment, there is one thing a college or university cannot economize on—its reputation. Prospective students and families need to be even more certain about the institution they select, about the quality of education it offers, and about the outcome, meaning the return on the investment of effort and money. Reputation now is more important than ever." Gehrung goes on to say, "Every mention of your college or university is an investment in its future, for it nourishes awareness that converts to respect. Like it or not, the public equates a high profile with quality."

Third, awareness of a college's name or reputation is a pivotal first step in foundation work. An advancement officer at a client college noted that it is significantly easier to make the case with a foundation when it knows all about you before you set a foot in the door: "You don't need to spend valuable time introducing yourself. If they already know you, you can begin discussing specifics almost immediately."

Foundation cultivation recognizes this point. Colleges often target foundations a year or more before contacting them with a grant or gift proposal. They use that year to heighten the institution's name recognition among foundation officials and in the region the foundation most often supports.

Fourth, institutions with strong images are able to recruit better faculty, and faculty are more likely to stay longer. During the next decade, the crisis in faculty hiring will have a greater impact on lesser-known institutions as a declining faculty pool flocks to institutions with strong names—names that will look better on curriculum vitae and names that are often more able to offer the resources good faculty need.

Fifth, institutions with strong images tend to have a greater percentage of annual fund participation. The national average is about 21 percent for all institutions. However, colleges such as the University of Chicago, Stanford, and Boston University have annual fund participation rates that are much higher. Centre College has an annual participation rate of 62.09 percent. Any effort to enhance the institution's reputation will increase the value of the degree and build pride and ownership among alumni, donors, and other key audiences.

And finally, image building is seen as a legitimate pre-recruiting function at a small but growing number of market-oriented institutions. As the diagram in Figure 5-1 of a recruiting funnel indicates, successful funnel strategies begin with image-enhancement strategies.

Let me offer two final bits of anecdotal evidence on the importance of image. The first is drawn from outside the educational community. A few years ago *Harvard Business Review* conducted an interview with Phil Knight, president of Nike. During the interview, Knight said Nike really began to soar when officials realized that they were not in the shoe business but in the image business. Sure, they make shoes, con-

> " **Institutions with strong images tend to have a greater percentage of annual fund participation.** "

ceivably some of the best shoes in world. But Nike sells much more than shoes—it sells the Nike swoosh.

Recently I had a conversation with a student interested in attending Yale. As you know, Yale is located in a very tough city—New Haven. The student and her parents were very much aware of Yale's location. When I asked if they were concerned about the city, they said yes. But they also said that though it was a concern, it wouldn't affect their final decision because "Yale is Yale." In other words, the image or reputation of Yale—that of a top-flight academic institution—is more important than other variables.

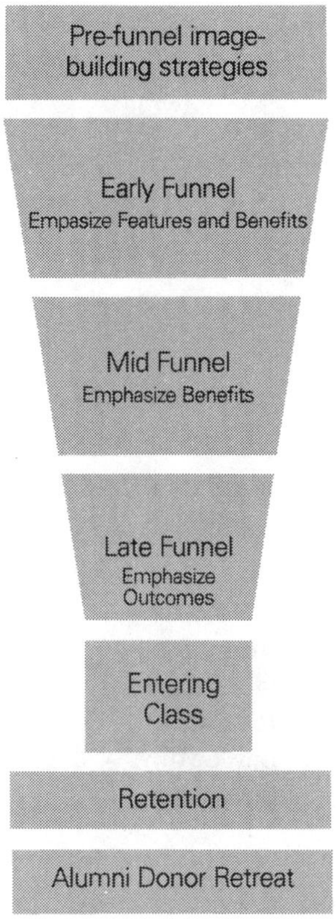

Understanding institutional images

An image is a set of attitudes or beliefs that a person or audience holds about an institution. An image is how you look, and an image is who you are. Though this may seem fairly straightforward, it is complicated by a few factors.

First, institutions have multiple images. Freshmen view the same institution differently than do seniors. Younger alumni view an institution one way while older alumni often view it another. Tenured faculty look at a college one way while untenured faculty look at it another. Everyone views the institution differently depending on context and perspective.

It is also useful to know that images sometimes lag behind institutional reality, that images change over time and often are not particularly accurate. For example, if you were ever an all-women's school with a strong nursing program, you will always be known, in some quarters, as that type of institution even if you are now coed and the nursing program was eliminated 10 years ago.

Third, whereas most impressions are built over time, they begin with a powerful first impression—an encounter upon which all future images are built. These first impressions, called "moments of truth," are so strong that it is difficult if not impossible to change the direction of an image after a poor first impression.

Fourth, images are relational in two directions—vertical and horizontal. An image's verticality means that if a person encounters one small element of a college such as a poor publication or an obnoxious faculty member, he or she is inclined to project that one small negative image to the entire college or university. At the same time, if he or she encounters a thoughtful publication that conveys its message well, that same positive impression is transferred to the entire institution. One colleague notes, "When they see our decal in the back window of a station wagon, the driver of that station wagon becomes the institution."

Images must also be considered in a horizontal context: People often compare one institution with another. Repeatedly we hear, "Yes, but it's not as good as . . ." This consideration is often overlooked. When colleges and universities develop an image strategy, they must clearly understand the image of the institutions and, in the case of fund raising, organizations with which they are most often compared. Images are seldom evaluated in a vacuum; they are best understood and improved in a context that includes your competition.

Figure 5-1.
Recruiting Funnel

Pre-funnel image-building strategies

Early Funnel
Empasize Features and Benefits

Mid Funnel
Emphasize Benefits

Late Funnel
Emphasize Outcomes

Entering Class

Retention

Alumni Donor Retreat

Characteristics of institutions with weak images

At a recent national conference I had an opportunity to make a presentation on images. During the session I asked participants to define the characteristics of institutions with weak images. They responded with the following:

Weak image:

- No sense of direction
- Weak academic core and unfocused or dated curriculum
- Poor morale
- High faculty and administrative turnover
- Frequent job-related grievances and high absenteeism
- Poor retention
- Difficulty in communicating a clear message
- Spending more to recruit a student
- Spending more to generate donations
- Low annual fund participation
- Lack of local/community support
- Vandalism

Truth vs. perception

There is one subtle aspect of image that must be explored further—the difference between truth and perception. One maxim of marketing is that perception is reality. In other words, how people perceive you is how—in their minds, hearts, and pocketbooks—you are. If they believe your academic programs are poor, then having the best academic programs in the country won't help. If prospective donors believe that the institution is ill-managed, they are less likely to contribute.

Al Cubbage, former director of marketing and communications at Drake University, now at Northwestern, is well aware of the difference between perception and reality. "A few years ago Drake conducted focus groups among high-school students in its main markets to learn more about how the college was perceived," he says. "The difference in image from market to market was striking. In the Chicago area, Drake was considered a 'pretty good school,' one that was quite acceptable for good students to attend but not a top-ranked institution. By contrast, students in the Minneapolis-St. Paul area viewed Drake as a 'prestige' institution, one that was difficult to get into and ranking just below Ivy League schools."

Which was correct? "Both," says Cubbage. "For the audience in each of these markets, the reality of Drake was how they perceived it. And Drake's success in attracting students in these markets depended to a great extent on meeting those perceptions."

Being good isn't good enough

It does little good to have solid programs, great faculty, outstanding students, and wonderful facilities if no one knows about them. Merely being good is not enough; people have to know you are good. Routinely, during a visit to a campus, the presi-

> "One maxim of marketing is that perception is reality."

dent and I have a chance to chat by ourselves. During the conversation she or he invariably says, somewhat proudly, "We are the best-kept secret east (or west) of the Mississippi (or Hudson or Kokosing or whatever)."

A key underlying assumption

Because there is sometimes the temptation to overstate the power of strong image, remember this important underlying assumption: A strong image will persist only if the institution is credible in an area valued by its clientele. For some and perhaps most institutions, this will be academic quality. Other institutions, however, may offer a relationship to the church or be known as an athletic powerhouse. Institutions with strong images generally have something they are known and valued for.

Managing your institution's image

Strong images don't just happen. They require the commitment of top administrators. They require a clear understanding of who your audiences are and how you are currently perceived. They require detailed planning and execution. And they require a long-term budgetary commitment. In short, images must be managed.

Image management begins by accepting the fact that an institution's most significant asset is its image. Image management recognizes that an institution's image must be continually built and maintained so that when people hear your institution's name, they immediately have a clear idea of who and what you are about.

Romancing the brand

David Martin calls this aspect of image management "romancing the brand." In his book by the same title, he examines how businesses create brand loyalty in the hearts and minds of consumers. Although the book focuses almost exclusively on businesses and consumers, its application to student recruiting, fund raising, and institutional marketing is as obvious as it is crucial. He writes that "brand mystique accrues by projecting a consistent personality over time. . . . Your creative selling message must build awareness of the brand and of its special advantages over a period of time. It must sustain this awareness so that the brand will be remembered when the need arises." Martin goes on to use an illustration from David Ogilvy in *Ogilvy on Advertising*:

> What would you think of a politician who changed his public personality every year? Have you noticed that Winston Churchill has been careful to wear the same ties and the same hats for 50 years—so as not to confuse us? Think of all the forces that work to change the personality and image of the brand from season to season. The advertising managers come and go. The copywriters, the art directors, and the account executives come and go. Even the agencies come and go. What guts it takes, what obstinate determination, to stick to one coherent creative policy, year after year, in the face of the pressures to "come up with something new" every six months.

Many institutions would do well to adopt Churchill's strategy.

Let me illustrate romancing the brand another way. A few years ago, when my son was attending preschool, he came home with a poster of the University of Iowa Hawkeye football team. When I asked about it, he said that everyone in his school, not just his class, received the same poster that morning. I later learned that the poster had been distributed to a number of preschools in the city. Through the distribution of the poster, the University of Iowa was romancing the brand and building name recognition and brand loyalty among a group of five-year-olds.

The image formula

Image management acknowledges a fundamental image formula that may be expressed as follows:

Institutional Image Formula
(Accuracy + Clarity + Consistency) x Continuity

First, *accuracy*. Everything that you do, tell, and show about your institution must be accurate. There is a strong tendency toward hype in many recruiting materials and fund-raising case statements. But if the college or university depicted in the video or publications is not the same college or university that students find when they arrive, they will leave. And if donors feel deceived or misled, they are increasingly likely to ask for their money back. At the very least, they will not give again. It is imperative that what you say about yourself be accurate, truthful, and demonstrable.

Clarity has several dimensions. First, are your individual messages clear and understandable? Second, do people know why they are receiving the message? And third, after reading (or hearing or seeing or touching) them, do they know what they are expected to do next?

William of Occum, a 12th-century philosopher, was fond of saying that the simple solution is usually the better solution. I believe he had a point. Often I will read a recruiting publication that does not contain the name of the institution on the cover. Some fund-raising publications are so elaborate and complex that you don't have any idea what they are trying to accomplish. I remember one capital campaign publication that clearly asked for the donation but didn't include information about where or to whom to send it. Sometimes in an effort to be clever, unique, and creative, we forget to be clear. And if people don't understand our messages, they are not likely to act on those messages.

Clarity has a second dimension—the need for your messages, especially publications messages, to compete successfully in the mail. Too often, publications and message strategies are designed in a vacuum. Designers do not understand that students and donors will be receiving a multitude of publications and solicitations from other institutions at the same time and that before your publications can be read, they must be opened, and before they are opened, they must be noticed.

The third critical component of a strong image is *consistency*. While this may seem obvious, few colleges and universities heed this bit of advice. Consistency means settling on a logo and family look and sticking to it. Consistency means developing an

> **Some fund-raising publications are so elaborate and complex that you don't have any idea what they are trying to accomplish.**

annual institutional fact sheet so that everyone at the institution uses the same facts and figures (number of majors, students, size of the endowment, books in the library) to describe it. And consistency means using the same look in fund raising and advertising and campus signage and vehicle identification and, well, you get the idea.

Perhaps the most important aspect of a strong image is *continuity*. Because it can take images years and years to develop fully, themes and messages must be given time to work.

Strong, well-conceived looks offer the best chance for continuity. They may require investing more time and money at the concept stage, but the resulting look will offer tremendous long-term value. Institutions such as Beloit and Cornell College and Westmont, with a keen eye toward stewardship of their resources, invest a considerable amount of time, money, and thought at the concept stage so their looks will last longer.

There is often a strong, even overwhelming feeling on the part of many that the visual aspects of an image—logos and "looks"—should be dramatically revised every year or two. Keep in mind, though, that your audiences change constantly. The worst reason to change a look is because you, your staff, or even your president is tired of it. A bigger and more important question is "is it still working?" If it is, don't mess with it. Your being tired of a look is not enough of a reason to change it. Often I counsel clients that it is far better to use an adequate logo wisely than to develop a new logo every couple of years.

It will take years and often hundreds of thousands if not millions of dollars to firmly establish a new look. With this in mind, there are only two good reasons for revamping a logo or look. First, the look is not working. Perhaps it never worked from the beginning, or maybe the marketplace or your institution has changed. If so, reevaluate. Second, you are responding to an opportunity. Perhaps you have an anniversary, special event, campaign, or name change in the works and you want to use a new look to help galvanize the campus and its constituents.

Steps to image management

Image management is both proactive and aggressive. It presumes a commitment to your environment and audiences. It means sunk costs with a long-term payoff. It is management by the numbers, not by institutional wishes and admonitions. It is, in its most complete and full sense, management and typically embraces the following steps:

- Getting top-down buy-in
- Organizing for action
- Defining your audiences
- Evaluating your current image
- Clarifying your goals
- Developing a plan
- Budgeting realistically
- Executing and evaluating

Begin with top-down buy-in

If image management doesn't have the active and aggressive support of top management, it will fail. Strategies will not be coordinated. Activities will not be sustained. And budgets will not be shared. Al Cubbage is quick to point out the need for top-down buy-in: "We're fortunate at Drake to have a president and other key administrators who understand the need for good marketing and provide the support to do it right. We don't spend much money on 'image' advertising; most of our efforts are aimed at eliciting a specific response. But we do spend money on making sure that all of our marketing efforts project a consistent image of our institution."

It is no coincidence, as we have seen from Chapter 4, that institutions with strong images are almost always institutions with strong leadership. This occurs for at least two reasons: because it takes visionaries who are willing to invest time and dollars and even a bit of themselves into building a strong image, and because the many variables that affect an institution's image cross so many departmental and divisional lines that the only way to avoid turf battles is to have decisions made and enforced from on high.

There is a clear "chicken and the egg" issue here. Did the president set about creating a strong image, or did an already strong image attract the president? Because most images take more than one president's tenure to establish, it is hard to establish clear cause and effect. Perhaps a strong president saw the need to begin building a strong image, and that emerging image attracted other strong presidents.

Organize for action

Most institutions have their image-enhancement strategies far too decentralized. The publications office reports to one administrator, media relations to another, and special events to a third. No one knows what the alumni office is up to, and the athletic office won't attend any planning meetings. There is no sharing of goals, no pooling of talent, no stewardship of resources. Where there could be a symphony, there is a cacophony.

Let's look at the scope of the problem. The following offices and individuals probably affect your institution's image:

- President's office
- Academic dean
- Graduate school deans
- Student recruiting office
- Development office
- Alumni office
- Public and community relations office
- Publications office
- Special events office
- Corporate relations office
- Institutional research office
- Athletics department
- Maintenance and grounds department

With this many people, offices, responsibilities, and agendas involved, there is little likelihood that any effective and long-term image-enhancement strategies will be developed, implemented, and maintained. The first step in image management is to deal with this organizational problem.

An ad hoc solution

In most cases, colleges and universities resist organizational change. Recognizing this reality, institutions interested in image management must be willing to establish two ad hoc committees: the image-policy committee and the image strategy committee.

The image policy committee (see Figure 5-2) includes the president; chief academic officer; enrollment management, development, and marketing officers; and the senior finance person. The committee also includes the marketing champion, the person designated by the president as the individual in charge of the overall marketing and image-building strategy. In many cases, but not all, this person will be the chief marketing officer. Finally, depending on the political climate on campus, the image-policy committee might also include a faculty representative appointed either by the academic dean or by the faculty governing body.

The primary purpose of this committee is to establish image policy and goals, cross territorial boundaries, and allocate resources and authority. It should not be mired down with technicians—they will have input in the image-strategy committee. (see Figure 5-3)

The first committee must be educated on the role and purpose of a strong image. Its members must become familiar with the tools, strategies, and mechanisms of image building. And they must have the same marketing and image goals. It is not oversimplifying this discussion to say that the image policy committee sets direction and provides guidance for the image/marketing champion. It is up to the champion, working through the image strategy committee, to figure out how to get there.

Under the leadership of the image/marketing champion, the image strategy committee is composed of such stakeholders as faculty, athletics, and even development. However, this committee also includes technocrats—people with the skills and expertise to achieve the image goals outlined by the image policy committee.

Figure 5-2.
Image Policy Committee

Figure 5-3.
Image Strategy Committee

In addition to the organizational change outlined above, the image-management model has one other important characteristic—the creation of soft alliances that allow regular policy-making input not only at the board and cabinet level but at the program level.

Through regular interaction, the chief marketing officer must have policy input in academics, student recruiting, fund raising, athletics, alumni, and other offices that are involved in building or projecting strong images.

The goal of this input is not to dictate policy but to educate policy-makers on the ramifications of their decisions. This soft alliance is a guiding and teaching relationship, not a controlling relationship. However, the chief marketing officer has a notable "big stick"—the image mandate from the president and the image-policy committee.

Demand accountability

Organizing for action presupposes the creation of an image czar, a single person responsible for executing the institution's image management strategies. Having a single person in charge is absolutely critical because group accountability means no accountability.

> "Having a single person in charge is absolutely critical because group accountability means no accountability."

As I write this I am flying from Washington, D.C., to Chicago. On the seat next to me is a image enhancement plan that a college president asked me to review. The plan is relatively well-conceived. The goals are carefully defined, the budgets seem adequate, and lots of people are involved. What is missing, however, is any sense of who will be in charge. No single person seems to be responsible for seeing that this plan is enacted.

A marketing professional

Who should this single responsible person be? She or he should be highly placed in the administration, having the ear and trust not only of the president but of the larger campus community. And that person must have a clear understanding of marketing and its tools. Often we have seen a seasoned manager, a political insider, a trusted confidant, fail because that person knows nothing about marketing. I must be adamant on this point. In Chapter 8 we will discuss the notion of a marketing champion. Whether you are talking about image management or larger marketing strategies, the need for a champion is paramount.

Define your audiences

Next you must bring order to your universe. Even a brief review of your market and environment will reveal dozens or perhaps hundreds of audiences that clamor for your attention. However, in an era of finite resources, it is impossible to meet everyone's needs. The solution is to set priorities.

Though the list of potential audiences can be extensive, usually only a handful directly affect an institution's future—and the composition of this handful often depends on the type of institution. Publics are interested in how they are perceived by taxpayers, community leaders, and legislators, whereas privates are more keenly interested in how they are perceived by alumni and parents. Some privates are interested in how sponsoring denominations see them, while some publics need the support of regional employers. Both types of institutions are interested in their perceptions among faculty, current students, and prospective students. Clearly, your institutional and environmental context plays a major role in defining what audiences are most significant to you.

Although your list of audiences is potentially endless, I suspect the primary ones might be drawn from the list in Table 5-1.

Evaluate your current image

As part of managing your image, you must know how you are already perceived. In their haste to set about improving their image, many institutions skip this important step.

Images are best evaluated along the following three dimensions:

- How the institution is perceived by primary audiences
- How the institution projects itself editorially and environmentally
- How the institution is compared with its cohort group

Table 5-1.
Audience Sources

Students	Donors	Others
Current students	Alumni	Parents
Traditional prospective students	Current donors	Faculty and staff
Nontraditional prospective students	Former donors	High school guidance counselors
Minority prospective students	Prospective donors	Business leaders
		Community residents
		Religious leaders

Perception studies

Determining how key audiences see you is relatively straightforward: Decide which of your many audiences are primary, and conduct image and perception studies to ascertain how these important audiences perceive you.

A guideline in image research is that you begin with the question to be answered. In other words, once you define the research question, you usually have a pretty good idea who has the answer. And once you know who has the answer, different research methods make a best fit for different types of audiences. For example, prospective students and parents may be reached through focus groups or mail or telephone surveys. Regional employers, on the other hand, are often best reached through personal or telephone interviews. Faculty often prefer the anonymity of a mail survey. State legislators will require a personal visit. And because alumni are dispersed, often the best way to reach them is through either a mail or a telephone survey.

Your best bet is to reason from the audience back to the methodology. In other words, ask yourself which audience has the answer to the question and then develop the best methodology to query that audience. It is also useful to keep in mind issues of anonymity, sensitivity, and complexity. If your audience might wish to remain anonymous, if the questions are sensitive, or if the questions are complex, a written survey might be a wise choice.

Obviously these are guidelines. Successful research sometimes involves a little trial and error and the ability to learn from your mistakes. However, if you keep in mind that the question dictates the audience and the audiences dictate the methodology, things should proceed smoothly.

After determining how primary audiences see you, you need to evaluate how you project yourself editorially and environmentally.

Evaluate yourself editorially

An editorial evaluation addresses your formal, written, image-building mechanisms. A realistic appraisal of your editorial media is extremely important because it is through these that most institutions project their image. This involves evaluating not only the product of these mechanisms but the abilities and talents of the people charged with this responsibility.

An editorial evaluation of your image involves not just print but direct mail, advertising, video, audio, and all the mass media. It includes publications as well as media relations. It addresses not only what you say about yourself but how you say it. It evaluates how you allocate dollars and time. It looks at budgets and talent and where you direct your energies. It seeks to answer such questions as these:

- What (and whose) institutional image do we wish to project? What data support this image?
- What is our short- and long-term vision for the institution?
- What are our institution's communication priorities?
- How have we defined our audiences and their needs and expectations?
- Do our communication efforts reflect the needs and expectations of the target audiences?
- How much time/budget/talent do we allocate to priority audiences?
- How and when do we evaluate the effectiveness of our current communication strategies?

Evaluate yourself environmentally

In addition to evaluating how you project yourself editorially, you must evaluate how you project yourself environmentally. How does your campus look? I call this the brick-and-mortar syndrome. It works like this. If you look good, people will assume you are good. If your campus is well groomed, if your signage is clear and consistent, if your buildings and windows are clean, people will assume that your entire campus is well managed. But if you do not tend to your campus, people will wonder what else has been ignored. It is simply amazing how many institutions have forgotten how important it is to wash their windows and sweep their walks.

Evaluate yourself comparatively

The third element of image evaluation is comparative. It is important to know how you compare with your cohort group.

> **"If you look good, people will assume you are good."**

A comparative evaluation is important because most students don't decide between attending your institution and not attending college at all. Rather, they decide between you and another institution. So understanding these other institutions and determining how they compare with you makes extraordinary sense.

Developing a list of cohort colleges can be more difficult than it appears. Refer to Table 5-2. When I consider a college's competition, I like to work with three groups. Assume, for this discussion, that a student has been accepted into your institution and another. If the student always elects to attend that other institution, this is a Category A competition. If the student always elects to attend your institution, this is a Category B competition. And finally, if the student decides to attend your institution half the time and the other institution half the time, this is a Category C competition.

Institutions should seek to preserve their edge with Category B institutions and should temper their efforts to win share from Category A institutions as any gains will be marginal and will come only at great cost.

Colleges and universities should concentrate image evaluation and enhancement on Category A rather than Category C institutions. This is where they will have the greatest chance to increase their share.

To determine how you compare with Category C institutions, you have to go back to the list of primary audiences. This entails asking, for example, prospective students how you compare on different dimensions with another institution.

Let me give you an example. Recently a client asked Stamats to complete a competitive positioning study. It wanted to know how it compared with seven other institutions on two dimensions—cost and quality. Using a five-point scale, we asked prospective students to evaluate the seven on these two dimensions. We then ran the mean of each response and prepared a scattergram graph like that shown in Figure 5-4. The result shows how the seven institutions compared with one another on cost and quality.

Comparative data such as these are extremely useful in helping to differentiate and position an institution. Chapter 7 will explore competitive positioning in greater depth.

Clarify your goals

Your perceptual, editorial, environmental, and comparative research has probably uncovered a multitude of image problems and opportunities. Now comes the sifting and evaluating. In the rush to develop and execute strategies, institutions often overlook the need to establish clear image goals that meet the needs of priority audiences.

When I work with clients to help write clear goals, I keep these basic rules in mind. First, list your goals in priority order. Focus on the truly important. Don't be distracted by whim or politics. Second, keep the list of goals as short as possible. It is deceptively easy to get bogged down.

Third, learn the difference between short-term and long-term goals. Short-term

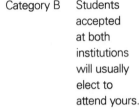

Table 5-2.
Competing Institutions

Type of Competition	Explanation
Category A	Students accepted at both institutions will usually elect to attend the other.
Category B	Students accepted at both institutions will usually elect to attend yours.
Category C	Half the students accepted at both institutions will enroll at yours, and half will enroll at the other.

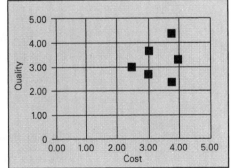

Figure 5-4.
Cost vs. Quality
Source: Stamats Communications, Inc.

goals are those you must accomplish immediately; long-term goals can wait. Or, as one wag says, achieving the short-term goals is what assures a long term.

Finally, good goals are quantifiable. Goals such as "improve our image" or "increase our popularity" are vague and ill-defined. Instead, build goals on the base-line data created in the perceptual research and quantify them. Rather than "improve our image," a better goal is "increase name recognition from 23 percent to 30 percent in the St. Louis metropolitan area during the next 12 months."

The new goal is built on research that established a baseline name-recognition level of 23 percent. Furthermore, the goal focuses on St. Louis. Finally, the goal includes a time period. This is a well-articulated goal.

Declaring your points of pride

An important, though sometimes overlooked, marketing goal is a simple declaration of your points of pride. Points of pride, or, as one client calls them, vivid descriptors, are those characteristics and qualities that you most want people to know about you. When people hear your name, what images do you want to have pop into their heads?

Points of pride must be mission-critical. They must express core values. And it is much more important that they are real than that they are distinctive. Successful points of pride often ring true with donors as well as prospective students.

Consider, for example, the following points of pride from an urban Catholic university:

- Friendly, supportive, safe
- Committed to the liberal arts in a Catholic tradition
- Focused on student learning
  (Note how this point is much more outcomes-oriented than simply saying that you are focused on teaching)

Some marketers overlook the simple, even elegant power of a handful of oft-repeated points of pride. Message theorists know, however, that simple messages repeated often are much more likely to be remembered than complex messages repeated less frequently.

It is very important that institutional points of pride be clarified as part of any image or marketing plan. Points of pride are then communicated and reinforced through recruiting publications, campaign case statements, advertising, tag lines, and any number of other media.

Develop a plan

By now you have set priorities among audiences, conducted the necessary research to identify image problems and opportunities, and articulated a series of concise image goals. Now you must write the plan.

In its most simple form, the image plan—much like a larger marketing plan—is the mechanism through which things get done. A plan addresses the who, what, when, and how.

> **Points of pride are those characteristics and qualities that you most want people to know about you.**

There is no magic to writing a good plan. But there are a couple of things to keep in mind. First, stay true to your goals. Every element of the plan must clearly support one or more image goals. If it doesn't, delete it.

Second, take advantage of the complete image mix. Earlier we quickly reviewed the many offices and individuals that have an impact on an institution's image. Effective plans take advantage of such media and activities as these:

- Publications
- Direct marketing including direct mail
- Advertising
  - Positional
  - Promotional
- Special events
  - Partnerships between the institution and local grade, junior high, and high schools
  - Science fairs
  - Talented-and-gifted student gatherings
  - Student leadership programs
  - Issues conferences (the environment, technology, human rights, etc.)
- High school relations
- Public relations
- Community relations
- Media relations
  - General news releases
  - Hometown news releases
  - Wild-art photo release (a visually striking photograph accompanied only by a caption)
  - Audio releases
  - Public service announcements
  - Pitch letters (ideas for feature stories pitched to media representatives)
  - Personal contact
  - Fax releases
  - Electronic news releases via autodial modem
  - Proactive speakers bureau and experts list
  - Faculty-penned columns
  - Talk shows
  - Tip sheets to local, regional, and select national media

Third, remember the image formula.

Institutional Image Formula
(Accuracy + Clarity + Consistency) x Continuity

Accuracy, clarity, consistency, and continuity. An image management plan won't work unless it is founded on these four cornerstones.

Fourth, keep it simple. Most image plans are far too complex.

Finally, give it time to work. Perhaps this is related to the need to keep it simple, but it is more than that. Even the most simple plans cannot be rushed. Images are notoriously nebulous and latent. It can take a great deal of time to change how people perceive you. Remember, neither Harvard nor McDonald's was built in a day.

Two final thoughts about your image enhancement plan. First, there is a strong temptation, especially among academics, to confuse process with product. Many institution officials think writing the plan is the same as executing the plan. They spend all their time in meetings and never actually get around to doing anything.

And second, beware of the false siren of perfection. There is no such thing as a perfect image enhancement plan, so don't needlessly delay implementation in the hopes that your plan will keep getting better. As George Patton said, "A good plan implemented today is better than a perfect plan implemented tomorrow."

Budget realistically

One of the most problematic aspects of image management is budgeting. Institutions often don't know how much to budget, and while there are no absolutes, there are some guidelines.

In general, plan to spend about 1.5 percent of your annual operating budget on disposable image activities. This is the amount you will spend on programs and strategies, not people. If your annual operating budget is $50 million, you can reasonably expect to spend $750,000 on publications, direct mail, advertising, special events, and other activities.

"It is most expensive to change a bad image."

It is also helpful to consider the levels of image difficulty. It is easiest and least expensive to maintain an already good image. It is more expensive to create a strong image. And it is most expensive to change a bad image. Adjust your budget accordingly.

Remember that as your image strategies begin to work, you can scale back their intensity. For example, if you might want to place a positional ad in each issue of a regional magazine for the first year, place only half that number of ads (every other issue) during the second year. Once the image is established, it takes less effort to maintain it. And once again, you can use baseline data to judge the effectiveness of your campaign and guide the allocation of resources.

You must also hire good, experienced people. In an effort to save a few dollars, institutions sometimes hire young, often inexperienced people to execute their plan. This is false economy. Although you may save on salaries, the mistakes, inexperience, missed deadlines, and lost opportunities will cost you dearly. Bite the budgetary bullet and hire people with experience. The knowledge and understanding of seasoned professionals will make these people a bargain.

Don't forget to support your plan with an adequate budget. It is far better to do fewer things well then to try to do a multitude of things poorly. Rather than under-fund high school visits so you can place limited advertising, it is probably better to halt the advertising and spend the money you need to visit the high schools you must.

Finally, manage the plan. I recently heard of a college that overspent its video-production budget by 50 percent. As a result, it had a wonderful video but no money to have it duplicated or distributed.

At a recent CASE meeting I talked with a woman from a small, relatively unknown college in the East. Her president had just asked her to develop an image-enhancement plan that would make their institution "a household word" in New England. She asked her president about additional staffing and funding. The president said that as a professional she should be able to manage the project with current resources. This president has no concept of what it takes to position an institution. It takes more than wishes and good intentions to improve an image, and without funding, any such plan will be doomed.

Execute and evaluate

Now that the plan is written and funded, it is time to act. Implement strategies and activities per the timeline you have established. But as you implement the plan, you must be evaluating its effectiveness.

There are two basic reasons for evaluating a marketing program: to provide data for modifying and increasing the effect of programs in progress (to make midcourse corrections), and to evaluate the effectiveness of completed strategies (so you can adjust ongoing plans).

The original research you conducted to help guide goal development will again prove invaluable because it contains baseline data against which you can evaluate your plan's effectiveness.

Conclusion

Each day, thousands of high school students around the country choose a college. As the data suggest, most of these students base their decision on their perception or image of the institution. The fact is, all educational institutions in the United States have an image. But is the image strong, weak, poor, or ambiguous? Is it accurate? Is it consistent? Is it widespread? And perhaps most important, is the image valued by prospective students and parents?

Smart, aggressive, well-administered institutions don't leave their image to chance. They look at their image as their most significant asset and manage that asset carefully. They set priorities among audiences. They conduct market research. They establish clear-cut goals. They write a plan. They support that plan with adequate resources. They do this because they have learned that perhaps image *is* everything.

> **"It takes more than wishes and good intentions to improve an image, and without funding, any such plan is doomed."**

6

Mixing and Matching
Developing an Effective Segmenting Strategy

There are two kinds of people in the world: those who divide people into groups and those who do not.
—William James

In the year 2000 and beyond, colleges and universities must move away from what Philip Kotler and others call "one size fits all" marketing strategies to strategies that focus on meeting the needs of subpopulations within their marketplace.

This notion of dividing large, heterogeneous populations into smaller, homogenous subpopulations is called segmentation. Segmentation is not a new idea for colleges and universities. For years, fund raisers have used different strategies for major donors than for annual fund participants, for foundations than for alumni.

Segmenting is also used on the recruiting side, though far less consistently. Most colleges use the same basic strategy to recruit the majority of their students. There has been some effort of late to develop separate strategies for nontraditional students, students of color, and even honors students, but these are more likely variations on the themes developed in the traditional recruiting funnel than new themes created specifically for these subpopulations. In addition, these segmented strategies are more likely to deal with promotional variables than with changes to product, price, or place.

A couple of quick terms

Before we can proceed with a detailed discussion of segmentation, let's introduce or reintroduce five terms:

- Segmentation
- Benefit segmentation
- Marketing mix
- Product mix
- Media mix

As stated earlier, *segmentation* is the dividing of heterogeneous populations into smaller homogeneous subsets of that target population. Ideally, the smaller subsets will contain like or very similar demographic, geographic characteristics. One example would be breaking a large donor pool into two smaller pools of major givers and alumni. Another example would be developing separate, distinct recruiting strategies for in-state, out-of-state, and international students.

The opposite of segmentation is aggregation—the use of an undifferentiated marketing strategy. Most colleges and universities, particularly publics, use this aggregated approach to student recruiting.

Benefit segmentation is the division of a mass market according to the benefits that people seek from a product. Benefit segmentation requires that the college or university determine the benefits that target audiences are seeking in the marketing mix. For example, a college, learning that its alumni have a keen interest in supporting the programs from which they graduated, may well organize alumni giving by academic major rather than by year of graduation.

The *marketing mix* is the four controllable variables—product, price, place, and promotion (the four Ps)—that a college or university emphasizes or mixes to meet the needs of its recruiting, fund-raising, and other target audiences.

Product mixes represent various product attributes. As we saw in Chapter 2, different kinds of students and donors value different product mixes. Students of high academic ability are attracted to a product mix that is heavily oriented toward academics. Students who are more social are keenly interested in campus and residence life. Different audience segments have different product-mix needs and expectations.

The *media mix* is the array of promotional strategies that a college or university uses to communicate its marketing mix to prospective target audiences. In many respects, the media mix is used to communicate the product, price, and place elements of the marketing mix.

> "Different audience segments have different product-mix needs and expectations."

Why segment?

At the outset, we must answer the basic question: Why develop a segmenting strategy? The reasons include these:

■ Segmentation allows you to monitor and survey the needs and expectations of critical target audiences more effectively, thereby continually refining your marketing, product, and media mixes.

■ Segmentation allows you to communicate with chosen target audiences more effectively and efficiently.

■ Segmentation cuts costs, so you spend less time and money on programs and communication strategies that are misguided and misdirected.

Ethical considerations

Segmentation raises a serious ethical concern. Because of its need to categorize, segmentation is a just a step away from stereotyping. If we segment a large population of prospective students into two categories—those who hope to be engineers and those who hope to teach—there will be a temptation to think that all students interested in engineering think and act alike. This point is illustrated more dramatically by how we segment students of color. Many well-meaning administrators have a tendency to put all students of color into the same segment (or should I say category) and assume that all African-American students and Hispanic students and Asian students pick and choose colleges the same way and have the same academic and social needs. Of course, this isn't so.

As we develop segmenting strategies, we must always take care that we are not playing to our stereotypes and prejudices.

A little segmenting theory

There are three basic approaches to segmentation:

■ Mass market strategy
■ Concentration strategy
■ Multisegment strategy

In a mass market strategy, every member of the target market receives marketing mix A (see No. 1, in Figure 6-1). Users of a mass market strategy make two assumptions: that their target audiences have very similar characteristics and needs that one marketing mix will satisfy, and that though different target audiences within their marketplace may have different needs, it is not worth the cost to clarify those needs and create different product or media mixes. Large public institutions often use a mass market strategy to recruit students. Every student, regardless of academic interest or ability, is recruited in the same fashion.

In a concentration strategy, efforts are focused on one segment of a larger market (see No. 2, Figure 6-1), and an appropriate product, price, place, and promotion mix is developed for that segment.

A concentration strategy offers some marketing benefits. For example, because all of its efforts are focused on a single segment of the total market, the institution can

Figure 6-1.
Marketing Mix Strategy

No Segmentation
1. Mass Market Strategy
All target audiences receive the same marketing and media mix.

Segmentation
2. Concentration Strategy
Organization recognizes diverse needs but targets only one segment.

3. Multisegment Strategy
Organization recognizes diverse needs and develops segments for each one.
Source: Schoell and Guiltinan

conduct the necessary research to ascertain the exact needs and expectations of its target market, then devote itself to meeting those needs. A college or university that specializes in aeronautics such as Embry-Riddle or in cooking such as the Culinary Institute of America uses a concentration strategy.

The major disadvantage of a concentration strategy is obvious: The institution is very dependent on one segment. If that segment diminishes in size, disappears, or has its needs met more effectively elsewhere, you are in trouble.

Finally, a multisegment strategy involves developing a manageable array of product, price, place, and promotion mixes (see No. 3, Figure 6-1) for each definable market segment. By using a multisegment rather than a concentration strategy, the institution is usually able to serve a greater number of potential audiences. Institutions that market themselves programmatically rather than institutionally often use a multisegment strategy. This, however, has one overarching disadvantage—it is possible to spread yourself too thin.

Traditional segments

As you can see from a quick look at the following pages, there are a great number of ways to segment potential target audiences. To compound the problem, there is seldom one best way. Audiences can be segmented via single variables, multiple variables, or different variables depending on where the audiences are in their relationship to the institution.

As colleges and universities consider segmenting options, they often turn to traditional geographic, demographic, and economic variables such as those outlined in Table 6-1.

The application of psychology and sociology has greatly expanded the array of segmenting options to include psychographics, personality descriptors, geodemographic clusters, and even product-usage segments.

Tables 6-2 and 6-3 present segments based on personality descriptors and geodemographic profiles and characteristics drawn from Claritas' PRIZM system.

One of the 62 "neighborhoods" listed in Table 6-2, Kids & Cul-de-sacs, is outlined below and in Table 6-3. As you can see, this profile offers a wide array of insightful data and perspectives.

Cluster 5: Kids & Cul-de-sacs

Near Executive Suites and Pools & Patios in all affluence measures, Cluster 5 is ranked first of the 62 PRIZM clusters in married couples with children and large (more than four-person) families. Because "family" governs its lives and activities, Kids & Cul-de-sacs is a noisy mix of bikes, dogs, carpools, music, and sports.

Additional segmenting possibilities

The segmenting array in Table 6-4, offered by Philip Kotler, focuses on benefits, user status, loyalty status, readiness stage, and attitude toward the institution. Because of these focuses, these segments have great potential for enhancing the effectiveness of

Table 6-2
Personality and Geodemographic Segments

Personality Descriptors	Affectionate	Passive	Stubborn	Experimenters
	Likable	Independent	Followers	Individualists
	Dominating	Self-assured	Leaders	
	Authoritative	Sociable	Conformists	

Geodemography*	Blue-blood Estates	Greenbelt Families	Boomtown Singles	Downtown
	Winner's Circle	Young Influentials	Starter Families	Hometown Retired
	Executive Suites	New Empty Nests	Sunset-city Blues	Family Scramble
	Pools & Patios	Boomers & Babies	Towns & Gowns	Southside City
	Kids & Cul-de-sacs	Suburban Sprawl	New Homesteaders	Golden Ponds
*The 62 clusters outlined in the adjacent columns are drawn from Claritas' PRIZM system. PRIZM is but one of an increasing number of geodemographic clusters. Geodemographic segmenting tools such as Claritas' PRIZM offer tremendous potential for both student recruiting and fund raising. In many respects, they combine the most useful of the geographic, demographic, and psychographic segmenting options.	Urban Gold Coast	Blue-chip Blues	Middle America	Rural Industrial
	Money & Brains	Upstarts & Seniors	Red, White, & Blue	Norma Rae-villes
	Young Literati	New Beginnings	Military Quarters	Mines & Mills
	American Dreams	Mobility Blues	Big-sky Families	Agribusiness
	Bohemian Mix	Gray Collars	New Ecotopia	Grain Belt
	Second-city Elite	Urban Achievers	River City USA	Blue Highways
	Upward Bound	Big-city Blend	Shotguns & Pickups	Rustic Elders
	Gray Power	Old Yankee Rows	Single-city Blues	Back-country Folks
	County Squires	Mid-city Mix	Hispanic Mix	Scrub-pine Flats
	God's Country	Latino America	Inner Cities	Hard Scrabble
	Big Fish, Small Pond	Middleburg Managers	Smalltown	

Table 6-3.
Social Group S1—Elite Suburbs

Predominant characteristics:
Households (% U.S.):   2,845,800 (3.0%)
Population (% U.S.):   9,032,900 (3.5%)
Demographic caption: Upscale suburban families
Ethnic diversity: Dominant white, high Asian
Family type: Married couples with children
Predominant age ranges: 35-44, 45-54
Education: College graduates
Employment level: White-collar/professional
Housing type: Owner/single unit
Density centile: 57 (1=sparse, 99=dense)
SER/median income: SER 10/middle $61,600

Education:

	U.S.	Cluster	Index
4+ years college	20.5	32.0	156
1-3 years college	25.1	32.1	128
High school graduate	29.9	25.1	84
Less than eighth grade	10.2	3.4	34

Occupation:

	U.S.	Cluster	Index
Professional/manager	26.6	35.4	133
Other white collar	31.8	36.5	115
Blue collar	26.1	18.3	70
Service	13.1	9.2	70
Farming/mining/ranching	2.4	0.7	28

Family type:

	U.S.	Cluster	Index
Married couples	28.1	30.5	108
Married couples with children	26.6	44.4	167
Single parents	9.1	6.0	66
Singles (not married)	36.2	19.1	53

Presence of children:

	U.S.	Cluster	Index
Under age 6	9.2	10.4	114
Age 6-13	11.6	14.0	121
Age 13-17	5.1	6.0	118
Household with 5+ persons	10.8	15.6	144

Age of population:

	U.S.	Cluster	Index
Under 24	10.1	87.7	76
25-34	16.2	16.1	100
35-44	15.8	20.8	131
45-54	11.1	12.7	114
55-64	8.1	6.4	79
65+	12.7	5.8	46
Median age	46.5	43.3	93

Race/ancestry:

	U.S.	Cluster	Index
White	83.2	86.7	104
Black	12.4	5.6	45
All other races	4.4	7.7	176
Hispanic	9.9	7.2	72
Asian	5.4	11.9	220

student recruiting and fund-raising strategies. The key, of course, is to develop research instruments that allow you to develop these profiles for donors and prospective students.

Similar to Kotler, consultant Bob Topor outlines a behavioral segmenting matrix that includes six stages that a prospective student, donor, or other constituent might be at relative to the institution. His segments, too, have great potential for student recruiting and fund-raising. See Table 6-5.

Topor makes the case that target audiences pass through one or more of these stages and that our job is to identify the stage that most members of the target audience are in and to develop effective communications that will motivate them to take the next step.

Viable segments for students and donors

The tables already cited offer a potentially dizzying array of segmenting options and ideas. However, with an eye to practicality, let's focus for a moment on the two audiences of critical interest to colleges and universities: prospective students and donors. See Table 6-6.

Determining whether a segmenting strategy is viable

Not every college or university should undertake a segmenting strategy. Schoell and Guiltinan offer five questions that must be addressed to determine whether creating a segmenting strategy is a sound idea for a particular institution.

1. *Are the characteristics and needs of target audiences—students, donors, and others—heterogeneous?*
   If the target market is homogenous, then one marketing mix is sufficient and a segmenting strategy is usually not necessary. However, the more divergent the characteristics and needs of a target audience, the more useful a segmenting strategy will become.

2. *Can segments be defined and evaluated in terms of relative attractiveness?*
   Not only must target audiences be diverse, but they must be diverse in obvious and measurable ways. For example, if you are recruiting prospective students, it is often wise to have separate recruiting strategies for traditional-age students, students of color, and nontraditional students. And in actuality, it is wise to examine the composition of your pool of students of color. Chances are that pool can be refined, or segmented even more.

3. *Is there at least one segment in the larger target audience large enough to warrant creating a separate segmenting strategy?*
   Unless your research identifies at least one segment that is large enough to be served profitably, there is little reason to develop a segmenting strategy.

4. *Can the segments be reached by developing a marketing and media mix that will respond to segments' needs?*
   If the research identifies one or more market segments, the next challenge is to develop an appropriate marketing mix (the four Ps) and media mix (how

Integrated Marketing for Colleges, Universities, and Schools

the four Ps are communicated). Generally, a separate marketing mix—and often a separate media mix—is created for each major segment. The college or university must possess the resolve, the resources, and the capabilities to mix and communicate the four Ps in an effective and timely fashion.

5. *Will the segments be responsive to the marketing mix developed for them?* If a segmenting strategy is to prove practical, the first question should be answered "no" while the remaining questions should be answered "yes."

Developing an effective segmenting strategy

For the most part, there are seven steps to the creation of an effective segmenting strategy:

- Make a commitment to a multisegment marketing strategy.
- Analyze the marketplace and the target audiences you now serve.
- Develop a list of potential segments.
- Create a marketing mix for chosen segments.
- Refine marketing and product mixes.
- Develop a communication grid.
- Evaluate the effectiveness of the segmentation strategy.

Make a commitment to a multisegment marketing strategy

The decision to move away from a mass market strategy to a multisegment strategy is a bold one, and it should be made carefully. On the downside, multisegment recruiting and fund-raising strategies will require more resources—of time, computers, expertise, and money. It will also require ongoing research and more institutional flexibility. However, multisegment strategies have a significant upside: They are more effective and efficient than a mass market strategy. Segmenting may sometimes be burdensome, but done correctly, it can become one of the most important tools in the marketer's arsenal.

Analyze the marketplace and target audiences you now serve

The second step in the segmenting process is to analyze your marketplace and the target audiences you currently serve.

As you look at the marketplace, ask yourself:

- Is its infrastructure (jobs and the economy) growing? If so, at what rate?
- Is it competitive? What colleges and universities are already serving it? Are they using a multisegment strategy?
- What is our image in the marketplace? How are we known? How well are we known? How are we compared with other institutions?
- With what institutions and entities do we compete for prospective students and donated dollars?

As you look at your target audiences, ask yourself:

- Are there enough prospective students in the marketplace to justify segmentation?

Table 6-4.
Psychographic, Attitudinal, and Motivational Segments

Benefits sought
Academic quality
Job skills
Social life

User status
Nonuser
Ex-user
Potential user
First-time user
Regular user
Completed user

Loyalty status
None
Medium
Strong
Absolute
Switcher

Readiness stage
Unaware
Aware
Informed
Interested
Desirous
Intend to apply/donate

Attitude toward institution
Enthusiastic
Positive
Indifferent
Negative
Hostile

Table 6-5.
Relationship Segments

Cognitive
Awareness
Knowledge

Affective
Liking
Preference
Conviction

Behavioral
Commitment

■ Do prospective students have the ability to pay?

■ Are prospective donors interested in our institution's mission and vision?

Create a list of potential segments

Because there are far more segments in a population than you can adequately serve, it is very important to clarify and refine your list of potential audience segments. As we have discussed, segmentation works best when you can identify common needs and expectations. And though there are several criteria you must consider as you evaluate the viability of potential segments, the following are minimums:

■ You must be able to quantify the segments effectively.

■ The segments must be accessible.

■ The segments must be large enough to justify your expenditures.

■ The segments must be nonvariable and sustainable over time.

■ The needs of each segment must be undermet.

Numerical goals

As early in the segmenting process as possible, you must set numerical goals to help gauge the efficacy of potential segments. For student recruiting, numerical goals might include:

■ The number of student segments

■ The number of prospective students in each segment

■ How much money it will require you to meet your recruiting goal for each segment

■ How much revenue each student segment will generate for the institution

■ How each type of student will affect student-support services

■ How many students in each segment are likely to persist

For fund raising, numerical goals might include:

■ The number of donor segments

■ How many donors will be in each segment

■ The amount of revenue each segment will contribute

■ How much it will cost to raise each dollar from each segment

■ The number or percentage of each segment that is likely to convert to a higher level of giving

For student recruiting, potential segments might include:

■ Traditional residential students

■ Full- and fuller-pay students

■ Women or men students

■ Students of color

■ Students from a particular denomination

■ Talented and gifted

■ In-state and out-of-state students

■ Students for specific majors that you are trying to grow

Table 6-6.
Segmentation Options for Prospective Students and Donors

Students	Donors
Demographic	*Demographic*
Age	Age
Gender	Gender
Ethnicity	Ethnicity
Academic profile (high school GPA, test scores)	
Academic interest	
Type of high school	
Geographic	*Geographic*
Distance from the institution	Distance from the institution
City, suburban, edge city, rural	City, suburban, edge city, rural
In state, out of state	
International	
Economic	*Economic*
Household income	Household income
Ability to pay	Disposable income
Need level	Tax status/rate
	Access to other dollars
Behavioral & psychographic	*Behavioral & psychographic*
Willingness to pay	Relationship to institution
Propensity to attend a specific type of college or university	Relationship to other donors
Motivation for attending college	Stage in life cycle
Postgraduation goals	Giving history
Family college-attendance pattern	Values, attitudes, and lifestyles
Relationship to institution	Geodemographic cluster
Values, attitudes, and lifestyle	
Geodemographic cluster	

For fund raising, potential segments might include:
- Alumni
- Trustees
- Faculty and staff
- Major donors
- Estate planners
- Foundations
- Corporate donors

Begin with a small rollout
Your initial list of recruiting and fund-raising segments should be fairly small. If you attempt to develop distinct marketing mixes for more than two or three segments, you will almost certainly be overwhelmed by the complexities and the drain on your resources. It is much better to begin small and add segments as you gain expertise and are more clearly able to evaluate results.

Create a marketing mix for each segment

The next step is carefully developing an appropriate marketing mix for each segment. This involves determining how the potential segments perceive you, gathering positioning and comparative data where appropriate, and identifying the benefits most attractive to each segment.

As you read in Chapter 5, image has a significant impact on decision-making; people, including students, are predisposed to institutions with which they are already familiar. It is very important to undertake legitimate image research. This will greatly affect the quality of the ensuing communications strategies.

While gathering data about how these market segments already perceive you, it is good to gather positional and comparative data. You must learn how students and donors position you in the marketplace and how they compare you with other, often competing, institutions.

While gathering image, positional, and comparative data, it is also important to gather benefit data—the needs and expectations of prospective students and donors. Often, these needs and expectations can be tied to the four Ps—product, price, place, and promotion.

Let's assume, for example, that we ask students of high academic ability, students of average academic ability, and parents to review the following list of 40 college-choice characteristics:

- Academic reputation of the institution
- Religious reputation of the institution
- Availability of specific programs or majors
- Recommendation of college guidebooks such as *Peterson's*
- Recommendation of such magazines as *U.S. News & World Report*
- Cost to attend (before financial aid)
- Cost to attend (after financial aid)
- Availability of scholarships
- Teaching emphasis
- Research emphasis
- Opportunity to be taught by faculty vs. graduate assistants
- Guaranteed undergraduate degree in four years
- Quality of the faculty
- Academic quality of students
- Student access to faculty
- Quality of academic/teaching facilities
- Availability of three-year undergraduate degree programs
- Quality of academic advising
- Quality of career counseling
- Academic support for underprepared students
- Support for students who are unsure about a major
- Job placement record

Quick Glance

Programmatic Marketing for Student Recruiting

One extraordinary variation on the use of segmentation for student recruiting is the use of programmatic marketing. In programmatic marketing, certain academic majors are marketed and promoted more heavily than others. In many respects, programmatic marketing is not true segmentation because it begins not with the target audience but with the product. However, it remains an extremely powerful approach to student recruiting.

- Graduate school placement record
- Opportunity to conduct research as an undergraduate
- Variety and quality of internship programs
- Opportunity to study abroad
- Computer and Internet availability in residence halls
- Ethnic diversity of the student body
- Proximity to a large city
- Geographic location
- Leadership opportunities on campus
- Friendliness of the campus
- Beauty of the campus
- Safety of the campus
- Opportunity to hold a job while attending college
- Quality of residence life
- The fact that someone I know attends the institution
- Availability and quality of recreational facilities
- Extracurricular clubs and activities

Quick Glance

Defining Benefit Segments
Benefit must be defined from the perspective and interest of the target audiences, not the institution. The target audience must automatically recognize the value of the benefit. If it doesn't, the "benefit" is not a benefit from its perspective. Don't waste time trying to convince students or donors that something is a benefit—either they will recognize it immediately or they will not.

After they have reviewed the list, we ask each group to indicate which five of the 39 characteristics are most important to them. The results are shown in Table 6-7.

How the three target audiences order their college-choice characteristics should offer significant insight into how you refine your product and message-mix strategies.

The same strategy can be used for donors. Through research it is possible to test quickly all case statements, appeals, and means of solicitation.

Refine marketing and product mixes

After you have gathered image-perception and product-mix data, it is time to refine your marketing and product mixes.

Remember, your marketing mix depends heavily on the four Ps—product, price, place, and promotion. You may find that some target audiences are keenly interested in your product and far less concerned about place or promotion. Some will focus intently on place. Others will be extremely price-sensitive. The only way to know how to develop a correct marketing mix is to ask each audience segment. Table 6-8 offers some potential mix strategies and options.

How target audiences perceive and value the mix is also important. Each different audience may expect a product with different emphases. Students, for instance, are often interested in different aspects of an institution than are their parents, and alumni donors are often interested in different aspects than are major donors. Table 6-9 is an oversimplification of how one college might mix aspects of its product.

Table 6-7
Top Five College Choice Characteristics

Students of high academic ability	Students of average academic ability	Parents
1. Academic reputation	Friendliness	Safety
2. Quality of faculty	Safety	Academic reputation
3. Availability of specific majors	Availability of specific majors	Cost
4. Cost	Cost	Job placement record
5. Graduate school placement	Academic reputation	Location

Table 6-8
Product, Price, Place, and Promotion Mixes

Product Mixes	Price Mixes	Place Mixes	Promotion Mixes
Academic	Gross cost	Single campus	Word-of-mouth communication
Social	Net cost	Satellite campus	Direct mail/publications
Physical	Ability to pay	WWW/Internet	Telemarketing
Spiritual	Willingness to pay	Travel abroad	Advertising (newspaper, magazine, radio, TV)
Reputational	Type of financial aid - merit-based - need-based	Day classes	Transit/outdoor
Value (cost vs. benefits)	Composition of aid package - scholarship/grant - loan - work-study	Evening classes	Electronic (video, audio, CDs, WWW, Internet)
		Weekend classes	Media relations Public relations Special events

Note: There is some debate about where time issues fit in the marketing mix. Some address time in the product mix. Others associate time with place. It really doesn't matter as long as time issues are addressed somewhere in the marketing mix.

Table 6-9.
Possible Product-Mix Emphases At One Institution

Target Audience	Product-mix Emphases
Prospective students	Strong emphasis on academics and social life
Parents	Stronger emphasis on academics, less emphasis on social life
Young alumni donors	Less emphasis on academics and stronger emphasis on social life and athletics
Older alumni donors	Increasing emphasis on academics
Major donors	Stronger emphasis on academics

Of course, the key to creating an effective product mix is to conduct research to determine the expectations of your target audiences and then mix the product within the range of possibilities established by your mission and vision.

Though there are several criteria for determining which academic programs are most suitable for programmatic marketing, the following are particularly useful:

■ The program has unused capacity.
■ The program has high operating and overhead costs.
■ The program is unique, not offered by competing colleges or universities.
■ The program has potential for high visibility in the marketplace.
■ The program has natural links to the surrounding community.
■ Graduation from the program leads to success in graduate school or high-income jobs.

Develop a communication grid
The next step in the segmentation process is to develop a communication grid that outlines potential message and communication strategies for each segment. Specifically, the grid addresses the following areas:

Integrated Marketing for Colleges, Universities, and Schools

- Audience segment
- Benefits/attributes the target audience segment values most
- Liabilities perceived by the audience segment
- Communication options

The use of a communication grid, as in Table 6-10, will help you keep track of the major messages and media for each segment.

A similar grid, as in Table 6-11, may be established for donors.

Evaluate effectiveness of segmenting strategy

Because you carefully defined your recruiting and fund-raising goals, it should be fairly straightforward to evaluate your response: Either you met your goals or you did

Table 6-10.
Communication Grid: Prospective Students

Audience Segment	Benefits/Attributes	Liabilities	Communication Options
Traditional/residential students	1. 2. 3.	1. 2. 3.	1. 2. 3.
Talented and gifted students	1. 2. 3.	1. 2. 3.	1. 2. 3.
Female students	1. 2. 3.	1. 2. 3.	1. 2. 3.
Engineering students	1. 2. 3.	1. 2. 3.	1. 2. 3.

Table 6-11.
Communication Grid: Donors

Audience Segment	Benefits/Attributes	Liabilities	Communication Options
Alumni	1. 2. 3.	1. 2. 3.	1. 2. 3.
Major Donors	1. 2. 3.	1. 2. 3.	1. 2. 3.
Corporate Donors	1. 2. 3.	1. 2. 3.	1. 2. 3.

not. However, determining why may be a bit problematic. If you failed to meet a goal, why not? Or if you greatly surpassed a goal, why? Careful determination will offer you tremendous insight into how you might improve the performance and effectiveness of your marketing strategies. Take the time to answer the question "why."

Good marketing plans are built on achievable, shared vision.

Section II

The Marketing Planning Process

> **"Plans are nothing. Planning is everything."**
> —Dwight Eisenhower

The Marketing Planning Process

Section I of this book was designed to help you develop a thorough understanding of marketing principles, tools, and techniques. Section II will help you use the tools and techniques presented in Section I to write your own marketing plan. Where Section I was theoretical and even a bit philosophical, Section II is decidedly practical.

To help organize what might at first be perceived as a daunting undertaking, Section II is divided into three chapters:

- Building the Foundation
- Writing the Plan
- Execution and Evaluation

These three chapters are organized around a series of steps that will help move you carefully yet deliberately through the planning process. These steps are presented in Table II-1.

Table II-1
Steps for Creating a Marketing Plan

Building the Foundation	Writing the Plan	Execution and Evaluation
Empower the process	Undertake a situational analysis	Execute the plan
Clarify your purpose	Make decision on research	Evaluate and modify the plan
Designate a champion	Finalize SWOT	Conduct a planning postmortem
Assemble the marketing team	Settle on vivid descriptors	
Build the team	Establish the marketing goals	
Define planning relationships and terminology	Clarify target audiences	
Affirm the unchangeable	Write marketing action plans	
Establish range of possibilities	Finalize the budget	
Make the decision to stay inside or go outside	Debug the plan	
Outline the planning process		

Why this approach

This multistep process was developed for several reasons. First, these steps outline the major and some often-overlooked minor issues that must be addressed as part of the planning process.

Second, these steps are sequential—they lend an order to the planning process. Rather than a large, complex, and often amorphous undertaking, the process is presented as a series of smaller, more easily defined and understood activities. This is especially important to people, teams, and organizations that begin the process without a thorough understanding of marketing.

Third, these steps emphasize the gathering of pertinent data at the beginning of the planning process where it will do the most good. Good plans are built on good data.

Fourth, these steps are designed to promote careful synthesis and debate. At the same time, they are designed to move you beyond prolonged synthesis and debate.

Next, these steps are designed to spread ownership among internal and external target audiences. And finally, these steps will keep you moving forward. Although debate and discussion are important parts of the process, our goal is to develop an effective comprehensive plan as quickly as possible.

Overview of the section

The section opens with Chapter 7, which covers building the foundation. One of the most comprehensive and lengthy chapters of the book, Chapter 7 will explore the issues that need to be addressed and the tasks that need to be accomplished before you can begin to write the plan. The 10 steps addressed in this chapter will show you how to empower the marketing process, choose a marketing champion, build a marketing team, and explore the relationship between marketing and strategic planning. Chapter 7 will conclude by introducing the planning process that the remainder of the book will follow.

Chapter 8 will move you, step by step, through the planning process outlined at the close of Chapter 7. It will begin with the situational or institutional analysis, discuss the creation of your SWOT (strengths, weaknesses, opportunities, and threats), move through goal-setting and the definition of target audiences, and conclude with writing a marketing action plan, budgeting, and debugging the plan.

Chapter 9 will wrap up the planning process by addressing three important topics: plan execution, ongoing evaluation, and the need to conduct a planning postmortem so future plans might benefit from the planning process you will soon undertake.

The importance of sequence

Each step in the planning process is designed to address a specific component of the planning process. Some of the steps will require you to gather information and complete worksheets. Others will force synthesis and appraisal. Many will require you to set priorities among options and opportunities. Some, such as Step 7, will be simple reminders not to overlook something important. And although individual steps may appear disparate at times, they have a common thread—to move you carefully through the planning process.

Before completing any of these steps, I encourage you to read all of Section II. This will help you achieve greater perspective on, and understanding of, the whole process. After you have read all the steps, the logic, order, and necessity behind individual steps will be more apparent.

7

> **❝ . . . I'm not laying bricks, I'm building a cathedral. ❞**
>
> —16th-century bricklayer

Building the Foundation

It is very difficult to hide a poor foundation. If the foundation is not solid, thoughtful, and true, sooner or later it will fail. And the structure that is built on this foundation, no matter how great or ornate, will crack, shift, distort, and perhaps even crumble.

The importance of a solid foundation is not limited to buildings. The analogy is also appropriate for the planning process. If you set about writing a plan without building a solid foundation, your marketing plan, too, will likely fail.

The purpose of this chapter is to help you build that foundation. It deliberately introduces and addresses topics that many marketing planners might ordinarily overlook. My purpose here is simple: to help you create a marketing plan that is on target, on track, and supported by the larger campus community.

Building the foundation

The 10 steps outlined in Table 7-1 will help you build the foundation you need to move ahead with certainty and confidence.

Let's begin by examining each step in detail. Remember, it is important and helpful to read through all the steps outlined in Chapters 7, 8, and 9 to gain an overview of the entire process before undertaking individual steps.

A quick reminder: As you read through these steps, notice how they stress two

Table 7-1.
Building the Foundation

1. Empower the process.
2. Clarify your purpose.
3. Designate a champion.
4. Assemble the marketing team.
5. Build the team.
6. Define planning relationships and terminology.
7. Affirm the unchangeables.
8. Establish the range of possibilities.
9. Decide whether to stay inside or go outside.
10. Outline the planning process.

important goals—the need to gather valid data early in the planning process and the need to create campus-wide ownership of the process and resulting plan.

Step 1: Empower the process

Empowering the marketing planning process begins with the active commitment of the president, or a very senior administrator with the backing of the president, to writing a marketing plan.

This commitment takes several forms. Foremost, it is a commitment to affirm the viability of the institution's mission. It is also a commitment to creating and communicating a strong, compelling institutional vision.

Second, it is a commitment to spend time, money, talent, and political capital on marketing. You simply cannot proceed in creating a marketing plan without this commitment.

Third, it is a commitment to make tough decisions—to change institutional priorities and remove organizational stumbling blocks and territorial imperatives that hinder the marketing planning process.

And finally, it is a commitment to choose a champion and empower both the team leader and the overall team.

Commitment is spelled $

A long time ago, my father and I talked about how organizations demonstrate commitment. He said that while mission statements were helpful, a better and often more realistic sense of commitment could come from a look at the budget. My dad was right. Commitment to the marketing planning process must include the commitment to spend dollars, often very contested dollars, first for the creation of a plan and later for short- and long-term implementation.

Often I hear presidents or senior administrators say, "Go ahead and write the plan, and we'll talk about funding it after it's done." However, when the plan is finished, the dollars more often than not never materialize. I have learned from experience that if the president is not willing to give you a firm idea of the dollars available for marketing at the outset of the planning process, you should seriously consider her or his commitment to marketing. Remember, for your own credibility, you cannot afford to be part of a process that makes promises to the organization's stakeholders and then fails to deliver.

Knowing the initial level of support is important for another reason—it helps define the range of possibilities. If the institution can afford to spend only $20,000 a year for five years, the marketing plan will be more modest than if the institution can spend $200,000 a year for five years.

Before you begin, make sure the president has committed the necessary resources. Remember, commitment is spelled with a $.

The presidential role in the planning process

Though the president may or may not be involved in the actual writing of the marketing plan, his or her role is still pivotal. As Figure 7-1 indicates, the president is involved in all key decisions beginning with the determination to proceed with marketing; the initial commitment of dollars; the selection of the marketing champion and team; and the establishment of the marketing goals, target audiences, and action plans. The marketing planning process outlined in these pages recognizes and supports the involvement of the president.

Step 2: Clarify your purpose

The second step in the planning process is to clarify why you want to create a marketing plan in the first place. The rationale is simple: If you don't have a clear understanding of why you are planning, it will be difficult to sell the process to the campus community. Most staff, administrators, and faculty are already burdened by more tasks than they can reasonably accomplish, and they will resist unless they can clearly see and appreciate, from their perspective, why it is being undertaken.

Other questions, too, will help clarify your purpose and spread ownership. It is often useful to ask these questions of all stakeholders, both internal and external, that might be directly affected by the planning process and the implementation of the marketing plan.

- What are the most significant marketing challenges our institution faces?
- What marketing opportunities are before us?
- Why are we interested in creating a marketing plan?
- What do we perceive as the benefits to writing a plan?
- What are our biggest concerns about writing a plan?

You should try to establish your needs as clearly and early in the process as possible. One college sends a newsletter out to campus audiences twice each year. Part of that newsletter includes a recurring article on "threats" that the college is facing. Faculty, staff, administrators, and even students are reminded that their marketplace is perilous and changing. Another institution places similar information on its internal computer bulletin boards. Keep in mind that the greater the number of stakeholders that recognize the legitimacy of the need to write a marketing plan, the less internal resistance you will meet.

It is often helpful to define your needs before you designate your marketing champion and select your team. The needs and problems your institution faces may affect whom you choose as champion and whom you invite to join your marketing team.

Figure 7-1.
Decision Points for the President

Decision to Proceed with Marketing Planning

Clarification of the Marketing Mandate

Appropriation of an Initial Marketing Budget

Approval of the Marketing Champion

Approval of Marketing Team Members

Approval of Prioritized Strengths, Weaknesses, Opportunities, and Threats

Approval of Vivid Descriptors

Approval of Prioritized Marketing Goals and Target Audiences

Approval of Final Marketing Plan, Timeline, and Budget

Step 3: Designate a champion

The next step is for the president to designate a champion, a single person responsible for the overall planning process.

Long ago I learned a fundamental lesson: Group accountability is no accountability. Every endeavor, every undertaking, every process must have someone, some single person, in charge. For our purposes, that person is the champion.

There are four essential characteristics of a strong marketing champion. First, she or he must have the respect of the campus community. Second, the champion must have both a theoretical and an experiential understanding of marketing. Third, the champion must have power and clout or access to power and clout. And finally, the champion must be able to lead and motivate people.

A strong marketing champion is important for several reasons:

- The variables that affect an institution's marketing efforts cross so many departmental and divisional lines that the only way to avoid turf battles is to have a strong champion actively involved.
- A respected champion will help spread ownership.
- Because many marketing issues are related to policy and strategic planning, the marketing champion must be closely related to the institution's policy-making body.
- Because marketing depends on appropriate funding, the champion—and by extension the president—must be able to authorize the reallocation of funds to support the marketing effort.

The marketing champion has one important task that must be highlighted: to serve as the interface or liaison between the marketing team and the institution's senior administrative staff, including the president.

At the outset, the marketing champion must be empowered with a clear and demonstrated mandate from the president. This will send an important message to the campus and increase the status and stature of the marketing effort. This is especially important because the marketing champion is often called to mediate between different power and organizational structures on campus.

A strong marketing champion also fulfills two other roles. She or he galvanizes and legitimizes your marketing efforts and provides accountability to the larger campus community.

There is a temptation—often a very strong one—to put the assistant of this or that in charge of the planning process. This is almost always a mistake, and most plans never recover from this error. If the planning process does not warrant the attention of a true champion, the institution is not serious enough about marketing.

While working with and through the marketing team, there are two skill sets the champion will depend on most—being a leader and being a delegator.

The champion as leader

The marketing champion is the team leader. It is her or his responsibility to set the tone and timbre of group interaction and dynamics. Of particular importance is the

> "The marketing champion must be empowered with a clear mandate."

champion's need to lead the team. Glenn Parker, writing in *Cross-Functional Teams: Working with Allies, Enemies, and Other Strangers*, notes that a team is an eclectic group with a variety of backgrounds, priorities, and interests—people who, given a choice, probably wouldn't work with one another.

This is often a valid description of a marketing team, and for the team to be successful, the champion must exhibit what Parker calls process skills, including these:

- Asking questions that will generate ideas and stimulate discussion
- Paraphrasing and using other listening skills to promote effective communication
- Managing discussions so that unassertive members will contribute ideas, outspoken members don't take over, and you can show that you value each person's input
- Creating a climate where members feel comfortable expressing their views
- Helping to reach decisions through consensus
- Involving all members in setting goals
- Ensuring that team members show respect to one another
- Celebrating accomplishments
- Motivating team members through recognition, job assignments, and other techniques

The champion as delegator

As important as the champion as leader is the champion as delegator. Few tactics for team-building are more efficient and effective than delegation. Delegation allows the champion to focus on the tasks that he or she can best complete, and the increased responsibility and recognition empower team members and bond them more tightly to the planning process.

There are several good books and articles on delegation. Robert Nelson's *Empowering Employees Through Delegation* is particularly helpful because it looks at delegation not simply as a way to reduce your workload but as an important strategy to empower those to whom you are delegating.

Nelson outlines several checklists and guides that are worth reviewing, including this delegation-planning checklist:

1. Develop a good attitude.
   - Give up some control.
   - Take risks.
   - Trust your team members.
   - Stay calm and patient.

2. Decide what to delegate.
   - Delegate whenever possible.
   - Delegate to both experienced and inexperienced employees.
   - Consider skill, motivation, and workload.

3. Select the right person.
   - Match skills and interests with tasks.
   - Motivate your employees.

4. Communicate responsibilities to team members.
   - Set and prioritize clear goals.
   - Share possible pitfalls.
   - Set performance standards.

5. Grant the appropriate level of authority.
   - Decide how much to give.
   - Inform team members of their authority.

6. Provide the appropriate level of support.
   - Tell the team what each member is doing.
   - Let your team know how and when you can help.
   - Share your resources.

7. Monitor the delegation.
   - Record employees' progress.
   - Ask for feedback on how you're delegating.

8. Evaluate the delegation.
   - Compare results with goals.
   - Evaluate the employee's role.
   - Discuss and give feedback.

The champion as leader and the champion as delegator are essential components of the marketing team.

Step 4: Assemble the marketing team

The selection of a strong marketing champion is the necessary first step. However, the champion cannot act alone—there must be a team.

Like the champion, the marketing team has several important tasks. The team must

- Oversee the planning process;
- Interface with the larger campus community and external stakeholders;
- Gather data and insight from internal and external sources;
- Clarify issues and options before the institution;
- Make preliminary decisions;
- Spread ownership of the marketing planning process;
- Oversee implementation of the plan; and

■ Monitor and evaluate the plan and plan activities at key junctures.

Who should be on the team . . . and yes, it is a team

Generally the question at this point is "who should be on the marketing team?" Although there is no single, universal answer, some guidelines provide direction. However, before we go on to discuss team composition, note that we have been calling this a marketing team rather than a marketing committee. This word choice was not accidental. All of us have been bamboozled into sitting on committees whose sole function seemed to be to meet, eat doughnuts, and generate lengthy and ultimately unacted-on reports. Second only to "task force," the term "committee" has way too much emotional, often negative, baggage in the academy.

This is one reason we use the term "team." The second, and perhaps more important, is because the creation of a marketing plan involves a true team effort—individuals working together with a unified goal in mind.

Organizational charts, titles, offices, and capabilities

It is difficult to discuss the exact composition of individual marketing teams because colleges and universities are neither organized the same way nor face the same challenges and opportunities. Institutions are rarely optimally organized from a marketing perspective. Half the marketing-related functions report to the advancement side, some to the president's office, others to the academic dean.

> **We need to look beyond titles and organizational charts...**

At some institutions, public relations includes community and media relations. At others, public relations is called public affairs. Some institutions have a separate marketing function. Many do not (at least not yet) have one at all. Sophisticated institutions have a separate donor relations function. Others have government or legislative relations.

Organizing the team

It does not really matter how you are organized or what you call what you do. If you spend all your time trying to chase down every dotted, solid, and straight line in every possible organizational chart, I fear that any hopes of real progress will be lost. Rather than positions and titles, let's focus on principles, philosophies, and outcomes. It does not matter what you call public relations as long as some people at your institution are charged with that responsibility. Nor does it matter who they report to. We need to look beyond titles and organizational charts and concentrate on involving essential capabilities and functions in the planning process and in implementing and monitoring the marketing plan.

While the exact composition of the marketing team will change depending on the president's mandate, most marketing teams include someone (or more) from the following areas:

■ Public relations
■ Recruiting and admissions
■ Academics/faculty

Figure 7-2.
**Composition of the
Marketing Team**

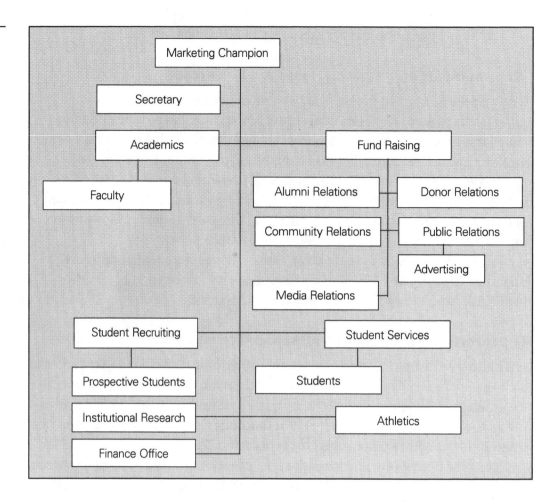

- ■ Student services
- ■ Fund raising
- ■ Athletics
- ■ Institutional research
- ■ Finance office

Figure 7-2 shows how a typical marketing team might be organized. As you set about selecting people for the team, keep in mind its two most important functions:

- ■ to gather insight and information from internal constituencies and the larger campus community, and
- ■ to spread ownership of the planning process and the resulting plan.

Figure 7-3 shows the relationship between the team and its internal and external constituencies.

Marketing-team members

Before we proceed with the next step in the planning process, let's take a few minutes to examine the role and function of individual team members.

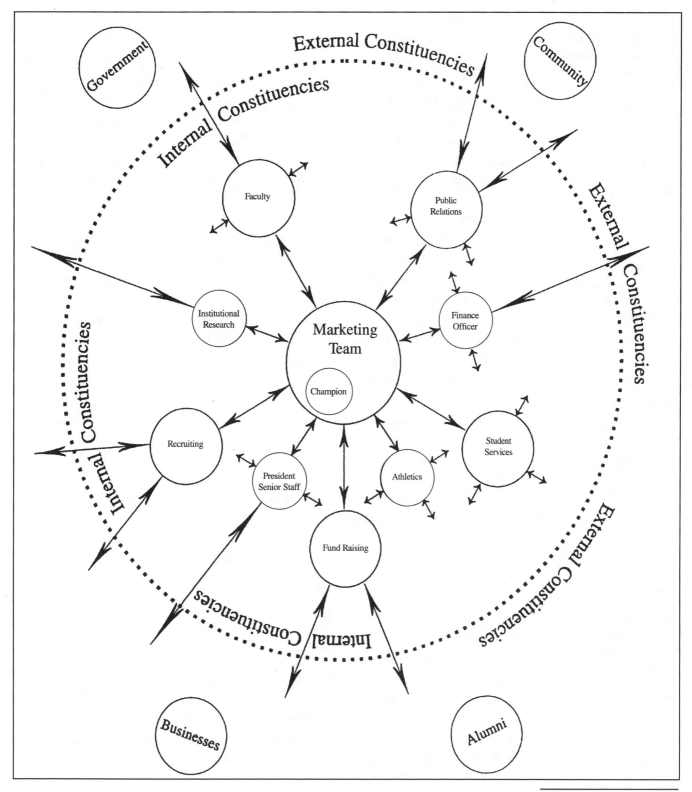

Figure 7-3.
Relationship Between Team and Constituencies

The champion

In most but not all cases, the champion is drawn from recruiting or advancement for the simple reason that these people generally have a greater understanding of and appreciation for not only marketing but the marketplace and its dynamics.

Once in a while the champion may be drawn from the faculty. This will work if the faculty member has all four of the characteristics of a champion and ample time.

Like all members of the marketing team, the champion is responsible for communicating with and managing the involvement of internal and external constituencies. For the champion, these constituencies include those in Table 7-2.

Secretary

Because of the great volume of information that will flow to and through the marketing team, it is helpful to have a secretary. This person may be a contributing member of the team or a clerical assistant recruited or appointed to serve. Ideally, this person should report directly to the champion.

The secretary is the chief recorder and document specialist. He or she is responsible for recording the minutes from each meeting; collecting, organizing, and distributing materials; handling correspondence; coordinating meetings and schedules; and generally keeping things under control. In most cases, the secretary is responsible for assembling and formatting the final, written plan.

The secretary should have one other important skill—the ability to keep confidences.

Public relations

The marketing team must include a representative from the PR office. This person must communicate with and gather insight and data from those constituencies listed in Table 7-3.

This involves assessing the perceptions, needs, and expectations of internal and external constituencies and involving staff in creating and executing action plans from their areas.

Academic representative

A strong academic representative is critical. Just as the team champion is responsible for interacting with senior administrators, the faculty representative must serve as a liaison with other faculty.

No one discipline necessarily offers the best faculty representatives to the marketing team. Contrary to popular notion, business faculty bring no essential skill set to the planning process. Rather, faculty who serve best in this role have a varied set of skills and attributes, including being

■ Perceived by other faculty as honorable and trustworthy
■ Able to consider all faculty needs—not just those of their department
■ Able to understand and appreciate all faculty ranks and categories including part-time and adjunct

■ Knowledgeable of the institution and its history

■ Knowledgeable of other institutions

■ Knowledgeable of the institution's obstacles and opportunities

■ Sensitive to students and their needs

After working with a number of faculty over the years, I have noticed other skills and attributes often found in the best faculty representatives:

■ They must be willing to examine issues critically from all sides.

■ They must be willing to interact with faculty from other disciplines.

■ They must be willing to do the homework—read the books, papers, reports; conduct the interviews; and complete the assignments.

■ They must be able to meet deadlines.

■ They must be thick-skinned because they will often serve as the lightning rod for all faculty concerns and complaints.

Perhaps most important, they must have an appreciation for the marketing planning process—believe that creating and implementing a marketing plan is in the best interests of all campus stakeholders, including faculty.

Fund raising

The marketing team must also include someone from the fund raising office. Like the representative from public relations, this person is responsible for serving as a communication and information-gathering liaison with internal and external constituencies. For the fund-raising office, these would include the constituencies listed in Table 7-4.

All fund-raising staff, working through the fund-raising representative, are involved in the planning process. And like the public relations representative, the fund-raising representative must see that the perceptions, needs, and expectations of key external constituencies are sought.

Recruiting and admissions

The representative from recruiting and admissions, too, is responsible for involving internal staff and constituencies and external constituencies in the planning process. The person from recruiting should represent all of the institution's student recruiting functions—not just undergraduate. In some cases, perhaps most, this will include graduate, nontraditional, continuing education, and recruiting for weekend and evening programs. See Table 7-5.

If your institution uses an enrollment management model that includes a separate student services area, it may not be necessary to include the student services representative. However, it has been my experience that representatives from student services often have unique insights into student needs that are of great importance to the planning process.

Student services

The representative from student services also plays an important role by serving as a

---

Table 7-5.
Constituencies With Whom the Recruiting Representative Communicates

Internal Staff
Field recruiters
Financial aid
Registrar

External Constituencies
Prospective students
- Traditional
- Of color
- International
- Nontraditional
- Graduate
Parents
High school influencers
- Guidance counselors
- Club advisers
- Coaches

Quick Glance

The Role of the Academic Dean
For a variety of reasons I do not recommend using the academic dean or provost as the academic representative. In my experience, this person does not have the time to complete this assignment, is not seen by most faculty as a legitimate faculty representative, is too often involved in faculty personnel matters, and generally has difficulty shedding his or her administrative cloak. It is much more effective and representative to have the involvement of a full-time faculty member or members.

Table 7-6.
Constituencies With Whom the Student Services Representative Communicates

Internal Staff
Orientation
Testing and evaluation
Counseling/advising
Campus life
Residence life
Health services
Career planning
Placement
Spiritual life

liaison with the internal constituencies outlined in Table 7-6.

Athletics

Surprisingly, few institutions include representatives from athletics on the marketing team. In most cases, this is a mistake. A strong or at least well-known athletic program has enormous marketing impact and offers tremendous opportunity for student recruiting, donor and alumni relations, and community relations. Coaches and sports information directors often have useful contacts in the media, among community residents, and among donors that could benefit not just athletics but the larger institution.

Institutional research

The marketing team will also benefit by including a member from institutional research. This representative has three possible functions: to assemble all relevant current research conducted by individuals and departments at the institution, to make sure the team does not initiate research now being undertaken by some other entity, and to oversee primary and secondary research completed as part of the planning process.

Finance office

The final member of the marketing planning team is a senior representative of the finance office. The inclusion of this person in the planning process is important for two reasons. First, only someone from the finance office is able to determine how much money all departments are currently spending on marketing and related activities. And second, the involvement of a person from finance early in the planning process increases the likelihood that he or she will more completely understand marketing, its potential benefits, and the importance of the institution providing long-term funding. Often these people become important allies when it comes time to develop or argue for a budget.

Quick Glance

Faculty Concerns About the Planning Process

Generally, faculty members are the biggest critics of marketing. However, the composition and size of the marketing team and how aggressively it seeks and manages faculty input can do a great deal to blunt criticism and even garner support.

As faculty look at the members of the marketing team and its leadership, they will ask themselves these questions:

■ Is the team interested in me and my ideas?
■ Are its members academically and experientially qualified?
■ Does the team understand the qualities and characteristics that make educational institutions unique and valued?
■ Will members work within current channels of governance and communication, or are they buckaroos who ride roughshod over the campus?
■ Does the team care about the institution, my department, and me as much as I do?

Who's missing?

Unless there is a compelling reason, I do not generally recommend that the marketing team include the following audiences:

- Current students
- Alumni
- Trustees
- Community residents
- Business leaders
- Donors
- The president

Table 7-7.
Solicitation of Input from Non-team Members

Audience	Team Members Solicits Input from ...
Current students	Student services or student recruiting
Alumni	Fund raising
Trustees	Champion or advancement
Community residents	Public relations
Business leaders	Fund raising or public relations
Donors	Fund raising
President	Champion

Of course, you're wondering why these people have been omitted from the planning process. Well, actually, they haven't. Rather than having them on the team, however, I believe that their needs and the institution's needs are best served by having other team members aggressively solicit their input, especially at the situational-analysis stage.

Table 7-7 outlines who will solicit input from each of these important cohorts.

Establishing the credibility of the marketing team

To help establish credibility, the champion and team members should get out and meet people, especially faculty. Attend divisional meetings. Tour facilities. Ask questions, listen, and keep confidences. Share success with everyone involved and even a few people who aren't. Nothing blunts criticism faster than sharing success. And finally, make your promises carefully. In some cases, your marketing effort will be measured more by what you failed to accomplish than by what you did accomplish.

Support among faculty for marketing must be earned. You'll know you have the support of the faculty when they look at you as a resource rather than an obstacle. And though you may never hear praise from faculty, if they start coming to you with information and ideas instead of just criticism, you have gone a long way toward earning their respect.

Some final comments about team composition

As you think about the composition of your marketing team, there are two other realities to address. First, the team should include people who will actually oversee the plan's implementation. If it doesn't, they will never have the necessary ownership, and you will miss the benefit of their experience and expertise. Second, though I have outlined a process for creating a fairly large team, you should always try to keep your marketing team as small as possible. It is difficult, if not impossible, for large teams to meet often enough to get the job done in a timely fashion.

Space and resources

Now that you have a marketing team, you need somewhere to meet and work. Your meeting room should have the following:

- An overhead projector
- A slide projector
- A screen
- Large chalkboards or dry-marker erasable boards with chalk and dry markers
- Flip charts
- A telephone
- Quick access to a photocopier
- A computer with access to the Internet
- Work tables
- Movable chairs and couches
- Quick access to coffee, soft drinks, and restrooms

You should also have copies of the following documents, reports, and data sets:

- Mission statement (if it's not in the catalog)
- Vision statement
- Strategic plan and initiatives
- Detailed institutional budget
- Campus master plan including
  - Planned renovations
  - Schedule of new buildings
  - Technology plan
- Annual report
- Most recent accreditation report
- All recent institutional research
- Local, regional, and/or national demographic, economic, and job-trend data
- Data on all competing colleges and universities
- College guides such as Barron's or Peterson's
- College catalog(s)
- Samples of all recruiting publications
- Campaign case statements
- Samples of all fund-raising literature
- Samples of literature from competing institutions
- Longitudinal recruiting and retention data
- Longitudinal annual fund and fund-raising data

Computer and software resources

If they are available, certain software and computer resources will make your work more efficient and effective.

A linked or network-based meeting scheduling software package such as Lotus Notes, Schedule Maker Pro, Team Agenda, or Sidekick Group Scheduling will make scheduling your meetings much easier.

E-mail can cut down on the need for so many meetings. You can use e-mail to query team members about a particular topic or issue, poll them about a decision, or even schedule meetings.

An idea generator such as Idea Fisher is a wonderful tool for facilitating group thinking and discussion. Ideas can be posed, expanded, and quickly evaluated.

I strongly suggest you also use planning software such as ManagePro, On Target, Fast Track Schedule, or Sure Track. This software will save you an enormous amount of time and frustration as the plan is developed, refined, implemented, and changed. We will explore the use of planning software in greater depth later in this chapter.

A computer-based projection system helps too. A good system will allow you to project your monitor's image to a large screen. This is especially useful when compiling initial lists and ideas, such as threats facing the campus. Using a computer to record and project the team's comments and ideas will make the process much more engaging and efficient. It is also helpful to use a projection system when examining World Wide Web sites.

Step 5: Build the team

In all likelihood, members of the marketing planning team will arrive with different expectations and different skill sets. There is a high probability that members have never worked together. Each one probably feels more responsibility to his or her own department or discipline than to the team, the process, and the institution. At this early stage, the members are a team in name only. The goal of this step is to help you coalesce the individual members into a team.

> **"Using planning software will save you time and frustration."**

What is a team?

Before we proceed too much further, let's clarify the term team. Jon Katzenbach and Douglas Smith describe a team as "a small number of people with complementary skills who are committed to a common purpose, performance goals, and approach for which they hold themselves mutually accountable." Teams agree on processes and rules and work toward a common goal or goals.

An expanded definition of teams

To help gain a more complete understanding of teams, it might be useful to explore Katzenbach and Smith's definition in greater detail. Drawing heavily from their book, *The Wisdom of Teams*, we note that teams…

… must develop the right mix of skills, generally in three categories:
- Technical or functional expertise
- Problem-solving and decision-making skills
- Interpersonal skills

… must be committed to a common purpose and performance goals. Teams develop direction, momentum, and commitment by working to shape a meaningful purpose.

... are committed to a common approach—a clear sense of how they will work together to accomplish their purpose.

... have mutual accountability. No group ever becomes a team until it can hold itself accountable as a team. Think, for example, about the subtle but critical difference between "the president holds me accountable" and "we hold ourselves accountable." At its core, team accountability is about the promises we make to ourselves and others, promises that underpin two aspects of teams: commitment and trust.

From individual behavior to team behavior

Table 7-8.
Individual Team Behaviors

Individual Behavior Trait	Group or Team Behavior or or Trait
Reticent	Communicative
Secretive or reserved	Open
Conflictual	Cooperative
Apprehensive	Trusting
Impersonal	Mutually concerned
Avoiding responsibility	Self-responsible
Sterile	Creative
Alienated	Committed
Confused about roles	Clear about roles
Individual-centered	Team-centered

Source: Glenn Parker

In many respects, what you have assembled, or will soon assemble, is a cross-functional team. This is composed of people from different departments and perspectives. For example, instead of having everyone on your team from the public relations office, the team will be composed of individuals from many different offices with different perspectives and backgrounds.

One of the most important first goals is to help what are at first cross-functional members coalesce into a true marketing team. Though it may never be possible for individuals to forget the constituencies they represent, it is possible for everyone to have a greater understanding of and appreciation for the team as a subset of the larger institution.

Glenn Parker and others define team-building as a structured attempt to improve or develop the effectiveness of a group of people who work together, temporarily or permanently. Representatives from internal and external constituencies will join your team with a number of behavioral traits. Most of these are positive. Others, however, are destructive or at least counterproductive. The champion must understand the need to move from individual behaviors to group behaviors. See Table 7-8.

Champion as team builder

In most cases, it is the champion's responsibility to build the team. However, in some instances it is helpful to use the services of a team building expert early on. This is especially important if the champion has neither the background nor the affinity for team building.

This section of Chapter 7 contains suggestions and recommendations that will help you not only build a strong marketing team but understand team dynamics, work with your team, recognize the characteristics of dysfunctional teams, and present options for rewarding your team. It is not designed to replace more comprehensive team building resources; rather, it is a primer on team building. The close of this section offers a number of excellent, comprehensive resources.

As the champion works to build the team, he or she should keep in mind the following suggestions:

- Maintain a sense of urgency and direction—the more urgent and meaningful the rationale, the more likely that a real team will emerge.
- Select team members by skills and skill potential, not personality. Skill sets of value include technical and functional, problem-solving, and interpersonal.
- Pay particular attention to first meetings and actions. When potential teams first gather, everyone alertly monitors others' signals to confirm, suspect, or dispel going-in assumptions and concerns. They pay particular attention to those in authority, especially the champion.
- Set up clear rules of behavior. The most critical rules pertain to attendance, discussion, confidentiality, analytic approach, end-product orientation, constructive confrontation, and contributions.
- Challenge the group regularly with fresh factions—new arrangements of work groups and new people—and additional information.
- Spend lots of time together.
- Exploit the power of positive feedback, recognition, and reward; even the strongest egos respond to positive feedback when it is real.

Team size

Earlier, when discussing the possible members of the marketing team, I noted the tension between having input from various internal and external stakeholders and the need to keep the team as small as possible. Katzenbach and Smith indicate that while it is theoretically possible to have a team of any size, critical interaction is often lost as team size expands: "Large numbers of people—by virtue of their size—have trouble interacting constructively as a group, much less agreeing on actionable specifics. Ten people are far more likely than 50 to successfully work through their individual, functional, and hierarchical differences toward a common plan and hold themselves jointly accountable for the results."

Step 6: Define planning relationships and marketing terminology

Perhaps you have just finished a strategic planning process, and some audiences with whom you will be working do not understand how marketing planning relates to strategic planning. It is important at the outset to explain how these two distinct but similar planning processes relate.

Strategic planning is designed to help institutions respond effectively to new situations. John Bryson noted, in *Strategic Planning for Public and Nonprofit Organizations*, that

> **Strategic planning is a disciplined effort to produce fundamental decisions and actions shaping the nature and direction of an organization.**

> ### Quick Glance
>
> **Team building**
> There are several excellent books and resources available for helping you build strong teams. Some favorites include Glenn Parker's *Cross-Functional Teams: Working With Allies, Enemies, and Other Strangers* and the *1996 Handbook of Best Practices for Teams,* Jon Katzenbach and Douglas Smith's *The Wisdom of Teams,* and Price Pritchett's *The Team Member Handbook for Teamwork.*
>
> Appendix D contains a brief primer for working with teams.

Others define strategic planning as a long-range planning process that focuses on adapting the organization to environmental change.

Both definitions contain the same outward and then inward view—the simple but often overlooked understanding that institutions must look outside and understand, even anticipate, their environment and marketplace before they can develop a plan.

Marketing looks outward and inward as well. In the literature and in practice, we know there is a fine line between strategic planning and marketing planning. The marketing goals that result from marketing planning are often very similar to the strategic initiatives that result from strategic planning.

Recently I began helping a small, private, liberal arts college in the Midwest develop a marketing plan. We began shortly after the college completed a strategic plan. As part of its strategic plan, the following seven strategic initiatives were developed:

- Enhance academic quality.
- Enroll and retain excellent students.
- Create a rich co-curricular experience.
- Establish an effective and unique program of leadership development and community service.
- Strengthen fund raising and endowment.
- Improve management and communication.
- Enhance facilities to support program initiatives.

Another client, this one a public four-year institution on the West Coast, has undertaken the following extraordinarily straightforward strategic initiatives:

- Increase enrollment.
- Increase endowment size.
- Increase academic quality of entering students.
- Develop a comprehensive facilities plan.

A third client, a two-year public institution in Illinois, has the following strategic initiatives:

- Provide the best education value in the region.
- Increase access.
- Recognize the importance of all people.
- Develop a mutually supportive relationship with the community.
- Build stronger ties to local high schools.
- Cultivate ties with local business and industry.
- Design a database form that clearly outlines the types of information we want to collect about each record or entry.

As you can see, these strategic initiatives have significant marketing overtones. For example, the desire to enhance academic quality, enroll and retain excellent students, and strengthen fund raising and endowment are very market- and marketing-oriented. However, although the strategic plan offers initiatives and goals, it does not outline specific methods for achieving the goals. Nor does it include budgets and methods of accountability.

Both strategic plans and marketing plans originate from the institutional mission and vision. However, whereas the vision and strategic plan provide a broad-sweep institutional direction, the marketing plan is often more concerned with the day-to-day. Or, as one president noted, the purpose of the marketing plan is to give "legs" to the strategic plan.

Settle on terms and definitions

As part of the planning process, you must make sure that all the parties involved define marketing the same way. There is nothing more frustrating than spending six months writing a comprehensive marketing plan only to find that the president didn't mean marketing—he or she really meant promotion.

At the outset, you must take the time to clarify how your president and dean and vice president for development define marketing. Make absolutely sure that everyone is using the same terminology. If their definition is really promotion, you have two options. You can try to educate them about the challenges facing your institution (take a look at Chapter 1 again) and show how a complete definition of marketing can help them address these challenges.** This will take time—especially if you want them, and you do, to have true ownership of the marketing planning process. The second option is to work with their definition of marketing, then write a great marketing/promotion plan—and as you and your plan succeed, begin slowly to expand, over time, everyone's working definition of marketing.

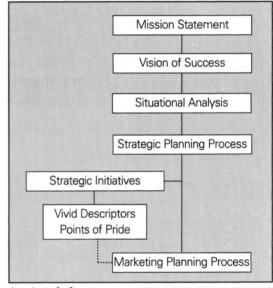

Figure 7-4.
Marketing, Mission, Vision, and Strategy

Step 7: Affirm the unchangeables

The next step in the process is to affirm the unchangeables—the institutional characteristics, qualities, and values that are not up for debate. In most, almost all, cases, the institution's mission is the foundation on which marketing plans are built. Missions are the marketing constants, not marketing variables. If your institution is a women's college, your marketing plan must affirm this important reality. If you work at a regional public with a long, proud history of teacher education, your marketing plan and activities must be consistent with this overarching reality.

Before you initiate a planning process, you absolutely must affirm, with internal and external campus constituencies, the institutional characteristics, qualities, and values that are mission-critical. Reinforce, as much as possible at this stage, your points

---

**If your senior administrators do not have a realistic appraisal of the challenges and opportunities facing the institution, you also need to take a look at any strategic planning documents. Chances are their founding assumptions and ensuing strategic initiatives are flawed as well.

of pride and vivid descriptors (more about these later). Clarify the geography you want to continue to serve. Focus on your mission and vision. See Figure 7-4.

It is very important that everyone involved in your planning process understands your *raison d'être* and that the entire campus community knows your planners have this understanding.

Step 8: Establish the range of possibilities

After you have thrown a philosophical fence around your *raison d'être,* it is time to establish a full range of possibilities. This is an enormously important and sometimes prickly step. Many years ago I read a wonderful book on problem-solving called *Conceptual Blockbusting: A Guide to Better Ideas.* The author, James Adams, made the point that too often we arrive at bad decisions, or are not able to conceptualize good decisions, because we unnecessarily limit the range of possible alternatives. We don't consider options because we too narrowly define the problem and/or range of possible solutions.

As I write this, I am working with a college that has served young women in the South for more than 100 years. Its target audiences have largely been traditional-age white women, and this institution is very concerned about the shrinking and competitiveness of this market. Helping some of its faculty, administrators, and staff understand that there are great numbers of nontraditional-age women and nonwhite women it might serve was an important first step in helping to establish a range of possibilities. That same college has a curriculum that is dominated by majors addressing traditional women's roles of teaching, nursing, secretarial studies, and homemaking. Helping the college review its curriculum in light of changing educational needs and expectations has greatly expanded the range of possibilities there.

As part of the planning process, I have found it useful to create a two-columned table that lists both institutional unchangeables and those characteristics or qualities that might, in fact, be modified or even replaced. For another client, I developed a grid that looked like the one in Table 7-9.

Table 7-9.
Unchangeables and Changeables

Institutional Characteristics We Will Not Change	Characteristics We Might Be Willing to Change
Commitment to academic quality	Serving only traditional-age students
Commitment to serving students in the Dallas/Fort Worth multiplex	Offering programs only on our campus
Commitment to the liberal arts	Stressing traditional teaching/learning models
	Not offering professional programs that complement the liberal arts
	Not serving nonresidential/commuter populations

As you use this table to help define your range of possibilities, take time to really examine your unchangeables. Some should be absolute—especially those that are mission-critical. Other unchangeables, with proper inspection, may not be as rigid as you think. For example, a college that historically offered classes only in the daytime felt that this was unchangeable. However, it was not really mission-critical, only convenient for faculty.

Step 9: Decide whether to stay inside or go outside

The next step in marketing planning is to decide whether to proceed with the planning process on your own or to bring in outside help. The decision to retain outside counsel may occur for a number of interrelated reasons, including that

- Administrators lack sufficient marketing expertise.
- The marketing process is unduly politicized, and you want objective help.
- A qualified outside firm, drawing on experience from other colleges and universities, is able to provide a unique perspective on the marketing problems and issues you face.
- An outside expert is able to complement the marketing champion's strengths and weaknesses.
- An outside expert may help legitimize the marketing effort to wary members of the campus community.
- An outside firm may have access to secondary data sources not immediately available to you.

Step 10: Outline the planning process

There are many ways to conceptualize the marketing planning process. One of my favorites is the use of the simple yet appropriate acronym S-O-S, which stands for situation, objectives, and strategy.

The first S, situation, helps formulate such questions as these:

- What's it like now?
- What's going on?

Table 7-10.
The Expanded Marketing-Planning Process

Situational Analysis	1. Internal/institutional analysis 2. External/environmental analysis 3. Creation of strengths, weaknesses, opportunities, and threats (SWOT)
Market Research	1. Perceptual 2. Needs analysis 3. Competitive 4. Environmental
Strategy Formation	1. Prioritize marketing goals 2. Prioritize target audiences 3. Write marketing action plans 4. Assemble the final plan
Strategy Execution	Implement the plan
Program Review and Evaluation	Evaluate the plan

Quick Glance

Faculty as Facilitators
I am often asked about the strengths and weaknesses of faculty as facilitators in the marketing planning process. Faculty can make great leaders as long as they have the time, are qualified, and are unbiased. However, potential faculty facilitators must understand their role. Are they serving as facilitators or champions? If facilitators, they must understand that their job is to support, not supplant, the champion. If they are to serve as the champion, they must work hard to look at problems and opportunities from the perspective of the whole institution, not just the faculty or their department. Finally, faculty facilitators must recognize that other faculty will place them under enormous pressure. They may even find themselves alienated, temporarily or permanently, from their peers.

■ What's happening to us?

■ And why?

O, objective, reminds us to examine such issues as these:

■ What are we going to do about this?

■ What are our options?

■ What are our goals?

The final S, strategy, invites us to outline options for achieving our objectives and goals:

■ What activities do we need to accomplish our goals?

■ Who will be doing what, when?

Though the planning process outlined in Table 7-10 may appear a bit more detailed and comprehensive, you will quickly see that it follows roughly the same basic S-O-S. The first stages—situational analysis and market research—are directed at defining the situation.

The second stage—strategy formation—involves establishing the objectives.

The final stages—strategy execution and program review and evaluation—are concerned with strategy.

The strategic marketing plan outline

There are many ways to organize a marketing plan. Over the years, however, I have found the outline in Figure 7-5 extremely useful.

This is the planning process and outline to be introduced and explained in Chapter 8.

Figure 7-5
Outline of the Strategic Marketing Plan

1. College or university mission statement
2. College or university vision statement
3. Situational analysis:
   ■ review of internal/institutional data
   ■ review of external/environmental data
   ■ synthesized and prioritized
     • strengths
     • weaknesses
     • opportunities
     • threats
4. Vivid descriptors/ points of pride
5. Prioritized marketing goals
6. Prioritized target audiences
7. Marketing action plans
8. Budgets
9. Timelines

8

Writing the Plan

"Write.
Write.
Write.
Write
it down."
—Lyric from *Sesame Street*

In Chapter 7 we focused on laying the foundation for a successful marketing planning process. Now it is time to build on that foundation and write the actual plan. To accomplish this task, we will work through the nine steps listed in Table 8-1.

Components of the marketing plan

Before we proceed, however, it will help to revisit the planning outline introduced at the close of Chapter 7 (Figure 7-5). That outline is a useful guide to what the final plan will look like.

The mission statement

As stated previously, it is very important that the marketing plan begin with a presentation of the institution's mission. This establishes the plan's general direction and tone and helps to affirm the unchangeables.

If you are not comfortable with putting mission at the opening of the plan, you must address possible incongruencies between the mission and your marketing goals and objectives. Either your mission or your plan must change.

Table 8-1.
Writing the Plan

Undertake a situational analysis

Decide on research

Prioritize and finalize SWOT

Settle on vivid descriptors

Establish marketing goals

Clarify target audiences

Write marketing action plans

Establish the budget

Debug the plan

The vision statement

Chapter 2 discussed vision at length and noted that whereas an institution's mission is a declaration of purpose, the vision helps clarify what the organization should look like as it fulfills its mission.

Vision provides a vital sense of direction or, as stated by Burt Nanus, "a realistic, credible, attractive future for your organization." Good marketing plans are built on achievable, shared vision.

Situational analysis

The situational analysis, sometimes called an institutional analysis, is the third component of a marketing plan. Philip Kotler and Patrick Murphy define it as "a systematic evaluation of the institution and its environment." They write further that "the goals of a situational analysis are to identify, evaluate, and prioritize your institution's external and internal environment." These data are coalesced and organized into what is called the SWOT: strengths, weaknesses, opportunities, and threats.

The situational analysis is often coalesced into a succinct position statement—a short paragraph that describes the "position" or status of the institution at the present time.

Marketing plans must include a realistic situational analysis. Many major marketing mistakes occur because the institution skipped or glossed over this step.

Vivid descriptors

Sometimes called points of pride, these are institutional characteristics or attributes that you want to communicate to your target audiences—the things for which you want to be known. Remember, though, that credible vivid descriptors must be valued by both the institution and the target audiences.

Prioritized marketing goals

As you work through the situational analysis, you will uncover myriad opportunities and obstacles you might address. The most important four or five of these will become formal marketing goals. A goal, sometimes called an objective, is something you wish to accomplish—increasing name recognition within your primary market, for example.

Because of time, budget, and talent limits, you must set priorities among your marketing goals. Keep in mind: It is much better to accomplish a few goals than to fail at accomplishing a larger number. At educational institutions, as in many organizations, you are often more remembered for what you failed to do than for what you did.

Marketing action plans (MAPs)

Marketing action plans are strategies that, when combined, help accomplish your marketing goals. If your goal, as noted above, is to increase name recognition in your

primary market, your MAPs might include these:
- Hiring a special events director
- Developing a stronger media relations effort
- Implementing a regional advertising campaign

As you will see later, MAPs carefully outline the specific strategy, note which marketing goal it supports, detail who will be responsible for its implementation, and indicate how it will be evaluated. MAPs also include a budget and timeline for completion.

Budgets

The next component of the marketing plan is presentation of the overall budget. This will be a compilation of the budgets established for each marketing action plan. Remember, the general budget was established with the president before the planning process began. The final budget is much more detailed and includes dollars allocated for each action plan.

Timelines

The final element of a marketing plan is a master timeline. Each MAP details when it will be implemented and how long it will run. The master timeline includes all MAPs so you have an exact understanding of what is happening when.

Now that we have a basic understanding of the components of the plan document, let's begin to draw them together.

Step 11: Undertake a situational analysis

Marketing plans begin with a thorough understanding of the institution and its marketplace. This process is called a situational or institutional analysis. This is a careful, systematic evaluation, from a marketing perspective, of your institution and its environment. The most important outcome is the gathering of data that will help guide the overall planning process. However, a properly conducted situational analysis is also a powerful means to help generate campus support for the planning process and the resulting plan.

If you have recently completed a strategic plan, you likely completed a situational analysis as part of it. If this is the case, examine the SWOT developed then and evaluate its completeness and currency before deciding to proceed with the situational analysis for the marketing plan.

Generally, the situational analysis is divided into two broad areas: internal/institutional and external/environmental.

Internal/institutional analysis

Depending on the degree of sophistication sought and the mandate from the presi-

> *Quick Glance*
>
> **How Comprehensive Should the Situational Analysis Be?**
> As you consider whether your situational analysis should be more or less comprehensive, you need to factor in a number of variables. Consider the deadline for finalizing the plan; the number, variety, and size of the marketing decisions you will be making; the mood of the campus; the knowledge of the senior staff and marketing team; the trust level of major constituents; and the quality of available data. All things considered, it is almost always better to err by being too comprehensive than by being not comprehensive enough. This is especially true when the atmosphere on campus is politically charged.

dent, the internal/institutional analysis may include the following activities:

- ■ Evaluate current leadership.
- ■ Review existing planning documents:
  - • Strategic plan
  - • Academic plan
  - • Marketing plan
  - • Recruiting plan
  - • Fund-raising plan
  - • Capital improvement plan
  - • Technology plan
- ■ Review current market research.
- ■ Review quality and currency of the institution's general core and curriculum.
- ■ Evaluate faculty competencies.
- ■ Evaluate success of recruiting and fund-raising strategies and activities.
- ■ Determine how such internal audiences as students, faculty, staff, administrators, and trustees perceive the institution.*
- ■ Examine current product, price, place, and promotion strategies.
- ■ Review facilities and the physical plant.
- ■ Evaluate deferred maintenance schedule.
- ■ Audit internal communication strategies.

  *Some may consider trustees an external constituency, and that's all right. The important thing is to make sure they are queried.

External/environmental analysis

The second component of the situational analysis is an audit of the external environment. In many cases, this analysis parallels the internal one. A comprehensive external/environmental analysis would include the following:

- ■ Review linkages and exchange relationships with such key external publics as business leaders, community leaders, local government officials, and area religious institutions (if applicable).
- ■ Determine how such external publics as these perceive the institution:
  - • Prospective students
  - • Parents
  - • High school influencers
  - • Regional employers
  - • Business leaders
  - • Alumni
  - • Community residents
  - • Community leaders
  - • Legislators and legislative staffs
  - • Donors
  - • Foundations

- Examine local, regional, national, and even international economic, demographic, and employment trends.
- Determine unmet educational need in primary service area.
- Complete an analysis/comparison of the institutions with which you compete for students, gifts, or media attention.
- Complete an audit of your external communication strategies.

The role of the marketing team

The marketing team, under the champion's leadership, is responsible for undertaking the situational analysis. The team can expect to conduct the following activities:

- Announce to internal and external audiences that the analysis is being undertaken; include information about its purpose and timeline.
- Gather and evaluate existing documents.
- Complete interviews with stakeholders.

As part of this analysis, the marketing team must commit to a basic set of rules:

- The team members are conduits, not filters. It is their job to collect all data whether they agree with it or not.
- The team should avoid using suspect, tainted, or anonymous data. All data sources must be cited.
- Great care must be taken to separate institutional myth and hype from marketing reality.
- As much as possible, data should be quantitative.
- This situational analysis should be as inclusive as possible.

Strategies for gathering data

Excellent strategies for gathering data as part of the institutional analysis include the following:

- Holding in-depth interviews with key constituents.
- Holding focus-group interviews with stakeholders.
- Putting broad questions on the campus electronic bulletin board.
- Sending individual surveys to faculty, staff, administrators, and students.
- Putting a survey instrument in campus newspapers or alumni magazines.
- Sponsoring campus-wide forums and discussions.
- Sending individual questionnaires to key administrators and faculty chairs.
- Obtaining local, regional, and national data from government agencies .
- Gathering data from such consortiums and professional associations as the Council for Advancement and Support of Education, National Society of Fund Raising Executives, American Association of College Registrars and Admissions Officers, American College Testing Program, American Council on Education, National Association of Independent Colleges and Universities, and Association of Governing Boards of Universities and Colleges.

Quick Glance

Dealing with Anonymous Data and Information

As part of the internal and external situational analyses, you are very likely to receive anonymous data from one source or another. This type of data is almost always suspect and should generally be disregarded. There is little to be gained by using anonymous data, and there is a high likelihood that decisions to use it will come back to haunt you if you do.

Asking and answering

As part of the situational analysis, you will be asking different constituents their opinions on different aspects of the college or university. These queries may occur one-on-one, in groups, or through survey research.

Your interviews or surveys should begin with a basic explanation of why you are seeking opinions and how you'll use them. Because many of the questions and answers are sensitive, you should, where appropriate and possible, offer respondents both anonymity and confidentiality.

With each group of stakeholders, ask the following general questions:

- From your perspective, what are the institution's major strengths?
- What do you believe are its major weaknesses?
- What do you believe are the major opportunities in our marketplace?
- What are the major threats or challenges in our marketplace?
- If you could change one aspect of the institution, what would it be?
- If you had a reasonable budget, what marketing activity would you tackle?
- I'd like to see the institution . . . .
- I choose to work here (or go to school here) because . . . .
- I think the institution can better respond to the future by . . . .
- I believe institutional quality entails . . . .
- For what should this institution be known? When people hear our name, what images would you like to have pop into their mind?

Appendix E contains a sample instrument for querying faculty. It is easy to modify for use with staff, administrators, and other constituents.

Organizing the data

During a situational analysis, you will quickly find yourself under an avalanche of data. It will help to begin organizing your findings into four broad categories:

- Strengths
- Weaknesses
- Opportunities
- Threats

Robert Smith uses the following definitions:

- Strengths: Comparative advantages over competitors. Resources that establish the institution's desired position or something on which you can capitalize. Examples:
  - Reputation for outstanding teaching
  - Stable or growing endowment
  - High placement rate for graduates

- Weaknesses: Problems, deficiencies, shortcomings, or flaws that detract from the institution's desired position. Weaknesses often consume resources that are better used elsewhere.

Examples:
- Lack of modern instructional technology equivalent to students' experiences in high school
- Untrained or inadequate staff in the development office
- Poor annual fund participation rate among alumni

■ Opportunity: An attractive, sometimes fleeting occurrence or trend where action is likely to produce a positive, competitive advantage. Responding to opportunities can propel the institution forward.

Examples:
- A new employer with educational needs moves into the area
- A national report lists the institution among the safest in the country
- A campus study reveals a strong and growing demand for graduate courses among local school systems

■ Threat: An unfavorable trend or specific event that would lead to stagnation, decline, or demise of the institution or one of its programs.

Examples:
- Decline in the number of area high school graduates
- Collapse of a major employer of the institution's graduates
- Erosion of tax base used to fund education in the state

As you think about conceptualizing and organizing your strengths, weaknesses, opportunities, and threats grid, it may be helpful to remember the following:

■ Strengths and weaknesses are usually internal/institutional, whereas opportunities and threats are generally external/environmental. See Table 8-2.

■ Something can be both a strength and a weakness or an opportunity and a threat. Consider, for example, an urban-based college. Because of its proximity to jobs, cultural events, and entertainment, students might consider its location a strength. However, these same students, concerned about safety, may look at the location as a weakness.

■ Different audiences may place the same characteristic in different categories. Students, for example, may consider strong campus life a strength while parents, concerned about time away from studies or the influence of a party school, consider it a weakness.

■ Not everyone on the team has to agree that something is a strength, weakness, opportunity, or threat before it can be added to the SWOT grid. It is perfectly acceptable to have civil disagreement at this point. It is more important to make the list as comprehensive as possible than it is to have unanimity.

■ Colleges and universities often approach a SWOT analysis with a tremendous amount of denial. Senior administrators and faculty who are often removed from day-to-day realities are especially guilty of looking at threats and weaknesses through rose-colored glasses.

Table 8-2.
Strengths, Weaknesses, Opportunities, and Threats

Internal/ Institutional	External Environmental
Strength	Opportunity
Weakness	Threat

Table 8-3.
SWOT Analysis

Strengths	Weaknesses	Opportunities	Threats
Faculty credentials and emphasis on teaching	Value vs. cost	College/business	Increased competition from publics and privates
Graduation rate	High cost to attend	Internships	Tuition gap between publics and privates
Presidential leadership	Dated, often antiquated facilities	Service/community relations	Uncertain government policies
Location	Low endowment	Leadership opportunities for students	Private college competition with more name recognition and financial aid
Current student research	Campus climate: anger and apathy	Summer school	Declining student pools
Commitment to customer service	Location	New recruiting markets	
Campus ambiance/ environment	Little institutional image, especially in emerging recruiting markets	Transfer market	
Many credible alumni	Poor retention rate	Experiential learning	
	Low level of student involvement in campus activities	Employer needs	
	Low annual fund participation	Summer camps/ conferences	
	Meager fund-raising ability		
	Lost alumni		
	Inability to make decisions in a timely manner		
	Too much faculty involvement in governance process		
	No common vision		
	Few noteworthy cultural events		

The SWOT grid

As you gather and organize your data, it is very likely that you will soon have a grid like the one in Table 8-3, prepared by a client in the West as it worked through its

Integrated Marketing for Colleges, Universities, and Schools

Table 8-4.
SWOT Analysis

Strengths	Weaknesses	Opportunities	Threats
Instructional environment	Lack of solid research data	Location in a growing, receptive community	Increased competition for prospective students
Safe, pristine environment	Poor regional image	Increasing number of high school graduates in service area	Location
Quality of life	Perception of overly rural/distant location	Budget allocation to support marketing activities	Closing of regional Air Force base
Strong academic programs	Misperceptions among high school counselors	Marketability of the campus	Poor perception of quality
Cost/value	Increased tuition hikes		Perception of tuition hikes
Increasingly diverse enrollment	Misperceptions among prospective students		Loss of power in state legislature
Admissions office	Climate		
Leadership opportunities for students			
Career preparation programs			
Two-year programs			
Tuition discount for graduate dependents			
Creation of a marketing task force			
Renewed emphasis placed on high school guidance counselors			
Honors program			
National academic awards			
Athletic programs			

strengths, weaknesses, opportunities, and threats.

As you read through the grid in Table 8-3, please note a couple of things. First, the grid contains summary statements that often represent more complex issues. Don't worry—the marketing-team secretary will capture the exact wording.

Second, the grid contains several characteristics that are labeled as both strengths and weaknesses or opportunities and threats. And third, note that these characteristics are marketing-oriented. The purpose of this grid is not to outline every ill and option your institution faces but to focus on those variables that might affect its ability to market itself more aggressively.

Another institution, this one a public university in Michigan, developed the list of strengths, weaknesses, opportunities, and threats found in Table 8-4. The analysis outlined above reveals several tendencies common among institutions seeking to undertake a comprehensive SWOT analysis. First, there is a disproportionate number of strengths, and many of them have at best a tangential effect on the institution's ability to market itself.

Second, there is a great degree of overlap between weaknesses and threats. Remember, weaknesses tend to be internal, and threats tend to be external. The majority of the weaknesses listed seem to focus on misperceptions, though tuition hikes and climate are also mentioned. Note, however, that this institution listed a lack of solid research data as its first weakness. Of course, the question comes to mind: If you don't have data, how do you know you are being misperceived?

Third, there is very little effort to develop a comprehensive list of opportunities and no attempt to tie them back to the institution's vision for success. Research would have helped to define educational needs and expectations in the marketplace that might provide some initial direction. In addition, a basic competitive analysis would have been helpful.

Finally, the list of threats seems to show the most thought and analysis.

One last comment. This SWOT analysis is strikingly political. Whereas the strengths are glowing and numerous, the weaknesses are either superficial or external. There is no real heartfelt analysis of internal weaknesses—of failed policies, poor practices, or dated programs.

One final SWOT grid in Table 8-5 is worth examining, this one from a large private institution in the South.

This SWOT analysis is much more realistic and less self-serving. It acknowledges a problem with administrative leadership and customer service—two areas that many institutions choose to ignore. It also correctly identifies competition with public institutions and declining family savings rates as major challenges.

> **Remember, weaknesses tend to be internal, and threats tend to be external.**

Step 12: Decide on market research

The situational analysis will often lead to a realization that you don't know enough, or even anything, about a particular issue. For example, the campus may not have recent data on how various internal or external audiences perceive it. Perhaps the institution has never examined unmet educational need in its service area. Maybe no one has undertaken a systematic evaluation of its curriculum.

At this point, the college must make a decision on whether it should undertake formal market research to gather the data it needs. This is often a tough decision. On the pro side, good data will provide extraordinarily valuable insight. On the con side,

Table 8-5.
SWOT Analysis

Strengths	Weaknesses	Opportunities	Threats
Location	Cost	Location	Competing public institution nearby
Small classes	Registration process	Proximity to one of the fastest growing counties in the country	Public higher education in general
Friendly atmosphere	Class scheduling—availability and timing	Growing nontraditional market	Falling family savings for college
Programs in premedicine, nursing, education, and business	Ill-conceived recruiting strategies	Strong corporate relations and opportunities	Location perceived as unsafe
Strong, accessible, friendly faculty	Career services	Strong Christian high school and church support	Tuition-reimbursement reductions
Christian environment	Student/campus life	Home schooling	Changing demography—more and more people do not know us
Quarterly calendar	Administrative leadership that is reactive rather than proactive	Able to build on reputations of a handful of majors	Not delivering on service
High annual fund participation	Student advising	Strong community interest in Christian higher education	Misperceptions about the institution
Strong donor relations	Takes too long to graduate		
	Lack of a consistent and persistent image		
	Limited facilities		
	Too many weak programs		
	Lack of a comprehensive retention strategy		

research requires time and money.

Though there is no simple rule that will help you determine whether you need to undertake research, keep in mind the following. If you …

■ Need perspective
■ Work in a politically charged environment
■ Need data to help you make major or difficult decisions
■ Plan to spend significant dollars over a number of years implementing your marketing plan

■ Politically simply cannot afford to be wrong

… then undertake market research. You won't regret it.

Step 13: Prioritize and finalize SWOT

Even a limited institutional analysis will uncover a potentially unmanageable number of interrelated problems and opportunities. For this reason, it is crucial to juxtapose data against institutional priorities so planners may accurately allocate resources. Many marketing plans founder because their designers tried to do too much at once. It's better to begin solving the most pressing marketing problems this year and save secondary problems for the future.

Organizing the SWOT

There are several ways to organize your SWOT data. Two of my favorites include the internal vs. external approach—similar to how the SWOT data were presented in Tables 8-3 – 8-5—and the task-area approach.

The internal vs. external approach

This way is very straightforward. As you can see from the SWOT analyses on the previous pages, the internal vs. external approach organizes the data in two large categories—internal strengths and weaknesses, and external opportunities and threats.

The task area approach

By contrast, the task area approach is designed to help you organize your SWOT around such critical task areas as fund raising, student recruiting, retention, or internal communication.

Table 8-6 focuses on the task area of student recruiting. Of course, your SWOT analysis would include more than one task area. The task area approach also includes a device in the far right column that asks you to indicate whether a strength, weakness, opportunity, or threat is distinctive, demonstrable, or critical. These criteria, or others you could customize for your institution, situation, and needs, are designed to help you identify SWOT that might be particularly important or helpful.

Both approaches assume that there will more of a distinction between strengths, weaknesses, opportunities, and threats than there often really is. Keep in mind that these grids are designed to help you organize and weigh the relative value of the data and perceptions you have collected. Use the grid to guide your thinking, but don't let it force you to overcategorize data. It is perfectly reasonable for data or an idea or a concern to be placed in more than one category. Keep in mind that it is more important at this stage to be inclusive rather than exclusive and that categories are less important than content.

Table 8-6
Task-Area SWOT Analysis

	Task Area: Recruiting	
Strengths	1.	☐ Distinctive ☐ Critical ☐ Demonstrable
	2.	☐ Distinctive ☐ Critical ☐ Demonstrable
	3.	☐ Distinctive ☐ Critical ☐ Demonstrable
	4.	☐ Distinctive ☐ Critical ☐ Demonstrable
Weaknesses	1.	☐ Distinctive ☐ Critical ☐ Demonstrable
	2.	☐ Distinctive ☐ Critical ☐ Demonstrable
	3.	☐ Distinctive ☐ Critical ☐ Demonstrable
	4.	☐ Distinctive ☐ Critical ☐ Demonstrable
Opportunities	1.	☐ Distinctive ☐ Critical ☐ Demonstrable
	2.	☐ Distinctive ☐ Critical ☐ Demonstrable
	3.	☐ Distinctive ☐ Critical ☐ Demonstrable
	4.	☐ Distinctive ☐ Critical ☐ Demonstrable
Threats	1.	☐ Distinctive ☐ Critical ☐ Demonstrable
	2.	☐ Distinctive ☐ Critical ☐ Demonstrable
	3.	☐ Distinctive ☐ Critical ☐ Demonstrable
	4.	☐ Distinctive ☐ Critical ☐ Demonstrable

Ballots, please

At this stage, your list of strengths, weaknesses, opportunities, and threats is probably very long and cumbersome—and you probably do not have the institutional resources to address every item on your list.

To solve this problem, I suggest that you use the SWOT list as a ballot and let team members vote on which items are most important.

The voting process works like this. Every team member gets a number of votes—say 12. The member can use three for each SWOT category. Members can give all three of their votes to one item, give one item two votes and another just one vote, or give one vote to three different items.

This voting accomplishes several important tasks. First, it sets priorities in the SWOT list. Second, because some additions to the list were not unanimous, the voting allows a final group evaluation. And third, because the voting is done in secret, individuals are protected from group dynamics and pressure. The SWOT is then retabulated on the basis of the votes. This new, prioritized list reflects the strengths, weaknesses, opportunities, and threats of most significance to the marketing team. A prioritized SWOT may look like Table 8-7.

Political realities

As part of SWOT analysis, the marketing team must determine how candid it wishes to be. Some campus climates can tolerate more frankness than others.

Let me give you two examples. I was helping a small college in Kansas work through a SWOT analysis. The marketing team was using a large white board in the administrative suite next to the president's office. The team was very reluctant to write

Table 8-7.
Prioritized SWOT Analysis

Strengths	Weaknesses	Opportunities	Threats
Faculty credentials and emphasis on teaching	High cost vs. perceived value	Improved retention	Declining annual fund participation
Location	Low endowment	Improve alumni involvement in recruiting and fund raising	Stalled capital campaign
Commitment to customer service	Campus climate: anger and apathy	Transfer market	Increased competition from publics and privates for prospective students
Many credible alumni	Little institutional image, especially in emerging recruiting markets	Adult market	Tuition gap between publics and privates
Facilities	Meager fund-raising ability		Private college competition with more name recognition and financial aid

anything critical or controversial on the board because it feared that the president would pop in at any minute. Our location and the team's reluctance to address critical yet obvious issues was problematic. It was clear that the range and honesty of our discussion were hindered.

At another campus, we had presented the final SWOT to the president. As he read the list of weaknesses we developed, he looked up and chided the marketing team for failing to put administrative leadership down as a weakness. "If we had good leadership," he said, "we wouldn't be in this mess."

Presidential "checkoff"

Now that the final SWOT grid has been assembled, it is time to seek approval from the president and perhaps the senior administrative team. As part of this presentation, it is helpful to provide an overview of the SWOT methodology. Write a short report that notes the definition of a situational analysis and individual SWOT components, who and what groups were surveyed, and how the items were assembled and prioritized. The report should emphasize that the SWOT analysis serves as the foundation for the marketing plan. If the SWOT is wrong or incomplete, the plan will likely be wrong or incomplete as well.

Often, after reviewing the list, the president will ask for some explanation, further detail, or even supporting data. Perhaps he or she will offer additional items for the list or ask that another individual or group be interviewed. These are all signs that the president is actively involved in the SWOT approval and should not be cause for alarm. Of more concern is the president who merely glances at the list and says "OK."

It is important that the team doesn't automatically make the adjustments that the president wants. Challenge his or her thinking. Make sure the president is really focused on major issues that relate to the institution's ability to improve its market position. Finally, though, settle on a SWOT that the president can support both politically and budgetarily.

It is very important that the president not only understand the prioritized SWOT but approve it before the next step in the planning can be undertaken.

> "Make sure the president is really focused on major issues that relate to the institution's ability to improve its market position."

After approval

After the president approves the SWOT analysis, it should be cleaned up and added to the marketing plan notebook being created by the team secretary. This will be the third component of the marketing plan, following the mission statement and the president's vision of success.

Step 14: Settle on vivid descriptors

Now that the situational analysis has been approved, it is time to begin clarifying your vivid descriptors and points of pride. A vivid descriptor is something for which you want to be known. It is the answer to this question:

When people hear your institution's name, what image do we want to pop into their minds?

Initial answers to this question were gathered as part of the SWOT analysis. However, it is also useful to consider answers to this question in light of your primary competition, the nature of your marketplace, and even your target audiences.

Because the vivid descriptors become a key component of your message flow to target audiences, they must have three qualities. First, they must represent core institutional values. Second, they must be widely shared and appreciated by key campus and external constituencies. And third, they must be enduring—something to which the institution can commit for a long period of time.

One point about vivid descriptors is somewhat confusing. Many people feel that vivid descriptors should be unique, and if they are, that's certainly helpful. But more important than being unique is that the descriptors be mission-critical and of value to your target audiences.

As you think about your vivid descriptors, they may well be "mixed," much like your four Ps. For example, donors may be more interested in some of the descriptors than students.

Sample vivid descriptors

Let's look at list of vivid descriptors developed by a public four-year institution in Texas. In response to the question "for what do we want to be known," the institution settled on the following vivid descriptors:

- A caring, supportive campus culture
- High-quality faculty, facilities, programs, and graduates
- A valuable economic, cultural, and intellectual asset to the region

Another institution, this one a public in Utah, wanted to be known for:

- Small classes
- Undergraduate focus
- Leadership in and partnership with the community
- Access to faculty
- Curriculum focused on real-world issues

A private institution in Ohio wanted to be known for:

- Respect of students, faculty, staff, alumni, donors, and the community
- Service to students
- Timely graduation
- Academic programs that lead to jobs

Creating a list of vivid descriptors involves looking in and looking out. They must reflect who you are as an institution. At the same time, they must also meet the needs and expectations of the marketplace.

The process for developing a list of vivid descriptors is not unlike the process for establishing your initial and then prioritized SWOT grid. There should be discussion, research, debate, and synthesis.

Often, the same survey and focus-group instruments used to gather initial SWOT data can be used to create the list of vivid descriptors. In fact, if you look at the list of potential SWOT questions presented in the section on asking and answering, you will find that the last question is specifically designed to help you develop a comprehensive list of vivid descriptors.

As we learned while developing the SWOT grid, it is not essential that everyone on the marketing team agree with the inclusion of every vivid descriptor. Remember, the same balloting process used to create the SWOT analysis can be used to evaluate the efficacy of individual descriptors.

As you gather and evaluate potential vivid descriptors, remember to keep their number as small as possible. Five or six descriptors is usually more than adequate. Any more and the list becomes unmanageable.

It is also important that the list of descriptors serve the entire institution—not just recruiting. Good descriptors and points of pride can also have a catalytic effect on fund raising and alumni relations.

Third, try to develop a list of descriptors that have the potential to differentiate you from your competition. Vivid descriptors should be just that—vivid. If they are too similar to those used by the competition, you have lost an important opportunity to distinguish yourself in the marketplace.

Finally, don't be afraid to launch some trial balloons with internal and external constituents. There is nothing wrong with asking potential donors or prospective students, for example, what they think of your list of vivid descriptors. Pretesting the relevance and efficacy of these descriptors with potential target audiences is a smart move.

Get the nod

Like the SWOT grid, the list of vivid descriptors must be presented to the president for her or his approval. After he or she approves them, it is time to begin developing your marketing goals. Before doing that, however, add the list of vivid descriptors to your marketing planning notebook. You have just completed the fourth component of your marketing plan.

Step 15: Establish marketing goals

The next step in the creation of your marketing plan is to coalesce the SWOT grid into a cogent set of manageable marketing goals.

Some may prefer to skip to the creation of a list of target audiences in Step 16 and then outline the marketing goals. It really doesn't matter which you do first. Marketing goals and target audiences are a chicken-and-egg kind of issue. It's hard to know which comes first, but the practical reality is that you need both before you can proceed with writing marketing action plans.

As we learned in the introduction to this chapter, a marketing goal is something you wish to accomplish. Sometimes called an objective, a good marketing goal is designed to build on a strength, address a weakness, realize an opportunity, or neutralize a threat.

Sample marketing goals might include these:

- Increase annual fund participation from 57 percent to 70 percent over five years.
- Increase the number of freshmen from our primary draw from 385 to 425 over the next three years.
- Raise the first-year to second-year retention rate from 76 percent to 85 percent over three years.

Characteristics of good marketing goals

Good marketing goals have specific characteristics that make them easier to conceptualize, achieve, and evaluate. Good marketing goals are:

- Important, usually based on your institution's mission and vision;
- Derived from your prioritized situational analysis;
- Founded on research;
- Realistic and achievable;
- As quantifiable as possible;
- Unambiguous and narrowly focused; and
- Usually directed at one or more clearly defined target audiences.

> **"One tangible goal of marketing is that it changes the behavior of people."**

Good marketing goals are important and usually based on your institution's mission and vision. Because marketing often means the reallocation of institutional resources, the marketing goal must be of sufficient importance to justify the effort.

Marketing goals should be derived from the prioritized institutional analysis. If the genesis of the goal cannot be found in your SWOT, either the SWOT was not complete or the goal needs some other rationale for inclusion.

Good marketing goals are also founded on research. Research not only helps shape the marketing goal but provides the necessary baseline data so you can effectively measure progress in meeting the goal. Additionally, marketing goals should be as quantifiable as possible. If you can't quantify, it will be very difficult to evaluate your progress.

Marketing goals are realistic and achievable. Nothing is more frustrating to a marketing team and campus community than a set of marketing goals that are clearly beyond their reach.

Marketing goals should also be unambiguous and narrowly focused. The descriptive terminology should be clearly defined, and the intent of the goals should be obvious.

Well-developed marketing goals are also directed at one or more target audiences. Remember, one tangible goal of marketing is that it changes the behavior of people.

Sample marketing goals

Let's look at some sample marketing goals as they were presented in their marketing plans. Consider these goals from a private liberal arts college in the Midwest:

1. Increase endowment.
2. Maintain enrollment.
3. Establish the college as a cultural, economic, and intellectual resource in key market areas.
4. Improve physical plant.
5. Develop a timely, accurate internal and external communication strategy.

Goals from a public university in the East include these:

1. Institutionalize the marketing function within the university.
2. Increase overall student enrollment.
3. Develop and use a family of video products to recruit students.
4. Develop an integrated marketing information system to assess and market the university.
5. Further refine and develop the university's positioning.
6. Develop and implement a comprehensive advertising strategy.
7. Develop a comprehensive means of tracking customer satisfaction.
8. Encourage and support decentralized marketing-oriented activities within the respective colleges and their departments.

As you look at these goals, several common characteristics become apparent. First, many of them are nonquantitative. Raise the endowment from what to what over what period of time? Increase enrollment from how many to how many? Without specifics, there is no accountability, and the goals will be difficult if not impossible to evaluate.

Second, people sometimes confuse goals with strategies. For example, the public university in the East has as a goal the hiring of a marketing director. Actually, the goal is to strengthen marketing within the institution. One strategy, then, is to hire a director. That same institution has as an action the creation of a comprehensive advertising strategy. This is correctly identified as a strategy or action to accomplish the goal of developing a strong institutional image or perhaps enhancing enrollment.

Third, notice the different emphases of these two sets of goals. The first set embraces a larger set of institutional needs and priorities and appears to be tightly bound to the strategic plan. I suspect these goals were developed by a campus-wide marketing team. The second set, however, is much more narrowly focused on student recruiting and retention. I suspect these goals were developed by a committee of people who work in these areas almost exclusively. These goals are more tactical and technical and do not have the same spirit demonstrated in the first set.

Now let's look at some marketing goals from a private institution in the West:

1. We will raise undergraduate enrollment by 20 percent, from 3,800 to 4,560, over the next six years.

2. We will increase freshman-to-sophomore retention from 63 percent to 75 percent over five years.

3. We will establish a campus culture that stresses the following qualities:
   - Outstanding academic quality
   - Programs and instruction that lead to jobs and graduate school
   - A friendly, safe, fun, and nurturing campus that stresses participation and individual responsibility and accountability
   - The economic, cultural, and social impact our institution has made and will continue to make in the region

4. We will establish a strong institutional image that focuses on a 150-mile radius. This image will stress the qualities outlined in Goal 3.

5. We will develop a comprehensive customer-service program that embraces prospective and current students, faculty, staff, administrators, and visitors to the campus.

6. We will increase annual fund participation from 39 percent to 50 percent over three years, and increase the average contribution from $22 to $45.

These goals are different for a number of important reasons. First, they all begin with "we." This is a small but significant point. The institution is stating from the beginning that these are our goals—not merely the goals of the marketing team.

Second, the tone of these goals is invigorating. There is a sense of mission and vision here. These goals are strategic and far-reaching.

Third, as much as is reasonably possible, these goals are built on baseline data. Enrollment growth and annual fund growth and participation levels are clearly documented. The radius of the institutional image is clearly outlined.

Fourth, these goals are both internal and external. Goal 3 outlines campus values, while Goal 4 stresses the promotion or marketing of these values to external audiences.

Integrating old goals with new ones

It is perfectly acceptable to include in your new marketing plan goals you are already working on, as long as those old goals survive the critical light of the SWOT and still meet the criteria of good marketing goals.

Work from the general to the specific

It is very helpful at this point to work from the general to the specific. I know, for example, that most marketing goals focus on one or more of the following general topic areas:
- Recruiting
- Retention
- Image building
- Fund raising
- Technology enhancement

- Curriculum evaluation and enhancement
- Facilities planning
- Customer service

I often ask clients to establish a general list like this from their SWOT. At this stage I am not interested in the nuances and subtleties of exact goals; rather, I want to help establish the range of goals they are considering. Once the general list of goals is developed, it is relatively easy to define goals in greater detail. This is an enormously effective way to establish the rough list of goals quickly and to keep up momentum.

Don't worry about wordsmithing

As you establish your list, it is tempting to debate and craft the exact, final wording of each one. If you do this, you're sure to lose momentum while getting bogged down by terms and definitions. At this stage, focus on the big concepts and themes and try to leave the wordsmithing until the general list is developed.

Keep the number of marketing goals manageable

As you assemble the goals, let me offer three quick final reminders. First, keep the number of goals as small as possible. As a start, I suggest no more than five or six. Any more and you run the risk of too large and cumbersome a plan. The only time to consider more goals is if you already have some experience with marketing plans and/or your SWOT analysis clearly indicates that you need more goals.

Second, try to keep the goals straightforward and universally accepted. If you can, begin with goals that most campus constituents believe should be accomplished. Not only will this help win initial acceptance of the plan, but it will allow you to gain experience and credibility you can use later as you seek to address more complex, perhaps controversial goals.

And finally, consider the timing. It is sometimes wise to implement some goals earlier in the plan and hold some until later. A good marketing plan is designed to run for five or more years. During the first couple of years, focus on goals that most constituents feel positive about. This will help you gain both credibility and momentum.

Underpromise and overdeliver

Remember, among some stakeholders, particularly those critical of the marketing process, you and your marketing plan are much more likely to be judged by what you failed to accomplish than by what you did accomplish.

The goal-approval process

Just as you sought approval for the SWOT grid and the vivid descriptors, you must now seek the president's buy-in for your list of marketing goals.

As you discuss the list of marketing goals with your president, keep in mind the following.

First, these goals represent a long-term commitment. Chances are your institution will be working with these goals for at least five years—probably longer. They deserve careful thought, even debate, before they are accepted.

Second, these marketing goals are a logical and obvious extension of the president's vision. He or she should be able to see clearly how they advance the institution's vision of success. If the vision cannot be seen in the marketing goals, something is wrong.

Third, goals clearly set a direction. By default, they also outline directions not taken. Fourth, these goals represent the likelihood of significant, usually very significant, financial expenditures. Often the funding of these goals will call for reallocation from elsewhere around campus. The goals must be of sufficient value to both the institution and the president so he or she is willing to face those battles confident of their importance.

One note: Early in the planning process the president committed to a rough budget. If in your opinion the goals he or she approves at this stage will require an appreciably larger budget, you must mention this. Failure to do so will greatly hinder your ability to capture the necessary dollars later in the planning process. It is better to have the president commit to a new amount now—when excitement is running high—than to try to get a new budget commitment later. If possible, get this commitment in writing from either the president or the chief finance officer. I have learned the hard way that memories often fail and priorities shift when it comes to the delivery of promised funds.

And finally, these goals also represent a commitment of time and prestige. They are a very obvious and very public declaration of intent.

Tweaking

In all likelihood the president will ask for a change or two in your list of goals. Perhaps he will question how they were prioritized or times set; maybe she wants some different wording. In most cases these changes are easily accommodated. However, if the president calls for major changes that seem to counter the previously approved SWOT grid, you have a problem. The marketing champion needs to have a private meeting with the president to discuss his or her reasoning, degree of commitment to the planning process, and degree of commitment to funding the plan once it is finished.

After the marketing goals have been approved, add them to the marketing planning notebook. This is the fifth component of the marketing plan.

Step 16: Clarify target audiences

For our purposes, a target audience is the person or group whose behavior or attitude you wish to change or whom you wish to influence or inform. Table 8-8 shows some oft-targeted audiences in higher education.

Table 8-8.
Potential Target Audiences

Students	College or University	External: Fund raising	External: Other
Current students	Faculty	Current donors: major	Parents
Prospective undergraduate, graduate, and continuing-education students	Staff	Current donors: minor	Legislators
Inquiring students	Administrators	Former donors	Church leaders
Applicants	Alumni	Prospective donors	Community residents
Matriculants	Trustees	Foundations	Community leaders
Nonmatriculants			Business leaders
Withdrawing students			High school contacts
Students of color			Media
International students			

Take the time to define your target audiences carefully. For example, if you include faculty, are you including part-timers as well as full-timers? If you are going to focus on alumni, do you include those alumni who didn't earn a degree as well as those who did?

As you think about potential target audiences, review Chapter 6. Chances are one of the segmenting strategies outlined there will help you define target audiences more critically.

The big questions

You will probably quickly find yourself with 15 to 20 likely candidates. This is OK—for now. After you establish this initial list, ask yourself the following questions. Of these audiences, which ones . . .

- Have you defined as critically as possible?
- Were consistently highlighted in the situational analysis?
- Have the most potential to advance the vision significantly?
- Are you able to realistically serve?
- Reside in your primary recruiting region?
- Are most advanced on the six-stage behavioral matrix?
- Are merely loud and persistent rather than truly important?

Qualify, qualify, qualify

As you and your marketing team think through the answers to these questions, you'll find yourself paring your list of target audiences. Ideally, you want to emerge with a list of five to seven, with each audience highly qualified according to one or more of

Table 8-9.
Qualification Variables

Target Audience	Qualification
Prospective students	Fit academic profile or profile to which you aspire, including segment of full- and fuller-pay students. Focus on students in primary and secondary recruiting regions.
Current students	Students who fit the profile of your graduates—those most likely to persist.
Faculty and staff	Not just full-time faculty, but part-time and adjunct faculty as well. All staff, especially those who interact with students or such key external constituencies as donors, community residents, or media.
Opinion leaders	Often called "movers and shakers." These people include not only the historic power structure in a community or region but the emerging power structure as well. Your development office should have identified these people.
Donors	Have a history or potential of giving. Have access to resources or to a person or entity that has resources.
Alumni	All alumni are important, but you should focus on those who fit one or more of these categories: alumni 1) who help you recruit, 2) who donate or have the clear potential to donate, 3) who have access to corporate wealth or power, 4) who participate in alumni activities, and 5) who are notable or powerful. Ideally your marketing strategies will help you move alumni to one or more of these categories.
Educational, science, business, and sports editors, writers, and reporters	You are not interested in all media—only the specific subsets that cater to a particular aspect of your institution. Breaking the media down into types makes them much easier to conceptualize and deal with.

the variables outlined in Table 8-9.

Sample target audiences

A private, church-related institution in Iowa targeted the following audiences in its marketing plan:

- Prospective college students
- Parents of prospective students
- Media
- Alumni and friends
- Business and professional leaders
- The general public

A large public institution in Ohio created this list:

- Prospective undergraduate, graduate, and continuing education students

- Parents of traditional-age prospective students
- High school influencers—guidance counselors, teachers, club advisers
- Community residents within 75 miles of the institution
- The education, business, sports, and science press
- Alumni
- Donors

Obtain approval

As with the SWOT, vivid descriptors, and marketing goals, you must now ask the president to approve your list of target audiences. This is the sixth component of the marketing plan.

Step 17: Write marketing action plans

The next step in the planning process is to create strategies or marketing action plans that will help you accomplish your goals. If goals are what you want done and target audiences are the people at whom goals are directed, then the marketing action plan is the means by which goals are accomplished.

In essence, the marketing action plan, or MAP, is a simple device that tells who will be doing what as you execute strategies. Consider, for example, the following goal:

> **Increase freshman-to-sophomore retention from 66 percent to 75 percent over five years**

This goal is straightforward, has clear definitions, and is eminently quantifiable. To accomplish this goal we develop marketing action plans that will be directed at the following four target audiences:

- Freshmen
- Faculty
- Staff
- Parents

After establishing the goal and target audiences, let's outline a handful of action-plan topics that will help accomplish the marketing goal:

- Define retention appropriately for each type of student—traditional, nontraditional, and graduate—and use this definition consistently.
- Conduct extensive research of current students' needs and expectations and of why students withdraw.
- Develop a more effective freshman orientation program.
- Target at-risk students.
- Implement a mentoring program.
- Create a profile of students who are more likely to persist in the funnel.
- Document to faculty the dollar and nondollar cost of each lost student.

Quick Glance

Quick Glance: Goals and Target Audiences
Goals are the things you want done; target audiences are the people whom you hope to affect with your goals. Let's say one of your marketing goals is to improve your institution's image. Because images rest in people's minds, you need to determine the target audiences you wish to influence, persuade, or inform. As you think about target audiences, it is very important to determine where these people live. Often marketing plans struggle because they are directed at too large a geography. One excellent way to get a better sense of your primary marketing geography is to create a map with software such as MapLinx or a geography database such as Access for Windows 97. These software packages will allow you to import the addresses of current students, alumni, and donors onto a single map. By using a different symbol for each group, you can get a clearer sense of where key overlaps occur. This will help you define your marketing geography.

- Offer an honors college with special orientation, advising, programs, scholarships, and privileges.
- Develop aggressive residence-life programs; use residence assistants as part of an early-warning system.
- Implement a campus ombudsman program.
- Discount tuition by five percent for sophomores, juniors, and seniors.
- Offer "one-stop shopping," a place where students can register, pay fees, and deal with financial aid.
- Increase quality of residence life.
- Train, motivate, and reward advisers and make them accountable for their mistakes.

Each of these strategies would be accomplished through the creation of one or more marketing action plans.

Goals, target audiences, and marketing action plans

We have just worked through the creation of a single marketing action plan that will support one marketing goal.

At this point it is important to again affirm the relationship among goals, target audiences, and marketing action plans. Remember:

- One goal can be directed at many audiences. For example, image goals may affect donors, community residents, prospective students, high school influencers, and so on. See Figure 8-1.
- One goal may require multiple marketing action plans, and these may run concurrently and sequentially. Building a strong annual fund, for example, may involve a plan for research that leads, later, to other plans involving communication with alumni donors, alumni events, changes in the alumni magazine, and the like.

Quick Glance

Strategies and Action Plans

A strategy is something you do to help accomplish a goal. A marketing action plan is the same thing as a strategy, though often in more detail. Whereas a strategy may describe what is to be done, a marketing action plan enumerates which goal the strategy is designed to help accomplish and then outlines who will be doing what when. For example, a strategy might be to hold an open house. The action plan would outline who will conduct it, when, what it will entail, how much it will cost, and so on.

Figure 8-1.
Directing Your Goals

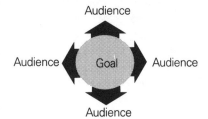

Quick Glance

Marketing Planning Software

I strongly recommend the use of marketing software. Although the bulk of your marketing plan—the mission, vision of success, situational analysis, vivid descriptors, goals, and target audiences—may be developed with a good word-processing package such as Word or WordPerfect, the creation and monitoring of your marketing action plans (MAPs), timelines, and budgets require the use of special planning software such as SureTrack, ManagePro, Fast Track Schedule, or On Target. Good marketing planning software is "linked." For example, it allows you to develop a template that includes the activity, who will do it, timeline, and cost. I can then create one master timeline that includes all the MAPs. Or I can assemble one budget or list all the MAPs that Jennifer or Tom is responsible for. Furthermore, if I make any changes to a MAP such as timing, cost, or who is responsible, that change is made automatically in every part of the plan. Of course, it is possible to create an effective marketing plan using only a word processor. But planning software will save you time. This software has a bit of a learning curve, so be prepared to spend some time figuring out its nuances.

Table 8-10.
Marketing Action Plan

Title of marketing action plan	
Description of the MAP	
Which goal(s) the plan supports	1.
	2.
	3.
	4.
	5.
Target audiences	1.
	2.
	3.
	4.
	5.
Action plan step-by-step	1.
	2.
	3.
	4.
	5.
Timeline	Begin date:
	End date:
Budget	$
	$
	$
	$
	$
MAP assigned to	
Evaluation mechanisms	
When to evaluate	
Who evaluates	
Report results to	

Marketing action plan template

It is useful to develop a standard template for all your marketing action plans. Some templates are fairly simple; others present the MAP in more detail. At minimum, a MAP template needs to describe the activity, when it will begin and end, who will be responsible, and how much it will cost. I have used variations of the template in Table 8-10 with great success.

Let's take a minute to detail a marketing action plan for one of the strategies outlined above: the creation of a mentoring program. See Table 8-11.

Working with action-plan topics

Earlier, when discussing creation of the list of marketing goals, I suggested you work with general goals and leave details and wordsmithing for later. I make this same recommendation here. Creation of your MAPs will proceed much more quickly if you work with MAP titles and avoid detail until later. Once the marketing team has

Table 8-11.
Marketing Action Plan for a Mentoring Program

Title of marketing action plan	Implement a mentoring program
Description of the MAP	The action plan will detail the creation of a mentoring program for entering freshmen.
Which goal(s) the plan supports	1. Increase freshman-to-sophomore retention from 66 percent to 75 percent over five years.
Target audiences	1. Freshmen
Action plan step-by-step	1. Examine mentoring programs at other colleges and universities.
	2. Undertake a literature search to review the pros and cons of mentoring programs.
	3. Discuss initial program concepts with the vice president for student affairs.
	4. Present the preliminary plan, budget, and timeline to senior administrators .
	5. Finalize plan.
	6. Launch the program.
Timeline	Begin date: April 15
	End date (to launch program): August 25
Budget	$1,500 to study programs at other institutions
	$500 for student help for literature review
	$20,000 to fund program for one year
MAP assigned to	Rachel H.
Evaluation mechanisms	Creation of initial plan, implementation of final plan, freshman focus groups, impact of mentoring program on freshman-to-sophomore retention
When to evaluate	May 15– initial program concepts
	June 15– preliminary plan, budget, and timeline
	July 30– finalize plan
	August 25– launch program
Who evaluates	Annette S.
Report results to	Steve K.

assembled the complete range of MAP topics, it can make some preliminary decisions about which MAPs to flesh out.

From software to paper and back to software again

To facilitate MAP creation, I suggest distributing paper copies of the MAP template to each member of the marketing team. Team members, often working with their constituencies, will develop the initial MAPs. The marketing planning team's secretary then assembles these hard copies.

The use of planning software

Let me illustrate the use of planning software. Suppose, for example, our SWOT supports creating two marketing goals:

■ Establish the on- and off-campus visibility of a new president.

■ Increase internal communication.

In response to these goals, the marketing team—or the subset charged with developing action plans for this activity—recommends the following:

■ Create a quarterly monthly newsletter for all faculty and staff.
■ Develop a campus-wide computer bulletin board and update it weekly.
■ Designate a campus ombudsman.
■ Implement a campus suggestion box.
■ Initiate a quarterly president's newsletter to faculty, staff, and students.
■ Write a six-times-yearly president's column for the student newspaper.
■ Implement a twice-yearly "ask senior administrators" brown-bag luncheon.
■ Launch a three-times-yearly audiotape from the president to board members.
■ Launch a twice-yearly audiotape from the president to community movers and shakers.
■ Hold one-on-one meetings with the president for each academic department.
■ Hold an open house at the president's home.
■ Manage by walking around.
■ Develop a topical forum series:
  • Forum 1: The changing marketplace
  • Forum 2: Strategic planning
  • Forum 3: Innovations in education
  • Forum 4: Capital and technology planning

Now let's use planning software to create a MAP template that includes the following:

■ The name of the MAP
■ The name of the person for completing the MAP
■ The cost of completing the MAP
■ The date it will be completed

With planning software, it is easy to assemble the details of individual MAPs so that you can more completely keep track of who is doing what, when. For example, let's consider a plan to enhance the image of a new president. See Figure 8-2.

Using planning software, we have developed a plan that will run for one academic year. As you can see in Figure 8-2, marketing action plan variables include:

■ Activity name
■ Manager (of that activity)
■ Cost
■ Start date
■ Finish date

Planning software easily coordinates the action-plan variables. More importantly, it also allows you to sort plan activities by cost, start date, or end date. For example, you could pull up all the activities that cost more than $1,500 or are scheduled to be completed in the first half of the academic year.

In addition, good planning software allows you to print individual GANTT* charts for each activity manager. For example, you could print out a calendar that includes only activities that Gwen is undertaking. See Figure 8-3.

And finally, planning software allows you to summarize all MAPs on one page, thereby giving a quick overview of the entire plan.

All good planning software includes a provision for tracking dollars. Some software also keeps a running tally on dollars spent and reminds you if projects are running ahead or behind budget.

Even the most basic software plots on a calendar when each action plan will be accomplished. By simply moving the symbol of the activity, you may change when something is to occur. Furthermore, by moving the timing symbol on the GANTT chart, you change all references to that activity everywhere in the plan.

The calendar function of planning software also allows you to display and print any portions of the plan you wish. For example, you can print the MAPs for July, one quarter (July, August, and September), an entire year, or multiple years.

Figure 8-2.
GANTT Chart

---

* A GANTT chart is a chronological overview of a series of activities in which each is represented as a bar or symbol on a calendar. GANTT charts allow you to see at a glance when everything is happening.

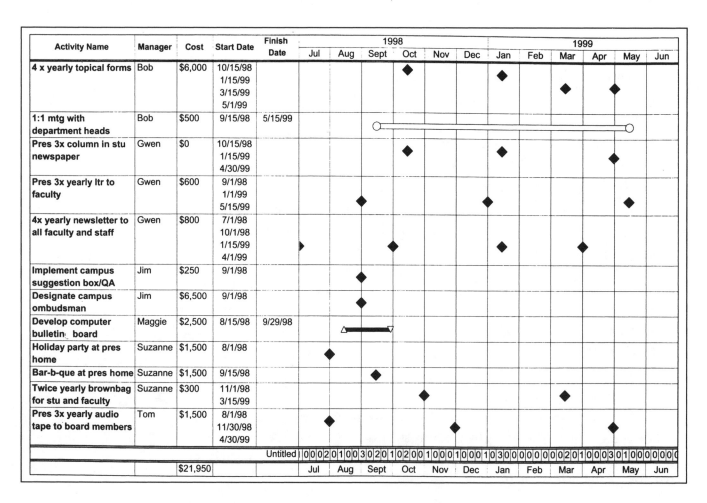

Activity Name	Manager	Cost	Start Date	Finish Date	1998						1999					
					Jul	Aug	Sept	Oct	Nov	Dec	Jan	Feb	Mar	Apr	May	Jun
Pres 3x column in stu newspaper	Gwen	$0	10/15/98 1/15/99 4/30/99					◆			◆			◆		
Pres 3x yearly ltr to faculty	Gwen	$600	9/1/98 1/1/99 5/15/99				◆				◆				◆	
4x yearly newsletter to all faculty and staff	Gwen	$800	7/1/98 10/1/98 1/15/99 4/1/99		▶		◆				◆		◆			
				Untitled	0000	0000	1000	101	0000	0000	0001 0 2 000	0000	0000 1000	101	0000	0000
		$1,400			Jul	Aug	Sept	Oct	Nov	Dec	Jan	Feb	Mar	Apr	May	Jun

Figure 8-3.
GANTT Chart for Individual Activity Manager

Step 18: Establish budget

The next step in the marketing planning process is to create a rough budget. Table 8-12 outlines a few resource allocation strategies, some good and some not so good: The worst resource allocation strategies ignore the planning process, are haphazard and arbitrary. The best, however, are planning-based and focus on institutional priorities. The worst are based on anecdotal data and impressions, while the best are based on mission, vision, and research.

A reasonable budgeting process

Two variables must be reconciled as part of the budgeting process: the rough budget established by your president at the outset, and the dollars required to accomplish the assembled MAPs.

With luck, these two amounts won't be too different. Chances are, though, that your MAPs require more money than your president anticipated. If this is the case, you must begin to make your case for more dollars. Thankfully, you will enter this discussion with two important assets: Your chief finance officer has been involved in the planning process, and the president has approved, as the plan progressed, the SWOT, goals, and target audiences.

Before discussing the actual budget, work carefully with the president through the SWOT, marketing goals, and target audiences that he or she previously approved. Show how the MAPs are designed to accomplish the marketing goals and, by extension, help achieve the president's vision.

If some of the goals and action plans will help increase revenue through the annual fund, a capital campaign, or tuition, give some reasonable projections. Remind the president that although the plan represents a multiyear commitment, chances are that plan expenditures will decrease once its effect begins to be felt. It is generally less expensive to maintain marketing efforts than to start them.

Even with the most ardent support of your president, you will probably have to go back and trim the budget. As you do so, focus on the prioritized marketing goals. Make every effort to preserve dollars, and the activities they represent, in the areas that matter most to the institution.

Table 8-12.
Resource Allocation Strategies

Worst Resource Allocation Strategies

Spend what you spent last year.

Match the competition.

Rely on consultant's suggestions.

Rely on vendor bids.

Determine what new efforts cost, and respond only if additional funding is available.

Assign resources to what we feel is important and we enjoy doing.

Best Resource Allocation Strategies

Develop a strategic marketing plan that links goals, strategies, and tactics to desired outcomes.

Determine annual plan that links priorities to results and resources.

Focus on 20/80s and not 80/20s (meaning the 20 things that accomplish 80 percent of your goals rather than the 80 things that accomplish 20 percent).

Evaluate, reprioritize, and reallocate.

Source: Laurence Smith, Eastern Michigan University

Remember one of the fundamental rules of budgeting: Put a little extra in earlier so you can take a little more out later.

Budgeting hints

With tight resources strangling most campuses, budgeting and cost issues will not go away, especially when marketing dollars are increasingly reallocated from other institutional sources. Although there are no absolutes to help you budget realistically, several guidelines will help.

First, consider the levels of image difficulty and budget accordingly. It is easiest and least expensive to maintain an already good image. It is more expensive to create a strong image. And it is most expensive to change a bad image.

Second, remember that as your image strategies begin to work, you can scale back their intensity. Once the image is established, it takes fewer dollars and less effort to maintain it.

Third, hire good people. To save a few dollars, institutions sometimes hire inexperienced people to execute their marketing strategies. This is false economy. Though you may save on salaries, the mistakes, missed deadlines, and lost opportunities will cost you dearly. I recommend biting the budgetary bullet and hiring people with experience. The knowledge and understanding of seasoned professionals will make these people a bargain.

Fourth, support your plan with an adequate budget. It is far better to do fewer things well than to try to do a multitude of things poorly. Rather than underfund high school visits so you can place limited advertising, it is probably better to halt advertising and spend the money necessary to visit priority high schools.

Fifth, manage the marketing plan. Remember the college that overspent its video production budget by 50 percent—then had a wonderful video but no money to duplicate or distribute it.

Finally, establish solid, measurable marketing goals and evaluate progress through systematic market research.

Step 19: Debug the plan

The final step is to debug the plan. Review each component. Make sure the SWOT is complete. Clarify that the goals are well-conceived and important. Working from the individual and collective MAPs and the assembled GANTT charts, evaluate the following:

- Are you spending 80 percent of your time and resources on the 20 most important activities?
- Is every MAP clearly supporting a goal? If it isn't, take it out or at least highlight it for cutting if a budget crunch occurs
- Is the viability of each MAP clearly borne out in the SWOT?

■ Has enough time been allocated for each MAP? Remember, things take longer the first time through.

■ Are the budgeted dollars realistic? If not, costs will cartwheel out of control.

■ Are too few people doing too many things? All major administrative departments should be involved in executing action plans.

■ Are first things being done first? Do what needs to be done now so that other things can be done later.

■ Are early MAPs primed for success? For morale and political reasons, make sure some of your early MAPs are highly successful and highly visible.

If your MAPs survive after you ask and answer these questions, you have gone a long way to developing a sound series of MAPs. Because you have used planning software, you can also run a total budget and timeline. When these are done, add them to the marketing planning notebook. Congratulations, you've written a marketing plan. Now it's time to put it into action.

9

Execution and Evaluation

Whereas Chapter 8 worked carefully through the steps required to actually write the marketing plan, this chapter will give you insights into executing and evaluating your plan and help you develop a strategy for refining the ongoing planning process.

In this chapter we will address the following three steps:

- Execute the plan.
- Evaluate and modify the plan.
- Hold a planning postmortem.

Step 20: Execute the plan

As you look at your completed plan, you will probably feel a bit anxious about implementing it. Before you panic, reconsider the master calendar you just assembled. The master calendar is more than a summary of all your marketing activities; it is a chronological guide of what should be done and when. By following your calendar, you keep the execution of the plan on time and on target.

The use of planning software

If you used planning software to assemble the plan, executing it will be even easier.

Planning software such as OnTarget, ManagePro, or Fast Track Schedule will allow you to establish "tickles" for each MAP. Rather than waiting for the due date, you can program your plan's software to remind you to check on specific MAPs at whatever point in their development you choose. Let's say that a MAP for creating a media database requires the following four steps to be accomplished over a two-month period:

■ Choose software.
■ Design database template.
■ Gather media directories.
■ Input data.

Software will allow you to monitor whether the person responsible for the action plan has completed each step, or it can remind you to check the person's progress at the halfway point. It will also allow you to organize MAPs by individual or by due date.

The key to keeping things on schedule is to not let a few missed deadlines derail the entire plan. In many respects, monitoring the execution of a marketing plan is similar to serving as an air-traffic controller. Most action plans will run on time. Some may be delayed, postponed, or rescheduled. And every now and then, for the good of the entire plan, you might have to cancel a MAP or two.

Most of the time, executing the plan is just this simple. Keep in mind, though, that a good marketing plan is fluid. Though it must have enough structure so people know what is happening, it must also be able to accommodate, even anticipate, changes and opportunities. You must always be willing to sacrifice existing MAPs if an even bigger opportunity . . . or crisis . . . arises.

Step 21: Evaluate and modify the plan

Types of evaluation

As you begin to execute the marketing plan, you are also beginning to evaluate and modify it. Evaluation occurs along two dimensions. First, you might evaluate whether a MAP is on schedule or completed and whether it ran on, under, or over budget. This is evaluation at its most basic.

However, you must also be prepared to determine whether the MAP helped accomplish the overarching goal or goals and even whether the goals themselves have been accomplished. This is a higher order, more complex type of evaluation.

As in the completion of a single MAP, you might assume at least at one level that if all the MAPs are completed, the goal was accomplished. However, even if you accomplish all your MAPs, you may or may not have accomplished your goal. This requires a different level of evaluation.

Measuring progress against the baseline

If your marketing goals are quantifiable and built on baseline data, it is relatively easy to measure progress. Consider the following example. In 1996, some 26 percent of your alumni contribute to the annual fund. One of your marketing goals is to increase that figure to 43 percent over three years. Action plans to help the institution meet this goal will be implemented.

Now let's skip ahead to 1999. We discover that this year 46 percent of alumni contributed to the annual fund. Was the goal accomplished? Of course. This example outlines the utility of baseline data. Without concrete baseline data to show where you started, it will be very difficult to evaluate progress. At the same time, your goals should be as quantified as possible. Without quantifiable goals, measuring progress will always be a guess at best.

Adding and modifying action plans

The ongoing evaluation may also lead you to the realization that action plans sometimes need to be added or modified. The odds are great that you, someone from the marketing planning team, or someone else on campus will have a great idea for a new action plan or whole series of action plans long after the plan is complete. This is OK. Remember, the written plan is less important than the planning process that accommodates this kind of modification.

Changing needs and priorities

Action plans and goals must be evaluated and sometimes modified in light of changing institutional needs and priorities. It is very important for the institution to develop ongoing mechanisms to evaluate changes and trends in the marketplace. A successful planning process recognizes the need for continued monitoring of internal and external marketing circumstances even after the plan is written.

Keeping track of dollars

Earlier we saw the need to monitor budgets. Again, good planning software will help track spent and unspent dollars. The ability to monitor costs is also useful if you notice that an important action plan or series of them is running over budget and you need to shift dollars from other, perhaps less important, action plans.

I know from experience that it is a much better management strategy to shift dollars within the plan than to ask for more money. This is especially true early in the plan's execution. After you have a record of success, it will be easier to ask for more money.

Keep raising the bar

One final thought about evaluation. You will find that the best goals are always a little bit beyond your reach. For example, let's say your goal is to increase retention from 45 percent to 60 percent over three years. After executing a number of MAPs, you find you've accomplished that. However, it is never a good strategy to rest on this accomplishment. Instead, after a period, raise the goal.

Asking the big question

Although achieving quantifiable goals is extraordinarily important, the overall success of your marketing plan can be evaluated, in part, by answering this question:

Has the financial condition of the college or university improved since it began marketing?

Some people will find this question overly simplistic, even crass. But think about it. Most marketing goals have as their logical end the improvement of the college or university's financial condition. You recruit more students because of the revenue they bring. You attract excellent faculty because they will attract better students and more grant money. Stronger images attract more students and donors. Satisfied students stay longer. Happy alumni contribute more. Tightening bonds with a local community will help preserve the flow of resources.

Is this oversimplified? Sure. But the point is an important one. One way to measure the overall effectiveness of your marketing plan is to see whether the institution is better off afterward than before.

Step 22: Hold a planning postmortem

Once the plan is under way and you have had a chance to reflect on the progress of individual MAPs and the overall planning process, it is time to hold a planning postmortem. The postmortem is designed to help you evaluate the process you just completed so your next planning cycle will be more effective and efficient.

There is no prescriptive postmortem process. The goal is to gather as much insight and information as possible. To this end, it is often best to begin with the president, the senior administrators, or both.

Begin at the top

After the plan has been under way for a period, ask the president how she or he feels about the planning process and the resulting plan. Was the president comfortable with her or his role? Was the budgeting method sensitive to other campus needs? Was the approval process well-engineered? Did the overall process live up to the president's expectations? What would he or she like done differently the next time around? Ask good questions. Listen closely. And probe.

Query the planning team

As part of the postmortem, it is also a good idea to spend time with the planning team. Take members out to lunch and query them about the planning process. What did they like and not like? What would they do differently? What do they wish they could undo? What was their favorite part of the planning process? What part surpassed their expectations? What part did they like least? Was enough time spent on each step; was too much time spent? How did the process affect their interaction with colleagues not directly involved?

Discuss each step. Focus on how the processes associated with each step could have been improved. Ask questions like these:

■ Was the process empowered correctly? Did it have the support of the campus community?

■ Did the team understand the purpose and communicate it to internal constituencies?

■ Was the right champion chosen?

■ Were the right people on the team? Who should be on the next team?

■ Did the team function as a team—or a committee?

■ Were planning relationships and terminology understood?

■ Did the team and the campus agree on and understand the unchangeables?

■ Did the team and the campus establish a range of possibilities?

■ Did the team make the correct decision to stay inside or go outside?

■ Was the planning process workable?

■ Was the SWOT analysis comprehensive enough? Too comprehensive? Did the process solicit enough input and provide adequate opportunity for synthesis? Did anyone feel left out?

■ Did the team have solid data with which to work?

■ Was the process for finalizing and prioritizing the SWOT appropriate?

■ Are the vivid descriptors relevant, reflective of the institution, and important?

■ Are the marketing goals significant? Will they unify the campus? Will they move it forward? Are they achievable?

■ Are the target audiences clearly defined? Is there consensus that they're important to the institution's future?

■ Are the MAPs well-conceived, focused on the marketing goals, well-timed, and well-funded?

■ Was all the promised money made available? Is the budget adequate? Is it sustainable over time?

■ Was the plan debugged appropriately? Were decisions made that will improve its performance and impact?

■ Is the plan's execution on time and on target?

■ Are criteria, tools, and procedures in place to modify the plan as it progresses?

And don't forget to ask the team the big question:

■ Was the planning process a good use of your time?

Talk to the campus community

It is also useful to talk to campus constituents. Perhaps working through the team and its liaisons with different groups, seek to answer the following questions:

- Do constituents feel that they were listened to?
- Do they feel sufficiently involved in the process?
- Do they understand the need for planning?
- Do they think their involvement was a good use of their time?
- Do they feel a sense of ownership with the plan?
- Are they committed to the plan and its success?
- Do they feel that things have improved?

And finally:

- Do they feel that marketing is/was a good use of campus resources?

It is always better to succeed with fewer goals than to fail at reaching more.

Section III
Putting It All Together

10

> **"Inch by inch, it's a cinch."**
> —Unknown

Putting It All Together
Some Thoughts and Reflections on Making Your Plan Work

We have come a long way. In Chapter 1, we established the critical case for marketing. Chapters 2 through 6 provided an extensive foundation for marketing by outlining basic and advanced marketing principles, tools, and techniques. Chapters 7, 8, and 9 presented a detailed marketing planning process. Now it is time to conclude.

Lessons learned

I have been helping colleges and universities develop marketing, recruiting, and strategic plans for nearly 20 years. During this time, I have seen dozens and dozens of institutions write and implement marketing plans. Thinking back to all the clients I have helped, I am particularly enamored with the institutions that succeeded, often with scant resources except heart and resolve. It is with some lessons learned from these institutions that I wish to close.

First, don't begin the marketing planning process unless your mandate is clear and widely accepted. The need for marketing must be articulated and understood by all major stakeholders. Whereas marketing may well be top-down, marketing efforts must be quickly assimilated by everyone at the institution. They must understand what marketing is, how it will help the institution—and themselves—and what their role is, not only in the planning process but in implementing the plan.

Generally, there are two ways to gain widespread support for marketing. First, show how changes in the marketplace will have a direct and long-term impact on the livelihood of people on campus. Second, actively involve these people in the marketing planning process. If faculty, staff, and administrators greet the decision to write a marketing plan with "here we go again," the mandate probably has not been made clear or demonstrated convincingly.

Second, administrators and faculty must be willing to make tough decisions. Many people believe, wrongly, that marketing will make problems go away, that resources will be more abundant, that decisions will be less political and choices clearer. This is seldom true, and it is especially not true early in the plan's implementation. Eventually, marketing may clarify options and deliver more resources, but the need to make tough decisions will never go away.

Third, balance the need for input with the need to act. As you proceed, you will quickly become aware of two tensions: the need to gain as much consensus as possible and the need to keep moving.

Although consensus from internal and external audiences is critical, an undue commitment to consensus can stall and even kill the marketing effort. This is especially true when there is confusion between stakeholders and target audiences and when too many groups assume that because they were asked for input, they are also part of the decision-making process. Your best strategy is to seek input from internal and external constituencies as part of situational analysis and perhaps as part of goal clarification.

Fourth, create an effective marketing team—and designate a true champion. Rather than yet another committee or task force, create and enable a marketing team. Keep in mind that talent is more important than title and that performance is more valued than position. Include the people who will actually be involved in implementing the plan, the people who will pay for the plan, and the people, especially as part of the decision-making process, who will have to defend the plan to naysayers of all stripes.

I well remember one marketing team. The seven people in the room were extremely frustrated. The president had "told" them that they were the new marketing team, but none had any interest or real understanding of marketing. All were already overwhelmed by their other duties. Two people were vying to become executive assistant to the president. To top it off, the team's first goal, as mandated by the president, was to cut programs. What a great start.

As you build the team, remember to choose and equip a qualified champion as its leader. The champion must have the respect of the campus community, must demonstrate both a theoretical and a practical understanding of marketing, must have power and clout or access to power and clout, and must be able to lead and motivate people.

The marketing team and the champion must manage the input of the entire campus, must clarify issues and options for the senior decision-makers, and must write a plan that involves the entire campus. And once in a while, perhaps when no one is looking, they should have some fun.

Fifth, make sure everyone is using the same definition of marketing. Will the plan embrace product—what is taught? Will it include price—how much is charged? Will it incorporate place—where you do what you do? Or will it simply focus on promotion—getting the word out?

It is absolutely critical that everyone from the president on down settle on a definition of marketing. I can't tell you how frustrating it is for a marketing team to spend months writing a comprehensive plan only to be told that what the president really had in mind was promotion.

Sixth, begin with solid research and establish baselines. One of the biggest and most costly mistakes colleges and universities make is developing a marketing plan without conducting legitimate market research. They usually decide not to undertake research for two reasons: to save money and to save time. Not surprisingly, because the resulting plan is flawed at its foundation, these institutions usually spend more money and time, often after making very public mistakes, than if they conducted the research in the first place.

Not undertaking market research because you need to save money is false economy. As part of the situational analysis, you must know how prospective students, donors, business leaders, alumni, and others perceive you. You need hard data to make tough decisions. And later, when the decisions turn political, you will be glad you have solid, quantitative data on hand to justify the choices you have made. And remember, good research is more than a focus group or a conversation overheard at an alumni gathering.

As you gather data, seek to establish baselines. Determine quantitatively how you are perceived, how many alumni give, how many students come from Chicago, and the number of first-year students who persist. These baselines are critically important.

Without them it will be very difficult to measure the progress of your marketing efforts.

Seventh, recognize the importance and power of a strong institutional image. After talking to hundreds of students, alumni, donors, and parents, I am convinced that an institution's image is its most important asset. If your institution is well-known and well-respected, prospective students will respond to your search, visit your campus, and apply; donors will give and give more; and you will attract better students, better faculty, and better administrators. Strong images won't make all your problems go away, but they will increase your ability to deal with them effectively.

Eighth, quickly settle on a marketing geography. Most marketing strategies are directed at much too large a geography. Though you may recruit students from and have alumni living in all 50 states and 17 foreign countries, the majority of your students and alumni surely live closer than farther away.

One important way to improve the quality of your marketing efforts quickly is to clarify and narrow your marketing area. Begin by using geographical database software such as Access for Windows 95 or Maplinx to plot, on a map, the following data sets:

- Distribution of current alumni
- Distribution of annual fund contributors
- Distribution of current students
- Distribution of prospective students who fit your profile
- Competing colleges and universities
- Feeder high schools, if applicable
- Feeder religious institutions, if applicable

The resulting map will give you a great deal of insight into the size and vitality of your marketing geography.

As you use these data to evaluate potential marketplaces, keep in mind one final thought: It is always less expensive to market yourself closer to where you are than farther away. Distant big cities and far shores may be enticing, but you will probably win or lose the marketing battle close to home.

Ninth, establish clear, reasonable goals. This is pivotal. Many plans founder under a set of goals that even in the best of circumstances is simply unreachable.

Sometimes it is an issue of funding. A lack of money can mean that even simple marketing goals will go unmet. Sometimes it is an issue of expertise. Even the most basic goals, in the hands of an inexperienced champion, may be elusive. Sometimes, too, it is the sheer number of goals. It is always better to succeed with fewer goals than to fail at reaching more.

As you think about complexity and number of goals, keep a couple of things in mind. First, stagger your goals over a multiyear period. If you are writing a five-year plan, work on a few goals the first year and add others as the plan progresses. Second, make your early goals as universally valued as possible; this will help spread ownership. And third, make sure your goals are truly important. Good goals should have an immediate payoff for fund raising, recruiting, or both. Avoid goals with undue fluff or posturing.

Tenth, develop a handful of simple, valued messages. Several years ago I read an extraordinary book—David Ogilvy's *Olgivy On Advertising*. The author noted that most communication strategies suffer from messages that are too complex or do not include a benefit from the audience's perspective.

Ogilvy's lessons are worth remembering. Successful messages are invariably simple or broken down into simple components that are repeated often. Ogilvy's second lesson is equally important: The message must contain a benefit for the audience. If the audience can't assign a benefit to your message, the message will probably get overlooked. Students are keenly interested in academic quality, but they often define quality differently than institutions do. They want access to faculty and facilities and service. Deans and presidents, however, talk about the size of the library or percentage of faculty with terminal degrees. Certainly these are attributes of academic quality, but are they the only messages your audiences want to hear?

As you can see, crafting messages is a complex yet critically important task. It asks and answers the simple question "for what do you want to be known?" In many respects, this is the essence of marketing; it is certainly the essence of image management and positioning.

For what do you want to be known? What do you want people to think about your institution? What are the four or five words or phrases you want to pop into their minds when they hear your name? Some colleges and universities call these "points of pride." My favorite term is "vivid descriptors." What words and phrases vividly describe you to prospective donors, students, parents, community members, religious leaders, and even legislators?

Eleventh, use a complete media mix. Too often, colleges and universities unnecessarily limit their media mix to publications and a bit of direct mail because they don't understand how to develop a complete media mix.

Earlier, in our discussion of promotion, I noted that promotion involves "marketing" the other three Ps through such avenues as advertising, publications, direct mail, publicity, personal contact, and environmentals. The key, of course, is how these media are mixed. Decisions affecting the mix of your media involve answering these questions:

- Who are our target audiences?

■ What are their values, attitudes, and lifestyles?
■ What are the character and complexity of our messages?
■ Where are our target audiences located?

As you evaluate the appropriateness of media-mix options, I suggest you carefully read the media section of any good book on advertising. This will provide a wealth of information and insight.

Twelfth, use benefit segments. Colleges and universities miss a great opportunity, and undermine their overall marketing strategy, when they fail to recognize that such large audiences as donors or prospective students are actually composed of smaller subgroups that often have very different product, price, place, and promotion needs and expectations. First defining segments and then refining benefits for them is an extremely effective marketing strategy that will have an almost immediate payoff.

Thirteenth, establish a realistic, sustainable marketing budget. One of the greatest challenges I have is helping clients reconcile everything they want to do with the amount of money they have to spend. I am always amazed at how quickly lofty marketing goals dissipate in the harsh light of budget realities. Though marketing may help increase revenues over the long run, this will occur only after initial up-front costs are paid. To reap the fund-raising and recruiting benefits of a stronger image, you must first build that image. Strong academic programs and majors will attract students only after the programs are built and publicized.

Not only must you budget significant dollars; you must make this commitment for a number of years. I have stressed this point a number of times, and it bears mentioning again. It is much better to spend $50,000 a year for five years than $250,000 for only one year. Resist the temptation to go for the big splash. You will have much more impact with a smaller campaign of longer duration.

Unfortunately, many administrators consider marketing dollars "spent" rather than "invested." I once attended a meeting of college and university business officers. One officer introduced me to a colleague, "No Way Ray," and explained that Ray's first response to every request for marketing money was no. Ray was convinced that his job was to safeguard the institution's coffers from the marauders in the marketing office. Ray had even prepared charts that showed how marketing expenditures had increased over the past several years. Unfortunately, Ray had not taken the time to show how much money these marketing efforts had returned to the institution.

Institutions that focus only on dollars spent and don't track how much those dollars return to the institution will never allocate sufficient resources to build and sustain an image and enable a marketing plan. When a friend at a college in the Midwest met resistance to his marketing efforts, he commissioned the business faculty to develop a formula whereby they could estimate how many dollars the marketing efforts brought in. Their study revealed that each dollar spent on marketing (image-building, public relations, advertising, etc.) returned eight dollars to the institution.

Next, remember to evaluate your plan's progress. Sometimes in the push to get things done, the last thing we want to do is find out whether they are working. But evaluating progress, from a resource-management and stewardship point of view, makes sense.

As noted earlier, the best time to think about evaluation is when developing your marketing goals and action plans. If these are quantifiable and built on baseline research, evaluation will be relatively easy.

Obviously, not all goals can be measured. But effective time, money, and staff management requires that you make every attempt to calculate progress.

And finally, don't forget internal marketing. Too often when we think about marketing, we focus only on external audiences. This is a mistake. Your ability to spread ownership of the marketing planning process and the resulting plan will increase dramatically if you remember that some of your most important audiences are internal. Some may find the notion of marketing a bit unsettling. Others will be threatened by changes to their routine or areas of responsibility. Some factions may use the pretext of marketing to advance personal agendas. Others may try to obstruct the process. And the rumors and misinformation will fly.

The only effective countermeasure is a strong internal marketing program—and a chief element must be timely, accurate, continual internal communication. Keeping people informed will go a long way toward winning them over.

Conclusion

The boundary-spanning process

This book was written to help you do more than simply write a marketing plan; it was written to help you develop an ongoing marketing planning process that will allow you to monitor your environment and continually refine your marketing goals and strategies.

After you carefully evaluate the data and insights obtained during the post-mortem, it is time to develop a strategy for continually monitoring your environment. Organizational theorists call this monitoring process "boundary spanning"—a wonderfully descriptive term that means to reach outside your organization to check the pulse of your marketplace.

I suggest three activities as part of your boundary-spanning strategy. First, keep at least a portion of the planning team intact. Not only is the team responsible for evaluating the plan's effectiveness; it is also ideally positioned to coordinate the boundary-spanning activities.

Second, the team should develop and initiate a research cycle such as the one outlined in Chapter 4. Nothing will keep you better informed about changes in your marketplace than a research cycle that systematically monitors constituencies and circumstances.

Third, the team should undertake a portion of the situational analysis each year. As with the research cycle, you might opt to devise a strategy that allows you to review your competition one year, factor demographic changes the second, and evaluate economic and employment trends the third.

Looking forward

Remember, your goal is not simply a marketing plan but a process that continually monitors the environment. It is this ongoing process that constantly measures strengths and weaknesses and assesses opportunities and threats. It is the process that spans the boundary from your institution to its environment. It is the process that synthesizes and sets priorities. It is the process that clarifies options.

At its best, the written marketing plan is an institution's organized, point-in-time response to the situational analysis. A solid planning process, however, recognizes—even anticipates—that the marketplace is fluid and dynamic. Things change, and an ongoing process will help keep the plan on track and on target.

As George Keller reminds us, "college presidents [and colleges] who do not look ahead become prisoners of external forces and surprises, most of them unpleasant." An ongoing marketing planning process will help make sure that all surprises are good ones.

Section IV
Resources

Appendix

Sources of Secondary Research

In an era of tight budgets, it is heartening to know there are some outstanding sources of inexpensive research data. These sources include, but are certainly not limited to, the following:

Your college or university library

Get to know the reference librarian and the tools he or she is able to offer. If you have access to batch searches, for instance, you will be able to ask the computer to provide a list of periodicals and books that address whatever topic you might be interested in. Also, check ERIC—a microfiche collection of documents relating to all facets of education.

Periodicals

In addition to specific publications for your areas of professional interest, you should be a regular reader of the following periodicals:
- *CASE Currents*
- *Admissions Strategist*

- *American Demographics*
- *Business Week*
- *Change*
- *Chronicle of Higher Education*
- *Chronicle of Philanthropy*
- *College and University*
- *Journal of College Admission*
- *Trusteeship*
- Major regional newspaper
- *Newsweek, Time,* or *U.S. News & World Report*
- Local newspaper

Your competition

The colleges with which you compete are a rich source of data. As soon as possible, have someone in your office get on their mailing lists. Keep track of their student-recruiting and fund-raising publications and correspondence. Pay particular attention to their positioning statements and what they are saying about themselves.

College guides

College guides are a valuable source of information. It is important to know not only how your college is depicted but what the guides are saying about your competition. While you're perusing the guide, read the detailed tables at the back of the book. They are valuable sources of comparative data and, when compared each year, trend data as well.

Trade and association newsletters

Many companies and associations produce newsletters that contain valuable information. CASE, NACAC, NCFR, AACRAO, and a multitude of other associations publish newsletters. A list of companies and associations is included in this Appendix.

The Web

One extremely useful resource is the World Wide Web. This Appendix contains more than 100 useful Web sites divided into seven key categories.

ACT/SAT data services

These services provide a wealth of comparative data.

The U.S. Government Printing Office

The United States government generates more data than any other body in the world, and most of these data are available at nominal cost through the U.S. Government Printing Office. When looking through its catalog of publications, don't forget the

Digest of Educational Statistics and the *Statistical Abstracts of the United States.*

U.S. Department of Commerce Bureau of the Census

The Census of Population is only one of the studies it publishes. In addition, it produces the censuses on housing, agriculture, business, manufacturers, mineral industries, transportation, and governments. Much of this information is available on floppy disk or CD, and importing it into your documents has never been easier.

Your own college database

Earlier we talked about using the application as a source of data. Don't forget to examine and possibly modify the forms and applications used by housing, the career center, financial aid, and other departments on your campus. Look, too, at your alumni data.

Consortium data

Consortia and associations are great sources of data. Whether you are a member of the Big Ten, Associated Colleges of the Midwest, or the Coalition of Christian Colleges and Universities, take advantage of the savings you can achieve through group association-wide projects.

Education organizations

At last count there were about 1,100 different educational organizations. Most of these organizations generate data. Check *Gale's Encyclopedia of Associations* for relevant educational organizations, and ask to be placed on their mailing lists.

Specialized publishers

There are several publishers that specialize in higher education. Jossey-Bass (especially its New Directions series), Barron's, Peterson's, College Board, Octameron Press, and others offer a variety of relevant books, periodicals, and annuals.

Media kits

To attract advertisers, magazines, newspapers, radio and television stations, and other media offer kits that contain demographic data about their audiences. These kits are a valuable source of information. If one of your constituent publics is served by a special magazine such as *Campus Life* or *Hispanic*, be sure to obtain those kits, also. And don't forget some of the professional publications like *Change* and the *Chronicle of Higher Education.* Their kits are extraordinarily helpful.

Local and regional Chambers of Commerce

Chambers of Commerce are valuable sources of demographic data and information relating to employment trends.

State economic development commissions

Like the chambers, state economic development commissions are also important sources of demographic, economic, and employment data.

Clipping file

A final source of data is your own clipping file. At Stamats, we have a file key of about 45 different topics. When someone in the company reads an article or attends a seminar that touches on one of those topics, the article or handout goes into the clipping file. Because much of this material is used in research, we make sure that each entry into the file includes a citation that lists the date and source of the information.

B

Organizations and Associations

American Association of Collegiate Registrars and Admissions Officers (AACRAO)
One Dupont Circle, Suite 330
Washington, DC 20036
(202) 293-9161
fax: (202) 872-8857

American College Personnel Association (ACPA)
One Dupont Circle, Suite 300
Washington, DC 20036
(202) 835-2272
fax: (202) 296-3286

American College Testing (ACT)
PO Box 4005
Iowa City, IA 52243
(319) 337-1000

American Council on Education (ACE)
One Dupont Circle, Suite 801
Washington, DC 20036
(202) 939-9300
fax: (202) 833-4760

American Marketing Association (AMA)
250 S. Wacker Dr., Suite 200
Chicago, IL 60606
(312) 648-0536
fax: (312) 993-7542

American Telemarketing Association
4605 Lankershim Blvd., Suite 824
North Hollywood, CA 91602
(818) 766-5324
fax: (818) 766-8168

Association of Governing Boards of Universities and Colleges (AGB)
One Dupont Circle, Suite 400
Washington, DC 20036
(202) 296-8400
fax: (202) 223-7053

Coalition for Christian Colleges and Universities
329 Eighth St., NE
Washington, DC 20002-6158
(202) 546-8713
fax: (202) 546-8913

The College Board
45 Columbus Avenue
New York, NY 10023-6992
(212) 713-8000
fax: (212) 713-8282

Council for Advancement and Support of
Education (CASE)
11 Dupont Circle, Suite 400
Washington, DC 20036
(202) 328-5900
fax: (202) 387-4973

Council for Independent Colleges
One Dupont Circle, Suite 320
Washington, DC 20036
(202) 466-7230

Direct Marketing Educational Foundation
1120 Avenue of the Americas
New York, NY 10036
(212) 768-7277
fax: (212) 790-1561

ERIC Clearinghouse for Higher Education
One Dupont Circle, Suite 630
Washington, DC 20036-1183
(202) 296-2597
fax: (202) 452-1844

National Association for College Admission
Counseling (NACAC)
1631 Prince St.
Alexandria, VA 22314
(703) 836-2222
fax: (703) 836-8015

National Association of Student Financial Aid
Administrators
1920 L St., NW, Suite 200
Washington, DC 20036
(202) 785-0453
fax: (202) 785-1487

National Association of Student Financial
Management Systems (NCHEMS)
PO Box 9752
Boulder, CO 80301
(303) 497-0392
fax: (303) 497-0338

National Association of College and University
Business Officers (NACUBO)
2501 M St., Suite 400
Washington, DC 20037
(202) 861-2500
fax: (202) 861-2583

National Association of Independent Colleges
and Universities (NAICU)
1025 Connecticut Ave., Suite 700
Washington, DC 20036
(202) 785-8866
fax: (202) 835-0003

National Association of Independent
Schools (NAIS)
1620 L St., NW
Washington, DC 20036-5605
(202) 973-9700
fax: (202) 973-9790

National Society of Fund Raising Executives
(NSFRE)
1101 King St., Suite 700
Alexandria, VA 22314
(703) 684-0410
fax: (703) 684-0540

University Microfilms International
300 N. Zeeb Rd.
Ann Arbor, MI 48106
(313) 761-4700

U.S. Department of Commerce Bureau of the
Census
Washington, DC 20233
(301) 457-3761

U.S. Government Printing Office
710 North Capitol St., NW
Washington, DC 20401
(202) 512-0132

Appendix
C

Valuable Web Sites

The following Web sites are divided into seven general categories:
- U.S. agencies
- Education associations and organizations (general)
- Admissions, student recruiting, financial aid, and student services
- Fund raising, alumni relations, and foundations
- Media and public relations
- Marketing, advertising, and direct mail
- Data and research resources

Some Web sites have been listed in multiple areas.

U.S. Agencies

Smithsonian Institution
http://www.si.gov

U.S. Bureau of the Census
http://www.census.gov

U.S. Bureau of Labor Statistics
http://www.bls.gov

U.S. Department of Education
http://www.ed.gov

U.S. Department of Education Office of Postsecondary Education
http://www.ed.gov/offices/ope/index.html

U.S. Department of Health and Human Services
http://www.os.dhhs.gov

U.S. House of Representatives
http://www.house.gov

U.S. Postal Service
http://www.usps.gov/

U.S. Senate
gopher.senate.gov

The White House
http://www.whitehouse.gov

Education Associations and Organizations (General)

American Association for Higher Education (AAHE)
http://www.ido.gmu.edu/AAHE/

American Association of Community Colleges (AACC)
http://www.aacc.nche.edu

American Association of University Professors (AAUP)
http://www.igc.apc.org/aaup/

American Association of University Women (AAUW)
http://www.aauw.org

American Council on Education (ACE)
http://www.acenet.edu

American Federation of Teachers (AFT)
http://www.aft.org

Association of Governing Boards (AGB)
http://www.agb.org

Association on Higher Education and Disability (AHEAD)
http://www.ahead.org

Association of Jesuit Colleges and Universities (AJCU)
http://www.ajcunet.edu/

Coalition of Christian Colleges and Universities (CCCU)
http://www.gospelcom.net/cccu/

Council of Independent Colleges and Universities (CIC)
http://www.cic.edu

European Council of International Schools
http://www.ecis.org

Historically Black Colleges and Universities
http://eric-web.tc.columbia.edu/hbcu

Internet College Exchange (ICX)
http://www.usmall.com/college/index.html

Multicultural Alliance
http://branson.org/mca

National Association of College and University Business Officers (NACUBO)
http://www.nacubo.org

National Association of Independent Schools (NAIS)
http://www.nais.org

National Association of State Boards of Education (NASBE)
http://www.nasbe.org

National Association of Student Personnel Administrators (NASPA)
http://www.naspa.org

National Community Education Association
http://www.idsonline.com/ncea

National Council of Educational Opportunity Associations
http://trio.ume.maine.edu/~nceoa/nceoa.html

National Education Association (NEA)
http://www.nea.org

National Information Center for Children and Youth With Disabilities
http://www.nichcy.org

National Institute for Educational Planning
http://www.niep.com

National Institute on the Education of At-Risk Students
http://www.ed.gov/offices

Telis (TeleLearning InfoSource)
http://www.telis.org

Universities (All)
http://www.mit.edu:8001/people/cdemello/
univ-full.html

University Continuing Education Association
(UCEA)
http://www.nucea.edu/main/html

United States Student Association
http://www.essential.org/ussa

Western Interstate Commission for Higher
Education
http://www.wiche.edu/

World-Wide Graduate School Directory
http://www.gradschools.com

Admissions, Student Recruiting, Financial Aid, and Student Services

American Association of Collegiate Registrars
and Admissions Officers (AACRAO)
http://www.aacrao.com

Association of Black Admission and Financial
Aid Officers of the Ivy League and Sister
Schools
http://web.mit.edu/afs/athena.mit.edu/org

Association for Multicultural Counseling and
Development
http://edap.bgsu.edu/AMCD

Athletic Scholarship Information Search
Techniques (ASIST)
http://www.athletes.com/assist.html

College Board Online
http://www.collegeboard.org/

College Express
http://www.collegexpress.com/

College NET
http://www.collegenet.com/

College Scholarship Service
http://www.collegeboard.org/css/html/
financialaidindx001.html

Educational Testing Service
http://www.ets.org/

Electronic Financial Aid Library
http://nt.scbbs.com/finaid/

Entrance Exams
http://www.cs.cmu.edu/afs/cs.cmu.edu/user/
mkant/

Financial Aid Information
http://www.finaid.org/

Loan Payment Estimator
http://www.student-loans.com/Repay.html

Minority Education Grants
http://www.grad.uiuc.edu/minority/
Education_Grants.html

National Association for College Admission
Counseling (NACAC)
http://www.nacac.com

National Association of Student Financial Aid
Administrators (NASFAA)
http://www.fuaud.org/nasfaa

National Association of Student Personnel
Administrators (NASPA)
http://www.naspa.org/

National College Fairs
http://www.nacac.com/faird&l.html

Nellie Mae Loan Link
http://www.nelliemae.org/

Performing & Visual Arts College Fairs
http://www.nacac.com

Peterson's Education
http://www.petersons.com

Preparing Your Child for College Science
http://www.ed.gov/pubs/Prepare/

Princeton Review
http://www.review.com/college/

Scholarship Scams
http://www.bcp/conline/edcamps/scholarship/

Student Services
http://www.studentservices.com

University Financial Aid Offices
http://www.finaid.org/finaid/fao-web.html

Fund Raising, Alumni Relations, and Foundations

Alumni Network
http://alumnet.com

American Society of Association Executives
http://www.asanet.org

Aspen Institute
http://www.aspeninst.org

Canadian Centre for Philanthropy
http://www.web.net/imagine

Chronicle of Philanthropy
http://www.philanthropy.com

Council for Advancement and Support of Education (CASE)
http://www.case.org

Council on Foundations
http://www.cof.org

Foundation Center
http://fdncenter.org/

Foundation for Independent Higher Education
http://www.fihe.org/

GrantsWeb
http://www.web.fie.com

National Society of Fund-raising Executives (NSFRE)
http://www.nsfre.org

NonProfit Times
http://www.nptimes.com

Philanthropy Journal OnLine
http://www.philanthropy-journal-org/

Philanthropy News Digest
http://fdncente.org/phil/philmain.html

Media Relations, and Public Relations

ABC Television
http:/www.abc.com

American Journalism Review
http://www.newslink.org/

Black Collegian
http://www.black-collegian.com/

Black Issues in Higher Education
http://www.blackissues.com

Business Wire
www.businesswire.com

CBS Television
http://www.cbs.com/

CNN
http://www.cnn.com

C-SPAN
http://www.c-span.org

Chronicle of Higher Education
http://www.thisweek.chronicle.com/

Columbia Journalism Review
http://www.cjr.org

Education News
http://biz.yahoo.com/news/education.html

Education Week
http:/www.edweek.org/ew/current/thisweek

ESPN
http:/www.espnet.com

Gebbie Press
http://www.gebbieinc.com

Los Angeles Times
http://www.latimes.com

MTV
http:/www.mtv.com

NBC Television
http:/www.nbc.com

National Public Radio
http://www.npr.org

New York Times
http://www.nytimes.com/

PBS Television
http:/www.pbs.org/

PR Newswire
http://www.prnewswire.com

Public Relations Society of America
http://www.prsa.org

Reuters
http://www.reuters.com

Rolling Stone
http://www.rollingstone.com

USA Today
http://usatoday.com

U.S. News Online
http://www.usnews.com

Wall Street Journal Interactive
http://www.wsj.com

Marketing, Advertising, and Direct Mail

Advertising Age
http://www.adage.com

American List Counsel
http://www.amlist.com

American Marketing Association
http:/www.ama.org

Beyond the Wall—Advertising
http://www.beyondthewall.com

Database America
http://www.databaseamerica.com

Dependable Lists
http://www.dependablelists.com

Direct Mail Underground
http://www.rdri.com

Direct Marketing News
http://www.dmnews.com

Direct Marketing University
http://www.communicomp.com

Direct Marketing World
http://www.dmworld.com

Direct Media
http://www.directmedia.com

Fishnet Electronic Magazine for Teens
http://www.jayi.com

Guerrilla Marketing
http://www.gmarketing.com

Horah Group—Direct Mail Resource
http://www.horah.com

Lycos—Personal Guide to the Web
http://point.lycos.com/

Marketplace 1 to 1 (Peppers and Rodgers)
http://www.m1to1.com

MaxiMarketing
http://www.maximarketing.com

National Research Center for College and
University Admissions (mailing lists)
http://www.nrccua.com

Softmail Direct
http://www.softmail.com

Target On Line
http://www.targetonline.com

Data and Research Resources

Academe Today (*Chronicle of Higher Education*)
http://www.chronicle.com

Amazon Bookstore
http://www.amazon.com

American Council on Education (ACE)
http://www.acenet.edu

American Demographics
http://www.demographics.com

AskERIC
http://ericir.syr.edu/

Business Directory
http://businessdirectory.dowjones.com

Education Commission of the States
http://www.ecs.org

Educational Resources Information Center
Clearinghouse (ERIC)
http://aspensys3.aspensys.com/eric/
barak.html#1

Educational Resources Information Center
Clearinghouse on Teaching and Teacher
Education (ERIC/SP)
http://www.ericsp.org

Electric Library
http://www.elibrary.com

Federal Web Locator
http://www.law.vill.edu/Fed-Agency/
Fedwebloc.html

Gale Encyclopedia of Associations
http://www.gale.com

Internet Resources for Institutional Research
http://apollo.gmu.edu/~jmilam/air95.html

Mead Data
http://www.meaddata.com

National Council of University Research
Administrators (NCURA)
http://softlib.rice.edu.ncura

Tattered Cover Bookstore
http://www.tatteredcover.com

Western Interstate Commission for Higher
Education
http://www.wiche.edu/

Yahoo: Education: Organizations: Student
Organizations
http://www.yahoo/Education/Organizations/
Student_Organizations

Yahoo: News/Newspapers: Universities
http://ww.yahoo.com/News/Newspapers/
University

D

A Primer for Working With Teams

Strategies for building the team

To help assemble and build the most effective marketing team possible, we suggest that the champion adapt the following nine strategies:

- Set the ground rules
- Meet off site
- Protect the team
- Draw the team together
- Settle on a basic decision-making procedure
- Monitor the performance of cross-functional teams
- Recognize dysfunctional traits and tendencies
- Deal effectively with resistance
- Reward the team

Set the ground rules

It is very important to set the ground rules as early as possible in the planning process. Ideally this has been done while that individual was being recruited for the team. However, it is always helpful to review with potential team members the answers to such questions as the following very early in the planning process:

- Why was I selected for this team?
- What is expected of me—what will I have to do?
- What are the limits of my time and commitment—how long will this take?
- Who is in charge of the team?
- Why was that person chosen?
- What is our purpose—what will be the practical outcomes of this team?
- What guarantees do I have that my contribution to this team will not be held against me in the future?
- How will my contribution to the team be recognized by the institution and my peers?

Glenn notes that it is not uncommon at the start to find that some team members may have some degree of hostility and suspicion. Often, as the ground rules are established and differences and expectations are talked out, this hostility and suspicion mellow to a genuine interest in the planning process.

Meet off-site

One of the most important things that you can do to help build a strong marketing team is to hold your first meeting or first meetings off-site. This is especially important if the team members have little prior experience working together.

Meeting off site is important for several reasons. First, it helps reduce territoriality. Second, off-site meetings isolate the team from day-to-day interruptions. Third, they are an ideal place to begin team-building experiences. And finally, off-site meetings can include not only time for work but time for play and relaxation.

Protect the team

As part of the team-building process, every effort must be made to protect the team from undue criticism. Often, team members become lightning rods for their constituencies and are unfairly criticized for actions of the team as a whole or for the institution's decision to pursue a more comprehensive marketing strategy. In an age of finite resources, marketing decisions often mean the reallocation of funds and institutional priorities. This can become a politically charged process, and team members will have a heightened sense of vulnerability.

These are some of the ways to help protect the team:

- Make clear to the community the challenges facing the institution and how marketing will help the college or university more successfully meet those challenges.
- Announce to the campus community why specific people were chosen to participate on the team.
- Invite campus-wide participation in the gathering of information.

- Keep the decision-making process as open and above-board as possible.
- Keep accurate notes and meeting minutes, and make them available to non-members of the committee.
- Encourage the team as often and as sincerely as possible.

Draw the team together

To help coalesce the team as quickly as possible, I suggest the use of team-building exercises. These exercises will help members learn more about each other, increase their level of trust, and help draw them together.

Generally, team-building exercises should be initiated during the first few meetings and then less frequently throughout the planning process. In some cases it is good to have a team-building facilitator. However, the champion is often able to guide the exercises as long as he or she also participates.

Here are some excellent sources for games and team-building exercises:

- Brandes, Donna, and Phillips, Howard: *Gamesters Handbook: Hundreds of Games for Teachers and Group Leaders*. Philadelphia: Trans Atlantic Publications, 1995.
- Francis, Dave, and Young, Don: *Improving Work Groups: A Practical Manual for Team-Building*. San Diego: University Associates, 1995.
- Pfeiffer, J. William: *The Encyclopedia of Team Building Activities*. San Diego: University Associates, 1990.
- Woodcock, Mike: *50 Activities for Teambuilding*. Brookfield, VT: Ashgate Publishing, 1989.

Settle on a basic decision-making procedure

Sooner or later the marketing team will have to make decisions—often very tough decisions—and how these are made is extraordinarily important. This is particularly true in higher education, where the process through which decisions are made is often at least as important as the resulting decision.

Moody, writing in *Decision-Making,* noted that capable decisions do not necessarily automatically arise from capable individuals. Although decision-making can at times be disconcerting, there are some handy tools that will help the process go more smoothly.

The high cost of perfect decisions

Before we can proceed too much further, we need to understand the difference between perfect decisions and pretty good decisions. Too often, colleges and universities try to make perfect decisions and spend far too much time and money contemplating their options. More likely than not, they never actually decide.

Our goal is not to help you make perfect decisions—they are too costly—but to help you make many satisfactory decisions in a timely fashion, decisions that keep things moving ahead and on schedule.

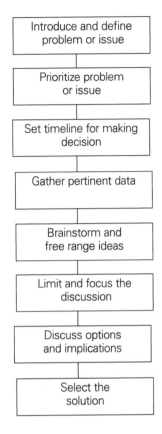

Figure A-1.
Decision-Making

- Introduce and define problem or issue
- Prioritize problem or issue
- Set timeline for making decision
- Gather pertinent data
- Brainstorm and free range ideas
- Limit and focus the discussion
- Discuss options and implications
- Select the solution

The schematic presented in Figure A-1 outlines a straightforward decision-making process that is worth exploring.

The first step is to introduce and define the problem or issue to be discussed. In some cases, this will involve establishing a context so all team members may understand the subtleties and implications being examined.

Next, juxtapose this problem or issue against others being contemplated. The goal, of course, is to set priorities. If the problem or issue pales when compared to the items already on the docket, it may be safely postponed. On the other hand, if its importance is quickly appreciated, it moves up the list.

The third step is to establish a timeline. This not only forces a decision but helps set a boundary for gathering data. Establishing a credible timeline—and sticking to it—is an important and often overlooked part of the decision-making process.

The fourth step is to gather pertinent data. Often, team members simply do not have enough information to make a learned and reasoned decision.

The next step is to brainstorm ideas and options. Brainstorming, sometimes called free-ranging, is an underutilized and underappreciated decision tool. For brainstorming to work well, the group must agree to the following guidelines:

- Work as fast as possible to reduce hindrances and generate more ideas.
- Set no restrictions; wild ideas are welcome.
- Aim for quantity, not quality.
- Encourage combinations and improvements.
- Don't judge until all ideas are introduced (this is the hardest rule to follow).

The keys to a successful brainstorming session are volume and variety. As in all dynamic situations, the better ideas have a tendency to percolate to the top.

At the conclusion of the brainstorming session, or perhaps in a later session, begin to limit and focus the discussion. At this time you are beginning to apply constraints of time, talent, and money. However, if the session was successful, you will still have a wonderfully diverse range of options from which to choose.

Next, discuss options and implications. One college president calls this "short-listing." Focus on the most salient ideas. In some cases, within the timeline you have established, you may require additional research before you can make a decision. The final step is to choose a course of action—to decide.

The schematic outlined above focuses on dealing with one issue or problem at a time. Of course, marketing teams will often confront multiple issues and problems, all clamoring for their share of attention.

The role of the champion

A good champion guides the team through the decision-making process. He or she facilitates members' contributions by performing several important functions:

- Initiating: The champion cites a problem and suggests a procedure for solving it
- Opinion-giving: The champion states his or her views without imposing them on the team

Integrated Marketing for Colleges, Universities, and Schools

- Clarification: The champion restates another's point to reduce misunderstanding
- Summarizing: The champion incorporates the views of the team into a solution for consideration
- Consensus testing: The champion frequently checks with members of the team to measure progress
- Group maintenance: The champion encourages the team, promotes harmony and compromise, facilitates communication, and sets group performance standards

Dampening enthusiasm

One of the quickest ways to dampen any enthusiasm that brainstorming may generate is to use "killer phrases" like these in Table A-1.

Monitor the performance of cross-functional teams

The need for the champion to monitor and appraise the performance of the team and its members is an extremely important undertaking that will help assure the success of the overall endeavor. Parker, writing in *Cross-Functional Teams*, notes that team players tend to fall into one of four general categories with good qualities:

Contributor

1. Shares relevant information with colleagues
2. Helps the team use its time and resources effectively
3. Pushes the team to achieve outstanding results
4. Successfully completes all work that affects the team's success
5. Accepts responsibility for team-oriented actions
6. Serves as a mentor for new team members
7. Has a clear set of priorities

Collaborator

1. Helps the team set and clarify long-term goals
2. Regularly reminds the team to review its goals and plans
3. Helps teammates who need it
4. Works hard to achieve team goals whether or not he or she agrees with them
5. Is open to new ideas or information that may alter team goals
6. Works outside defined roles to help achieve team goals
7. Shares credit with teammates

Communicator

1. Helps resolve technical or interpersonal problems
2. Listens objectively while withholding judgment
3. Recognizes and praises colleagues for their efforts
4. Shows enthusiasm and a sense of urgency for the team's work

Table A-1.
Killer Phrases

A good idea, but . . .

Be practical . . .

We tried that . . .

Against school policy . . .

It needs more study . . .

All right in theory . . .

Don't start anything yet . . .

It's not budgeted . . .

It's not our job . . .

That's not our problem . . .

Let's turn it over to a committee . . .

The faculty won't go for it . . .

We've been doing it this way for a long time . . .

We've never done it this way before . . .

What other schools are trying this . . .

We're not a business, we're a college . . .

If this idea is so good, why isn't someone else doing it?

5. Tries to achieve consensus among teammates
6. Encourages others to participate in discussions and decisions
7. Provides other members with specific, helpful feedback on their performance

Challenger

1. Frankly shares opinions about the team's work
2. Disputes conventional wisdom, even if it means disagreeing with the team leader or the majority
3. Questions the team's goals
4. Pushes the team to set high ethical standards
5. Asks why, how, and other relevant questions at team meetings
6. Challenges the team to take calculated risks
7. Reports team progress and problems honestly
8. Backs off when views are rejected; supports a legitimate team consensus

Recognize dysfunctional traits and tendencies

As you begin to work as a team, the champion and all members keep in mind some of the symptoms of dysfunctional teams. Berelson and Steiner outlined a number of typical symptoms, including these:

- Cautious or guarded communication: Fear of some form of punishment, ridicule, or negative reaction may cause people to say nothing or be guarded in what they do say.
- Formal or structural communication: This is happening when people substitute letters and e-mail for personal communication, send copies of their letters to people outside the team, or use legal terminology in correspondence.
- Lack of disagreement: When there is little or no disagreement among a group, it is very possible that the members, for whatever reason, are unwilling to share true feelings or ideas. When there are healthy differences, people will make such statements as "I have a thought on that," or "Here's another way to think about this."
- Failure to share information: Team members often have valuable experience relating to a point of discussion. When they hold back that information or perspective, the destructiveness of poor teamwork is in motion.
- Reliance on criticism: Criticism, particularly when delivered in the presence of others, is a form of punishment that will inhibit people from sharing ideas and making suggestions.
- Lack of individual feedback: When teams are working well, members receive frequent, constructive, and specific feedback, given in a positive way. In a poor team, there is little or no feedback—and what there is is usually negative.
- Poor meetings: It is likely that a counterproductive team is at work if, when a team meets, the following symptoms are present:
  - nonexistent or unclear agenda

- general boredom or lack of enthusiastic participation
- long, poorly structured meetings
- failure to reach decisions
- one or two people dominating all discussions
- people being put down and stymied

■ Unclear goals: All team members should be able to articulate team goals.

■ Low commitment: When goals are dictated rather than reached through consensus, team members are likely to respond, "These are not my goals."

■ Unrealistic goals: Poor teams draft goals that are unreachable.

■ Conflict within the team: If there is a destructive conflict among team members, it will lead to a suspicious and combative environment.

■ Failure to use team members' talents: Ineffective teams are often unaware of the diversity and different levels of members' skills.

■ Competition: When members are openly competing with one another, they often withhold information that would benefit the entire team and the planning process.

■ Conformity: Poor teams stress conformity and a follow-the-norm approach.

■ Tension: When people are uncomfortable together and the atmosphere is tense, a team is unable to function in an open and sharing manner.

■ Misunderstanding of jobs or roles: Members of poorly functioning teams often express confusion: "That's not my job," "He was going to do that," or "I have no idea what we are doing."

■ Low confidence in others: In an effective team, individuals not only know the roles of other team members but also have confidence that other members will carry out their parts of the job.

■ One-person decisions: Poor teamwork can be a result of the way members participate in decisions. In poor teams, decisions are boss-directed, with only marginal team-member input actually counting in the final decision.

Deal effectively with resistance

Sooner or later, members of any team resist an idea or direction. This is a time of great vulnerability for both the individual and the team. The individual may feel threatened and even ostracized, while team members watch to see how the individual is treated.

Dealing constructively with this is a very important part of team dynamics. Laurence Smith, Vice President of Marketing and Student Affairs at Eastern Michigan University, offers ten ways to work with resistance:

■ Maintain two-way communication at all times.

■ Never punish resistance.

■ Involve potential resisters in fact-gathering.

■ Help those affected to make their feelings known.

■ Do not predetermine what is "illegitimate."

- Try to change the norms of the group.
- Engage communication directly aimed at confronting, sharing, and probing resisters' feelings.
- Look for opportunities to negotiate "win-win" solutions.
- Build a sense of confidence and competence about new situations.
- Never mandate. Remember, people support what they build.

Reward the team

A strong, dynamic champion will only get you so far. The institution must also be willing to reward or compensate the team in positive ways. Here are some options for rewarding the team and its members:

- Provide release time from other activities and responsibilities.
- Hold planning retreats that include time and allowances for recreation.
- Allow members to present progress on key marketing initiatives to the campus community.
- Help members, through the planning process, to increase their level of expertise in an area that they value.

Appendix

E

Sample SWOT Analysis Survey of Faculty

As you know, the college is involved in creating a comprehensive, institutionwide marketing plan. An essential part of this process is gaining input from faculty. To facilitate that input, would you please take a few minutes to complete this survey. Please feel free to attach other sheets as necessary.

This survey is both anonymous and confidential. It is designed to be returned directly to Stamats, and it will not be seen by any XYZ faculty, staff, administrator, or trustee. Data will be presented in the aggregate, and anecdotally, as part of our final report and presentation to the college.

To be included in this study, this survey must be completed and returned in the envelope provided no later than _____.

Thank you for your help.

Name
Title et al.

Integrated Marketing for Colleges, Universities, and Schools **201**

1. What three or four national/external trends do you feel will have the most impact on XYZ's future?

_____

_____

_____

_____

_____

2. Overall, how would you assess XYZ's vulnerability in today's recruiting marketplace?

    Not vulnerable = __ __ __ __ __ = Very vulnerable

3. From your perspective, what should be the college's top three academic priorities?

_____

_____

_____

_____

_____

4. How do you define academic quality?

_____

_____

_____

_____

_____

5. From your perspective, what are the strengths and weaknesses of XYZ's general education requirements?

Strengths:

_____

_____

_____

Weaknesses:

_____

_____

6. What is your best idea for improving the quality of the classroom experience?

_____

_____

_____

_____

_____

7. What new/additional AV (audiovisual) resources would most help you improve the teaching/learning experience for your students?

_____

_____

_____

_____

_____

8. What new/additional technology/technological resources would most help you improve the teaching/learning experience for your students?

_____

_____

_____

_____

_____

9. What resources (within reason) do you need to do a better job teaching?

_____

_____

_____

_____

10. Overall, how would you rate the quality of XYZ's advising program?

_____

_____

_____

_____

_____

11. What ideas do you have for improving advising?

_____

_____

_____

_____

_____

12. What ideas (other than those outlined above) do you have for enhancing the intellectual growth and career preparation of XYZ's students?

_____

_____

_____

_____

_____

13. What ideas do you have for improving XYZ's retention programs and strategies?

_____

_____

_____

_____

_____

14. Aside from your own, what is the strongest academic program on campus?

_____

_____

_____

_____

15. Within present or reasonable resources, and based on your understanding of XYZ's mission and the ABC area, what major(s) should the college consider adding to its curriculum?

_____

_____

_____

_____

_____

Undergraduate:

_____

_____

_____

_____

_____

Graduate:

_____

_____

_____

_____

_____

Post-baccalaureate/certificate curricula:

_____

_____

_____

_____

_____

16. What ideas do you have for improving the manner in which XYZ evaluates its current academic programs and majors?

_____

_____

_____

_____

17. What ideas do you have for improving the manner in which XYZ evaluates potential (new) academic programs and majors?

_____

_____

_____

_____

18. In your opinion, what new building or renovation of an existing building would have the most impact on the College's ability to meet the educational needs of its students?

_____

_____

_____

_____

_____

19. From your perspective, how can the college improve its ability to more effectively and consistently take advantage of the ideas of faculty like you?

_____

_____

_____

_____

_____

20. If there was one thing you could change about XYZ, what would it be?

_____

_____

_____

_____

_____

A little bit about you:

21. Do you teach at XYZ: ☐ Full-time   ☐ Part-time

22. Do you primarily teach:
        ☐ Day classes (before 5 p.m.)   ☐ Evening classes (after 5 p.m.)

23. Are you tenured?   ☐ Yes   ☐ No

24. How long have you taught at XYZ? (number of years) ____

Thank you for your help with this survey.

Bibliography

Aaker, David A.: *Building Strong Brands*. New York: Free Press, 1995.

Aaker, David A.: *Managing Brand Equity: Capitalizing on the Value of a Brand Name*. New York: Free Press, 1991.

Absher, Keith, and Crawford, Gerald: "Marketing the Community College Starts With Understanding Students Perspectives." *Community College Review*, 23, no. 4 (Spring 1996): 59-67

Adams, James L.: *Conceptual Blockbusting: A Guide to Better Ideas*, 3rd ed. Reading, MA: Addison-Wesley-Longman Publishing, 1990.

Albrecht, Karl: *The Northbound Train: Finding the Purpose, Setting the Direction, Shaping the Destiny of Your Organizations*. New York: AMA-COM, 1994.

Ambrose, Sandra, and Hellmuth, Daniel: *Telemarketing Skills Training Manual.* Englewood Cliffs, NJ: Prentice-Hall, 1990.

Andreasen, Alan R., and Kotler, Philip: *Marketing for Nonprofit Organizations.* Englewood Cliffs, NJ: Prentice-Hall, 1995.

Arbetier, Solomon: *Minority Enrollments in Higher Education Institutions: A Chronological View.* New York: College Board, May 1986.

Arnold, David: *The Handbook of Brand Management.* Reading, MA: Addison-Wesley-Longman Publishing, 1993

Assessing the Cost of Student Recruitment at Smaller Independent Colleges and Universities. Washington, DC: The National Association of College and University Business Officers, 1989.

✓ Astin, Alexander W., and Green, Kenneth C., and Korn, William S.: *The American Freshman: Twenty-Year Trends, 1966-1985.* Cooperative Institutional Research Program—UCLA, CA: UCLA and the American Council on Education, 1987.

✓ Astin, Alexander: *Minorities in American Higher Education.* San Francisco: Jossey-Bass Publishers, 1982.

Barker, Joel A.: *The Future Edge: Discovering the New Rules of Success.* New York: William Morrow and Company, 1992.

Barker, Joel: *Paradigms: The Business of Discovering the Future.* New York: Harper Business Publishers, 1993.

✓ Particularly recommended

Batra, Rajeev, and Myers, John G., and Aaker, David A.: *Advertising Management*, 5th ed. Englewood Cliffs, NJ: Prentice-Hall, 1996.

✓ Beckworth, Harry: *Selling the Invisible: A Field Guide to Modern Marketing*. New York: Warner Books, 1997.

✓ Belasco, James A.: *Teaching the Elephant to Dance: Empowering Change in Your Organization*. New York: Crown Publishing Group, 1990.

✓ Belasco, James A.: *Flight of the Buffalo: Soaring to Excellence, Learning to Let Employees Lead*. New York: Warner Books, 1993.

Bennis, Warren: *On Becoming a Leader*, 2nd ed. Reading, MA: Addison-Wesley-Longman Publishing, 1994.

✓ Bennis, Warren: *Why Leaders Can't Lead: The Unconscious Conspiracy Continues*. San Francisco: Jossey-Bass Publishers, 1990.

Bennis, Warren, and Nanus, Burt: *Leaders: Strategies for Taking Charge*. New York: Harper & Row, 1997.

Bensimon, Estela, and Tierney, William G.: "Shaping the Multicultural Campus: Strategies for Administrators." *College Board Review*, no. 166 (Late Winter 1992-93):4-7, 30.

Bingham, F. Jr.: "Marketing the Institutions of Higher Learning: A Research Analysis Enrollment Model." *Journal of Marketing for Higher Education*, 4, no. 1-2(1993).

Birnbaum, Robert: *How Colleges Work: The Cybernetics of Academic Organization and Leadership*. San Francisco: Jossey-Bass Publishers, 1988.

✓ Blanchard, Kenneth H.: *The One Minute Manager Meets the Monkey*. New York: William Morrow and Company, 1989.

Block, Peter: Stewardship: *Choosing Service Over Self-Interest*. San Francisco: Berrett-Koehler Publishers, 1993.

✓ Bloom, Allan: *The Closing of the American Mind*. New York: Scribner's, 1987.

Bok, Derek C.: *Beyond the Ivory Tower: Social Responsibilities of the Modern University*. Cambridge, MA: Harvard University Press, 1982.

Bolman, Lee G., and Deal, Terrence E.: *Modern Approaches to Understanding and Managing Organizations*. San Francisco: Jossey-Bass Publishers, 1984.

Bowen, William G., and Breneman, David W.: "Student Aid: Price Discount or Educational Investment?" *College Board Review*, no. 167 (Spring 1993):2-5, 35-36.

Bowles, Jerry, and Hammond, Joshua: *Beyond Quality: New Standards of Total Performance That Can Change the Future of Corporate America*. New York: Berkley Publishing Group, 1992.

✓ Boyer, Ernest L.: College: *The Undergraduate Experience in America*. Princeton, NJ: Carnegie Foundation for the Advancement of Teaching, 1997.

Bradburn, Norman M.: *Polls and Surveys: Understanding What They Tell Us*. San Francisco: Jossey-Bass Publishers, 1996.

Brand, Miles: "The Challenge to Change: Reforming Higher Education." *Educational Record*, Fall 1993.

Brandes, Donna, and Phillips, Howard: *Gamesters Handbook: Hundreds of Games for Teachers and Group Leaders*. Philadelphia: Trans Atlantic Publications, 1995.

Brimelow, Peter: "Taxation Without Representation." *Forbes*, 153, no. 2 (January 17, 1994).

Brooks, L., and Hammond, J.: "Has Higher Education Been Using the Wrong Marketing Approach?" *Journal of Marketing for Higher Education*, 4, no. 1-2 (1993):27-.

Brown, H.: "Positioning the Undervalued Metropolitan University." *Journal of Marketing for Higher Education*, 4, no. 1-2 (1993):159-175.

Bryson, John M.: *Strategic Planning for Public and Nonprofit Organizations: A Guide to Strengthening and Sustaining Organizational Achievement*. San Francisco: Jossey-Bass Publishers, 1995.

Burnett, Edward: *Database Marketing: The New Profit Frontier*. Rosemont: Morris Lee Publishing Group, 1996.

Byham, William C., and Cox, Jeff: *Zapp! The Lightning of Empowerment*. New York: Fawcett Book Group, 1992.

Carter, Lindy Keane: "Righting the Wrongs: Advice on Avoiding the Most Common Mishaps in Marketing Communications." *CURRENTS*, 19, no.2 (February 1993):46-49.

Cetron, Marvin, and Davies, Owen: *American Renaissance: Our Life at the Turn of the 21st Century*. New York: St. Martin's Press, 1990.

Chaleff, Ira: *The Courageous Follower: Standing Up To and For Our Leaders*. San Francisco: Berrett-Koehler Publishers, 1995.

Clark, Neil: *Team Building: A Practical Guide for Trainers*. New York: McGraw-Hill Companies, 1994.

Clemens, John K., and Mayer, Douglas F.: *The Classic Touch: Lessons in Leadership from Homer to Hemingway*. New York: Dow Jones-Irwin, 1987.

Cohen, Michael, and March, James: "A Garbage Can Model of Organizational Choice." *Administrative Science Quarterly* (March 17, 1972).

✓ Coplin, William D., and O'Leary, Michael K.: *Everyman's Prince: A Guide to Understanding Your Political Problems*. North Scituate, MA: Duxbury Press, 1976.

Cornesky, Robert A.: *Using Deming to Improve Quality in Colleges and Universities*. Madison, WI: Magna Publications, 1992.

✓ Cowan, John: *Small Decencies: Reflections and Meditations on Being Human at Work*. New York: Harper Business Publishers, 1992.

Cowan, Ruth: "Prescription for Small-College Turnaround." *Change*, January/February 1993.

Crispell, Diane, et al.: "What's in a Brand?" *American Demographics*, 15, no. 5 (May 1993):26-32.

Crosby, Philip: *Absolutes of Leadership*. San Francisco: Jossey-Bass Publishers, 1997.

Cubbage, Alan, Vice President for University Relations, Northwestern University. Personal interviews (ongoing).

✓ Cutlip, Scott M., Center, Allen H., and Broom, Glen M.: *Effective Public Relations*, 7th ed. Englewood Cliffs, NJ: Prentice-Hall, 1994.

Dalziel, Murray M., and Schoonover, Stephen C.: *Changing Ways: A Practical Tool for Implementing Change Within Organizations*. New York: AMACOM, 1988.

Dennis, Marguerite J.: *Mortgaged Futures: How to Graduate from School Without Going Broke*. Washington, DC: Hope Press, 1986.

DePree, Max: *Leadership Is an Art*. New York: Dell Publishing Company, 1989.

✓ DePree, Max: *Leadership Jazz*. New York: Doubleday, 1992.

✓ Dilenschneider, Robert L.: *Power and Influence: Mastering the Art of Persuasion*. New York: Prentice-Hall, 1990.

✓ Dillman, Don A.: *Mail and Telephone Surveys: The Total Design Method*. New York: John Wiley and Sons, 1978.

Dillon, William R.: *Marketing Research in a Marketing Environment*, 2nd ed. Burr Ridge, IL: Richard D. Irwin, 1989.

Dixon, Pam: *Virtual College: A Quick Guide to How You Can Get the Degree You Want with Computer, TV, Video, Audio, and Other Distance Learning Tools*. Princeton, NJ: Peterson's, 1996.

Dolence, Michael G., and Rowley, Daniel James, and Lujan, Herman D.: *Working Toward Strategic Change: A Step-by-Step Guide to the Planning Process*. San Francisco: Jossey-Bass Publishers, 1997.

✓ Dovel, George P.: "Stake It Out: Positioning Success, Step by Step." *Business Marketing*, 15, no. 7 (July 1990): 43-51.

Dyke, Stewart Bradford, Director of Public Affairs, Denison University. Personal interviews (ongoing).

Edmondson, Brad: "Colleges Conquer the Baby Bust." *American Demographics*, 9, no. 9 (September, 1987):26-31.

Ehrenberg, Ronald, and Murphy, Susan: "What Price Diversity: The Death of Need-Based Financial Aid at Selective Private Colleges and Universities?" *Change*, 25, no. 4 (July/August 1993):64-73.

Farson, Richard E.: *Management of the Absurd: Paradoxes in Leadership*. New York: Simon and Schuster, 1996.

✓ Fisher, Roger, and Ury, William L.: *Getting to Yes: Negotiating Agreement Without Giving In*. Boston: Houghton Mifflin, 1991.

Francis, Dave, and Young, Don: *Improving Work Groups: A Practical Manual for Team Building*, University Associates, 1995.

Franzak, F: "Viewing the Curriculum as a Product: Implications from a Marketing Research Study." *Journal of Marketing for Higher Education*, 1993.

Gardner, John: *Excellence: Can We Be Equal and Excellent Too?* Rev. ed. New York: W.W. Norton and Company, 1995.

✓ Garreau, Joel: *The Nine Nations of North America.* Boston: Houghton-Mifflin, 1981.

Garreau, Joel: Edge City: *Life on the New Frontier.* New York: Doubleday and Company, 1992.

Gehrung, Fred, President, Gehrung and Associates. Personal interviews and conversations.

Gilmoure, James H., and Pine, B. Joseph: "The Four Faces of Mass Customization." *Harvard Business Review,* January-February 1997.

✓ Grabowski, Stanley M.: Marketing in Higher Education.: *AAHE - Eric Higher Education Research Report No. 5.* Washington, DC: American Association for Higher Education, 1981.

Gregory, James, with Wiechmann, Jack G.: *Marketing Corporate Image: The Company As Your Number One Product.* Lincolnwood, IL: NTC Contemporary Publishing Company, 1991.

Habecker, Eugene B.: *Leading with a Follower's Heart: Practicing Biblical Obedience and Humility in the Workplace.* Wheaton, IL: Victor Books, 1990.

Hall, Cindy: "Demystifying Marketing: Campuses Use and Confuse This Concept. To Understand It, Start by Cutting Through the Fog." *CURRENTS,* 19, no. 2 (February 1993): 30-31.

Hamel, Gary, and Prahalad, C.K.: *Competing for the Future.* Cambridge, MA: Harvard Business School Publishing, 1994.

Hammond, Ray, and Howard, Jeff: "Rumors of Inferiority—Barriers to Black Success in America." *New Republic* (September 9, 1985).

Handy, Charles: *The Age of Paradox.* New York: McGraw-Hill Companies, 1995.

Henry, Rene A. Jr.: *Marketing Public Relations: The Hows That Make It Work.* Ames, IA: Iowa State University Press, 1995.

Hersch, Richard H.: *Intentions and Perceptions: A National Survey of Public Attitudes Toward Liberal Arts Education.* New York: Hobart and William Smith Colleges, 1996.

Higher Education Directory. Falls Church, VA: Higher Education Publications, 1997.

Holmes, Arthur F.: *The Idea of a Christian College.* Grand Rapids, Michigan: William B.Eerdmans, 1975.

Hossler, Don: *Enrollment Management: An Integrated Approach.* New York: College Board, 1995.

Ingersoll, Ronald J.: *The Enrollment Problem: Proven Management Techniques.* New York: American Council on Education and Collier Macmillan Publishing, 1988.

Ingram, Richard T.: *Ten Basic Responsibilities of Nonprofit Boards.* Washington, DC: National Center for Nonprofit Boards, 1996.

Johnson, Spencer: *The One Minute Sales Person.* New York: Avon Books, 1991.

✓ Jones, John Philip: *What's in a Name? Advertising and the Concept of Brands.* Lexington, MA: Lexington Books, 1986.

✓ Kanter, Rosabeth Moss: *The Change Masters: Innovation for Productivity in the American Corporations.* New York: Simon and Schuster, 1985.

✓ Kaplan, Abraham: *The Conduct of Inquiry: Methodology for Behavioral Science.* New Brunswick, NJ: Transaction Publishers, 1998.

Katz, Donald: "Triumph of the Swoosh." *Sports Illustrated* (August 16, 1993)

Katz, Ron: *Advertising and Marketing Checklist.* Chicago: NTC Business Books, 1990.

Katzenbach, Jon R., and Smith, Douglas K.: *The Wisdom of Teams: Creating the High-Performance Organization.* New York: Harper & Row, 1994.

Keller, George: *Academic Strategy: The Management Revolution in American Higher Education.* American Association for Higher Education, Baltimore: Johns Hopkins University Press, 1983.

Keller, George: "The Vision Thing in Higher Education." *Planning for Higher Education,* 23, no. 4 (Summer 1995):8-14.

Kerr, Clark: *The Uses of the University*, 4th ed. Cambridge, MA: Harvard University Press, 1995.

Kerr, Clark: *Troubled Times for American Higher Education: The 1990's and Beyond*. Albany, NY: State University of New York Press, 1994.

Kinnear, Thomas C.: *Marketing Masters*. Chicago: American Marketing Association Publications, 1991.

Knowlton, Steven: "Hyping Numbers at Colleges: With Competition Keen for Freshmen, Admissions Officers Learn to Compile Figures That Create an Air of Exclusivity." *New York Times* (Education Life) (January 8, 1995):4A.

Kobs, Jim: *Profitable Direct Marketing*, 2nd ed. Chicago: NTC Contemporary Publishing Company, 1994.

Kotler, Philip, and Fox, Karen: *Strategic Marketing for Education Institutions*. Englewood Cliffs, NJ: Prentice-Hall, 1995.

Kotler, Philip, and Murphy, Patrick E.: "Strategic Planning for Higher Education." *Journal of Higher Education*, 52, no. 5 (September-October 1981): 70-89.

Kotter, John P.: *The Leadership Factor*. New York: Free Press, 1988.

Kouzes, James M., and Posner, Barry Z.: *The Leadership Challenge: How to Get Extraordinary Things Done in Organizations*. San Francisco: Jossey-Bass Publishers, 1987.

Kouzes, James M., and Posner, Barry Z.: *Credibility: How Leaders Gain and Lose It, Why People Demand It*. San Francisco: Jossey-Bass Publishers, 1993.

Kramer, Martin: "Lengthening Time-to-Degree." *Change*, 25, no. 3 (May/June 1993):5-7.

✓ Kriegel, Robert J.: *Sacred Cows Make the Best Burgers: Developing Change-Ready People and Organizations*. New York: Warner Books, 1997.

✓ Kuhn, Thomas S.: *The Structure of Scientific Revolutions*, 3rd ed. Chicago: University of Chicago Press, 1996.

Larson, Erik: *The Naked Consumer: How Our Private Lives Become Public Commodities*. New York: Henry Holt, 1992.

Larson, Erik: "Why Colleges Cost Too Much." *Time*, 149, no. 11 (March 17, 1997):46-50, 52-54.

Lenzer, Robert, and Johnson, Stephen S.: "Seeing Things as They Really Are: An Interview With Peter Drucker." *Forbes* (March 10, 1997).

Leonhardt, David: "Two-Tier Marketing." *Business Week*, no. 3518 (March 17, 1997):82-90.

Lesly, Philip: *Lesly's Handbook of Public Relations and Communications*, 4th ed. New York: AMACOM, 1991.

Levine, Arthur: *Higher Learning in America: 1980-2000*. Baltimore: Johns Hopkins University Press, 1993.

Levine, Arthur: *Shaping Higher Education's Future*. San Francisco: Jossey-Bass Publishers, 1989.

Levinson, Jay C.: *Guerrilla Advertising*. Cost-Effective Techniques for Small-Business Success. Boston: Houghton Mifflin, 1994.

✓ Levinson, Jay: *Guerrilla Marketing Attack: New Strategies, Tactics, and Weapons for Winning the Big Profits for Your Small Business*. Boston: Houghton Mifflin, 1989.

Levinson, Jay: *Guerrilla Marketing Excellence: The 50 Golden Rules for Small-Business Success*. Boston: Houghton Mifflin, 1993.

✓ Levinson, Jay: *The Guerrilla Marketing Handbook*. Boston: Houghton Mifflin, 1995.

✓ Levinson, Jay: *Guerrilla Marketing: Secrets for Making Big Profits from Your Small Business*. Boston: Houghton Mifflin, 1993.

Levitt, Theodore: *The Marketing Imagination*. New York: Collier Macmillan, 1986.

Lewis, Herschell Gordon: "Before I Forget... The Core of Any Successful Direct Marketing Strategy Has to Be the Ability to Convince the Reader, Viewer, or Listener. That Ability Stems from Astute Word Choice." *Direct Marketing*, 58, no. 12 (April 1996):38-39.

Loden, D. John: *Megabrands: How to Build Them, How to Beat Them*. Homewood, IL: Business One Irwin, 1992.

Magrath, Allan J.: *The Six Imperatives of Marketing: Lessons From the World's Best Companies*. New York: AMACOM, 1992.

Martin, David N.: *Romancing the Brand*. New York: AMACOM, 1989.

Martin, Don: *TeamThink: Using the Sports Connection to Develop, Motivate, and Manage a Winning Business Team.* New York: Dutton, 1993.

✓ Mayhew, Lewis B., and Ford, Patrick L., and Hubbard, Dean L.: *The Quest for Quality: The Challenge for Undergraduate Education in the 1990s.* San Francisco: Jossey-Bass Publishers, 1990.

Mayhew, Lewis B.: *Surviving the Eighties.* San Francisco: Jossey-Bass Publishers, 1980.

McKenna, Regis: *Real Time: Preparing for the Age of the Never Satisfied Customer.* Cambridge, MA: Harvard Business School Press, 1997.

McKenna, Regis: *Relationship Marketing: Successful Strategies for the Age of the Customer.* Reading, MA: Addison-Wesley-Longwood Publishing, 1991.

Menand, Louis: "Everybody Else's College Education." *New York Times Magazine* (April 20, 1997):48.

Metzler, Ken: *Creative Interviewing: The Writer's Guide to Gathering Information by Asking Questions,* 3rd ed. Boston: Allyn and Bacon, 1997.

✓ Merriam, Sharon B., and Cunningham, Phyllis M.: *Handbook of Adult and Continuing Education.* San Francisco: Jossey-Bass Publishers, 1989.

Mickelthwait, John, and Wooldridge, Adrian: *The Witch Doctors: Making Sense of Management Gurus.* New York: Times Books, 1996.

Mintzberg, Henry: *The Rise and Fall of Strategic Planning: Reconceiving Roles for Planning, Plans, Planners.* New York: Free Press, 1994.

Moll, Richard: *Playing the Private College Admissions Game,* rev ed. New York: Penguin Books, 1986.

Moll, Richard: *The Public Ivys: A Guide to America's Best Public Undergraduate Colleges and Universities.* New York: Viking Books, 1985.

Moll, Richard: "The Scramble to Get the Class." *Change,* 26, no. 2 (March/April 1994):10-17.

Moody, Paul E.: *Decision-Making: Proven Methods for Better Decisions.* New York: McGraw-Hill, 1983.

Morganthau, Tom, and Nayyar, Seema: "Those Scary College Costs." *Newsweek,* 127, no. 18 (April 29, 1996): 52-56.

Murphy, John M: *Branding: A Key Marketing Tool.* New York: McGraw Books, 1987.

Musashi, Miyamoto: *A Book of Five Rings.* New York: Overlook Press, 1974.

Naisbitt, John: *Megatrends 2000.* New York: Warner Books, 1996.

Naisbitt, John: *Reinventing the Corporation: Transforming Your Job and Your Company for the New Information Society.* New York: Warner Books, 1985.

✓ Nanus, Burt: *Visionary Leadership: Creating a Compelling Sense of Direction for Your Organization.* San Francisco: Jossey-Bass Publishers, 1992.

Nanus, Burt: *The Leader's Edge: The Seven Keys to Leadership in a Turbulent World.* Chicago: Contemporary Books, 1989.

Nash, Edward L.: *Database Marketing: The Ultimate Marketing Tool.* New York: McGraw-Hill Companies, 1993.

Nelson, Robert B.: *Empowering Employees Through Delegation.* Burr Ridge, IL: Irwin Professional Publishing, 1994.

Neustadt, Richard E.: *Thinking in Time: The Uses of History for Decision-Makers.* New York: Free Press, 1986.

✓ Ogilvy, David: *Ogilvy On Advertising.* New York: Crown Publishing, 1983.

Parker, Glenn M.: *Cross-Functional Teams: Working With Allies, Enemies, and Other Strangers.* San Francisco: Jossey-Bass Publishers, 1994.

Parker, Glenn M., and Kropp, Richard: *Fifty Activities for Self-Directed Teams.* Amherst, MA: Human Resource Development Press, 1994.

Parker, Glenn M., and Kropp, Richard: *Fifty Activities for Team Building.* Amherst, MA: Human Resource Development Press, 1992.

Parker, Glenn M.: *Team Players and Teamwork: The New Competitive Business Strategy.* San Francisco: Jossey-Bass Publishers, 1996.

Parker, Glenn M.: *1996 Handbook of Best Practices for Teams.* Amherst, MA: Human Resource Development Press, 1996.

Patterson, James, and Kim, Peter: *The Day America Told the Truth: What People Really Believe About Everything That Matters.* New York: Prentice-Hall, 1991.

Payne, Stanley: *The Art of Asking Questions.* Princeton, NJ: Princeton University Press, 1951.

Peppers, Don, and Rogers, Martha: *Enterprise One to One: Tools for Competing in the Interactive Age.* New York: Currency Doubleday, 1997.

Peppers, Don, and Rogers, Martha: *The One to One Future: Building Relationships One Customer at a Time.* New York: Doubleday, 1993.

Peters, Tom, and Austin, Nancy: *A Passion for Excellence: The Leadership Difference.* New York: Random House, 1985.

Peters, Tom: *The Circle of Innovation: You Can't Shrink Your Way to Greatness.* New York: Alfred A. Knopf, 1997.

Peters, Tom, and Waterman, Robert Jr.: *In Search of Excellence: Lessons from America's Best-Run Companies.* New York: Harper & Row, 1982.

Peters, Tom: *Liberation Management: Necessary Disorganization for the Nanosecond Nineties.* New York: Alfred A. Knopf, 1992.

Peters, Tom: *The Pursuit of Wow!: Every Person's Guide to Topsy-Turvy Times.* New York: Vintage Books, 1994.

Peters, Tom: *Thriving on Chaos: A Handbook for Management Revolution.* New York: Alfred A. Knopf, 1987.

Pfeffer, Jeffrey: *Competitive Advantage Through People: Unleashing the Power of the Workforce.* Cambridge, MA: Harvard Business School Press, 1994.

Pfeffer, Jeffrey: *Managing With Power: Politics and Influence in Organizations.* Cambridge, MA: Harvard Business School Press, 1992.

Pfeiffer, J. William: *The Encyclopedia of Team Building Activities.* San Diego: University Associates, 1990.

Pine, B. Joseph: *Mass Customization, The New Frontier in Business Competition.* Cambridge, MA: Harvard Business School Press, 1993.

Popcorn, Faith, and Marigold, Lys.: *Clicking: 16 Trends to Future Fit Your Life, Your Work, and Your Business.* New York: HarperCollins, 1996.

Popcorn, Faith: *The Popcorn Report: Faith Popcorn on the Future of Your Company.* New York: Doubleday, 1991.

Postman, Neil: *Amusing Ourselves to Death: Public Discourse in the Age of Show Business.* New York: Viking, 1985.

Pritchett, Price: *The Employees Handbook of New Work Habits for a Radically Changing World: 13 Ground Rules for Job Success in the Information Age.* Dallas: Pritchett and Associates, 1994.

Pritchett, Price: *Firing Up Commitment During Organizational Change: A Handbook for Managers,* 2nd ed. Dallas: Pritchett and Associates, 1996.

Pritchett, Price: *The Team Member Handbook for Teamwork.* Dallas: Pritchett and Associates, 1992.

Ray, Michael, and Rinzler, Alan: *The New Paradigm in Business: Emerging Strategies for Leadership and Organizational Change.* New York: Perigee, 1993.

Ries, Al: Focus: *The Future of Your Company Depends on It.* New York: Harper & Row, 1997.

Ries, Al, and Trout, Jack: *Bottom-Up Marketing.* New York: McGraw-Hill, 1989.

Ries, Al, and Trout, Jack: *Marketing Warfare.* New York: McGraw Hill, 1986.

Ries, Al, and Trout, Jack: *Positioning: The Battle for Your Mind,* rev ed. New York: McGraw-Hill, 1986.

Ries, Al, and Trout, Jack: *The 22 Immutable Laws of Marketing: Violate Them at Your Own Risk!* New York: Harper & Row, 1993.

Ritchie, Karen: *Marketing to Generation X.* New York: Lexington Books, 1995.

Robbins, Harvey, and Finley, Michael: *Why Teams Don't Work: What Went Wrong and How to Make It Right.* Princeton, NJ: Peterson's Pacesetter Books, 1995.

Robert, Michael: *Strategy Pure and Simple: How Winning CEOs Out-Think Their Competition.* New York: McGraw-Hill Companies, 1993.

Rowley, Daniel James, et al.: *Strategic Change in Colleges and Universities: Planning to Survive and Prosper.* San Francisco: Jossey-Bass Publishers, 1997.

Rudolph, Frederick: *The American College and University: A History.* Georgia: University of Georgia Press, 1990.

Russo, J. Edward, and Shoemaker, Paul J.H.: *Decision Traps: Ten Barriers to Brilliant Decision Making and How to Overcome Them.* New York: Currency Doubleday, 1989.

Safire, William, and Safir, Leonard: *Leadership.* New York: Simon and Schuster, 1990.

Schlossberg, Nancy K., and Lynch, Ann Q., and Chickering, Arthur W.: *Improving Higher Education Environments for Adults: Responsive Programs and Services from Entry to Departure.* San Francisco: Jossey-Bass Publishers, 1989.

Schoell, William F., and Guiltinan, Joseph: *Marketing: Contemporary Concepts and Practices,* 6th ed. Englewood Cliffs, NJ: Prentice-Hall, 1995.

Schultz, Don E. and Barnes, Beth. *Strategic Advertising Campaigns,* 4th ed. Lincolnwood, IL: NTC Business Books, 1995.

Schultz, Don E., and Tannenbaum, Stanley, and Lauterborn, Robert F.: *Integrated Marketing Communications: Putting It Together and Making It Work.* Chicago: NTC Business Books, 1993.

Schultz Don E., Tannenbaum, Stanley, and Lauterborn, Robert F.: *Integrated Marketing Communications: The New Marketing Paradigm.* Lincolnwood, IL: NTC Business Publishing, 1997.

Schwartz, Peter: *The Art of the Long View: Planning for the Future in an Uncertain World.* New York: Currency Doubleday, 1995.

Senge, Peter M.: *The Fifth Discipline: The Art and Practice of the Learning Organization.* New York: Currency Doubleday, 1990.

Sevier, Robert A.: "Acting Strategically: A Handful of Breakthrough Strategic Moves That Will Strengthen Your Position in the Marketplace." *White Paper No. 4,* Cedar Rapids: Stamats Communications Inc., 1997.

Sevier, Robert A.: "Conducting Focus Group Research." *Journal of College Admissions,* no. 122 (Winter, 1989):4-9.

Sevier, Robert A.: "Developing an Effective Recruitment Funnel." *Admission Strategist* (Fall 1992).

✓ Sevier, Robert A.: "Hooked on You: Convincing Admitted Students to Enroll with These Creative Yield Strategies." *CURRENTS ,* 14, no. 8 (September 1988):21-25.

Sevier, Robert A.: "How Quality Point Systems Can Improve Recruiting Effectiveness and Reduce Costs." *Admission Strategist* (Spring 1994).

✓ Sevier, Robert A: "Image is Everything: Strategies for Measuring, Changing, and Maintaining Your Institution's Image." *College and University,* 69, no. 2 (Winter 1994):60-75.

, Sevier, Robert A.: "Is Demography Destiny?" *Journal of College Admissions,* no. 135 (Spring 1992):13-22.

Sevier, Robert A.: "Recruiting African-American Undergraduates: A National Survey of the Factors That Affect Institutional Choice." *College and University,* 68, no. 1 (Fall 1992/Winter 1993):48-52.

Sevier, Robert A.: "Those Important Things: What Every College President Needs to Know About Marketing and Recruiting." *White Paper No. 2,* Cedar Rapids: Stamats Communications Inc., 1996.

Sevier, Robert A., and Kappler, Steven D.: "What Students Say: Results of Two National Surveys on How Students Choose a College." *White Paper No. 3,* Cedar Rapids: Stamats Communications Inc., 1997.

Sevier, Robert A.: "Why Marketing Plans Fail: Nine Reasons Student Recruitment Efforts Break Down—And How to Avoid Them." *CURRENTS,* 20, no. 10 (November/December 1994):48-53.

Sewell, Carl, and Brown, Paul B.: *Customers for Life: How to Turn that One-Time Buyer Into a Liftetime Customer.* New York: Doubleday, 1990.

Shanklin, William L., and Ryans, John K. Jr.: *Thinking Strategically: Planning for Your Company's Future.* New York: Random House Business Division, 1985.

Shea, Christopher: "Concept of a 3-Year Bachelor's Degree Gains Support Among Campus Leaders." *Chronicle of Higher Education* (February 10, 1993).

Siegel, Fred: "The Cult of Multiculturalism." *New Republic*, 204, no. 7 (February 18, 1991):34-38.

✓ Simon, Raymond: *Public Relations: Concepts and Practices*, 3rd ed. New York: John Wiley and Sons, 1984..

Smith, Laurence N., Vice President for Marketing and Student Services, Eastern Michigan University. Personal interviews (ongoing).

✓ Smith, Page: *Killing the Spirit: Higher Education in America*. New York: Viking, 1989.

Smith, Robert, Dean, School of Arts and Sciences, University of Tennessee-Martin. Personal interviews (ongoing).

Soares, Eric: *Cost-Effective Marketing Research: A Guide for Marketing Managers*. New York: Quorum Books, 1988.

Speer, Tibbett: "A Nation of Students." *American Demographics*, 18, no. 8 (August 1996):32-38, 45.

Stecklow, Steve: "More Colleges Offer Degrees in Three Years." *Wall Street Journal* (February 28, 1994):B1.

Stecklow, Steve: "Universities Face Trouble for Enhancing Guide Data." *Wall Street Journal* (October 12, 1995):B1.

Stone, Robert: *Successful Direct Marketing Methods*, 6th ed. Lincolnwood, IL: NTC Business Publishing, 1997.

Stumpf, Stephen A., and Mullen, Thomas P.: *Taking Charge: Strategic Leadership in the Middle Game*. Englewood Cliffs, NJ: Prentice-Hall, 1992.

Taylor, Robert F: *Back to Basic Selling: Unique Sales Tips for Sure-Fire Success*. Englewood Cliffs, NJ: Prentice-Hall, 1985.

Tinto, Vincent: *Leaving College: Rethinking the Causes and Cures of Student Attrition*. Chicago: University of Chicago Press, 1993.

Topor and Associates: "Athletics and Marketing: An Appeal to Change Perceptions About the Value of Athletics in Marketing Higher Education." *Marketing Higher Education* (March 1995).

Topor, Robert S.: *Institutional Image: How to Define, Improve, and Market It*. Washington, DC: Council for Advancement and Support of Education, 1986.

Topor, Robert S.: *Marketing Higher Education: A Practical Guide*. Washington, DC: Council for Advancement and Support of Education, 1983.

Topor, Robert S.: *Media & Marketing: A Powerful New Alliance for Higher Education*. Mountain View, CA: Topor and Associates, 1993.

Treacy, Michael, and Wiersema, Fred: *The Discipline of Market Leaders: Choose Your Customers, Narrow Your Focus, Dominate Your Market*. Reading, MA: Addison-Wesley-Longman Publishing, 1995.

Tully, Shawn: "Finally, Colleges Start to Cut Their Crazy Costs." *Fortune* (May 1, 1995).

Vavra, Terry G.: *Aftermarketing: How to Keep Customers for Life Through Relationship Marketing*, rev ed. Chicago, IL: Irwin Professional Publishing, 1995.

Waldman, Steven: "Too Old, Too Fast—Millions of American Teenagers Work But May be Squandering Their Futures." *Newsweek* (November 16, 1992).

Wallace, Thomas P.: "Public Higher Education Finance: The Dinosaur Age Persists." *Change*, 25, no. 4 (July/August 1993):56-63.

Walters, James C.: "Market Research: The First Step in Your Marketing Program." *College and University* (Fall 1994).

Walters, Laurel Shaper: "Colleges Grade Degree-in-Three Program." *Christian Science Monitor* (March 21, 1994): 14.

Weaver, Richard: *Ideas Have Consequences*. Chicago: University of Chicago Press, 1948.

Weinstein, Art: *Market Segmentation: Using Demographics, Psychographics, and Other Segmentation Techniques to Uncover and Exploit New Markets*. Chicago: Probus Publishing Company, 1987.

Weinstein, Art. Market Segmentation: *Using Demographics, Psychographics, and Niche Marketing Techniques to Predict and Model Customer Behavior*. Chicago: Probus Publishing Company, 1993.

Weiss, Michael J.: *The Clustering of America.* New York: Harper & Row, 1988.

Willigan, Geraldine E.: "High-Performance Marketing: An Interview with Nike's Phil Knight." *Harvard Business Review*, 70, no. 4 (July-August 1992):90-101.

Willimon, William H., and Naylor, Thomas H.: *The Abandoned Generation: Rethinking Higher Education.* Grand Rapids, MI: William B. Eerdmans Publishing Company, 1995.

✓ Willingham, Ron: Best Seller: *The New Psychology of Selling and Persuading People.* Englewood Cliffs, NJ: Prentice-Hall, 1984.

Willingham, Ron: *Integrity Selling: How to Succeed in Selling in the Competitive Years Ahead.* Garden City, NY: Doubleday, 1987.

Wong, Frank: "Diversity & Community: Right Objectives and Wrong Arguments." *Change* (July/August, 1991).

Woodcock, Mike: *50 Activities for Teambuilding.* Brookfield, VT: Ashgate Publishing, 1989.

Woodcock, Mike: *Team Development Manual,* 2nd ed. Brookfield, VT: Ashgate Publishing, 1989.

World's Greatest Brands: An International Review. New York: John Wiley & Sons, 1992

Wurman, Richard S.: *Information Anxiety.* New York: Doubleday, 1989.

Yale, David R.: *Publicity and Media Relations Checklists: 59 Proven Checklists to Save Time, Win Attention and Maximize Exposure with Every Public Relations and Publicity Contact.* Lincolnwood, IL: NTC Business Books, 1995.

✓ Zemsky, Robert, and Oedel, Penny. *The Structure of College Choice.* New York: College Board, 1983.

Zemsky, Robert. "Shared Purposes." *Pew Policy Perspectives*, 6, no. 4. (April 1996). Washington, DC: American Council on Education.

Zollo, Peter: "Talking to Teens." *American Demographics*, 17, no. 11 (November 1995):22-28.

Zollo, Peter: *Wise Up to Teens: Insights into Marketing and Advertising to Teenagers.* Ithaca, New York: New Strategist Publications, 1995.

_____: "Black Like Who? Rap, Respect and the New Generation Gap." *Newsweek.* (March 17, 1997).

_____: "Students of the '90s: What Do They Want From College?" *Change* (September/October 1993).

About the Author

Robert Sevier is the vice president for research and marketing at Stamats Communications, Inc., an integrated marketing, publications, interactive media, and consulting company serving higher education. Each year, Sevier directs more than 100 research studies of such audiences as prospective students (both traditional and nontraditional), parents, community residents, current and former donors, business leaders, faculty and staff, trustees, and others.

He has written extensively for *CASE CURRENTS*, the *Journal of College Admissions, Communication World, Admission Strategist, College and University Journal*, and conducted more than 300 seminars and presentations for CASE, NAICU, NACAC, ACT, AACRAO, NACCAP, the AMA, NCMPR, the College Board, and other organizations on such topics as:

- Social, demographic, economic, and governance trends affecting higher education
- Integrated marketing communication
- Analyzing and improving institutional images
- Marketing, recruiting, and competitive positioning plan development
- Designing search and direct mail strategies
- Enrollment management
- Developing more effective recruiting funnels

Sevier directs the Stamats Working Smart seminars, and is a frequent contributor to *Applications, ACCESS, re:Quest*, and *Advantage* newsletters. He is also responsible for the Stamats' White Papers, a series of monographs for presidents and senior administrators that address such issues as strategic planning, marketing, student recruiting, and leadership. From CASE, he has received the coveted Steuben Apple Award for teaching excellence.

Prior to Stamats, Sevier worked as director of Media Relations for the Oregon Health Sciences University and served as director of marketing communications for Denison University. He taught journalism and public relations at the college level for 10 years.

Sevier earned a Ph.D. from The Ohio State University in 1986 in policy analysis and higher education administration with an emphasis on marketing. He also holds an M.S. degree in journalism/public relations from the University of Oregon (1979).

He may be reached at: Stamats Communications, 427 Sixth Avenue SE, Cedar Rapids, IA 52406, 800-553-8878, bob-sevier@stamats.com.